D1556948

DISCUSSIONS AND ARGUMENTS

ON VARIOUS SUBJECTS

THE WORKS OF
CARDINAL JOHN HENRY NEWMAN
BIRMINGHAM ORATORY
MILLENNIUM EDITION
VOLUME VII

SERIES EDITOR

JAMES TOLHURST DD

DISCUSSIONS
AND
ARGUMENTS
ON VARIOUS SUBJECTS

BY

JOHN HENRY CARDINAL NEWMAN

with an Introduction by JAMES TOLHURST and
Notes by the late GERARD TRACEY, completed by
JAMES TOLHURST

Gracewing.

NOTRE DAME

BR
85
.N43
2004

First published in 1872 by
Basil Montague Pickering
Published in the Birmingham Oratory Millennium Edition in 2004
jointly by

Gracewing
2 Southern Avenue
Leominster
Herefordshire HR6 0QF

University of Notre Dame Press
310 Flanner Hall
Notre Dame
IN 46556 USA

The right of James Tolhurst to be identified as the author of the Introduction and of James Tolhurst and Gerard Tracey as authors of the Editor's Notes to this work has been asserted in accordance with the Copyright, Designs and Patents Act 1988.

Library of Congress Cataloging-in-Publication Data

Newman, John Henry, 1801–1890.
    Discussions and arguments on various subjects/by John Henry
    Newman ; with an introduction by James Tolhurst and notes by the
    late Gerard Tracey, completed by James Tolhurst.
        p. cm. – (The works of Cardinal John Henry Newman:
    Birmingham oratory millennium edition; v. 7)
    ISBN 0-268-03600-4 (cloth: alk. paper)
        1. Christianity.   I. Tolhurst, James.   II. Title.

BR85.N43 2004
230'.2–dc22   2003070255

UK ISBN 0 85244 453 2
US ISBN 0-268-03600-4

Additional typesetting by Action Publishing Technology Ltd, Gloucester, GL1 5SR
Printed in England by MPG Books Ltd, Bodmin PL31 1EG

CONTENTS

ABBREVIATIONS

Apo.	*Apologia pro Vita Sua*
Ari.	*Arians of the Fourth Century*
A.S.	*Alternative Sermons*
Ath. I, II	Select Treatises of St Athanasius, 2 volumes
A.W.	*John Henry Newman: Autobiographical Writings* ed. Henry Tristram
BCP	*The Book of Common Prayer*
BOA	Birmingham Oratory Archives
Call.	Callista
D.A.	*Discussions and Arguments on Various Subjects*
Dev.	*An Essay on the Development of Christian Doctrine*
Diff. I, II	*Certain Difficulties felt by Anglicans in Catholic Teaching*, 2 volumes
DNB	Dictionary of National Biography, to 1900
Ess. I, II	*Essays Critical and Historical*, 2 volumes
G.A.	*An Essay in Aid of a Grammar of Assent*
H.S. I, II, III	*Historical Sketches*, 3 volumes
Idea	*The Idea of a University defined and illustrated*
Jfc.	*Lectures on the Doctrine of Justification*

K.C.	*Correspondence of John Henry Newman with John Keble and others, 1839–1845*
L.D.	*Letters and Diaries of John Henry Newman*
Mix.	*Discourses addressed to Mixed Congregations*
OED	*Oxford English Dictionary*
O.S.	*Sermons preached on Various Occasions*
P.S.	*Parochial and Plain Sermons*
Prepos.	*Present Position of Catholics*
S.D.	*Sermons bearing on Subjects of the Day*
S.N.	*Sermon Notes of John Henry Newman 1849–1878*
U.S.	*Fifteen Sermons preached before the University of Oxford*
V.M. I, II	*The Via Media,* 2 volumes

NOTE ON THE TEXT

Basil Montague Pickering published four editions: 1872, 1873, 1878 and 1882. An index was added in the second edition. In Newman's copy of the third edition there is a marginal note on page 292, line 10 which suggests replacing 'impracticable' with 'unimaginible' (sic). It was not incorporated in the fourth or subsequent editions. Longmans, Green & Co published four editions, one in 1885, two in 1888 and one in 1890. Apart from small stylistic corrections, the text is the same throughout.

INTRODUCTION

Newman had written to Monsignor Talbot in 1867 that he was an old man, perhaps within a few years of his death.[1] However, four years later he was very much alive, in the midst of re-publishing earlier works. The 1870s thus saw the re-appearance of his *Essay on Miracles, Fifteen Sermons Preached before the University of Oxford, The Idea of a University, Callista,* and *Loss and Gain.* But in addition Newman dusted down his earlier pieces for the two-volume *Essays Critical and Historical,* his three-volume *Historical Sketches* and his *Discussions and Arguments on Various Subjects.*

When he was thinking of a title for the six essays in the book he thought 'Arguments' would be a better descriptions than 'Discussions', although he conceded 'the first of the papers is a discussion'.[2] Pickering, the publisher, played safe and opted for both words. The book appeared in the Spring of 1872. It was reprinted in 1873 and 1878.

It shares a relationship with *Essays Critical and*

[1] 26 May 1867. *Letters and Diaries (L.D.)* XXIII, p. 241.
[2] To B. M. Pickering, 23 January 1872, *L.D.* XXVI, p. 12.

Historical which brought together articles from the *British Critic*, but it differs from that and all of Newman's works in its rather haphazard nature of literary pieces which stem from the 1830s, 1840s, 1850s and 1860s. There is no attempt at making any connection, and therefore each portion will be treated separately in order to understand its chronological context and its background in Newman's own life.

By 1872, with the publication of the *Apologia*, Newman was able to enter a period of enjoyment of his labours. With the help of his friends, especially the Duke of Norfolk and Hope Scott, he built the cloister in front of the church with its handsome pillars and memorials to deceased Oratorians and bought land for the Oratory School playing fields. He would soon be made a Fellow of Trinity College and then a cardinal.

The publishers knew that his works would sell, such was his reputation, and Newman was easily persuaded to dig out all his old literary pieces. The *Guardian* said that he must be very sure of his position to republish articles with scarcely any correction or refutation. There is a remarkable consistency which binds earlier and later works, so that no apologies were necessary. But in addition Newman remarks that if he had attempted any revision 'it would come to pieces and he would have to write it over again'.[3] Newman is probably being modest as he completely re-worked his *Essay on the Development of Doctrine* for Pickering in 1878.

When he came to publish what became *Discussions and Arguments* he asked Richard Church to comment

[3] To W. S. Lilly, 27 June 1887, *L.D.* XXX, p. 105.

on his letters to the *Catholic Standard* which was to bear the title 'Who's to Blame?' Church replied, 'It would be a great pity not to preserve them and I am sure they would be read just now with real interest. They seem to be written for this session of parliament.'[4]

Newman duly included the letters and rounded off the selection with a long review article which he had written for the Jesuit periodical, *The Month*. As it stands, the volume comprises articles from the *British Magazine*, two Tracts, a series of letters to *The Times*, letters to *The Catholic Standard* and the review article mentioned earlier.

How to Accomplish it

Originally published in Hugh James Rose's publication *The British Magazine* in 1834 under the title 'Home Thoughts Abroad', this chose the setting of a meeting in Rome between three friends, Ambrose, Basil and Cyril. Newman had visited the city with the Froudes in 1832 during his Mediterranean excursion. He had met Christian von Bunsen on that occasion, and he was re-incarnated as Ambrose. The choice of the other names, Cyril for Newman himself and Basil possibly for William Wilberforce or Pusey, was much influenced by his immersion in the writings of the Fathers which occasioned *Arians*.

When Newman returned from the Mediterranean, he was confronted with the beginnings of the Oxford Movement and the subsequent need for the Tracts for the Times. The question of Rome's position loomed large in discussions between Newman's friends. In a

[4] *L.D.* XXV, p. 380n.

letter to Hurrell Froude Newman said, 'We mean the Tracts should formally take up the Popish question. If you saw my Home Thoughts Number 2 (= *How to Accomplish it*) you would understand my line very completely.'[5] What was the particular position of the Church of England, if union with Rome was precluded? Newman wrote to Hugh James Rose, 'There is the probability of the whole subject of Church authority, power, claims, etc. etc. being opened. I am persuaded that half solutions which have hitherto really been enough, will not do in time to come.'[6] The solution would seem to be found in making the Church more popularly based. In an article in the *British Magazine*, Newman argued: 'The Church is thought invaluable as a promoter of good order and society; but is regarded as nothing more'.[7] To Rose he said, 'I wish to encourage churchmen to look boldly at the Church's being made to dwell in the affections of the people at large.'[8] This was the message which he sent to Hurrell Froude, 'The idea has broken on me, as it did a little before on yourself, that the Church is essentially a popular institution'.[9] The underlying theme of *How to Accomplish it* is the lack of popular attraction which is driving congregations to the dissenting Churches and the need to recover what Rome possesses without conceding Rome's position. The tentative solution

[5] 10 September 1835, *L.D.* V, p. 140.

[6] 10 April 1836, *L.D.* V, p. 274.

[7] 'Vincentius of Lerins', *British Magazine*, XVI (August 1836); *L.D.* IV, p. 341.

[8] 10 April 1836, *L.D.* V, p. 275.

[9] 2 September 1833, *L.D.* IV, p. 583. This is discussed more fully in Tolhurst J., *The Church, A Communion*, Gracewing, Leominster, 1988, pp. 32–42.

would seem to be monasticism and religious sisterhoods.

Newman uses the three characters to toss around the nature of the *Via Media* of the Anglican Church. Ambrose (Bunsen) points out that there is a Catholic body and Anglicans have separated themselves from it. Cyril (Newman) counters that purity of faith is more precious than unity, and if Rome has erred then it is the duty of Anglicans to separate themselves. Anglicans should not look to Rome but to Archbishop Laud.

Basil then intervenes and endorses the appeal to Laudian principles, saying that although the system of Laud cannot be expected to return, it is possible to hope for the development and continuation of his principles. He faces the question of union with Rome and dismisses it:

> It is to lose our *position* as a Church, which never answers to any, whether body or individual. If, indeed, salvation were not in our Church, the case would be altered; as it is, were Rome as pure in faith as the Church of the Apostles, which she is not, I would not join her, unless those about me did so too, lest I should commit schism. Our business is to take what we have received, and build upon it: to accept, as a legacy from our forefathers, this 'Protestant' spirit which they have bequeathed us, and merely to disengage it from its errors, purify it, and make it something more than a negative principle; thus only have we a chance of success.[10]

[10] *Discussions and Arguments (D.A.)*, p. 31. However, Newman noted in 1834, 'Protestantism has been tried and failed – it goes into Socinianism', *Subjects for Lectures on the Via Media* (1834), Birmingham Oratory Archives (*BOA*), D.6.3.

Ambrose interjects that there is no firm foundation such as Rome possesses, but Basil dismisses that by saying that one should be content with the spiritual heritage of Anglicanism, in particular its liturgy. 'On these foundations, properly understood, we may do anything'.[11] Cyril (Newman) then rounds off the debate by arguing that the Anglican Church must become more attractive (as well as more apostolic) by drawing on the Catholic heritage, not by some ersatz imitations but by the liturgy as advocated by the Caroline divines and by the resurgence of monachism and religious sisterhoods, to which Basil gives his wholehearted support. In fact Pusey (if Basil *is* Pusey) was instrumental in the formation of Anglican sister-hoods. In June 1841 he wrote to Newman that he had just received the vows of Marian Rebecca Hughes, who had been influenced by reading Newman's *The Church of the Fathers* (see n. p. 40).

The Patristical Idea of Antichrist

Newman explains that this contribution to the volume was Tract 83. It takes the form of four Advent sermons which were originally preached in November and December 1835 (MS Sermons 394–397).

It is possible that the impetus for the sermons – apart from the obvious liturgical context of the Letter to the Thessalonians – was Newman's correspondence with his brother Frank (Francis William Newman 1805–1897) who had joined the Plymouth Brethren in 1831 and had followed the founder, J. N. Darby, to Persia. Newman berates his brother for 'that

[11] *D.A.*, p. 35.

wretched, nay (I may say) cursed Protestant principle, (not a principle in which our Church has any share, but the low arrogant cruel ultra-Protestant principle) – your last letter showed me you had so imbibed it as to be in great peril – but I had no notion you had gone so far'.[12] In the interests of putting the balanced understanding of the Scriptural position on Antichrist, Newman undertakes his series of Advent sermons which fit unevenly between the second volume of his *Parochial Sermons* and his *Lectures on The Prophetical Office of the Church*.

The rise of millenary sects, like the Plymouth Brethren (1830), the Church of Jesus Christ of the Latter Day Saints (1830), the Adventists (1831), the Catholic Apostolic Church (1832) and the Christadelphians (1848) focused people's minds on the Second Coming of Christ and its implications. Edward Bickersteth wrote in 1831, 'The good folk here [in the Midlands] are all afloat prophesying, and the immediate work of the Lord is disregarded for the uncertain future.'[13]

There are and were two main positions on the ultimate millennium: pre-millenary and post-millenary. Protestant pre-millenarianism originated in the seventeenth century under writers such as Joseph Mede (1586–1638). It taught that the dead would rise before the coming of Christ, and all the 'saints' would rejoice in Christ's presence when he came. In 1842 The Prophecy Investigation Society was founded in St

[12] 23 November 1835, *L.D.* V, p. 166. Newman returned to the subject in 1840 in his review of Dr Todd's Discourses which he published in the *British Critic, Essays Critical & Historical (Ess)* II, pp. 112–85.

[13] *Memoir*, II, p. 43.

George's, Bloomsbury, and two years later E. B. Elliott published his four-volume *Horae Apocalypticae* which urged that there should be no alliance with the papal anti-Christian religion. Post-millenarianism looked expectantly for signs of the last days and the happiness and rapture which awaited the faithful. Edward Irving's Catholic Apostolic Church and John Nelson Darby's Plymouth Brethren were both post-millenaries, as were the Owenites. There was general disagreement as to whether there would be signs preceding the rapture (the 'being caught up with Christ' as stated in I Corinthians 15:51ff.) or not.

Newman distanced himself from any Protestant anti-Romanism. He would maintain that the Church of Rome was never identified as Antichrist, merely the Roman Empire as an entity and political system and individuals such as Antiochus Epiphanes, Julian the Apostate, and (a firm favourite of Newman's) Mahomet 'the false prophet, who propagated his imposture about 600 years after Christ came'.[14] Newman is far from being alone in his stance. Bishop Horsley numbered Islam among 'the most pestilent heresies'.[15] Newman was by no means alone in refusing to identify Antichrist.

Archbishop Whately, who had been Newman's mentor at Oriel, stated 'I should keep clear of the conflicting opinions as to the precise interpretation of the prophecy respecting the "Man of Sin" ... I should dwell on the "sin", not on the "Man"; and lead the

<hr/>

[14] *D.A.*, p. 55. He writes: 'O that thy Creed were sound/ for thou dost soothe the heart, thou Church of Rome', 'Lyra Apostolica XXXIII', in *British Magazine*, February 1836, p. 147.
[15] *D.A.*, p. 107.

reader to judge of the tree by its fruits, rather than of the fruits by the tree'.[16] In fact Newman was quite certain that he considered Antichrist 'to be a person, yet future'.[17] Those who bear the mark of Antichrist are very clearly the French revolutionaries, who introduced Roman divinities (like the Emperor Julian) and a new worship which was in fact a sort of official paganism.[18] As to the city of Antichrist, Rome or Babylon (not the Roman Church) was a type of many cities or something more than Rome or Babylon, yet to come, 'of a proud and deceiving world'.[19]

The persecution which will precede the Last Days is yet to come. There will indeed be violence but not necessarily convulsions (is Newman being squeamish?). The signs are already there in the total decline of the old Roman Empire and – he optimistically hopes – 'the approaching destruction of the Mahometan power'.[20] Nemesis will be achieved by the Chinese, it would seem, who 'are gathering strength, and beginning to frown over the seat of the Roman Empire'.[21]

In such a situation his hearers are not urged to quake in their shoes or to await the rapture, but 'if they be Christians in heart, pilgrims, watchers, waiting for the light' [22] then they wait in faith. The Lord will come and bring an end to sin and wickedness and

---

[16] Letter to a friend. *Life & Correspondence of Archbishop Whately*, ed. Jane Whately, 2 vols, London, 1866. Vol. 1, p. 60.

[17] To H. E. Manning, 28 February 1837, *L.D.* VI, p. 34.

[18] *D.A.*, p. 69ff.

[19] *D.A.*, p. 90.

[20] *D.A.*, p. 103.

[21] *D.A.*, p. 105. Samuel Waldegrave in his *New Testament Millenarianism* (London 1855), spoke of the movement in the Far East 'which is revolutioning the teeming millions of Chinese', p, 396.

[22] *D.A.*, p. 106.

'accomplish the number of His elect, and perfect those who at present struggle with infirmity'.[23] This is perfectly orthodox Christian doctrine which leaves open to discussion the precise nature of the Second Coming. But Newman did not rule out the idea of some pre-millennial 'reign'. In private correspondence, Newman wrote 'As to the Millenum (sic), as Christ was at once a sufferer and a conqueror, the Son and Lord of David, yet it appeared not now beforehand, so it may be true that when He comes there may be little faith on the earth yet a millennium of peace and purity immediately precede the final judgment'.[24] It is interesting that these sentiments do not find expression in the text which he publishes.

Although he states that this is the *Patristical* idea of Antichrist, and under 'the exclusive guidance of the Fathers of the Church'[25] the force of the argument is really scriptural. Gibbon is quoted quite as much as the Fathers, and there are only scattered references to Chrysostom, Jerome, Cyril of Jerusalem, Irenaeus, Hippolytus and Augustine. However, even though Newman would regard one of the Fathers as 'a prophet for Truth's Creed',[26] this would not be universally appreciated. Dean Thomas Gaisford is not untypical in referring to the Fathers in Christ Church Library as 'sad rubbish'.[27] A clergyman 'of the Puritan school' was characteristically blunt when

---

[23] *D.A.*, p. 106.

[24] To Unknown Correspondent, 24 February 1837, *L.D.* VI, p. 34.

[25] *D.A.*, p. 45.

[26] Of St. Ambrose in 'Lyra Apostolica XV' in *British Magazine VI* (August 1834), p. 151.

[27] Mozley T., *Reminiscences of Oriel College & The Oxford Movement*, 1882, vol. 1, p. 356.

he said that the Fathers were 'stinking puddles of tradition.'[28]

Holy Scripture in its Relation to the Catholic Creed
In the same year, Newman embarked on twelve lectures in Adam de Brome's chapel in St Mary's on consecutive Tuesdays between 8 May and 7 August (excluding 10 and 17 July when he was in London). He published eight of these in Tract 85 (he entitled them Part I) and republished them in *Discussions and Arguments*. In a letter to his bishop in 1841, he wrote 'In defending such doctrines and practices of the Church as Infant Baptism or the Episcopal Succession, the Tracts have argued that they rested on substantially the same basis as the Canon of Scripture, viz. the testimony of ancient Christendom. But to those who think this basis weak, the argument becomes a disparagement of the Canon not a recommendation of the Creed'.[29]

Tract 83 deals with the Scriptural basis for the system of Christian doctrine summarised in the Creed. Newman intends to answer the question, Where can you find support in the Bible for what the Church preaches and represents?

The initial problem is that many of the teachings of the Church are not 'insisted on with such frequency and earnestness as might be expected'.[30] The plenary remission of sin by baptism; no usage of the word 'priest'; so little said about ordination; the word 'altar' being used only once or twice and fasting is

---

[28] Liddon H. P., *Life of E. B. Pusey*, London, 1893, vol. 1, p. 434.

[29] To Richard Bagot, 29 March 1841, *L.D.* VIII, p. 136.

[30] *D.A.*, p. 115.

mentioned very rarely. There is plainly a need to 'submit to the indirectness of the Scripture evidence'[31] and accept that because there is no clear proof does not mean that there is no basis for our Christian practice. In certain cases we must accept that there are arguments against particular doctrines as much as there is supporting evidence. In other cases we have to infer the teaching from other unrelated passages of Scripture: 'It does not follow that a doctrine or a rite is not divine, because it is not strictly stated in Scripture'.[32]

Newman then outlines the two attitudes to Scripture with which he disagrees. The Roman position is unacceptable because of its stress on the role of Tradition as an alternative source. But far more odious is the liberal philosophy (or latitudinarian, as it was generally termed then) which denies any basis for Christian teaching.

Newman's battle with latitudinarianism would be a lifetime's work for him. When he received his *biglietto* in Rome as a cardinal, he took the occasion to outline his position: 'For thirty, forty, fifty years I have resisted, to the best of my powers, the spirit of Liberalism in religion ... Liberalism in religion is the doctrine that there is no positive truth in religion, but that one creed is as good as another, and this is the teaching which is gaining substance and force daily. It is inconsistent with

---

[31] *D.A.*, p. 113. Newman asks 'When a passage of Scripture ... is obscure and perplexing it is as well to ask ourselves whether this may not be owing to some insensibility in ourselves or in our age, to certain peculiarities of the Divine Law or government therein involved.' *Parochial and Plain Sermons* (*P.S.*) IV, p. 27 (preached April 2 1837).

[32] *D.A.*, p. 125.

the recognition of any religion as truth. It teaches that all are to be tolerated as all are matters of opinion. Revealed religion is not a truth, but a sentiment and a taste – not an objective fact, not miraculous; and it is the right of each individual to make it say just what strikes his fancy.'[33] In 1838, in Tract 85, Newman would argue that a serious man could not be 'a consistent Latitudinarian' if he knew what he was speaking about, because he would have to reject every doctrine, not just those he finds unpalatable.[34]

But the rejection of any creed contained in Scripture, argues Newman, does not mean that there is no divine message anywhere at all. In fact 'it would make me look *out* of Scripture for it ... if there is a Revelation, there must be a doctrine'.[35] It may be hard to discern and so obscure that every person will have his own interpretation of it. But this would 'drive me, not into Latitudinarianism, but into Romanism. Yes, and it will drive the multitude of men. It is far more certain that Revelation must contain a message, than that that message must be in Scripture. It is a less violence to one's feelings to say that part of it is revealed elsewhere, than to say that nothing is revealed anywhere'.[36] Newman will argue the scriptural basis for doctrine in the rest of the Tract, but he has already conceded the power of the Romanist position. It explains the atmosphere of

[33] May 17 1879 in *Sayings of Cardinal Newman*, 1890, p. 18. Compare the almost identical language in *D.A.*, p. 129.

[34] *D.A.*, p. 131. 'They say that the object of the Gospel Revelation is merely practical, and therefore, that theological doctrines are altogether unnecessary.' *P.S.* II, (1834), p. 261.

[35] *D.A.*, p. 132.

[36] *D.A.*, p. 133.

unease that surrounded the publication of the Tracts which saw the authors as fifth columnists for Rome, even if they themselves loudly proclaimed otherwise.

In the third section Newman comes to the central point of his argument, examining Scripture 'antecedently' and then 'in matter of fact'. He already stated that 'we must submit to the indirectness of Scripture'.[37] In Anglican terms this means submitting to what Newman terms 'an inconvenience which certainly does attach to our Church' that Christian doctrines have in fact been revealed *and* that they are in Scripture.[38] The only alternative is to accept the Roman position, which does not believe in 'sola Scriptura'.[39] But Newman says Romanism for the time being is put aside.[40] Therefore any religious system must be contained obscurely and indirectly in Scripture. Thus 'solemn and important truths may be silently taken for granted or alluded to in a half sentence, or spoken of indeed, yet in such unadorned language that we may fancy we see through it and see nothing'.[41]

The question of the authority or canonicity of Scripture occupies the sixth and seventh section, and Newman maintains that those who oppose Church doctrine ought consistently to oppose the authority of Scripture: 'a battle for the Canon of Scripture is but the next step after a battle for the Creed ... and that if we were not defending the Creed, we should at this

---

[37] *D.A.*, p. 141. 'When a passage of Scripture ... is obscure and perplexing it is as well to ask ourselves whether this may not be owing to some insensibility in ourselves.' *P.S.* IV, p. 27.

[38] *D.A.*, p. 142.

[39] *D.A.*, p. 144. See under notes p. 127.

[40] *D.A.*, p. 152.

[41] *D.A.*, p. 192.

moment be defending the Canon'.[42]

Newman brings in the Fathers of the Church (in particular, the fourth and fifth centuries) in evidence of Church doctrine and in support of the scriptural basis (which rather seems to support the Roman position). He argues that those who pick and choose among the primitive Church system should in all consistency pick and choose of the Canon of Scripture.[43]

The last section summarises the argument. The Creed with its various doctrines rests for its authority on Scripture, and it in turn relies on the testimony of the ancient Church Fathers, who bear witness to the Canon we possess. This cannot be accidental, but faith is needed. Ultimately there is no other choice. 'Shall we go to Mahometanism or Paganism ... some heresy or sect: true, we may; but why are they more sure? are they not a part while the Church is the whole? Why is the part true, if the whole is not?'[44]

Newman concludes with his personal statement of faith: 'Why should not the Church be divine? The burden of proof surely is on the other side. I will accept her doctrines, and her rites, and her Bible ... It is, I feel, God's will that I should do so; and besides, I love all that belong to her, – I love her Bible, her doctrines, her rites, and therefore I believe.'[45]

The Tamworth Reading Room
The fourth essay introduces Newman at his controversial best. We ought to bear in mind that Tract 90

[42] *D.A.*, p. 198.
[43] *D.A.*, p. 209.
[44] *D.A.*, p. 252.
[45] *D.A.*, p. 253.

is in the offing – with its dire consequences for the Tracts and the movement in general.

The occasion was a speech made by Sir Robert Peel at Tamworth in Staffordshire. He spoke in support of, and contributed handsomely to, the new library and reading room which was part of the 'apostolate' of Lord Brougham and his followers. The founder of the *Penny Magazine* and the *Penny Encyclopaedia* in the 1830s saw it as his particular mission to bring enlightenment to the masses. For this purpose the Society for the Diffusion of Knowledge and the Mechanics Institute were founded. All very laudable one would agree.

Many saw beyond such utilitarian motives and sensed it in Peel's speech when he spoke of the new building being 'open to all persons, of all descriptions, without reference to political opinions or to religious creed'.[46] John Walter of *The Times* dispatched his son John, a recent graduate on 30 January, to ask Newman to contribute a series of letters to the newspaper. The letters, by *Catholicus*, duly appeared 5–26 February 1841. The five letters do not oppose the principle of access to education for the masses – this would be insulting to intelligence. The theory of the wide diffusion of useful knowledge, especially scientific and mechanical, could be considered 'a kind of neutral ground, on which men of every shade of politics and religion may meet together, disabuse each other of their prejudices, form intimacies and secure co-operation'.[47] But it turns out that this is not so neutral after all because the delivery of knowledge involves freeing

[46] *L.D.* VIII, p. 526.
[47] *D.A.*, p. 256.

the inquiring spirit from religious encumbrance (as took place at the time of the French Revolution ...). People must be delivered from tyranny and persecution and the depression caused by those (inspired by religious principles) who want to keep you 'to the level of their own contented ignorance'.[48]

It now becomes plain that 'with reference to religious Creed' does not simply imply that the Test Act will not be demanded before readers take out a book, but that the Church of England in particular must take its place among all denominations – and presumably those with no affiliation at all 'without the asperities of party feeling'[49] – as if Christianity was a catalyst for infighting just like politics itself. It is possible to glimpse the twentieth-century liberal version which moves to the exclusion of religion altogether in the name of Science and the betterment of humanity: 'the great truth has gone forth to all the ends of the earth, that man shall no more render account to man for his belief, over which he has himself no control'.[50]

In his second letter, Catholicus (i.e. Newman) attacks the assumption that the mere acquiring of knowledge will bring about moral improvement, that 'in becoming wiser, a man will become better'.[51] He asks ironically how the input of scientific knowledge can make people virtuous: 'does it act like a dose or a charm which comes into general use empirically?'[52]

[48] *D.A.*, p. 259. Cf. *L.D.* VIII, pp. 525–33 for the published version of the Address.
[49] *D.A.*, p. 259.
[50] *D.A.*, p. 259.
[51] *D.A.*, p. 261.
[52] *D.A.*, p. 262.

It would seem that we need to understand virtue in utilitarian not Christian terms – not the brutal self-interest of Bentham but a more generous sentiment. Knowledge is 'fair and glorious, exalted above the range of ordinary humanity'.[53] But how does such knowledge deal with the disordered and passionate state of the labouring classes 'in a severe winter, snow on the ground, glass falling, bread rising, coal at 20d the cwt, and no work'?[54] The recipe is a constant and changing course of knowledge – diversion plus excitement[55] (and Newman could not imagine cable television). But if we are honest, such remedies will hardly serve their purpose as much as 'digestive pills half an hour before dinner, and a posset at bedtime at the best; and at the worst dram-drinking and opium'. Who, he asks 'was ever consoled in real trouble by the small beer of literature or science?'[56] There is something faintly ludicrous about a Prime Minister (he was, and would be again that year) addressing a potential audience of the working class on a treatise he had just received, *A Report on the Disease to which the Wheat Plant is Liable*.[57] It has just that touch of inconsequentiality which we have come to expect from government experts. Newman blames Peel and his Utilitarian friends for dredging up Cicero's philosophy when they had already been enlightened by

---

[53] *D.A.*, p. 263. In Note A on Liberalism Newman says that one of the criteria is that, 'Virtue is the child of knowledge'. *Apologia pro Vita Sua* (*Apo*), p. 296.

[54] *D.A.*, p. 268. 20d = 20 old pence. Coal was sold in hundredweight bags (20 cwt = 1 ton).

[55] *D.A.*, p. 266.

[56] *D.A.*, p. 266. Notice that he contrasts his bedtime posset with the small *beer* of science.

[57] *L.D.* VIII, p. 528.

Christianity: 'these Christian statesmen cannot be content with what is divine without as a supplement hankering after what was heathen'.[58] There is a desire for what Christianity brings, but at the same time a desire to go beyond the confines of religion. But knowledge by itself is not power; 'it merely aims at disposing of his [man's] existing powers and tastes, as is most convenient, or is practicable under the circumstances'.[59] Moral goodness which is bound up with mastery of the mind, not acquisition of information, cannot be conjured out of a book; it remains a gift: '"Grace" or the "Word", by whichever name we call it, has been from the first a quickening, renovating, organizing principle. It has new created the individual, and transferred and knit him into a social body, composed of members each similarly created. It has cleansed man of his moral diseases, raised him to hope and energy, given him to propagate a brotherhood among his fellows, and to found a family or rather a kingdom of saints all over the earth; – it introduced a new force into the world, and the impulse which it gave continues in its original vigour down to this day.'[60]

Yet those who advocate 'The Diffusion of Knowledge' have an in-built prejudice against aspects of Christianity. They would regard themselves as moderate, balanced and enlightened. They would insist upon a ticket from a public minister of religion as evidence of proficiency in Christian knowledge[61] but exclude from the Library any example of

[58] *D.A.*, p. 270.
[59] *D.A.*, p. 272.
[60] *D.A.*, pp. 270–1.
[61] *D.A.*, p. 280.

'controversial divinity'[62] – no Tracts for the Times obviously. Christianity is thus considered part of the general knowledge package. Newman makes the point that *doctrine* is Christian knowledge and cannot be simply excluded, because Christianity is something more than useful and entertaining, 'I want faith to come first, and utility and amusement to follow'.[63]

As eminent and worthy people intent on good works often lack a sense of humour and do not think that their words could ever be taken amiss, Newman decides to poke a little fun at them. Sir Robert Peel proposes that the institution at Tamworth 'be open to the well-educated and virtuous women of this town and neighbourhood'.[64] The obvious corollary is put: Does it mean to exclude women not virtuous? 'Does it mean to exclude them while bad *men* are admitted?'[65] But if Sir Robert were really doing his job he would above all want to encourage the unvirtuous so that they could benefit from improvement through contact with scientific influence! One can well imagine how people would have roared heartily as they buttered their toast and toyed with their kipper, taking up their *Times* on those cold February mornings, at the picture conjured up of pickpockets and card-sharps being ushered into the Library while madams and street walkers are looking through the windows with longing for literary satisfaction. Although the promoters of the Tamworth Reading Room would dismiss bias against religion, in fact they

[62] *D.A.*, p. 280.
[63] *D.A.*, pp. 280–1.
[64] *D.A.*, p. 281 and *L.D.* VIII, p. 526.
[65] *D.A.*, p. 281.

take from Christianity what they give to science.[66]
Christianity is in effect down-graded (as we have now
come to expect, but here we see the beginning of a
long process). Faith is seen as a spirit of division which
gives rise to parties and controversy. In the interest of
general harmony we must discard all that disunites and
cultivate all that will amalgamate.[67] Religion must be
abandoned in favour of the pursuit of knowledge:
'Knowledge can do for Society what has hitherto been
supposed to be the prerogative of Faith'.[68]

Robert Peel is firmly of the opinion that 'an
increased sagacity will administer to an exalted faith;
that it will make men not merely believe in the cold
doctrines of Natural Religion, but that it will so
prepare and temper the spirit and understanding, that
they will be better qualified to comprehend the great
scheme of human redemption'.[69] In that outpouring
of claptrap we can see ahead into the multiple
speeches made by twentieth-century dictators who
have removed religion from the scene and have to
inspire their citizens to sacrifice. But ultimately
knowledge cannot inspire, only faith (even Stalin had
to make use of the Orthodox Church during The
Great Patriotic War). It can be stated categorically,
that there has never been a religion of physics or
philosophy but only of revelation. 'It has never been a
deduction from what we know: it has ever been an
assertion of what we are to believe. It has never lived

[66] *D.A.*, p. 280.
[67] *D.A.*, p. 285. Cf '... to pretend to cultivate love at the expense of faith' *MS Sermon* 485, *BOA*.
[68] *D.A.*, p. 287.
[69] *D.A.*, p. 292.

in a conclusion; it has ever been a message, or a history, or a vision.'[70]

Sir Robert Peel sincerely believed that such a pursuit of knowledge without the constraints of too much dogma would lead to thoughts of religion. Newman turns to history and laments the fact that 'in the history of heathen Greece ... her most eminent empirical philosophers were atheists, and that it was their atheism which was the cause of their eminence'.[71] This does not mean that the study of science (or Nature, as Newman puts it) leads to atheism, but when there is no religion – or when it is excluded – the mind tends in that direction. It is true that scientific research can produce a great feeling of exaltation. We can marvel at the intricacies of the computer as the Victorians were fascinated by steam engines, but, points out Newman, 'wonder is not religion, or we should be worshipping our railroads'.[72]

Those who would 'improve' mankind are often guilty of taking from him and her the very ingredient that alone makes it possible. The pursuit of knowledge leaves on one side the inconvenient fact of sin and the need for repentance: it makes irrelevant the notion of Divine Providence of God's love and justice and mercy which alone can inspire and ultimately build a society worthy of those whom God has created. Newman ends with a touching but

[70] *D.A.*, p. 296. Cf. 'Faith outstrips argument ...' *Via Media (V.M.)* I, p. 86.

[71] *D.A.*, p. 298.

[72] *D.A.*, p. 302. Cp. the remark 'the establishment of Societies, in which literature or science has been the essential bond of union, to the exclusion of religious profession'. *Fifteen Sermons preached before the University of Oxford (U.S.)* p. 72.

firm analysis of Sir Robert Peel: 'How melancholy is it that a man of such exemplary life, such cultivated tastes, such political distinction, such Parliamentary tact and such varied experience, should have so little confidence in himself, so little faith in his own principles, so little hope of sympathy in others, so little heart for a great venture, so little of romantic aspiration, and of firm resolve, and stern dutifulness to the Unseen!'[73]

Who's to Blame?

With the last two literary pieces in *Discussions and Arguments* we are dealing with Dr Newman, now a Roman Catholic. Those who maintained that with the loss of his Anglican faith, he would somehow forfeit much of his appeal were to be sadly disillusioned. *Who's to Blame?* marks Newman's first real attempt at political theory (it can be contrasted with his lectures on Turkish history which he gave to the Catholic Institute of Liverpool in 1853). If anything, freedom from the Established Church allowed Newman to feel unconstrained to comment on the Establishment.

As with *The Tamworth Reading Room*, this took the form of letters to the Irish newspaper *The Catholic Standard* 3 March–21 April, 1855. Thomas Richardson, the Catholic publisher, had offered the editorship to Newman's friend, Henry Wilberforce, who had resigned his living of East Farleigh (to which he had been presented by Prince Albert) when he had become a Catholic in 1850. On 4 June 1854 Newman was

[73] *D.A.*, p. 305. Cf. 'Obedience, the Remedy for Religious Perplexity', *P.S.* I, pp. 229–43.

formally installed as Rector of the Catholic University, and he gave his inaugural lecture on 9 November. He would be back and forth between Dublin and Birmingham over the next four years, and having finished *Who's to Blame?* he would take up work on his novel *Callista* which he completed in August 1855.

Newman wrote to Wilberforce in 1854 to discuss the matter of his salary: 'Richardson won't give any decent terms. He picks the brains of authors, and there is the whole of it'.[74] He broached the question of literary contributions, pointing out, 'You must be able to say to a friend, "Here is the Trust Question – or the War question – or the Anglican Convocation Question, making a row"'.[75] The war in question was the Crimean campaign which began in January 1854, involving Britain and France and the Ottoman Turks on the one side, and Russia on the other. Newman's position on the war was unequivocal. He thought it 'a simple piece of Johnbullism'.[76] But he used the circumstances of the war and the administrative chaos that seems to have reached every level of the enormous Whitehall and military bureaucracy to examine the implications for the British Constitution. Despite his criticisms he was fulsome in his praise, writing in *Who's to Blame?* 'I have a decided view that Catholicism is safer and more free under a constitutional *regime* such as our own, than under any other ... that remarkable polity, which the world never saw before or elsewhere,

[74] 14 February 1854, *L.D.* XVI, p. 45.

[75] 3 March 1855, *L.D.* XVI, p. 400.

[76] To J. Walker of Scarborough, 1 January 1855, *L.D.* XVI, p. 340: 'I have hated the war heartily from the first, thought it unnecessary, and considered Whig pride to be the moving principle of it'. By February 1855, 1000 British soldiers were dying each week.

and which it is so pleasant to live under'.[77] But the action of the war seemed to put many of the instruments of government on hold and Newman did not like the implications.

The Crimean War, which like many campaigns of the British army had its fierce opponents, by all accounts was a shambles. More soldiers died of disease than in battle, and the logistics of supply seem to show all the aspects of a vaudeville turn. This may not have mattered in the past, but for the first time a newspaper, *The Times*, had a war correspondent, in the person of William Howard Russell, at the front sending daily dispatches which presented the grim story to the breakfast tables of the British public.

Newman thought that war was 'a most inconvenient, expensive, tedious process; it takes much money, many men, and many lives'.[78] He did not see much advantage as a Catholic in prising Turkey from Russia, if that meant installing Protestant Liberalism instead (he need not have worried).[79] But in the heat of war the very democratic institutions which are the pride of British people may be altered 'under the immediate pressure, in order to make them work easier ... because the British Constitution is made for a state of peace, and not for a state of war'.[80] The State and the Constitution depend on each other. The State is necessary for the well-being and fundamental

[77] *D.A.*, pp. 307, 310. Also 'I suppose, England is, in a political and national point of view, the best country to live in the world.' p. 353.

[78] *D.A.*, p. 308. The Crimea left a lasting impression on the British with names like 'raglan', 'cardigan' and 'balaclava' entering the language and a plethora of Inkerman Terraces.

[79] *D.A.*, p. 310.

[80] *D.A.*, pp. 309, 311.

freedom of the individual and yet has to possess the
authority and administrative capacity to enforce law
and order. But there is a price to be paid for the
amount of power you put in the hands of the State. If
you limit that power then the State is feeble, but if
invigorated it can be high-handed.[81] Newman comes
to the conclusion that 'a despotic government is the
best for war, and a popular government the best for
peace'.[82] He then analyses the Athenian democratic
system and draws parallels with the individualism
shown by Miltiades and Themistocles and that of the
ordinary British citizen: 'that inward spring of restless
independence, which makes a State weak, and a
Nation great'.[83]

There is no doubt in Newman's mind that Athens
lacked firmness and consistency as a State but that lack
was made up by the brilliance of intellectual activity.
In a similar way, if the nation is strong then enterprise
can take on the running of State-controlled businesses
such as postal services and railways and even education
which are otherwise government monopolies. Not
that Newman is necessarily advocating that all these
things should be privatized, but he would be broadly
in favour of a partnership between government and
private ownership. This brings him to state that
managing wars is not something which the State seems
to do well. 'I do not say that a Constitutional State
never must risk war, never must engage in war, never
will conquer in war; but that its strong point lies in the
other direction. If we would see what liberty,

[81] *D.A.*, p. 326.
[82] *D.A.*, p. 326.
[83] *D.A.*, p. 330. Cf *Historical Sketches* (*H.S.*) III, pp. 81–8.

independence, self-government, a popular Constitution, can do, we must look to times of tranquillity. In peace a self-governing nation is prosperous in itself, and influential in the wide world.'[84] Newman is a good propagandist for the British character. 'An Englishman likes to take his own matters into his own hands. He stands on his own ground, and does as much work as half a dozen men of certain other races. He can join too with others, and has a turn for organizing, but he insists on its being voluntary. He is jealous of no one, except kings and governments, and offensive to no one except their partisans and creatures ... Protected by the sea, and gifted with a rare energy, self-possession, and imperturbability, the English people have been able to carry out self-government to its limits, and to absorb into its constitutional action many of those functions which are necessary for the protection of any country, and commonly belong to the Executive; and triumphing in their marvelous success they have thought no task too hard for them.'[85] But at the same time the English character is so individualistic that it wants as little of government as is possible: 'a system of checks and counter-checks, the division of power, the imperative concurrence of disconnected officials, and his own supervision and revision, – the method of hitches, cross-purposes, collision, deadlocks ...'[86] This was well demonstrated in the chaos surrounding the conduct of the Crimean War because with the multiplication of committees nobody was effectively in charge. Yes, the concentra-

[84] *D.A.*, p. 332.
[85] *D.A.*, pp. 336, 339.
[86] *D.A.*, p. 342.

tion of power in the Executive does present problems
(this is a constant subject of debate in the United
States which has a supreme executive with far more
powers than the British monarch), but if you forbid
the concentration of power then you will make its
operation inevitably open to inefficiency ('roundabout, clumsy, slow, intermittent and disappointing')
and with nobody willing to take responsibility, to
negligence and the eventual waste of life, which the
Irish famine and the Crimean War abundantly
demonstrated.[87] Despite all the committees of the War
Department, the army was only reorganized when
Edward Cardwell was Secretary for War 1868–75.

Newman makes the observation that English people
consider it better if the State executive 'should work
badly, than work to the inconvenience and danger of
our national liberties ... The Nation's object never
was that the Executive should be worked in the best
possible way, but that the Nation should work it. It is
altogether a family concern on a very large scale: the
Executive is more or less in commission, and the
commission is the Nation itself'.[88] One wonders if
Newman as vicar of St Mary's would ever have been
as detached so as to see the greatness of the British
Constitution and its very obvious shortcomings.

This concept of sharing in the Executive means that
the people in fact divide among themselves the power
both of the Crown and the judiciary. The people
administer the Crown lands, and the courts are

---

[87] *D.A.*, p. 341. Newman much earlier wrote to Keble on 3 January
1842 about Convocation, saying 'The Bishops are a real and existing
power – Convocation is not'. *L.D.* VIII, p. 411

[88] *D.A.*, p. 347.

governed by the law of precedents which must be in keeping with the national consensus. Newman rather bitterly maintains that 'satisfaction, peace, liberty, conservative interests' were the supreme end of the law, and not mere raw justice as such.[89] National utility is to be the watchword and 'injustice is the exception improvement may make things worse',[90] even though bribery is rife!

Why does Newman take such a jaundiced view even of the jury system? He says that 'the good of the country is made to take the lead of private interest' and that an unjust verdict is the price one has to pay.[91] This is more than passing interest as many countries have suspended the right to trial by jury and this is now being considered in England (although initially rejected by the House of Lords). It is bound up by his attitude to democracy which he cannot disassociate from the French Revolution, the revolutions of 1848 and the Chartist riots.

Newman does not advocate despotism, the rule of 'knout and tar barrel',[92] but he despairs of the English attitude towards any exercise of power as somehow limiting the essential liberties bestowed by Magna Carta. It is a particularly English characteristic to hamstring both the army and the National Church, so that they can never threaten the commonweal. When not engaged in combat, the army is run down to subsistence level and the Church is deprived of 'such ecclesiastical belonging

[89] *D.A.*, p. 351.
[90] *D.A.*, p. 352.
[91] *D.A.*, pp. 349, 353.
[92] *D.A.*, p. 309 and cf. *H.S.* I, p. 180. For Newman's politics *see* J. Derek Holmes 'Factors in the Development of Newman's Political Attitudes' in *Newman and Gladstone*, ed James Bastable, Dublin, 1978, p. 74ff.

as the ritual and ceremonial of religion, synods, religious orders, sisters of charity, missions, and the like, necessary instruments of Christian faith'.[93] It is also told to confine itself to cultivating theology in private and avoiding controversy and extremism.[94]

But having said all this, Newman concludes by saying that he is exposing the weak side of the Constitution 'not exactly because I want it altered, but because people should not consider it the strong side. I think it is a necessary weakness; I do not see how it can be satisfactorily set right without dangerous innovations'.[95] All in all, it is a very balanced judgement on an institution that like Topsy 'has just growed'. Newman acknowledges that it works, but wartime stretches it and reveals its weaknesses. But as Churchill was to maintain, 'Democracy is the worst form of government except all those other forms that have been tried from time to time'.[96] But at the same time, the people have to accept the blame for their desire to limit the power of their rulers.

An Internal Argument for Christianity

In 1864 Newman published the work for which he will always be remembered, his *Apologia*. It vindicated him triumphantly and gave him a certain public notoriety which never really left him. He published *A Letter to Pusey* in January 1866 and received Bishop Ullathorne's request to open an Oratory at Oxford which was to afford him much heartache. In the midst

[93] *D.A.*, pp. 358–9. See infra p. 39ff.
[94] *D.A.*, p. 359.
[95] *D.A.*, p. 360.
[96] Speech. Hansard, 11 November 1947, column 206

of all this he told his friend, Sir Frederic Rogers, Secretary of State for the Colonies, that he had sent for Sir Robert Seeley's theological best-seller *Ecce Homo*. He goes on to say that he saw very few books and that composition was for him 'a child-birth' and 'the consequence is I have nothing in writing which has not been published'.[97] Yet within six months he was working on the problem of certitude which would result in *A Grammar of Assent*.

When Newman finally got down to reading *Ecce Homo* he wrote again to Rogers, apologizing for not writing sooner, since Rogers was obviously impressed by the work. He did not share Roger's enthusiasm. 'Let me be honest, and say that I had the greatest difficulty to get on with the book ... There seemed to me little new in it, but what was questionable, or fanciful. And it seemed to me that the author treated things as discoveries, when they were only new to him. At the same time the book, I grant, is full of interest as a sign of the times – and as likely to influence the course of thought as it is now running in the religious world.'[98]

Rogers ought to have recognized the warning notes – Newman had already completed his review by May 1865 and sent it to Fr Coleridge, the Editor of the Jesuit periodical *The Month*. It was published in June 1866 and was not complimentary. He damned it with faint praise as the best-seller it was: 'This is what we especially mean by calling his book "remarkable". It

[97] 18 January 1866, *L.D.* XXII, p. 129.
[98] 13 May 1866, *L.D.* XXI, p. 231. John Robert Seeley (1834–1895) was Professor of Latin at University College London. In 1869 he became Professor of Modern History at Cambridge. There is a photograph of Newman reading *Ecce Homo* which is reproduced in Meriol Trevor's *Newman Light in Winter*, Macmillan, London, 1972, on p. 338.

deserves remark, because he has excited it'.[99] Sir John
Seeley aimed in his work to present an image of Christ
taken from the pages of the Gospels, in such a way that
'the recorded picture of our Lord is its own evidence,
that it carries with it its own reality and authority'.[100]

Newman plainly found the book exasperating.
There was an obvious superficial appeal, such as a
coffee-table book would have today, but it did not
measure up to any criteria of greatness. It was 'a
Volume in which what is trite and what is novel, what
is striking and what is startling, what is sound and
what is untrustworthy, what is deep and what is
shallow, are so mixed up together, or at least so
vaguely suggested, or so perplexingly confessed –
which has so much of occasional force and circum-
nambient glitter, of pretence and seriousness – as to
make it impossible either with a good conscience to
praise it, or without harshness and unfairness to
condemn.'[101] Needless to say, Newman is not
dissuaded from his course, which comes down firmly
against the book.

He begins pointing out how at a time of scepticism it
is unwise to presume faith in our Saviour without
establishing the foundations of such faith. These would
include the veracity of the Gospels themselves (so
continuing the debate which we saw in *Holy Scripture in
its relation to the Catholic Creed*) and the means by which
those Gospels reached us, which Newman (and
Augustine) would link to the Catholic Church.

The very attraction of the book, especially 'among

[99] *D.A.*, p. 364.
[100] *D.A.*, p. 372.
[101] *D.A.*, p. 363.

Anglicans of the Oxford school, after the wearisome doubt and disquiet of the last ten years',[102] is that it sidesteps so many issues and leaves all controversy to one side, appealing to Liberal and Catholic alike and all shades between:

These are the men who, if they could, would unite old ideas with new; who cannot give up tradition, yet are loth to shut the door to progress; who look for a more exact adjustment of faith with reason than has hitherto been attained; who love the conclusions of Catholic theology better than the proofs, and the methods of modern thought better than its results; and who, in the present wide unsettlement of religious opinion, believe indeed, or wish to believe, Scripture and orthodox doctrine, taken as a whole, and cannot get themselves to avow any deliberate dissent from any part of either, but still, not knowing how to defend their belief with logical exactness, or at least feeling that there are large unsatisfied objections lying against parts of it, or having misgivings lest there should be such, acquiesce in what is called a practical belief, that is, accept revealed truths, only because such acceptance of them is the safest course, because they are probable, and because to hold them in consequence is a duty, not as if they felt absolutely certain, though they will not allow themselves to be actually in doubt.[103]

---

[102] *D.A.*, p. 370. These saw the publication of the collection *Essays and Reviews* (1860).
[103] *D.A.*, p. 371.

Newman almost apologizes to the author for having to criticize someone who sees Christ as the founder of a visible Church and who was both King and Judge. But Sir John Seeley ruins it all by emphasizing that Jesus was human like us in all respects. Newman notes that the author does not draw on the Gospel of St John and thus has Christ after his baptism filled with 'agitation of mind' and then maturing his plan of action in the wilderness, 'becoming conscious of miraculous power'.[104] *Ecce Homo* interprets Christ's words to Nicodemus 'Unless a man is born again' as a demand to be open and not visit in secret! In the encounter with the woman taken in adultery, Jesus stoops down 'in His burning embarrassment and confusion ... so as to hide His face'.[105]

Newman cannot help saying 'Taking his work as it lies we can but wish he had kept his imagination under control'.[106] But apart from an over-stimulated imagination, Sir John Seeley also had an inbuilt resistance to the response which Catholics have to their Lord and God. Was this unconnected with his decision to exclude most of St John's Gospel? For Catholics, says Newman, 'their faith is as indelible as the pigment which colours their skin, even though it is skin-deep'.[107] This could not be otherwise, given the whole sacramental system and the Real Presence. 'Do we not believe in a Presence in the sacred Tabernacle, not as a form of words, or as a notion but as an Object as real as we are real?'[108]

[104] *D.A.*, p. 382.
[105] *D.A.*, p. 385.
[106] *D.A.*, p. 386.
[107] *D.A.*, p. 386.
[108] *D.A.*, p. 388.

Yet the author of *Ecce Homo* maintains that Jesus' denunciation of hypocrites extends to those who take 'the *short cut to belief* ... when, overwhelmed with difficulties which beset their minds, and afraid of damnation, they *suddenly* resolve to strive no longer but, giving their minds a holiday, to rest content with *saying* that they believe, and acting *as if* they did'.[109] He goes on to say, 'Assuredly, those who represent Christ as presenting to man an abstruse theology, and saying to them peremptorily, "Believe or be damned", have the coarsest conception of the Saviour of the world'.[110] Yet that is exactly what Jesus did say on many occasions with brutal frankness. Newman's judgement is surprisingly harsh because he sees the impact which the book may have on unsuspecting readers. So he says he presents a view of Christianity that is selective: 'You either accept Christianity, or you do not: if you do, do not garble and patch it; if you do not, suffer others to submit to it ungarbled'.[111]

Discussions and Arguments

Pickering (Newman's publisher) was pleased to have the volume. It went into a second edition the following year and a third and fourth edition in 1878 and 1882. It sold steadily, and when Longmans took over the publication in 1885 it was reprinted twice in 1888 and again in 1890.

The appeal of the book – apart from the fame of the author – depends very much on the particular nature

[109] *D.A.*, p. 390.
[110] *D.A.*, p. 390.
[111] *D.A.*, p. 398.

of the readership. For those wishing to study the evolution of the Oxford Movement, the first article would hold a special interest as it puts forward the growing problem of how to 'romanise' the Anglican Church without going over to Rome. Newman is very fair in his presentation of the individual opinions. In fact Newman always regretted any exaggeration or denigration of individual views. He would later write to Fr Coleridge, Editor of *The Month*, about an article which had appeared in the periodical, 'It has pained me to find that in *The Month* the Anglican Sacrament has been said to be probably a slice of quartern loaf, and nothing else. What good such expressions can do, I know not – but I feel keenly what harm they can do'.[112]

For those who want to understand the Oxford Movement the Tracts are essential reading. The two included in this volume are fairly representative of their type. The first sixty or so Tracts were pamphlets of between four and sixteen pages. In September 1835, they started to expand, led by Pusey's *Scriptural views of Holy Baptism* (Tr. 67–9). Tracts giving the views of the Anglican authorities on Baptism, Apostolical Succession and the place of Scripture and Tradition followed, together with Newman's Tract on Purgatory.

The lectures on the Patristical idea of Antichrist have perhaps the least interest – one wonders what his own congregation would have made of them – because he so studiously avoids any identification of Rome as the 'scarlet woman' that it is almost painful. He also does not really deal with the prevailing

[112] 21 October 1866, *L.D.* XXII, pp. 303–4.

millenary sentiments which had obviously found a receptive audience and continue to recruit adherents in our own day.

The Tract on Scripture in its relation to the Creed is a scholarly piece of work which gives the basis for the place of Scripture in Anglicanism while not being bound by the strictures of 'sola Scriptura'. He argues that the teaching of the Fathers of the Church fills in the gaps and apparent inconsistencies in the revealed word, but of course this is not the Catholic doctrine of Tradition! The strictures on Latitudinarianism are totally consistent with all that Newman will say about Liberalism. He maintained that it was the graveyard of all faith where no one view is better than any other.

When we come to *The Tamworth Reading Room* we find Newman at his most incisive and humorous. He lauds the high-minded benefactors who out of the generosity of their hearts will provide a library for the working classes of Staffordshire. But he then dissects the whole enterprise, pointing out that it is attempting to make people virtuous by scientific knowledge and information. Behind the philanthropy lies the in-built rationalist understanding of religion as the enemy of free thought and action. Newman was concerned that because libraries were good things, people might be persuaded to accept the underlying argument and be open to further attempts to free them from religion. As such, it was the forerunner of so many humanist campaigns which assume that religion now has no place in society, and indeed no right to a say. Secular States, having benefitted from religious institutions and foundations seem to consider it a duty to disassociate themselves from any sacred affiliation. The same arguments are brought forward to substantiate Sunday trading ('in the interests of the consumer'), non-denominational education ('it breaks down prejudice') and in recent times the new constitution of the European Union which dispenses with any mention of God ('so as not to antagonize ...'). It may appear enlightened, but it breathes the very spirit of the Enlightenment with its desire to overcome the hold that religion still possesses and evokes, even if subconsciously, in the minds and hearts of nations which owe their origin to Christianity.

The most interesting contribution in many ways is *Who's to Blame?* Newman uses the blunders which marked the conduct of the Crimean War to examine the workings of British democracy. Nobody could accuse him of any disloyalty to all things British. But he is also objective. Steeped in classical history, with Athens an ever-present and vivid model, he points out the strengths and weaknesses of the British system. The desire on the part of British citizens to limit the power of the executive neatly avoids despotism but leads to endless bureaucracy and worse. Since every aspect of rule has to be shared out, there is an inevitable proliferation of committees, which often take on a life of their own. The points raised in Newman's essay have contemporary relevance on both sides of the Atlantic. There is an ongoing debate in the United States on the balance between federal and state powers, and in Britain, concerning the amount of power new regional authorities can exert as well as the coherence of public-private partnerships. In Britain, many have asked whether the Prime Minister, with a substantial majority in parliament is assuming semi-presidential powers.

It is interesting that the question was being asked also in the context of a military campaign, which, like the Crimea, has its critics.

In his review of *Ecce Homo* Newman introduces us to a book of which the style of writing is now very familiar. It does not try to rival German and French rationalism but it presents a Jesus of Nazareth who is all too human, questioning his mission and showing his embarrassment in the face of sin. A presentation that for all its 'humanity' despises those who see in Jesus the Christ, the Son of God and are ready to believe and worship because he alone can take away the sins of the world.

The Style of Discussions and Arguments
Reference has been made throughout to Newman's use of irony. This can be noted especially in *The Tamworth Reading Room* and *Who's to Blame?* Of Lord Brougham, Newman can write 'No one can equal the great sophist. Lord Brougham is inimitable in his own line'.[113] Those who like him try to improve human nature while ignoring moral weaknesses 'do but play a sort of "hunt the slipper"'.[114] When people of all persuasions are included to aid the acquisition of knowledge, Newman describes them as being, 'all admitted by this writer [Peel] to one beatification in proof of the Catholic character of his substitute for faith'.[115]

Those who think in terms of knowledge as providing diversion for the mind are like the nurserymaid,

[113] *D.A.*, p. 260.
[114] *D.A.*, p. 274.
[115] *D.A.*, p. 289.

who 'when a child cries ... dances it about, or points to the pretty horses out of the window, or shows how ashamed poll-parrot, or poor puss must be of its tantrums'.[116] Nor does the mention of the wonders of Nature escape Newman's withering touch: 'Rather stay your hunger with corn grown in Jupiter, and warm yourself by the Moon'[117] and, already quoted 'Wonder is not religion or we would be worshipping our railroads'.[118]

In *Who's to Blame?* Newman contrasts the heights of Inkerman with the depths of Exeter Hall (the venue for revivalist meetings). Newman blaming the British public for the ultimate failures of the Crimea cannot resist a final irony: 'Such is the will of the Nation, which had rather that its institutions should be firm and stable, than that they should be effective'.[119] Those who consider Newman to lack a sense of humour, who kept his nose in books, are in for a very pleasant surprise.

The untimely death of Gerard Tracey has deprived us of an invaluable and ever courteous friend and unique resource. It is to be hoped that some way will be found to continue the assistance he gave to researchers, because with his historical scholarship and complete mastery of the Newman archives and the library, Gerard could identify the most obscure reference. He had clearly demonstrated this in his

[116] *D.A.*, p. 264.
[117] *D.A.*, p. 304.
[118] *D.A.*, p. 302.
[119] *D.A.*, p. 348.

editorship of Volumes VI, VII and VIII of the *Letters and Diaries*, as well as numerous articles and interviews.

He was working on Volume IX and this edition of *Discussions and Arguments* which he chose especially for its challenge (he was proved right!). I was honoured to work with him throughout the present Newman Millennium Edition, and like others will miss his friendship. As a particular mark of respect he was given the privilege of being buried in the Oratorian community graveyard at Rednall in the Lickey Hills outside Birmingham, which had been purchased in 1854, just prior to Newman's *Who's to Blame?* He shares that part of the graveyard reserved for those who are not professed members of the community with Mrs Frances Wooten, the widow of Newman's doctor in Oxford.[120]

I have endeavoured to complete the notes to this volume in the same spirit in which they were begun. The credit for most of these are Gerard's; the responsibility for the rest is mine.

James Tolhurst
September 2003

---

[120] She was received into the Church by Newman in 1850 and became his loyal supporter and friend. She was the first matron of the Oratory School and died in 1876.

THE REV. HENRY ARTHUR WOODGATE, B.D.,

MY DEAR WOODGATE,

Half a century and more has passed since you first allowed me to know you familiarly, and to possess your friendship.

Now, in the last decade of our lives, it is pleasant to me to look back upon those old Oxford days, in which we were together, and, in memory of them, to dedicate to you a Volume, written, for the most part, before the currents of opinion and the course of events carried friends away in various directions, and brought about great changes and bitter separations.

Those issues of religious inquiry I cannot certainly affect to lament, as far as they concern myself: as they relate to others, at least it is left to me, by such acts as you now allow me, to testify to them that affection which time and absence cannot quench, and which is the more fresh and buoyant because it is so old.

I am, my dear Woodgate,

Your attached and constant friend,

JOHN HENRY NEWMAN.

January 5, 1872.

I.

HOW TO ACCOMPLISH IT.*

I.

WHEN I was at Rome, I fell in with an English acquaintance, whom I had met occasionally in his own county, and when he was on a visit at my own University. I had always felt him a pleasant, as rather engaging companion, and his talent no one could question; but his opinions on a variety of political and ecclesiastical subjects were either very unsettled or at least very uncommon. His remarks had often the effect of random talking; and though he was always ingenious, and often (as far as I was his antagonist) unanswerable, yet he did not advance me, or others, one step towards the conviction that he was right and we were wrong in the matter which happened to be in dispute. Such a personage is no unusual phenomenon in this day, in which every one thinks it a duty to exercise the "sacred right of private judgment;" and when, consequently, there are, as the grammar has it, "quot homines, tot

---

* [The discussion in this Paper is carried on by two speculative Anglicans, who aim at giving vitality to their Church, the one by uniting it to the Roman See, the other by developing a nineteenth-century Anglo-Catholicism. The narrator sides on the whole with the latter of these.]

sententiæ;" nor should I have distinguished my good friend from a score of theorists and debaters, producible at a minute's notice in any part of the United Kingdom, except for two reasons—first, that his theories lay in the different direction from those now in fashion, and were all based upon the principle of "bigotry," (as he, whether seriously or paradoxically, avowed)—next, that he maintained they were not novelties, but as old as the Gospel itself, and possessing as continuous a tradition. Yet, in spite of whatever recommendations he cast about them, they did not take hold of me. They seemed unreal; this will best explain what I mean:—*unreal*, as if he had raised his structure in the air, an independent, self-sustained pile of buildings, *sui simile*, without historical basis or recognized position among things existing, without discoverable relations to the wants, wishes, and opinions of those who were the subjects of his speculations.

We were thrown together at Rome, as we had never been before; and, getting familiar with him, I began to have some insight into his meaning. I soon found him to be quite serious in his opinions; but I did not think him a wit the less chimerical and *meteoros* than before. However, as he was always entertaining, and could bear a set-down or a laugh easily, from the sweetness and amiableness of his nature, I always liked to hear him talk. Indeed, if the truth must be spoken, I believe, in some degree, he began to poison my mind with his extravagances.

One day I had called at the Prussian Minister's, and found my friend there. We left together. The landing from which the staircase descended looked out over Rome; affording a most striking view of a city which the Christian can never survey without the bitterest, the most loving, and the most melancholy thoughts. I will not describe the details of the prospect ; they may be found in every book; nothing is so common now as panoramic or dioramic descriptions. Suffice it to say, that we were looking out from the Capitol all over the modern city ; and that ancient Rome, being for the most part out of sight, was not suggested to us except as the basis of the history which followed its day. The morning was very clear and still : all the many domes, which gave feature to the view before us, rose gracefully and proudly. We lingered at the window without saying a word. News of public affairs had lately come from England, which had saddened us both, as leading us to forebode the overthrow of all that gives dignity and interest to our country, not to touch upon the more serious reflections connected with it.

My friend began by alluding to a former conversation, in which I had expressed my anticipation, that Rome, as a city, was still destined to bear the manifestation of divine judgments. He said, " Have you really the heart to say that all this is to be visited and overthrown ?" His eye glanced at St. Peter's. I was taken by surprise, and for a moment overcome, as well as he ; but the parallel of the Apostles' question in the Gospel soon came to my aid, and I said, by way of answer, " Master, see what manner of stones and what buildings are here !" He smiled ; and we relapsed into our meditative mood.

At length I said, " Why, surely, as far as one's imagination is concerned, nothing is so hard to conceive as that evil is coming on our own country : fairly as the surface of things still promises, yet you as well as I expect evil. Not long before I came abroad, I was in a retired parish in Berkshire, on a Sunday, and the inestimable blessings of our present condition, the guilt of those who are destroying them, and moreover, the difficulty of believing they could be lost, came forcibly upon me. When everything looked so calm, regular, and smiling, the church bell going for service, high and low, young and old flocking in, others resting in the porch, and others delaying in the churchyard, as if there were enjoyment in the very cessation of that bodily action which for six days had worried them, (but I need not go on describing what both of us have seen a hundred times,) I said to myself, ' What a heaven on earth is this! how removed, like an oasis, from the dust and dreariness of the political world! And is it possible that it depends for its existence on what is without, so as to be dissipated and to vanish at once upon the occurrence of certain changes in public affairs ?' I could not bring myself to believe that the foundations beneath were crumbling away, and that a sudden fall might be expected."

He replied by one of his occasional flights—" If Rome itself, as you say, is not to last, why should the daughter who has severed herself from Rome ? The amputated limb dies sooner than the wounded and enfeebled trunk which loses it."

" Say this anywhere in Rome than on this staircase," I answered. " Come, let us find a more appropriate place for such extravagances ; " and I took him by the arm, and we began to descend. We made for the villa on the Palatine, and in our way thither, and while strolling in its walks, the following discussion took place, which of course I have put together into a more compact shape than it assumed in our actual conversation.

2.

" What I mean," said he in continuation, " is this : that we, in England, are severed from the centre of unity, and therefore no wonder our Church does not flourish. You may say to me, if you please, that the Church of Rome is corrupt. I know it; but what then? If (to use the common saying) there are remedies even worse than the disease they practise on, much more are remedies conceivable which are only not as bad, or but a little better. To cut off a limb is anyhow a strange mode of saving it from the influence of some constitutional ailment. Indigestion may cause cramp in the extremities, yet we spare our hands or feet, notwithstanding. I do not wish to press analogies; yet, surely, there is such a religious *fact* as the existence of a great Catholic body, union with which is a Christian privilege and duty. Now, we English are separate from it."

I answered, "I will grant you thus much,—that the present is an unsatisfactory, miserable state of things; that there is a defect, an evil in existing circumstances, which we should pray and labour to remove; yet I can grant no more. The Church is founded on a doctrine— the gospel of *Truth;* it is a means to an end. Perish the Church Catholic itself, (though, blessed be the promise, this cannot be,) yet let it perish *rather* than the Truth should fail. Purity of faith is more precious to the Christian than unity itself. If Rome has erred grievously in doctrine (and in so thinking we are both of one mind), then is it a duty to separate even from Rome."

"You allow much more," he replied, "than most of us; yet even you, as it seems to me, have not a deep sense enough of the seriousness of our position. Recollect, at the Reformation we did that which is a sin, *unless* we prove it to be a duty. It was, and is, a very solemn protest. Would the seraph Abdiel have made his resistance a triumph and a boast,—spoken of the glorious stand he had made,—or made it a pleasant era in his history? Would he have gone on to praise himself, and say, 'Certainly, I am one among a thousand ; all of them went wrong but I, and they are now in hell, but I am pure and uncorrupt, in consequence of my noble separation from those rebels'? Now, certainly, I have heard you glory in an event which at best was but an escape as by fire,—an escape at a great risk and loss, and at the price of a melancholy separation."

I felt he had, as far as the practical question went, the advantage of me. Indeed it must be confessed that we Protestants are so satisfied with intellectual victories in our controversy with Rome as to think little of that charity which " vaunteth not herself, is not puffed up, doth not behave herself unseemly."

He continued :—" Do you recollect the notion entertained by the primitive Christians concerning Catholicity ? The Church was, in their view, one vast body, founded by the Apostles, and spreading its branches out into all lands,—the channel through which the streams of grace flowed, the mystical vine through which that sap of life circulated, which was the possession of those and those only who were grafted on it. In this Church there can be no division. Pass the axe through it, and one part or the other is cut off from the Apostles. There cannot be two distinct bodies, each claiming descent from the original stem. Indeed, the very word *catholic* witnesses to this. Two Apostolic bodies there may be without actual contradiction of terms ; but there is necessarily but one body Catholic." And then, in illustration of this view, he went on to cite from memory the substance of passages from Cyril and Augustine, which I suspect he had picked up from some Romanist friend at the English College. I have since turned them out in in their respective authors, and here give them in translation.

The first extract occurs in a letter written by Augustine to a Donatist bishop :—

" I will briefly suggest a question for your consideration. Seeing that at this day we have before our eyes the Church of God, called Catholic, diffused throughout the world, we think we ought not to doubt that herein is a most plain accomplishment of holy prophecy, confirmed as it was by our Lord in the Gospel, and by the Apostles, who, agreeably to the prediction, so extended it. Thus St. Paul preached the Gospel, and founded churches, etc. John also writes to seven Churches, etc. With all these churches we, at this day, communicate, as is plain ; and it is equally plain that you Donatists do not communicate with them. Now, then, I ask you to assign some reason why Christ should . . . all at once be pent up in Africa, where you are, or even in the whole of it. For your community, which bears the name of Donatus, evidently is not in all places —that is, catholic. If you say ours is not the Catholic, but nickname it the Macarian, the rest of Christendom differs from you ; whereas you yourselves must own, what every one who knows you will also testify, that yours is known as the Donatist denomination. Please to tell me, then, how the Church of Christ has vanished from the world, and is found only among you ; whereas our side of the controversy is upheld, without our saying a word, by the plain fact, that we see in it a fulfilment of Scripture prophecy." *

The next is from one of the same Father's treatises, addressed to a friend :—

" We must hold fast the Christian religion, and the communion of that Church which is, and is called, Catholic, not only by its members, but even by all its enemies. For, whether they will or no, even heretics themselves, and the children of schism, when they speak, not with their own people, but with strangers, call that Church nothing else but Catholic ? Indeed they would not be understood, unless they characterized it by that name which it bears throughout the world." †

* Ep. 49, Ed. Benedict. † De vera Rel., c. 7, n. 12.

The last was from Cyril's explanation of the doctrine of the One Holy Catholic Church :—

"Whereas the name (*church*) is used variously . . . . as (for instance) it may be applied to the heresy or persuasion of the Manichees, etc., therefore the creed has carefully committed to thee the confession of the One Holy Catholic Church, in order that thou mayest avoid their odious meetings, and remain always in the Holy Catholic Church, in which thou wast regenerated.   And if perchance thou art a traveller in a strange city, do not simply ask, 'Where is the house of God?' for the multitude of persuasions attempt to call their hiding-places by that name ; nor simply, 'Where is the Church?' but, 'Where is the *Catholic* Church?' for such is the peculiar name of this the holy Mother of us all, who is the spouse of the Only-Begotten Son."[*]

3.

After giving some account of these passages, he continued : "Now, I am only contending for the *fact* that the communion of Rome constitutes the main body of the Church Catholic, and that we are split off from it, and in the condition of the Donatists ; so that every word of Augustine's argument to them, could be applied to us.   This, I say, is a *fact;* and if it be a grave fact, to account for it by saying that they are corrupt is only bringing in a second grave fact.   Two such serious facts —that we are separate from the great body of the Church, and that it is corrupt—should, one would think, make us serious ; whereas we behave as if they were plus and minus, and destroyed each other.   Or rather, we *triumph* in the Romanists being corrupt, and we *deny* they are the great body of Christians, unfairly merging their myriad of churches under the poor title of '*the* Church of Rome ;' as if unanimity destroyed the argument from numbers."

* Cyril Hieros. Catech., xviii. 12.

"Stay! not so fast!" I made answer; "after all, they are but a part, though a large part, of the Christian world. Is the Greek communion to go for nothing, extending from St. Petersburg to Corinth and Antioch? or the Armenian churches? and the English communion which has branched off to India, Australia, the West Indies, the United States, Canada, and Nova Scotia? The true state of the case is this: the condition of the early Church, as Augustine and Cyril describe it, exists no more; it is to be found nowhere. You may apply, indeed, the terms which they used of it to the present time, and call the Romanists Catholics, as they claim to be; but this is a fiction and a theory, not the expression of a visible fact. Is it not a mere theory by which the Latin Church can affect to spread itself into Russia? I suspect, in spite of St. Cyril, you might ask in vain for their churches under the name of Catholic throughout the autocrat's dominions, or in Greece, as well as in England or Scotland. Where is the Catholic Bishop of Winchester or Lincoln? where the Catholic Church in England as a visible institution? No more is it such in Scotland; not to go on to speak of parts of Germany or the new world. All that can be said by way of reply is, that it is a very considerable communion, and venerable from its consistency and antiquity."

"That is the point," interrupted my companion; "they maintain that, such as they are, such they ever have been. They have been from the first 'the Catholics.' The schismatical Greeks, the Nestorians, the Monophysites, and the Protestants have grown up at different times, and on a novel doctrine or foundation."

"Have a care," I answered, "of diverging to the question of Apostolicity. We are engaged upon the Catholicity of the Latin Church. If we are to speak of

Antiquity, you yourself will be obliged to abandon its cause, for you are as decided as myself upon its corruptions from primitive simplicity. Foundation we have as apostolical as theirs, (unless you listen to the Nag's-head calumny,) and doctrine much more apostolical. Please to keep to the plain tangible *fact*, as you expressed it when you began, of the universal or catholic character of the Roman communion."

He was silent for a while, so I proceeded.

"Let me say a word or two more on the subject I had in hand when you interposed. I was observing that the state of things is certainly altered since Augustine's time—that is, in matter of fact, divisions, cross divisions, and complicated disarrangements have taken place in these latter centuries which were unknown in the fifth. We cannot, at once, apply his words as the representatives of things now existing; they are, in great measure, but the expression of principles to be adopted. May I say something further without shocking you? I think dissent and separatism present features unknown to primitive Christianity—so unknown that in its view of the world a place is not provided for them. A state of things has grown up, of which hereditary dissent is an element. All the better feelings of stability, quietness, loyalty, and the like, are in some places enlisted in its favour. In some places, as in Scotland, dissent is the religion of the state and country. I am not supposing that such outlying communities have blessings equal to the Church Catholic; only, while I condemn them as outlying, I would still contend that they retain so much of privilege, so much of the life and warmth of that spiritual body, from the roots of which they spring, as irregular shoots, as to secure their individual members from the calamity of being altogether cut off from it. In the latter ages of Judaism, the ten tribes, and afterwards the Samaritans, and then the proselytes of the gate, present a parallel, as having a position beyond the literal scope of the Mosaic law. I shall scruple, therefore, to apply the strong language which Cyprian uses against schismatics to the Scottish presbyterians or to the Lutherans. At least, they have the Scriptures. You understand why I mention this—to show, by an additional illustration, that not every word that the Fathers utter concerning the Church Catholic applies at once to the Church of this day. The early Christians had not the complete canon, nor were books then common, nor could most of them read. Other differences between their Church and our Church might be mentioned ;—for instance, the tradition of the early Church was of an historical character, of the nature of testimony ; and possessed an authority superadded to the Church's proper authority as a divine institution. It was a witness, far more perfect in its way, but the same in kind, as the body of ancient writers may be for the genuineness of Cæsar's works. It was virtually infallible. Now, however, this accidental authority has long ceased, or, at least, is indefinitely weakened ; and to resist it is not so obviously a sin against light. Here, then, is another reason for caution in applying the language of the Fathers concerning schism to our own times, since they did not in their writings curiously separate the Church's intrinsic and permanent authority as divine, from her temporary office of bearing witness to the Apostolic doctrine as to an historical fact."

"I must take time to think of this," he replied; "meanwhile, you at least grant me that the Latin communion is the main portion of Christendom—that participation with it is especially our natural position—and that our

present separation from it is a grievous calamity as such,
and, under the circumstances, nothing short of a solemn
protest against corruptions in it, of which we dare not
partake."

"I grant it," said I.

"And, in consequence, you discard, henceforth and for
ever, the following phrases, and the like—' our glorious
emancipation from Rome,' 'the noble stand we made
against a corrupt church,' 'our enlightened times,' 'the
blind and formal papists,' etc. etc."

"We shall see," I answered—"we shall see."

4.

We walked some little way in silence; at length, he
said, "I wonder what use you intend to make of the
view you just now so eagerly propounded, of the difference of circumstances between the present and the
ancient Church. It leads, I suppose, to the justification
of some of those ill-starred theories of concession which
are at present so numerous?"

To tell the truth, I did not see my way clearly how
far my own view ought to carry me. I saw that, without care, it would practically tend to the discarding the
precedent of Antiquity altogether, and was not unwilling
to have some light thrown by my friend upon the subject; so I affected, for the moment, a latitudinarianism
which I did not feel.* "Certainly," I replied, "it would
appear to be our duty to take things as we find them;
not to dream about the past, but to imitate, under
changed circumstances, what we cannot fulfil literally.
Christianity is intended to meet all forms of society; it
is not cast in the rigid mould of Judaism. Forms are
transitory — principles are eternal: the Church of the

* [*Vid.* Note on "Essays Crit. and Histor.," vol. i., p. 288; also p. 308.]

day is but an accidental development and type of the invisible and unchangeable. It will always have the properties of truth ; it will be ever (for instance) essentially conservative and aristocratic ; but its policy and measures will ever vary according to the age. Our Church in the seventeenth century was inclined to Romanism ; in the nineteenth, it was against Catholic emancipation. The orange ribbon, the emblem of a whig revolution, is now the badge of high tory confederations. Thus, the spirit of the Church is uniform, ever one and the same ; but its relative position and ordinances change. At least, all this might be said ; and I should like to see how you would answer it."

" That is," he interposed, " you grant that a Jew *would* have been wrong in philosophizing after the pattern you are setting, and talking of the nature of things, and transitory forms, and eternal truths, though you are privileged to do so ? "

" May we not suppose that the rules of the early Church were expedient then—nay, expedient now—as far as they could conveniently be observed, without considering them absolutely binding ? "

"Will you allow," he asked, in reply, "that St. Cyprian would have been in sin had he dispensed with episcopal Ordination, or St. Austin had he recognized the Donatists, or St. Chrysostom had he allowed the deacons to consecrate the elements ? "

" They would have committed sin," I answered.

" And in what would that sin have consisted ? "

" I suppose in doing that which they thought to be contrary to the continued usage of the Church."

" That is," he said, "in doing what they thought contrary to *apostolic* usage ? "

I granted it.

"And, of course," he said, "what they thought to be of apostolic usage, in such matters, was really such?"

I allowed this also.

"So it seems," he continued, "that they might not, and we may, do things contrary to apostolic usage."

"That," I said, "is the very assertion I am making; outward circumstances being changed, we may alter our rule of conduct."

He made answer: "I will give you my mind in a parable. Not many days since, I had scrambled into the rubbish yonder, which marks the site of the Apollo library, when I found what would be a treasure in the eyes of all the antiquarians in Europe, but which, to me, has a value of another kind—a MS. vindication of himself by a Jewish courtier of Herod the Great, for not observing the rites and customs of Judaism. It is well argued throughout. He sets out with owning the divinity of the Mosaic law, its beauty and expediency; the associations of reverence and interest cast around it; the affection it stirs within the mind; and the abstract desirableness of obeying it. 'But, after all, I confess,' he continues, 'I do not think its precepts binding at this day, because we are at such a distance from the age of Moses, and all the nations around us, not to say ourselves are changed, though the Law is not.' He proceeds to argue that he is not bound to go up to Jerusalem at the Passover, because there are synagogues about the country, which did not exist in the time of Moses; and, though it is true that purifications may be performed at the Temple, which the synagogues do not allow of, yet, 'after all,' he asks, 'how can we possibly know that the line of priests and Levites has been kept pure? Who can tell what irregularities may not have been introduced into their families during the captivity? Then, again,

what a set of men these said priests are ! Tainted with
pharisaical pride, or rather polluted with pharisaical
hypocrisy : especially the high priests : the very office
has become altogether secular—very much changed, too,
in form and detail from the original institution. What
enormities have occurred in the history of the Asmoneans ! Who can suppose that they have any longer
extraordinary gifts, prophecy, or the like, as of old time?
Besides, there is a temple at Alexandria now, not to say
another at Gerizim. Again, Herod, a man of Edom, is
king, and has remodelled the state of things ; for centuries we have had secular alliances, and religion is now
to be supported by ordinary, not extraordinary, means.
From the time that these political changes took place,
the rites have been superfluous. Events have proved
this. A number of Jews once attempted to keep the
Sabbath strictly, when an enemy came who surprised
them in consequence, and killed them. They were pious
but plainly narrow-minded and extravagant men. In
short, since the Captivity, the former system has been
superseded.' "

" Enough, enough," I interrupted ; " perhaps I have
spoken more strongly than I meant as to our liberty of
acquiescing in innovations. However, I still must hold
that we have no right to judge of others at this day, as
we should have judged of them, had all of us lived a
thousand years earlier. I do really think, for instance,
that in the presbyterianism of Scotland we see a providential phenomenon, the growth of a secondary system
unknown to St. Austin—begun, indeed, not without sin,
but continued, as regards the many, ignorantly, and
compatibly with some portion of true faith : I cannot
at once apply to its upholders his language concerning
schismatics."

" Well, perhaps I may grant you this, under explanations," he replied, " if you, indeed, will grant that we, on our part, should deviate in practice from primitive rules *as little* as we can help—only so much as the sheer necessity of our circumstances obliges us. For instance, no plain necessity can ever oblige us to bury an unbaptized person ; though a necessity (viz., of climate), may be urged for baptizing by sprinkling, not by immersion. This will serve as an illustration."

I assented to him, and was glad to have gained a clearer view on this point than I had ever obtained before. I have since seen the principle expressed, in a Tract that has fallen in my way, as follows, the immediate point argued in it being the Apostolical Succession :—

" Consider the analogy of an absent parent, or dear friend, in another hemisphere. Would not such an one naturally reckon it one sign of sincere attachment, if, when he returned home, he found that in all family questions respect had been shown especially to those in whom he was known to have had most confidence? . . . If his children and dependents had searched diligently where, and with whom, he had left commissions, and, having fair cause to think they had found such, had scrupulously conformed themselves, as far as they could, to the proceedings of those so trusted by him, would he not think this a better sign than if they had been dexterous in devising exceptions, in explaining away the words of trust, and limiting the prerogatives he had conferred?"*

The principle herein set forth is one which the law manifestly acts upon, as does every prudent statesman or man of business—viz., to go as near as he can to the rules, etc., which come into his hands, when he cannot observe them literally in all respects. But, to continue our conversation.

* [By Mr. Keble.]

5.

My companion went on in his ardent way: "After all, there is no reason why the ancient unity of Christendom should not be revived among us, and Rome be again ecclesiastical head of the whole Church."

"You will," said I, "be much better employed, surely, in speculating upon the means of building up our existing English Church, the Church of Andrewes and Laud, Ken and Butler, than attempting what, even in your own judgment, is an inconsistency. Tell me, can you tolerate the practical idolatry, the virtual worship, of the Virgin and Saints, which is the offence of the Latin Church, and the degradation of moral truth and duty which follows from these?"

"These are corruptions of the Greek Church also," he answered.

"Which only shows," said I, "that we are in the position of Abdiel—one against a many, to take your own comparison. However, this is nothing to the purpose. It is plain, to speak soberly and practically, we never can unite with Rome; for, even were we disposed to tolerate in its adherents what we could not allow in ourselves, they would not listen to our overtures for a moment, unless we began by agreeing to accept all the doctrinal decrees of Trent, and that about images in the number. No; surely, the one and only policy remaining for us to pursue is, not to look towards Rome, but to build up upon Laud's principles."

"Here you are theorizing, not I," returned he. "What is the ground of Andrewes and Laud, Stillingfleet and the rest, but a theory which has never been realized? I grant that the position they take in argument is most admirable, nearer much than the Romanist's to that of the primitive Church, and that they defend and develop their peculiar view most originally and satisfactorily; still, after all, it is a *theory,*—a fine-drawn theory, which has never been owned by any body of churchmen, never witnessed in operation in any system. The question is not, how to draw it out, but how to do it. Laud's attempt was so unsuccessful as to prove he was working upon a mere theory. The actual English Church has never adopted it: in spite of the learning of her divines, she has ranked herself among the Protestants, and the doctrine of the Via Media has slept in libraries. Nay, not only is Anglicanism a theory; it represents, after all, but an imperfect system; it implies a return to that inchoate state, in which the Church existed before the era of Constantine. It is a substitution of infancy for manhood. Of course it took some time, after its first starting, to get the Ark of Religion into her due course, which was at first somewhat vacillating and indeterminate. The language of theology was confessedly unformed, and we at this day actually adopt the creeds and the canons of the fourth century; why not, then, the rites and customs also?"

"I suppose," said I, "no follower of Laud *would* object to the rites and customs then received."

"Why, then," he asked, "do not we pay to the See of Rome the deference shown by the Fathers and Councils of that age?"

"Rome is corrupt," I answered. "When she reforms, it will be time enough to think about the share of honour and power belonging to her in the Universal Church. At present, her prerogative is, at least, suspended, and that most justly."

"However, what I was showing," continued he, "was that the Anglican principle is scarcely fair, as fastening the Christian upon the very first age of the Gospel for evidence of all those necessary developments of the elements of Gospel truth, which could not be introduced throughout the Church except gradually. On the other hand, the Anglican system itself is not found complete in those early centuries ; so that the principle is self-destructive. Before there were Christian rulers, there was no doctrine of ' Church and King,' no union of ' Church and State,' which we rightly consider to be a development of the Gospel rule. The principle in question, then, is both in itself unfair and unfairly applied, as it is found in our divines. It is also the result of a very shallow philosophy : as if you could possibly prevent the completion of given tendencies, as if Romanism would not be the inevitable result of a realized Anglicanism, were it ever realized.* However, my main objection to it is, that it is not, and never has been, realized. Protestantism is embodied in a system ; so is Popery : but when a man takes up this Via Media, he is a mere doctrinarian —he is wasting his efforts in delineating an invisible phantom ; and he will be judged, and fairly, to be trifling, and bookish, and unfit for the world. He will be set down in the number of those who, in some matter of business, start up to suggest their own little crotchet, and are for ever measuring mountains with a pocket ruler, or improving the planetary courses. The world moves forward in bold and intelligible parties ; it has its roads to the east and north—nay, to points of the compass

---

* [" As to the resemblance of the author's opinions to Romanism,—if Popery be a perversion or corruption of the Truth, as we believe, it must, by the very force of the terms, be like that Truth which it counterfeits ; and therefore the fact of a resemblance, as far as it exists, is no proof of any essential approximation in his opinions to Popery. Rather, it would be a serious argument against their primitive character, if to superficial observers they bore no likeness to it. Ultra-Protestantism could never have been silently corrupted into Popery."—*Advert. 3rd vol. Par. Serm., Ed.* I.]

between them, to the full number of the thirty-two ; but not to more than these. You *must* travel along a ready-made road ; you cannot go right ahead across-country, or, in spite of your abstract correctness, you will be swamped or benighted. When a person calling himself a ' Reformed Catholic,' or an ' Apostolical Christian,' begins to speak, people say to him, ' What are you ? If you are a Catholic, why do you not join the Romanists ? If you are ours, why do you not maintain the great Protestant doctrines ?' Or, in the words of Hall of Norwich, addressed, it is said, to Laud :

' I would I knew where to find you ; then I could tell how to take direct aims ; whereas now I must pore and conjecture. To-day you are in the tents of the Romanists—to-morrow in ours ; the next day between both—against both. Our adversaries think you ours—we, theirs ; your conscience finds you with both and neither. I flatter you not : this of yours is the worst of all tempers. Heat and cold have their uses—lukewarmness is good for nothing, but to trouble the stomach. . . . How long will you halt in this indifference ? Resolve one way, and know, at last, what you do hold— what you should. Cast off either your wings or your teeth, and, loathing this bat-like nature, be either a bird or a beast.'

" This was the character of his school down to the Non-jurors, in whom the failure of the experiment was finally ascertained. The theory sunk then, once and for all."

" My dear fellow," I made answer, " I see you are of those who think success and the applause of men everything, not bearing to consider, *first*, whether a view be true, and then to incur boldly the ' reproach ' of upholding it. Surely, the Truth has in no age been popular, and those who preached it have been thought idiots, and died without visible fruit of their labours."

He smiled, and was silent, as if in thought.

I continued : " Now listen to me, for I have it in purpose to turn your own words against yourself, to show
that you are the theorist, and I the man of practical
sense ; and at the same time to cheer you with the hope,
that the Anglican principle, though the true one, yet
may perchance be destined, even yet, in the designs of
Providence, to be expanded and realized in us, the
unworthy sons of the great Archbishop.

6.

As I said these words, I caught a sight of one of
the companions of my excursion making towards us,
who was well known to the friend with whom I was con-
versing. Instead, then, of beginning my harangue
upon the prospects of the English Church, I said,
" Here comes a friend in need, just in time. I was but
going to repeat what I have picked up from him. He
is the great theorist, after all, and he will best do justice
to his own views himself."

We went forward to meet him ; and, after some
indifferent topics had passed between us, I told him
the position in which he had found us, and asked him to
take upon himself the exposition of his own speculations.
I will pass over all explanations on his part, hesitations,
disclaimers of the character I gave of him, and the like,
and will take up the conversation when he was fairly
implicated in the task which we had imposed upon him.
For the future, I will call him Basil, and my first friend
Ambrose, to avoid circumlocution.

" Nothing seems so chimerical, I confess," said he, " as
the notion that the Church temper of the seventeenth
century will ever return in England ; nor do I ever expect it will, on a large scale. But the great and small in
extent are not conditions of moral or religious strength

and dignity. The Holy Land was not larger than Wales. We can afford to give up the greater part of England to the spirit of the age, and yet develop, in a diocese, or a single city, those principles and tendencies of the Caroline era which have never yet arrived at their just dimensions."

"You presuppose, of course, a King like the Martyr, in these anticipations ?" said Ambrose.

"In speaking of a *single* diocese, or city," returned the other, " I have obviously implied a system of which political arrangements are not the mainspring. Alas! we can no longer have such a king. The Monarchy is not constitutionally now what it was then ; nay, the Church, perchance, may not even be allowed the privilege of being loyal in time to come, though obedient and patient it always must be. The principle of national religion is fast getting out of fashion, and we are relapsing into the primitive state of Christianity, when men prayed for their rulers, and suffered from them, neither giving nor receiving temporal benefits. The element of high-churchmanship (as that word has commonly been understood) seems about to retreat again into the depths of the Christian temper, and Apostolicity is to be elicited instead, in greater measure.

' 'Tis true, 'tis pity ; pity 'tis, 'tis true.'

It would be well, indeed, were we allowed to acknowledge the magistrate's divine right to preside over the Church; but if the State declares it has itself no divine right over us, what help is there for it ? We must learn, like Hagar, to subsist by ourselves in the wilderness. Certainly, I never expect the *system* of Laud to return, but I do expect the due continuation and development of his *principles*. High-churchmanship—looking at the matte_ historically—will be regarded as a temporary stage of a course. The (so-called) union of Church and State, as it then existed, has been a wonderful and most gracious phenomenon in Christian history. It is a realization of the Gospel in its highest perfection, when both Cæsar and St. Peter know and fulfil their office. I do not expect anything so blessed again. Charles is the King, Laud the prelate, Oxford the sacred city, of this principle ; just as Rome is the city of Catholicism, and modern Paris of infidelity. I give up high-churchmanship. But, to return——"

"First, however," interrupted Ambrose, "I have it in purpose to imprison you in a dilemma, which you must resolve before you can discuss your subject with any ease or convenience. Either you expect this substitution of apostolicity for high-churchmanship at an early or at a distant date. If you say at an early, such keen anticipation of so deplorable a calamity as the unchristianizing of the State savours of disloyalty ; if at a distant, of fanaticism, as if the spirit of the seventeenth century could, on ever so contracted a field, revive centuries hence."

"I intend," he answered, "neither to be disaffected nor fanatical, and yet shall retain my anticipations. As to the charge of disloyalty, I repel it at once by stating, that I *am* looking forward to events as yet removed from us by centuries. It is no disloyal or craven spirit to suppose that, in the course of generations, changes may occur, when change is the rule of the world, and when, in our own country especially, not one hundred and fifty years perhaps has ever passed without some great constitutional change, or violent revolution. It is no faintness of heart to suppose that the eras of 1536, 1649, and 1688 are tokens of other such in store.

We all know that dynasties and governments are, like individuals, mortal ; and to provide against the un-churching of the monarchy, is not more disrespectful to it than to introduce a regency bill beforehand, in the prospect of a minority. The Church alone is eternal ; and, being such, it must, by the very law of its nature, survive its friends, and is bound calmly to anticipate the vicissitudes of its condition. We are consulting for no affair of the day ; we are contemplating our fortunes five centuries to come. We are labouring for the year 2500. By that time we may have buried our temporal guardians : their memory we shall always revere and bless ; but the Successors of the Apostles will still have their work—if the world last so long—a work (may be) of greater peril and hardship, but of more honour, than now.

"Nor, on the other hand, is it idle to suppose that former principles, long dormant, may, like seed in the earth, spring up at some distant day. History is full of precedents in favour of such an anticipation. At this very time the nation is beginning to reap the full fruits of the perverse anti-ecclesiastical spirit to which the Re-formation on the Continent gave birth. Three centuries and more have not developed it. Again, three centuries and more were necessary for the infant Church to attain her mature and perfect form, and due stature. Atha-nasius, Basil, and Austin are the fully instructed doctors of her doctrine, discipline, and morals."

7.

I could not but look at Ambrose, and smile at hearing the argument he had used, before the other came up incidentally made available against himself. Basil continued :

"Again, Hildebrand was the first to bring into use the donations made by Pepin and Charlemagne to the Church; yet these were made between A.D. 750—800, and Hildebrand's papacy did not commence till 1086. The interval was a time of weakness, humiliation, guilt, and disgrace to the Church, far exceeding any ecclesiastical scandals in our own country, whether in the century before or after the Caroline era. Gibbon tells us that the Popes of the ninth and tenth centuries were 'insulted, imprisoned, and murdered by their tyrants;' that the illegitimate son, grandson, and great grandson of Marozia, a woman of profligate character, were seated in St. Peter's chair; and the second of these was but nineteen when elevated to that spiritual dignity. He renounced the ecclesiastical dress, and abandoned himself to hunting, gaming, drinking, and kindred excesses. This, too, was the season of anti-popes, one of whom actually opposed Hildebrand himself, and eventually obliged him to retreat to Salerno, where he died. Yet now that celebrated man stands in history as if the very contemporary and first inheritor of Charlemagne's gifts, and reigns in the Church without the vestige of a rival. So little has time to do with the creations of moral energy, that Guiberto ceases in our associations to have lived with him, or the first Carlovingians to have been before him. He obliterated an interval of three hundred years."

"You were somewhat too conceding, methinks, when you began," said Ambrose, "if you are not exorbitant now. It is not much more to ask that a king like Charles should ascend the throne, than that a mind like Hildebrand's should be given to the Church."

"And yet Father Paul, a sagacious man," Basil answered, "did look with much anxiety towards the English hierarchy of his day (1617), as likely to develop an

apostolical spirit which even kings could not control
So far, indeed, he was mistaken in his immediate anticipation, because the English Church was far too loyal to
be dangerous to the State; yet it may chance that, in
the course of centuries there is no king to whom to be
loyal. His words are these :—

'Anglis nimium timeo ; episcoporum magna illa potestas, licet
sub rege, prorsus mihi suspecta est. Ubi vel regem desidem nacti
fuerint, vel magni spiritûs archiepiscopum habuerint, regia authori-
tas pessundabitur, et episcopi ad absolutam dominationem aspira-
bunt. Ego equum ephippiatum in Angliâ videre videor, et ascen-
surum propediem equitem antiquum divino.' *

"Now, is it not singular that this Church should so
close upon these words have developed Laud, a prelate
(if any other) aspiring and undaunted ? And again, that
within fifty years of him the king actually was in the
power of the primate, as the umpire between him and
the nation, though Sancroft (as he himself afterwards
understood) was not alive to his position, nor equal to
the emergency ? These are omens of what may be still
to come, inasmuch as they show the political and moral
temper, the presiding genius of the Anglican Church,
which had produced, at distant intervals, before Laud,
prelates as high-minded, though doubtless less enlightened and more ambitious. It is not one stroke of fortune, one political revolution, which can chase the *genius
loci* from his favourite haunt. Canterbury and Oxford
are a match for many Williams of Nassau."

I here interrupted him to corroborate his last remarks,
without pledging myself to approve his mode of conveying them. I said that "Leslie, one of the last of

* [I think this is to be found in Sarpi's Letters, a book lent to me by
Dr. Routh.]

the line of apostolical divines, had expressed the same
opinion concerning the Church at large, in his Case of
the Regale and Pontificate. His words are as follows:

> 'I say, if the Church would trust to Him more than to the arm
> of flesh, she need not fear the power of kings. No ; Christ would
> give her kings, not as heads and spiritual fathers over her, but as
> nursing fathers, to protect, love, and cherish her, to reverence and
> to save her, as the Spouse of Christ. Instead of such fathers as
> she has made kings to be over herself, and of whom she stands in
> awe, and dare not exert the power Christ has given her, without
> their good liking, she should then have " children whom she might
> make princes in all the earth." Kings would become her sons and
> her servants, instead of being her fathers.
> 'My brethren, let me freely speak to you. These promises must
> be fulfilled, and in this world, for they are spoke of it, and belong
> not to the state of heaven, but to the condition of the Church in all
> the earth. All the prophets that have been, since the world began,
> have spoken of these days ; therefore, they will surely come ; and
> " though ye have lien among the pots, yet she shall be as the wings
> of a dove, that is covered with silver, and her feathers like gold." '

"Having been led to quote from an author who wrote
a century since, let me here add the witness of an acute
observer of our own century, whose Letters and Remains
have been published since the date of the conversation I
am relating—Mr. Alexander Knox. The following was
written just two centuries after Sarpi's letter :

> 'No Church on earth has more intrinsic excellence, [than the
> English Church,] yet no Church, probably, has less practical influ-
> ence. Her excellence, then, I conceive, gives ground for confiding
> that Providence will never abandon her ; but her want of influence
> would seem no less clearly to indicate, that Divine Wisdom will not
> always suffer her to go on without measures for her improvement.
> . . . Shall then the present negligence and insensibility always
> prevail? This cannot be ; the rich provision made by the grace
> and providence of God, for habits of a noble kind, is evidence that

those habits shall at length be formed, that men shall arise, fitted, both by inclination and ability, to discover for themselves, and to display to others, whatever yet remains undisclosed, whether in the words or works of God.   But if it be asked, how shall fit instruments be prepared for this high purpose, it can only be answered, that in the most signal instances times of severe trial have been chosen for divine communications.—Moses, an exile, when God spoke to him from the bush ; Daniel, a captive in Babylon, where he was cheered with those clearest rays of Old Testament prophecy ; St. John, a prisoner in Patmos, where he was caught up into heaven, and beheld the apocalyptic vision. . . . . My persuasion of the radical excellence of the Church of England does not suffer me to doubt, that she is to be an illustrious agent in bringing the mystical kingdom of Christ to its ultimate perfection.'"

8.

When the conversation had arrived at this point, my friend Ambrose put in a remark. "It must be confessed," he said, "that your triumphant Church will, after all, be very much like what the papal was in its pride of place. The only difference would seem to be, that the Popes deposed kings ; but you, in effect, wait till there are no kings to depose, leaving it to the (so-called) 'radical reformers' to bring upon themselves the odium of the acts which are to introduce you. Why not, then, avail ourselves of what is ready to our hands in the Church of Rome ? Why attempt, instead, to form a second-best and spurious Romanism ?"

"Pardon me," I said, in answer, "Basil thinks the Roman Church corrupt in doctrine. We cannot join a Church, did we wish it ever so much, which does not acknowledge our Orders, refuses us the Cup, demands our acquiescence in image worship, and excommunicates us, if we do not receive it and all other decisions of the Tridentine Council. While she insists on this, there must be an impassable line between her and us ; and while she claims infallibility, she must insist on what she has once decreed; and when she abandons that claim she breaks the principle of her own vitality. Thus, we can never unite with Rome."

"This is true and certain," said Basil; "but even though Rome were as sound in faith as she is notoriously unsound, our present line would remain the same. What, indeed, might come to pass at a distant era, when monarchies had ceased to be, it would be impertinent to ask; but, though I have been anticipating the future, we have nothing really to do with the future. Our business is with things as they are. We want to *begin* at once, and must not, dare not start upon a basis which is not to be realized for some hundred years to come. Of course;—and to do anything effectually, we must build upon principles and feelings already recognized among us. I grant all this: let us leave the future to itself: we are concerned, not with illusions, (as the French politicians say,) but with things that are. But this holds of other illusions besides those against which you have warned such as me. For what we know, by the time we are without kings Rome may be without a Pope; and it would be a strange policy to go over to them now, by way of anticipating a distant era, which, for what we know, may, in the event, be preceded by their coming over to us. You have heard of the two brothers in the seventeenth century, papist and puritan, who disputed together and convinced each other. Let us take warning from them.

"I repeat, to do anything effectually, certainly we must start upon *recognized* principles and customs. Any other procedure stamps a person as wrong-headed, ill-judging, or eccentric, and brings upon him the contempt and ridicule of those sensible men by whose opinions society is necessarily governed. Putting aside the question of truth and falsehood—which of course is the main consideration—even as aiming at success, we must be aware of the great error of making changes on no more definite basis than their abstract fitness, their alleged scripturalness, their adoption by the ancients. Such changes are rightly called *innovations;* those which spring from existing institutions, opinions, or feelings, are called *developments,* and may be recommended without invidiousness as being *improvements.* I adopt, then, and claim as my own, that position of yours, 'that we must take and use what is ready to our hands.' To do otherwise, is to act the *doctrinaire,* and to provide for simple failure : for instance, if we would enforce observance of the Lord's Day, we must not, at the outset, rest it on any theory (however just) of Church authority, but on the authority of Scripture. If we would oppose the State's interference with the distribution of Church property, we shall succeed, not by urging any doctrine of Church independence, or by citing decrees of General Councils, but by showing the contrariety of that measure to existing constitutional and ecclesiastical precedents among ourselves. Hildebrand found the Church provided with certain existing means of power ; he vindicated them, and was rewarded with the success which attends, not on truth as such, but on this prudence and tact in conduct. St. Paul observed the same rule,— whether preaching at Athens or persuading his countrymen. It was the gracious condescension of our Lord Himself, not to substitute Christianity for Judaism by any violent revolution, but to develop Judaism into Christianity, as the Jews might bear it. Now, Popery is *not* here ready to our hands ; on the contrary, we find among us, at this day, an intense fear and hatred of Popery ; and that, ill-instructed as it confessedly is, still based upon truth. It is mere headstrong folly, then, to advocate the Church of Rome. It is to lose our *position* as a Church, which never answers to any, whether body or individual. If, indeed, salvation were not in our Church, the case would be altered ; as it is, were Rome as pure in faith as the Church of the Apostles, which she is not, I would not join her, unless those about me did so too, lest I should commit schism. Our business is to take what we have received, and build upon it : to accept, as a legacy from our forefathers, this 'Protestant' spirit which they have bequeathed us, and merely to disengage it from its errors, purify it, and make it something more than a negative principle ; thus only have we a chance of success. All your arguments, then, my dear Ambrose, in favour of Romanism, or rather your regrets on the subject—for you are not able to go so far as to design, or even to hope on the subject—seem to me irrelevant, and recoil upon your own professed principle ; and, instead of persuading others, only lead them to ask the pertinent question, 'Why do you stay among us, if you like a foreign religion better ?'"

The other smiled with an expression which showed that he was at once entertained and as unconvinced as before. For myself, I was not quite pleased with the tone of political expedience which my friend had assumed, though I agreed in his general sentiment ; except, indeed, in his patience towards the word "Protestant," which is a term as political as were his arguments.

"You have surely been somewhat carried beyond your own excellent judgment," I said, "by your earnestness in advocating a view. A person who did not know you as well as I do would take such avowals as the offspring of a Florentine, not an English school. It is certainly *safer* in so serious a matter to go upon more obvious, more religious grounds than those you have selected ; for I agree with you most entirely in the conclusion you arrive at. I will give you a reason, which has had particular weight with me. Of course, one must not say, ' Whatever is, is right,' in such a sense as to excuse what is wrong, whether committed or permitted, violence or cowardice ; yet, at the same time, it certainly is true, that the external circumstances under which we find ourselves, have a legitimate influence, nay, a sort of claim of deference, upon our conduct. St. Paul says that every one should remain in the place where he finds himself. This, so far, at least, applies to our ecclesiastical position, that, unless where conscience comes in, it is our duty to submit to what we are born under. I do not insist here on the engagements of the clergy to administer the discipline of Christ as the Church and Realm have received the same ; here, I only assert that we find the Church and State united, and must therefore maintain that Union."

" The said Union," interrupted Ambrose, " being much like the union of the Israelites with the Egyptians, in the house of bondage."

" So it may be," I replied,—" but recollect that the chosen people were not allowed to disenthral themselves without an intimation of God's permission. When Moses attempted, of himself, to avenge them, he only got into trial and distress. It was in vain he killed the Egyptian, there was neither voice, nor any to answer, nor any that regarded. Providence always says, ' *Stand still*, and see the salvation of God.' We must not dare to move, except He bids us. How different was the success of Moses afterwards, when God sent him ! In like manner, the deliverers of Israel, in the period of the Judges, were, for the most part, expressly commissioned to their office. At another time, 'the Lord delivered Sisera into the hand of a woman.' It is not for us 'to know the times and the seasons which the Father hath put in His own power.'

"And so, once more, Daniel, though he prayed towards the Temple during his captivity, made no attempt to leave Babylon for his own country, to escape from the mass of idolaters and infidels, scorners and profligates, among whom his lot was cast in this world. We, too, who are in captivity, must *bide our time.*"

9.

Here there was a pause in the conversation, as if our minds required rest after sharing in it, or leisure to digest it. We were in the terrace walk overlooking the Trastevere: we stood still, and made such disconnected remarks as the separate buildings and places in the view suggested. At length, the Montorio, where St. Peter was martyred, and some discourse it suggested, recalled us to our former subject, and we began again with fresh life.

"Hildebrand," said Ambrose, "had a basis to go upon; and we, in matter of fact, have none. However true your policy may be of our availing ourselves of things existing, I repeat we have no *church* basis,—we have nothing but certain merely political rights. Hildebrand had definite powers, though dormant or obsolete. The Exarchate of Ravenna had been formally ceded to the popedom by Pepin, though virtually wrested from it in the interval. The supposed donation of Constantine and the Decretals were recognized charters, which churchmen might fall back upon. We have nothing of this kind now."

⁎⁎   3

" Let us make the most of what we have," returned the other ; "and surely we have enough for our purpose. Let us consider what that purpose is, and what it is we want : our one tangible object is to restore the connexion, at present broken, between bishops and people ;—for in this everything is involved, directly or indirectly, which it is a duty to contend for ;—and to effect this, we want no temporal rights of any sort, as the Popes needed, but merely the recognition of our Church's existing spiritual powers.   We are not aiming at any kingdom of this world ; we need no Magna-Chartas or Coronation oaths for the object which we have at heart : we wish to maintain the faith, and bind men together in love.   We are aiming, with this view, at that commanding moral influence which attended the early Church, which made it attractive and persuasive, which manifested itself in a fascination sufficient to elicit out of paganism and draw into itself all that was noblest and best from the mass of mankind, and which created an internal system of such grace, beauty, and majesty, that believers were moulded thereby into martyrs and evangelists.   Now let us see what materials we have for a similar spiritual structure, if we keep what, through God's good providence, has descended to us.

"First, we have the Ordination Service, acknowledging three, and three only, divinely appointed Orders of ministers, implying a Succession, and the bishop's divine commission for continuing it, and assigning to the presbytery the power of retaining and remitting sins : these are invaluable, as being essential, possessions.

"Next, we have the plain statements of the general necessity of the sacraments for salvation, and the strong language of the services appointed for the administration of them.   We have Confirmation and Matrimony

recognized as spiritual ordinances. We have forms of
absolution and blessing.

"Further, we have the injunction of daily service, and
the solemnization of fast and festival days.

"Lastly, we have a yearly confession of the desirable
ness of a restoration of the primitive discipline.

"On these foundations, properly understood, we may
do anything."

"Still you have not touched upon the real difficulty,"
interrupted Ambrose. "Hildebrand governed an existing body, and was only employed in vindicating for it
certain powers and privileges; you, on the other hand,
have to make the body, before you proceed to strengthen
it. The Church in England is not a body now, it has
little or no substantiveness; it has dwindled down to its
ministers, who are as much secular functionaries as they
are rulers of a Christian people. What reason have you
to suppose that the principles you have enumerated will
interest an uninstructed, as well as edify an already disciplined, multitude? Still the problem is, How to do it?"

10.

When he stopped, Basil looked at me. "Cyril," said
he, mentioning my name, "has much to say on this
argument, and I leave it to him to tell you how to do
it." Thus challenged, I began in my turn.

"I will tell you," I said, "Hildebrand really had to
create as well as we. If the Church was not in his time
laid prostrate before the world, at least it was incorporated into it—so I am told, at least, by those who have
studied the history of his times: the clergy were dissolved
in secular vocations and professions; a bishop was a
powerful baron, the feudal vassal of a temporal prince,
of whom he held estates and castles, his Ordination being

virtually an incidental form, necessary at the commencement of his occupancy; the inferior clergy were inextri-
cably entangled in the fetters of secular alliances, often
criminal and scandalous.   In planting his lever, which
was to break all these irreligious ties, he made the *received*
forms and rules of the Church his fulcrum.   If master-
minds are ever granted to us, to build us up in faith and
unity, they must do the same; they must take their
stand upon that existing basis which Basil has just now
described, and must be determined never to extravagate
from it.   They must make that basis their creed and
their motive; they must persevere for many years, in
preaching and teaching, before they proceed to act upon
their principles, introducing terms and names, and impressing members of the Church with the real meaning
of the truths which are her animating element, and
which her members verbally admit.   In spite of opposition, they must persevere in insisting on the episcopal
system, the apostolical succession, the ministerial commission, the power of the keys, the duty and desirableness of Church discipline, the sacredness of Church rites
and ordinances.

"So far well; but you will say, how is all this to be
made interesting to the people?   I answer, that the
topics themselves which they are to preach are of that
striking and attractive nature which carries with it its own
influence.   The very notion, that representatives of the
Apostles are now on earth, from whose communion we
may obtain grace, as the first Christians did from the
Apostles, is surely, when admitted, of a most transport-
ing and persuasive character; it will supply the desideratum which exists in the actual teaching of this day.
Clergymen at present are subject to the painful experience of losing the more religious portion of their flock,

whom they have tutored and moulded as children, but who, as they come into life, fall away to the dissenters. Why is this? Because they desire to be stricter than the mass of Churchmen, and the Church gives them no means; they desire to be governed by sanctions more constraining than those of mere argument, and the Church keeps back those doctrines, which, to the eye of faith, give a reality and substance to religion. He who is told that the Church is the treasure-house of spiritual gifts, comes for a definite privilege; he who has been taught that it is merely a duty to keep united to the Church, gains nothing, and is tempted to leave it for the meeting-house, which promises him present excitement, if it does nothing more. He who sees Churchmen identified with the world, naturally looks at dissent as a separation from it. The first business, then, of our Hildebrand will be to stop this continual secession to the dissenters, by supplying those doctrines which nature itself, I may say, desiderates in our existing institutions, and which the dissenters attempt to supply. This should be well observed, for it is a remarkable circumstance, that most of the more striking innovations of the present day are awkward and unconscious imitations of the provisions of the old Catholic system. 'Texts for every day in the year' are the substitute for the orderly calendar of Scripture Lessons; prayer-meetings stand for the daily service; farewell speeches to missionaries take the place of public Ordinations; public meetings for religious oratory, the place of the ceremonies and processions of the middle ages; charitable societies are instead of the strict and enthusiastic Religious Institutions. Men know not of the legitimate Priesthood, and therefore are condemned to hang upon the judgment of individual and self-authorized preachers; they defraud their chil-

dren of the initiatory sacrament, and therefore are forced
to invent a rite of dedication instead of it ; they put up
with legends of private Christians, distinguished for an
ambiguous or imperfect piety, narrow-minded in faith,
and tawdry and discoloured in their holiness, in the
place of the men of God, the meek martyrs, the saintly
pastors, the wise and winning teachers of the Catholic
Church.   One of the most striking illustrations of this
general remark, is the existing practice and feeling
about psalmody :—formerly great part of the public service was sung ; part of this, as the Te Deum, being an
exhibition of the peculiar gospel doctrines.   We let this
practice go out ; then, feeling the want of singing, we
introduce it between the separate portions of the services.   There is no objection to this, so far; it has
primitive sanction.   But observe,—we have only time for
one or two verses, which cannot show the drift and spirit
of the Psalm, and are often altogether unintelligible, or
grammatically defective.   Next, a complaint arises, that
no *Christian* hymns constitute part of the singing ; so,
having relinquished the Te Deum, we have recourse to
the rhymes of Watts, Newton, and Wesley.   Moreover,
we sing as slow as if singing were a penitential exercise.
Consider how the Easter hymn affects a congregation,
and you will see their natural congeniality to musical
services of a more animated, quicker, and more continued
measure.   The dissenters seem to feel this in their adoption of objectionable secular tunes, or of religious tunes
of a *cantabile* character ; our slow airs seem to answer
no purpose, except that of painfully exhausting the
breath—they will never allure a congregation to sing.
So, again, as to the Services generally; they are scarcely
at all adapted to the successive seasons and days of the
Christian year : the Bible is rich in materials for illus

trating and solemnizing these as they come; but we make little use of it. Consider how impressive the Easter anthem is, as a substitute for the *Venite:* why should not such as this be appointed at other Seasons, in the same and other parts of the service ? How few prayers we possess for particular occasions ! Reflect, for instance, upon Jeremy Taylor's prayers and litanies, and I think you will grant that, carefully preserving the Prayer Book's majestic simplicity of style, we might nevertheless profitably make additions to our liturgical services. We have but matins and evensong appointed : what if a clergyman wishes to have prayers in his church seven times a day ?

"I touched just now on the subject of the Religious Institutions of the middle ages. These are imperatively called for to stop the progress of dissent; indeed, I conceive you necessarily must have dissent or monachism in a Christian country;—so make your choice. The more religious minds demand some stricter religion than that of the generality of men; if you do not gratify this desire religiously and soberly, they will gratify it themselves at the expense of unity. I wish this were better understood than it is. You may build new churches, without stint, in every part of the land, but you will not approximate towards the extinction of Methodism and dissent till you consult for this feeling; till then, the sectaries will deprive you of numbers, and those the best of your flock, whom you can least afford to lose, and who might be the greatest strength and ornament to it. This is an occurrence which happens daily. Say that one out of a number of sisters in a family takes a religious turn; is not her natural impulse to join either the Wesleyans or the irregulars within our pale ? And why ? all because the Church does not provide innocent outlets for the sober relief of feeling and excitement: she would fain devote herself immediately to God's service—to prayer, almsgiving, attendance on the sick. You not only decline her services yourself,—you drive her to the dissenters: and why? all because the Religious Life, though sanctioned by Apostles and illustrated by the early Saints, has before now given scope to moroseness, tyranny, and presumption."

II.

"I will tell you," interrupted Basil, "an advantage which has often struck me as likely to result from the institution (under sober regulations) of religious Sisterhoods—viz., the education of the female portion of the community in Church principles. It is plain we need schools for females: so great is the inconvenience, that persons in the higher ranks contrive to educate their daughters at home, from want of confidence in those schools in which alone they can place them. It is speaking temperately of these to say, that (with honourable exceptions, of course, such as will be found to every rule) they teach little beyond mere accomplishments, present no antidotes to the frivolity of young minds, and instruct in no definite views of religious truth at all. On the other hand, what an incalculable gain would it be to the Church were the daughters, and future mothers, of England educated in a zealous and affectionate adherence to its cause, taught to reverence its authority, and to delight in its ordinances and services! What, again, if they had instructors, who were invested with even more than the respectability which collegiate foundations give to education in the case of the other sex, instructors placed above the hopes and fears of the world, and impressing the thought of the Church on their pupils' minds, in association with their own refinement and heavenly serenity! But, alas! so ingrained are our unfortunate prejudices on this head, that I fear nothing but serious national afflictions will give an opening to the accomplishment of so blessed a design."

"For myself," said I, "I confess my hopes do not extend beyond the vision of the rise of this Religious Life among us; not that even this will have any success, as you well observe, till loss of property turns the thoughts of the clergy and others from this world to the next. As to the rise of a high episcopal system, that is, again to use your notion, a dream of A.D. 2500. We can but desire in our day to keep alive the lamp of truth in the sepulchre of this world till a brighter era: and surely the ancient system I speak of is the providentially designed instrument of this work. When Arianism triumphed in the sees of the eastern Church, the Associated Brethren of Egypt and Syria were the witnesses prophesying in sackcloth against it. So it may be again. When the day of trial comes, we shall be driven from the established system of the Church, from livings and professorships, fellowships and stalls; we shall (so be it) muster amid dishonour, poverty, and destitution, for higher purposes; we shall bear to be severed from possessions and connexions of this world; we shall turn our thoughts to the education of those middle classes, the children of farmers and tradesmen, whom the Church has hitherto neglected; we shall educate a certain number, for the purpose of transmitting to posterity our principles and our manner of life; we shall turn ourselves to the wants of the great towns, and attempt to be evangelists in a population almost heathen.

"Till then, I scarcely expect that anything will be devised of a nature to meet the peculiar evils existing in a densely peopled city. Benevolent persons hope, by increasing our instruments of usefulness, to relieve them. Doubtless they may so relieve them ; and no charitable effort can fail of a blessing. New churches and lay co-operation will do something ; but, I confess, I think that some instrument different in kind is required for the present emergency: great towns will never be evangelized merely by the parochial system. They are beyond the sphere of the parish priest, burdened as he is with the endearments and anxieties of a family, and the secular restraints and engagements of the Establishment. The unstable multitude cannot be influenced and ruled except by uncommon means, by the evident sight of disinte-rested and self-denying love, and elevated firmness. The show of domestic comfort, the decencies of furniture and apparel, the bright hearth and the comfortable table, (good and innocent as they are in their place,) are as ill-suited to the missionary of a town population as to an Apostle. Heathens, and quasi-heathens, (such as the miserable rabble of a large town,) were not converted in the beginning of the Gospel, nor now, as it would appear, by the sight of domestic virtues or domestic comforts in their missionary. Surely Providence has His various means adapted to different ends. I think that Religious Institutions, over and above their intrinsic recommendations, are the legitimate instruments of working upon a populace, just as argument may be accounted the medium of conversion in the case of the educated, or parental authority in the case of the young.

12.

" I have been watching with some interest," said Ambrose, who had been silent all this while, "how near, with all your protestations against Popery, you would advance towards it in the course of your speculations. I am now happy to see you will go the full length of what you yourselves seem to admit is considered one of its most remarkable characteristics—monachism."

"I know," answered I, "that is at present the popular notion ; but our generation has not yet learned the distinction between Popery and Catholicism. But, be of good heart ; it will learn many things in time."

The other laughed ; and, the day being now someway advanced into the afternoon, we left the garden, and separated.

March, 1836.

II.

THE PATRISTICAL IDEA OF ANTICHRIST.

IN FOUR LECTURES.

I.

The Times of Antichrist.

THE Thessalonian Christians had supposed that the coming of Christ was near at hand. St. Paul writes to warn them against such an expectation. Not that he discountenances their looking out for our Lord's coming,—the contrary ; but he tells them that a certain event must come before it, and till that had arrived the end would not be. " Let no man deceive you by any means," he says ; " for that Day shall not come, except there come a falling away first,"—and he proceeds " and " except first " that man of sin be revealed, the son of perdition."

As long as the world lasts, this passage of Scripture will be full of reverent interest to Christians. It is their duty ever to be watching for the advent of their Lord, to search for the signs of it in all that happens around them ; and above all to keep in mind this great and awful sign of which St. Paul speaks to the Thessalonians. As our Lord's first coming had its forerunner, so will the second have its own. The first was "One more than a prophet," the Holy Baptist: the second will be more than an enemy of Christ; it will be the very image of Satan, the fearful and hateful Antichrist. Of him, as described in prophecy, I propose to speak; and, in doing so, I shall follow the exclusive guidance of the ancient Fathers of the Church.

I follow the ancient Fathers, not as thinking that on such a subject they have the weight they possess in the instance of doctrines or ordinances. When they speak of doctrines, they speak of them as being universally held. They are witnesses to the fact of those doctrines having been received, not here or there, but everywhere. We receive those doctrines which they thus teach, not merely because they teach them, but because they bear witness that all Christians everywhere then held them. We take them as honest informants, but not as a sufficient authority in themselves, though they are an authority too. If they were to state these very same doctrines, but say, "These are our opinions: we deduced them from Scripture, and they are true," we might well doubt about receiving them at their hands. We might fairly say, that we had as much right to deduce from Scripture as they had; that deductions of Scripture were mere opinions; that if our deductions agreed with theirs, that would be a happy coincidence, and increase our confidence in them; but if they did not, it could not be helped—we must follow our own light. Doubtless, no man has any right to impose his own deductions upon another, in matters of faith. There is an obvious obligation, indeed, upon the ignorant to submit to those who are better informed; and there is a fitness in the young submitting implicitly for a time to the teaching of their elders; but, beyond this, one man's opinion is not better

than another's. But this is not the state of the case as
regards the primitive Fathers. They do not speak of
their *own private* opinion ; they do not say, " This is
true, *because* we see it in Scripture "—about which there
might be differences of judgment—but, " this is true,
because in matter of fact it is held, and has ever been
held, by all the Churches, down to our times, without
interruption, ever since the Apostles : " where the question is merely one of testimony, viz., whether they had
the means of knowing that it had been and was so held ;
for if it was the belief of so many and independent
Churches at once, and that, on the ground of its being
from the Apostles, doubtless it cannot but be true and
Apostolic.

This, I say, is the mode in which the Fathers speak as
regards *doctrine ;* but it is otherwise when they interpret
prophecy. In this matter there seems to have been no
catholic, no formal and distinct, or at least no authoritative traditions ; so that when they interpret Scripture
they are for the most part giving, and profess to be
giving, either their own private opinions, or vague, float-
ing, and merely general anticipations. This is what might
have been expected ; for it is not ordinarily the course
of Divine Providence to interpret prophecy before the
event. What the Apostles disclosed concerning the
future, was for the most part disclosed by them in private,
to individuals—not committed to writing, not intended
for the edifying of the body of Christ,—and was soon
lost. Thus, in a few verses after the passage I have
quoted, St. Paul says, " Remember ye not, that when
I was yet with you, I told you these things ? " and he
writes by hints and allusions, not speaking out. And
it shows how little care was taken to discriminate and
authenticate his prophetical intimations, that the Thes-

salonians had adopted an opinion, that he had said—
what in fact he had not said—that the Day of Christ
was immediately at hand.

Yet, though the Fathers do not convey to us the interpretation of prophecy with the same certainty as they
convey doctrine, yet, in proportion to their agreement,
their personal weight, and the prevalence, or again the
authoritative character of the opinions they are stating,
they are to be read with deference; for, to say the least,
they are as likely to be right as commentators now; in
some respects more so, because the interpretation of prophecy has become in these times a matter of controversy
and party. And passion and prejudice have so inter-
fered with soundness of judgment, that it is difficult to
say who is to be trusted to interpret it, or whether a private Christian may not be as good an expositor as those
by whom the office has been assumed.

I.

Now to turn to the passage in question, which I shall
examine by arguments drawn from Scripture, without
being solicitous to agree, or to say why I am at issue,
with modern commentators: "That Day shall not
come, except there come a falling away first." Here
the sign of the second Advent is said to be a certain frightful apostasy, and the manifestation of the man of sin,
the son of perdition—that is, as he is commonly called,
Antichrist. Our Saviour seems to add, that that sign
will immediately precede Him, or that His coming will
follow close upon it; for after speaking of "false prophets" and "false Christs," "showing signs and wonders," "iniquity abounding," and "love waxing cold,"
and the like, He adds, "When ye shall see all these
things, know that it is near, even at the doors." Again

He says, "When ye shall see the Abomination of Desolation . . . stand in the holy place . . . then let them that be in Judea flee into the mountains."* Indeed, St. Paul also implies this, when he says that Antichrist shall be destroyed by the brightness of Christ's coming.

First, then, I say, if Antichrist is to come *immediately* before Christ, and to be the sign of His coming, it is manifest that Antichrist is not come yet, but is still to be expected ; for, else Christ would have come before now.

Further, it appears that the time of Antichrist's tyranny will be three years and a half, or, as Scripture expresses it, "a time, and times, and a dividing of time," or "forty-two months,"—which is an additional reason for believing he is not come ; for, if so, he must have come quite lately, his time being altogether so short ; that is, within the last three years, and this we cannot say he has.

Besides, there are two other circumstances of his appearance, which have not been fulfilled. First, a time of unexampled trouble. "Then shall be great tribulation, such as was not from the beginning of the world to this time, no, nor ever shall be ; and except those days should be shortened, there should no flesh be saved."† This has not yet been. Next, the preaching of the Gospel throughout the world—"And this Gospel of the kingdom shall be preached in all the world for a witness unto all nations, and then shall the end come."‡

2.

Now it may be objected to this conclusion, that St. Paul says, in the passage before us, that "the mystery of iniquity doth already work," that is, even in *his* day, as if Antichrist had in fact come even then. But he would

* Matt. xxiv. 16, 33.　　　† Ib. 21, 22.　　　‡ Ib. 14.

seem to mean merely this, that in his day there were shadows and forebodings, earnests, and operative elements, of that which was one day to come in its fulness. Just as the types of Christ went before Christ, so the shadows of Antichrist precede him. In truth, every event of this world is a type of those that follow, history proceeding forward as a circle ever enlarging. The days of the Apostles typified the last days : there were false Christs, and risings, and troubles, and persecutions, and the judicial destruction of the Jewish Church. In like manner, every age presents its own picture of those still future events, which, and which alone, are the real fulfilment of the prophecy which stands at the head of all of them. Hence St. John says, " Little children, it is the last time ; and as ye have heard that the Antichrist shall come, *even now* are there many Antichrists ; whereby we know that it is the last time."* Antichrist was come, and was not come ; it was, and it was not the last time. In the sense in which the Apostles' day 'might be called the "last time," and the end of the world, it was also the time of Antichrist.

A second objection may be made as follows : St. Paul says, "Now ye know what withholdeth, that he (Antichrist) might be revealed in his time." Here a something is mentioned as keeping back the manifestation of the enemy of truth. He proceeds : " He that now withholdeth, will withhold, until he be taken out of the way." Now this restraining power was in early times considered to be the Roman Empire, but the Roman Empire (it is argued) has long been taken out of the way ; it follows that Antichrist has long since come. In answer to this objection, I would grant that he "that withholdeth," or "hindereth," means the power of Rome, for all the ancient

* 1 John ii. 18.

4

writers so speak of it. And I grant that as Rome, according to the prophet Daniel's vision, succeeded Greece, so Antichrist succeeds Rome, and the Second Coming succeeds Antichrist.* But it does not hence follow that Antichrist is come : for it is not clear that the Roman Empire is gone. Far from it : the Roman Empire in the view of prophecy, remains even to this day. Rome had a very different fate from the other three monsters mentioned by the Prophet, as will be seen by his description of it. "Behold a fourth beast, dreadful and terrible, and strong exceedingly ; and it had great iron teeth : it devoured and brake in pieces, and stamped the residue with the feet of it : and it *was diverse from all the beasts that* were before it, and it *had ten horns.*"† These ten horns, an Angel informed him, "are ten kings that shall rise out of this kingdom" of Rome. As, then, the ten horns belonged to the fourth beast, and were not separate from it, so the kingdoms, into which the Roman Empire was to be divided, are but the continuation and termination of that Empire itself,—which lasts on, and in some sense lives in the view of prophecy, however we decide the historical question. Consequently, we have not *yet* seen the end of the Roman Empire. "That which withholdeth" still exists, up to the manifestation of its ten horns ; and till it is removed, Antichrist will not come. And from the midst of those horns he will arise, as the same Prophet informs us : "I considered the horns, and behold, there came up among them another little horn ; . . . and behold, in this horn were eyes like the eyes of a man, and a mouth speaking great things."

Up to the time, then, when Antichrist shall actually appear, there has been and will be a continual effort to manifest him to the world on the part of the powers

* Chrysostom in loco.   † Den. vii. 7.

of evil. The history of the Church is the history of that long birth. " The mystery of iniquity doth *already* work," says St. Paul. "*Even now* there are many Antichrists," * says St. John,—"every spirit that confesseth not that Jesus Christ is come in the flesh, is not of God ; and *this* is that spirit of the Antichrist, whereof ye have heard that it should come, *and even now already is it in the world.*"† It has been at work ever since, from the time of the Apostles, though kept under by him that "withholdeth." At this very time there is a fierce struggle, the spirit of Antichrist attempting to rise, and the political power in those countries which are prophetically Roman, firm and vigorous in repressing it. And in fact, we actually have before our eyes, as our fathers also in the generation before us, a fierce and lawless principle everywhere at work—a spirit of rebellion against God and man, which the powers of government in each country can barely keep under with their greatest efforts. Whether this which we witness *be* that spirit of Antichrist,‡ which is one day at length to be let loose, this ambitious spirit, the parent of all heresy, schism, sedition, revolution, and war—whether this be so or not, at least we know from prophecy that the present framework of society and government, as far as it is the representative of Roman powers, is that which withholdeth, and Antichrist is that which will rise when this restraint fails.

3.

It has been more or less implied in the foregoing re-marks, that Antichrist is one man, an individual, not a power or a kingdom. Such surely is the impression left on the mind by the Scripture notices concerning him, after taking fully into account the figurative character

---

* 1 John ii. 18. † Ib. iv. 3. ‡ [ὁ ἄνομος.]

of prophetical language. Consider these passages together, which describe him, and see whether we must
not so conclude. First, the passage in St. Paul's Epistle :
" That day shall not come, except there come a falling
away first, and that man of sin be revealed, the son of
perdition, who is the adversary and rival of all that is
called God or worshipped ; so that he sitteth as God in
the temple of God, proclaiming himself to be God. . . .
Then shall that Wicked One be revealed, whom the Lord
shall consume with the spirit of His mouth, and shall
destroy with the brightness of His coming . . . . whose
coming is after the working of Satan, with all power and
signs and lying wonders."

Next, in the prophet Daniel: "Another shall rise after
them, and he shall be diverse from the first, and he shall
subdue three kings. And he shall speak great words
against the Most High, and shall wear out the saints of
the Most High, and think to change times and laws : and
they shall be given into his hand until a time and times,
and the dividing of time. But the judgment shall sit,
and they shall take away his dominion, to consume and
to destroy it unto the end." Again : "And the king shall
do according to his will ; and he shall exalt and magnify himself above every god, and shall speak marvellous
things against the God of gods, and shall prosper till the
indignation be accomplished. . . . Neither shall he regard the God of his fathers, nor the Desire of women, nor
regard any god ; for he shall magnify himself above all.
But in his estate shall he honour the God of forces, and
a god whom his fathers knew not shall he honour with
gold and silver, and with precious stones, and pleasant
things." * Let it be observed, that Daniel elsewhere describes other kings, and that the event has shown them

* Dan. vii., xi.

certainly to be individuals,—for instance, Xerxes, Darius, and Alexander.

And in like manner St. John : "There was given unto him a mouth speaking great things, and blasphemies ; and power was given unto him to continue forty and two months.   And he opened his mouth in blasphemy against God, to blaspheme His Name, and His tabernacle, and them that dwell in heaven.   And it was given unto him to make war with the saints, and to overcome them ; and power was given him over all kindreds and tongues and nations.   And all that dwell upon the earth shall worship him, whose names are not written in the book of life of the Lamb slain from the foundation of the world."†

Further, that by Antichrist is meant some one person, is made probable by the anticipations which, as I have said, have already occurred in history, of the fulfilment of the prophecy.   Individual men have arisen actually answering in a great measure to the above descriptions ; and this circumstance creates a probability, that the absolute and entire fulfilment which is to come will be in an individual also.   The most remarkable of these shadows of the destined scourge appeared before the time of the Apostles, between them and the age of Daniel, viz., the heathen king Antiochus, of whom we read in the books of Maccabees.   This instance is the more to the purpose, because he is actually described, (as we suppose) by Daniel, in another part of his prophecy, in terms which seem also to belong to Antichrist, and, as belonging, imply that Antiochus actually was what he seems to be, a type of that more fearful future enemy of the Church.   This Antiochus was the savage persecutor of the Jews, in their latter times, as Anti-

† Rev. xiii.

christ will be of the Christians. A few passages from
the Maccabees will show you what he was. St. Paul in
the text speaks of an Apostasy, and then of Antichrist as
following upon it ; and thus is the future of the Christian
Church typified in the past Jewish history. " In those
days went there out of Israel wicked men, who persuaded
many, saying, Let us go and make a covenant with the
heathen that are round about us : for since we departed
from them, we have had much sorrow. So this device
pleased them well. Then certain of the people were so
forward herein, that they went to the king, who gave
them licence to do after the ordinances of the heathen ;
whereupon they built a place of exercise at Jerusalem,
according to the custom of the heathen ; and made
themselves uncircumcised, and forsook the holy covenant,
and joined themselves to the heathen, and were sold to
do mischief." Here was the Falling away. After this
introduction the Enemy of truth appears. " After that
Antiochus had smitten Egypt, he returned again, ...
and went up against Israel and Jerusalem with a great
multitude, and entered proudly into the sanctuary, and
took away the golden altar, and the candlestick of light
and all the vessels thereof, and the table of the shew-
bread, and the pouring vessels, and the vials, and the
censers of gold, and the veil, and the crowns, and
the golden ornaments that were before the temple ;
all which he pulled off. And when he had taken all
away, he went into his own land, having made a great
massacre, and spoken very proudly." After this he set
fire to Jerusalem, " and pulled down the houses and
walls thereof on every side. . . . Then built they the
city of David with a great and strong wall, . . . and
they put therein a sinful nation, wicked men, and fortified themselves therein." Next, " King Antiochus wrote

to his whole kingdom, that all should be one people,
and every one should leave his laws: so all the heathen agreed according to the commandment of the king.
Yea, many also of the Israelites consented to his religion, and sacrificed unto idols, and profaned the sabbath." After this he forced these impieties upon the
chosen people. All were to be put to death who would
not " profane the sabbath and festival days, and pollute
the sanctuary and holy people, **and** set up altars, and
groves, and chapels of idols, and sacrifice swine's flesh
and unclean beasts," and " leave their children uncircumcised." At length he set up an idol, or, in the words of
the history, " the Abomination of Desolation upon the
altar, and builded idol altars throughout the cities of
Juda on every side. . . . And when they had rent in
pieces the books of the law which they found, they burnt
them with fire." It is added, " Howbeit many in Israel
were fully resolved and confirmed in themselves not to eat
any unclean thing, wherefore they chose rather to die . . .
and there was very great wrath upon Israel." * Here we
have presented to us some of the lineaments of Antichrist,
who will be such, and worse than such, as Antiochus.

The history of the apostate emperor Julian, who lived
between 300 and 400 years after Christ, furnishes us
with another approximation to the predicted Antichrist,
and an additional reason for thinking he will be one
person, not a kingdom, power, or the like.

And so again does the false prophet Mahomet, who
propagated his imposture about 600 years after Christ
came.

Lastly, that Antichrist is one individual man, not a
power,—not a mere ethical spirit, or a political system,
not a dynasty, or succession of rulers,—was the universal

* 1 Mac. i.

tradition of the early Church. " We must say," writes St. Jerome upon Daniel, "what has been handed down to us by all ecclesiastical writers, that, in the end of the world, when the Roman Empire is to be destroyed, there will be ten kings, to divide the Roman territory between them, and that an eleventh will rise up, a small king, who will subdue three of the ten, and thereupon receive the submission of the other seven. It is said that 'the Horn had eyes, as the eyes of a man,' lest we should, as some have thought, suppose him to be the evil spirit, or a demon, whereas he is one man, in whom Satan shall dwell bodily. 'And a mouth speaking great things ;' for he is the man of sin, the son of perdition, so that he dares to 'sit in the Temple of God, making himself as if God.' 'The beast has been slain, and his carcase has perished ;' since Antichrist blasphemes in that united Roman Empire, all its kingdoms are at one and the same time to be abolished, and there shall be no earthly kingdom, but the society of the saints, and the coming of the triumphant Son of God."   "And Theodoret : " Having spoken of Antiochus Epiphanes, the prophet passes from the figure to the Antitype ; for the Antitype of Antiochus is Antichrist, and the figure of Antichrist is Antiochus. As Antiochus compelled the Jews to act impiously, so the Man of Sin, the son of perdition, will make every effort for the seduction of the pious, by false miracles, and by force, and by persecution. As the Lord says, ' Then will be great tribulation, such as never was from the beginning of the world till this time, nor ever shall be.' " *

What I have said upon this subject may be summed up as follows :—that the coming of Christ will be immediately preceded by a very awful and unparalleled

* Jerom. in Dan. vii ; Theodor. in Dan. xi.

outbreak of evil, called by St. Paul an Apostasy, a falling away, in the midst of which a certain terrible Man of sin and Child of perdition, the special and singular enemy of Christ, or Antichrist, will appear ; that this will be when revolutions prevail, and the present framework of society breaks to pieces ; and that at present the spirit which he will embody and represent is kept under by "the powers that be," but that on their dissolution, he will rise out of their bosom and knit them together again in his own evil way, under his own rule, to the exclusion of the Church.

4.

It would be out of place to say more than this at present. I will but insist on one particular circumstance contained in St. Paul's announcement which I have already in part commented on.

It is said there will "come a falling away, and the man of sin will be revealed." In other words, the Man of Sin is born of an Apostasy, or at least comes into power through an apostasy, or is preceded by an apostasy, or would not be except for an apostasy. So says the inspired text: now observe, how remarkably the course of Providence, as seen in history, has commented on this prediction.

First, we have a comment in the instance of Antiochus previous to the actual events contemplated in the prophecy. The Israelites, or at least great numbers of them, put off their own sacred religion, *and then* the enemy was allowed to come in.

Next the apostate emperor Julian, who attempted to overthrow the Church by craft, and introduce paganism back again : it is observable that he was preceded, nay, he was nurtured, by heresy ; by that first great heresy which disturbed the peace and purity of the Church.

About forty years before he became emperor, arose the pestilent Arian heresy which denied that Christ was God. It ate its way among the rulers of the Church like a canker, and what with the treachery of some, and the mistakes of others, at one time it was all but dominant throughout Christendom. The few holy and faithful men, who witnessed for the Truth, cried out, with awe and terror at the apostasy, that Antichrist was coming. They called it the "forerunner of Antichrist."* And true, his Shadow came. Julian was educated in the bosom of Arianism by some of its principal upholders. His tutor was that Eusebius from whom its partizans took their name ; and in due time he fell away to paganism, became a hater and persecutor of the Church, and was cut off before he had reigned out the brief period which will be the real Antichrist's duration.

And thirdly, another heresy arose, a heresy in its consequences far more lasting and far-spreading ; it was of a twofold character; with two heads, as I may call them, Nestorianism and Eutychianism, apparently opposed to each other, yet acting towards a common end : both in one way or other denied the truth of Christ's gracious incarnation, and tended to destroy the faith of Christians not less certainly, though more insidiously, than the heresy of Arius. It spread through the East and through Egypt, corrupting and poisoning those Churches which had once, alas! been the most flourishing, the earliest abodes and strongholds of revealed truth. Out of this heresy, or at least by means of it, the impostor Mahomet sprang, and formed his creed. Here is another especial Shadow of Antichrist.

---

* πρόδρομος 'Αντιχρίστου.—" Now is the Apostasy ; for men have fallen away from the right faith. This then is the Apostasy, and the enemy must be looked out for."—*Cyril. Catech.*, 15, n. 9.

These instances give us warning :— Is the enemy of Christ, and His Church, to arise out of a certain special falling away from GOD ? And is there no reason to fear that some such Apostasy is gradually preparing, gathering, hastening on in this very day ? For is there not at this very time a special effort made almost all over the world, that is, every here and there, more or less in sight or out of sight, in this or that place, but most visibly or formidably in its most civilized and powerful parts, an effort to do without Religion ? Is there not an opinion avowed and growing, that a nation has nothing to do with Religion ; that it is merely a matter for each man's own conscience ?—which is all one with saying that we may let the Truth fail from the earth without trying to continue it in and on after our time. Is there not a vigorous and united movement in all countries to cast down the Church of Christ from power and place ? Is there not a feverish and ever-busy endeavour to get rid of the necessity of Religion in public transactions ? for example, an attempt to get rid of oaths, under a pretence that they are too sacred for affairs of common life, instead of providing that they be taken more reverently and more suitably ? an attempt to educate without Religion ?—that is, by putting all forms of Religion together, which comes to the same thing ;—an attempt to enforce temperance, and the virtues which flow from it, without Religion, by means of Societies which are built on mere principles of utility? an attempt to make *expedience*, and not *truth*, the end and the rule of measures of State and the enactments of Law? an attempt to make numbers, and not the Truth, the ground of maintaining, or not maintaining, this or that creed, as if we had any reason whatever in Scripture for thinking that the many will be in the right, and the

few in the wrong? An attempt to deprive the Bible of
its one meaning to the exclusion of all other, to make
people think that it may have an hundred meanings all
equally good, or, in other words, that it has no meaning
at all, is a dead letter, and may be put aside? an attempt to supersede Religion altogether, as far as it is
external or objective, as far as it is displayed in ordinances, or can be expressed by written words,—to confine it to our inward feelings, and thus, considering how
variable, how evanescent our feelings are, an attempt, in
fact, to destroy Religion?

Surely, there is at this day a confederacy of evil,
marshalling its hosts from all parts of the world, organizing itself, taking its measures, enclosing the Church of
Christ as in a net, and preparing the way for a general
Apostasy from it. Whether this very Apostasy is to
give birth to Antichrist, or whether he is still to be
delayed, as he has already been delayed so long, we
cannot know; but at any rate this Apostasy, and all its
tokens and instruments, are of the Evil One, and savour
of death. Far be it from any of us to be of those simple
ones who are taken in that snare which is circling around
us! Far be it from us to be seduced with the fair
promises in which Satan is sure to hide his poison! Do
you think he is so unskilful in his craft, as to ask you
openly and plainly to join him in his warfare against the
Truth? No; he offers you baits to tempt you. He
promises you civil liberty; he promises you equality;
he promises you trade and wealth; he promises you a
remission of taxes; he promises you reform. This is
the way in which he conceals from you the kind of work
to which he is putting you; he tempts you to rail against
your rulers and superiors; he does so himself, and in-
duces you to imitate him; or he promises you illumina-

tion,—he offers you knowledge, science, philosophy, enlargement of mind. He scoffs at times gone by ; he scoffs at every institution which reveres them. He prompts you what to say, and then listens to you, and praises you, and encourages you. He bids you mount aloft. He shows you how to become as gods. Then he laughs and jokes with you, and gets intimate with you ; he takes your hand, and gets his fingers between yours, and grasps them, and then you are his.

Shall we Christians allow ourselves to have lot or part in this matter ? Shall we, even with our little finger, help on the Mystery of Iniquity which is travailing for birth, and convulsing the earth with its pangs? " O my soul, come not thou into their secret ; unto their assembly, mine honour, be not thou united." * " What fellowship hath righteousness with unrighteousness ? and what communion hath light with darkness ? Wherefore, come out from among them, and be ye separate," . . . lest you be workers together with God's enemies, and be opening the way for the Man of Sin, the son of perdition.

2

The Religion of Antichrist.

ST. JOHN tells us that "every spirit that confesseth not that Jesus Christ is come in the flesh, is that spirit of Antichrist, which even now already is in the world." It was the characteristic of Antichrist, that he should openly deny our Lord Jesus Christ to be the Son of God come in the flesh from heaven. So exactly and fully was this description to answer to him, that to deny Christ might be suitably called the spirit of Antichrist; and the deniers of Him might be said to have the spirit of Antichrist, to be like Antichrist, to be Antichrists. The same thing is stated in a former chapter. "Who is the Liar, but he that denieth that Jesus is the Christ? he is the Antichrist, that denieth the Father and the Son. Whosoever denieth the Son, the same hath not the Father;"* from which words, moreover, it would appear that Antichrist will be led on from rejecting the Son of God to the rejecting of God altogether, either by implication or practically.

I shall now make some further observations on the characteristic marks of the predicted enemy of the Church; and, as before, I shall confine myself to the interpretations of Scripture given by the early Fathers.

My reason for doing so is simply this,—that on so difficult a subject as unfulfilled prophecy, I really can

* 1 John ii. 22, 23.

have no opinion of my own, nor indeed is it desirable I should have, or at least that I should put it forward in any formal way. The opinion of any one person, even if he were the most fit to form one, could hardly be of any authority, or be worth putting forward by itself; whereas the judgment and views of the early Church claim and attract our special regard, because for what we know they may be in part derived from traditions of the Apostles, and because they are put forward far more consistently and unanimously than those of any other set of teachers. Thus they have at least greater claims on our attention than those of other writers, be their claims little or great; if they are little, those of others are still less. The only really strong claim which can be made on our belief, is the clear fulfilment of the prophecy. Did we see all the marks of the prophecy satisfactorily answered in the past history of the Church, then we might dispense with authority in the parties setting the proof before us. This condition, however, can hardly be satisfied, because the date of Antichrist comes close upon the coming of Christ in judgment, and therefore the event will not have happened under such circumstances as to allow of being appealed to. Nor indeed is any history producible in which are fulfilled all the marks of Antichrist clearly, though some are fulfilled here and there. Nothing then is left us, (if we are to take up any opinion at all,—if we are to profit, as Scripture surely intends, by its warnings concerning the evil which is to come,) but to go by the judgment of the Fathers, whether that be of special authority in this matter or not. To them therefore I have had recourse already, and now shall have recourse again. To continue, then, the subject with the early Fathers as my guides.

I.

It seems clear that St. Paul and St. John speak of the same enemy of the Church, from the similarity of their descriptions. They both say, that the spirit itself was already at work in their day. "That spirit of the Antichrist," says St. John, "is *now already* in the world." "The mystery of iniquity doth *already* work," says St. Paul. And they both describe the enemy as characterized by the same especial sin, open infidelity. St. John says, that "he is the Antichrist that *denieth the Father and the Son;*" while St. Paul speaks of him in like manner as "*the adversary and rival of all that is called God, or worshipped;*" that "he sitteth as God in the Temple of God, setting forth himself that he is God." In both these passages, the same blasphemous denial of God and religion is described; but St. Paul adds, in addition, that he will oppose all existing religion, true or false, "*all* that is called God, or worshipped."

Two other passages of Scripture may be adduced, predicting the same reckless impiety; one from the eleventh chapter of Daniel: "The king shall do according to his will; and he shall exalt himself and magnify himself *above every god,* and shall speak marvellous things *against the God of gods,* and shall prosper till the indignation be accomplished. . . . Neither shall he regard the *God of his fathers,* nor the Desire of women, nor *regard any god*—for he shall magnify himself *above all.*"

The other passage is faintly marked with any prophetic allusion in itself, except that all our Saviour's sayings have a deep meaning, and the Fathers take this in particular to have such. "I am come in My Father's Name, and ye receive Me not; if *another shall come in his own name,* him ye will receive." * This they consider

* John v. 43.

to be a prophetic allusion to Antichrist, whom the Jews
were to mistake for the Christ.   He is to come "in *His
own* name."   Not from God, as even the Son of God
came, who if any might have come in the power of His
essential divinity, not in God's Name, not with any pretence of a mission from Him, but in his own name, by a
blasphemous assumption of divine power, thus will
Antichrist come.

To the above passages may be added those which
speak generally of the impieties of the last age of the
world, impieties which we may believe will usher in and
be completed in Antichrist :—

"Many shall run to and fro, and knowledge shall be
increased. . . . Many shall be purified, and made white,
and tried : but the wicked shall do wickedly ; and none
of the wicked shall understand, but the wise shall
understand."*   "In the last days perilous times shall
come, for men shall be lovers of their own selves,
covetous, boasters, proud, blasphemers, disobedient to
parents, unthankful, unholy, without natural affection,
trucebreakers, false accusers, incontinent, fierce, despisers
of those that are good, traitors, heady, high-minded,
lovers of pleasures more than lovers of God, having a
form of godliness but denying the power thereof :"†
"scoffers walking after their own lusts, and saying, Where
is the promise of His coming ?"‡ "despising government, presumptuous . . . self-willed, not afraid to speak
evil of dignities . . . promising men liberty, while themselves the servants of corruption :"§ and the like.

2.

I just now made mention of the Jews : it may be well

* Dan. xii. 4, 10.   ‡ 2 Pet. iii. 3, 4.
† 2 Tim. iii. 2—5.   § 2 Pet. ii. 10, 19.

then to state what was held in the early Church concerning Antichrist's connexion with them.

Our Lord foretold that many should come in His name, saying, "I am Christ." It was the judicial punishment of the Jews, as of all unbelievers in one way or another, that, having rejected the true Christ, they should take up with a false one ; and Antichrist will be the complete and perfect seducer, towards whom all who were previous are approximations, according to the words just now quoted, "If another shall come in his own name, him ye will receive." To the same purport are St. Paul's words after describing Antichrist ; "whose coming," he says, "is . . . with all deceivableness of unrighteousness in them that perish, because they received not the love of the Truth, that they might be saved. And *for this cause* God shall send them strong delusion that they should believe a lie, that they all might be damned who believed not the Truth, but had pleasure in unrighteousness."

Hence, considering that Antichrist would pretend to be the Messiah, it was of old the received notion that he was to be of Jewish race and to observe the Jewish rites.

Further, St. Paul says that Antichrist should "sit in the Temple of God ;" that is, according to the earlier Fathers, in the Jewish Temple. Our Saviour's own words may be taken to support this notion, because He speaks of "the Abomination of Desolation" (which, whatever other meanings it might have, in its fulness denotes Antichrist) "standing in the *holy place*." Further, the persecution of Christ's witnesses which Antichrist will cause, is described by St. John as taking place in Jerusalem. "Their dead bodies shall lie in the street of the great city, (which spiritually is called Sodom and Egypt,) where also our Lord was crucified."

Now here a remark may be made. At first sight, I suppose, we should not consider that there was much evidence from the Sacred Text for Antichrist taking part with the Jews, or having to do with their Temple. It is, then, a very remarkable fact, that the apostate emperor Julian, who was a type and earnest of the great enemy, should, as he did, have taken part with the Jews, and set about building their Temple. Here the history is a sort of comment on the prophecy, and sustains and vindicates those early interpretations of it which I am reviewing. Of course I must be understood to mean, and a memorable circumstance it is, that this belief of the Church that Antichrist should be connected with the Jews, was expressed long before Julian's time, and that we still possess the works in which it is contained. In fact we have the writings of two Fathers, both Bishops and martyrs of the Church, who lived at least one hundred and fifty years before Julian, and less than one hundred years after St. John. They both distinctly declare Antichrist's connexion with the Jews.

The first of them, Irenæus, speaks as follows : " In the Temple which is at Jerusalem the adversary will sit, endeavouring to show himself to be the Christ."

And the second, Hippolytus : "Antichrist will be he who shall resuscitate the kingdom of the Jews." *

3.

Next let us ask, Will Antichrist profess any sort of religion at all ? Neither true God nor false god will he worship : so far is clear, and yet something more, and

---

* Iren Hær. v. 25. Hippol. de Antichristo, § 25. St. Cyril of Jerusalem also speaks of Antichrist building the Jewish Temple ; and he too wrote before Julian's attempt, and (what is remarkable) prophesied it would fail, because of the prophecies.—*Vide* Ruff. Hist. i. 37.

that obscure, is told us.   Indeed, as far as the prophetic
accounts go, they seem at first sight incompatible with
each other.   Antichrist is to " exalt himself over all
that is called God or worshipped."   He will set himself
forcibly against idols and idolatry, as the early writers
agree in declaring.   Yet in the book of Daniel we read,
" In his estate *shall he honour the god of forces ; and a
god whom his fathers knew not shall he honour* with
gold and silver, and with precious stones and pleasant
things.   Thus shall he do in the most strongholds with
a *strange god, whom **he** shall acknowledge* and increase
with glory." *   What is meant by the words translated
" god of forces," and afterwards called " a strange god,"
is quite hidden from us, and probably will be so till the
event ; but anyhow some sort of false worship is certainly predicted as the mark of Antichrist, with this
prediction the contrary way, that he shall set himself
against *all idols*, as well as against the true God.   Now
it is not at all extraordinary that there should be this
contrariety in the prediction, for we know generally that
infidelity leads to superstition, and that the men most
reckless in their blasphemy are cowards also as regards
the invisible world.   They cannot be consistent if they
would.   But let me notice here a remarkable coincidence,
which is contained in the history of that type or shadow
of the final apostasy which scared the world some forty
or fifty years ago,—a coincidence between actual events
and prophecy sufficient to show us that the apparent
contradiction in the latter may easily be reconciled,
though beforehand we may not see how ; sufficient to
remind us that the all-watchful eye, and the all-ordain-
ing hand of God is still over the world, and that the
seeds, sown in prophecy above two thousand years since,

* Dan. xi. 38, 39.

are not dead, but from time to time, by blade and tender shoot, give earnest of the future harvest. Surely the world is impregnated with the elements of preternatural evil, which ever and anon, in unhealthy seasons, give lowering and muttering tokens of the wrath to come!

In that great and famous nation over against us, once great for its love of Christ's Church, since memorable for the deeds of blasphemy, which leads me here to mention it, and now, when it should be pitied and prayed for, made unhappily, in too many respects, our own model— followed when it should be condemned, and admired when it should be excused,—in the Capital of that powerful and celebrated nation, there took place, as we all well know, within the last fifty years, an open apostasy from Christianity; nor from Christianity only, but from every kind of worship which might retain any semblance or pretence of the great truths of religion. Atheism was absolutely professed;—and yet in spite of this, it seems a contradiction in terms to say it, a certain sort of worship, and that, as the prophet expresses it, "a strange worship," was introduced. Observe what this was.

I say, they avowed on the one hand Atheism. They prevailed upon a wretched man, whom they had forced upon the Church as an Archbishop, to come before them in public and declare that there was no God, and that what he had hitherto taught was a fable. They wrote up over the burial-places that death was an eternal sleep. They closed the churches, they seized and desecrated the gold and silver plate belonging to them, turning, like Belshazzar, those sacred vessels to the use of their impious revellings; they formed mock processions, clad in priestly garments, and singing profane hymns. They annulled the divine ordinance of marriage, resolving it

into a mere civil contract to be made and dissolved
at pleasure.   These things are but a part of their
enormities.

On the other hand, after having broken away from all
restraint as regards God and man, they gave a name to
that reprobate state itself into which they had thrown
themselves, and exalted it, that very negation of religion,
or rather that real and living blasphemy, into a kind of
god.   They called it LIBERTY, and they literally worshipped it as a divinity.   It would almost be incredible,
that men who had flung off all religion should be at the
pains to assume a new and senseless worship of their
own devising, whether in superstition or in mockery,
were not events so recent and so notorious.   After
abjuring our Lord and Saviour, and blasphemously
declaring Him to be an impostor, they proceeded to
decree, in the public assembly of the nation, the adoration of Liberty and Equality as divinities: and they
appointed festivals besides in honour of Reason, the
Country, the Constitution, and the Virtues.   Further,
they determined that tutelary gods, even dead men,
may be canonized, consecrated, and worshipped; and
they enrolled in the number of these some of the most
notorious infidels and profligates of the last century.
The remains of the two principal of these were brought
in solemn procession into one of their churches, and
placed upon the holy altar itself; incense was offered to
them, and the assembled multitude bowed down in worship before one of them—before what remained on earth
of an inveterate enemy of Christ.

Now, I do not mention all this as considering it the
fulfilment of the prophecy, nor, again, as if the fulfilment
when it comes will be in this precise way, but merely to
point out, what the course of events has shown to us in

these latter times, that there *are* ways of fulfilling sacred announcements that seem at first sight contradictory,— that men may oppose every existing worship, true and false, and yet take up a worship of their own from pride, wantonness, policy, superstition, fanaticism, or other reasons.

And further, let it be remarked, that there was a tendency in the infatuated people I have spoken of, to introduce the old Roman democratic worship, as if further to show us that Rome, the fourth monster of the prophet's vision, is not dead. They even went so far as to restore the worship of one of the Roman divinities (Ceres) by name, raised a statue to her, and appointed a festival in her honour. This indeed was inconsistent with exalting themselves "above *all* that is called god;" but I mention the particular fact, as I have said, not as throwing light upon the prophecy, but to show that the spirit of old Rome has not passed from the world, though its name is almost extinct.

Still further, it is startling to observe, that the former Apostate, in the early times, the Emperor Julian, he too was engaged in bringing back Roman Paganism.

Further still, let it be observed that Antiochus too, the Antichrist before Christ, the persecutor of the Jews, he too signalized himself in forcing the Pagan worship upon them, introducing it even into the Temple.

We know not what is to come; but this we may safely say, that, improbable as it is that Paganism should ever be publicly restored and enforced by authority for any period, however short, even three years and a half, yet it is far less improbable now than it was fifty years ago, before the event occurred which I have referred to. Who would not have been thought a madman or idiot, before that period, who had conjectured such a porten-

tous approximation towards Paganism as actually then
took place?

4.

Now let us recur to the ancient Fathers, and see
whether their further anticipations do not run parallel
to the events which have since happened.

Antichrist, as they considered, will come out of the
Roman Empire just upon its destruction;—that is, the
Roman Empire will in its last days divide itself into ten
parts, and the Enemy will come up suddenly out of it
upon these ten, and subdue three of them, or all of them
perhaps, and (as the prophet continues) "shall speak
great words against the Most High, and shall wear out
the saints of the Most High, and think to change times
and laws, and they shall be given into His hand until a
time, and times, and the dividing of time."* Now it is very
observable, that one of the two early Fathers whom I
have already cited, Hippolytus, expressly says that the
ten states which will at length appear, though kingdoms,
shall also be *democracies.* I say this is observable, considering the present state of the world, the tendency of
things in this day towards democracy, and the instance
which has been presented to us of democracy within the
last fifty years, in those occurrences in France to which
I have already referred.

Another expectation of the early Church was, that the
Roman monster, after remaining torpid for centuries,
would wake up at the end of the world, and be restored
in all its laws and forms ; and this, too, considering those
same recent events to which I have referred, is certainly
worth noticing also. The same Father, who anticipates
the coming of democracies, expressly deduces from a
passage in the xiiith chapter of the Apocalypse, that

* Dan. vii. 25.

"the system of Augustus, who was founder of the Roman Empire, shall be adopted and established by him (Antichrist), in order to his own aggrandizement and glory. This is the fourth monster whose head was wounded and healed; in that the empire was destroyed and came to nought, and was divided into ten diadems. But at this time Antichrist, as being an unscrupulous villain, will heal and restore it; so that it will be active and vigorous once more through the system which he establishes." *

I will but notice one other expectation falling in with the foregoing notion of the re-establishment of Roman power, entertained by the two Fathers whom I have been quoting; viz., one concerning the name of Antichrist, as spoken of in the xiiith chapter of the Revelation: "Here is wisdom," says the inspired text; "let him that hath understanding count his number, for it is the number of a man, and his number is six hundred threescore and six." Both Irenæus and Hippolytus give a name, the letters of which together in Greek make up this number, characteristic of the position of Antichrist as the head of the Roman Empire in its restored state, viz., the word Latinus, or the Latin king.

Irenæus speaks as follows: "Expect that the empire will first be divided into ten kings; then while they are reigning and beginning to settle and aggrandize themselves, suddenly one will come and claim the kingdom, and frighten them, having a name which contains the predicted number (666); him recognize as the Abomination of Desolation." Then he goes on to mention, together with two other words, the name of Lateinos as answering to the number, and says of it, "This is very probable, since it is the name of the last empire;—for the Latins" (that is, the Romans) "are now in power." †

---

* Ibid., 27, 49.   † He adds, that he himself prefers one of the other words.

And Hippolytus : " Since . . the wound of the first monster was healed . . . . and it is plain that the Latins are still in power, therefore he is called the Latin King (Latinus), the name passing from an empire to an individual." *

Whether this anticipation will be fulfilled or not, we cannot say. I only mention it as showing the belief of the Fathers in the restoration and re-establishment of the Roman Empire, which has certainly since their day been more than once attempted.

It seems then, on the whole, that, as far as the testimony of the early Church goes, Antichrist will be an open blasphemer, opposing himself to every existing worship, true and false,—a persecutor, a patron of the Jews, and a restorer of their worship, and, further, the author of a novel kind of worship. Moreover, he will appear suddenly, at the very end of the Roman Empire, which once was, and now is dormant ; that he will knit it into one, and engraft his Judaism and his new worship (a sort of Paganism, it may be) upon the old discipline of Cæsar Augustus ; that in consequence he will earn the title of the Latin or Roman King, as best expressive of his place and character ; lastly, that he will pass away as suddenly as he came.

5.

Now concerning this, I repeat, I do not wish to pronounce how far the early Church was right or wrong in these anticipations, though events since have seriously tended to strengthen its general interpretations of Scripture prophecy.

It may be asked, however, What practical use is there in speaking of these things, if they be doubtful ?

* Hippol. de Antichristo, § 50.   The Greek text seems corrupt.

I answer, first, that it is not unprofitable to bear in mind that we are still under what may be called a miraculous system. I do not mean to maintain that literal miracles are taking place now every day, but that our present state is a portion of a providential course, which began in miracle, and, at least at the end of the world, if not before, will end in miracle. The particular expectations above detailed may be right or wrong; yet an Antichrist, whoever and whatever he be, is to come; marvels are to come; the old Roman Empire is not extinct; Satan, if bound, is bound but for a season; the contest of good and evil is not ended. I repeat it, in the present state of things, when the great object of education is supposed to be the getting rid of things supernatural, when we are bid to laugh and jeer at believing everything we do not see, are told to account for everything by things known and ascertained, and to assay every statement by the touchstone of experience, I must think that this vision of Antichrist, as a supernatural power to come, is a great providential gain, as being a counterpoise to the evil tendencies of the age.

And next, it must surely be profitable for our thoughts to be sent backward and forward to the beginning and the end of the Gospel times, to the first and the second coming of Christ. What we want, is to understand that we are in the place in which the early Christians were, with the same covenant, ministry, sacraments, and duties;— to realize a state of things long past away;—to feel that we are in a sinful world, a world lying in wickedness; to discern our position in it, that we are witnesses in it, that reproach and suffering are our portion,—so that we must not "think it strange" if they come upon us, but a kind of gracious exception if they do not; to have our hearts awake, as if we had seen Christ and

His Apostles, and seen their miracles,—awake to the hope and waiting of His second coming, looking out for it, nay, desiring to see the tokens of it; thinking often and much of the judgment to come, dwelling on and adequately entering into the thought, that we individually shall be judged. All these surely are acts of true and saving faith; and this is one substantial use of the Book of Revelation, and other prophetical parts of Scripture, quite distinct from our knowing their real interpretation, viz., to take the veil from our eyes, to lift up the covering which lies over the face of the world, and make us see day by day, as we go in and out, as we get up and lie down, as we labour, and walk, and rest, and recreate ourselves, the Throne of God set up in the midst of us, His majesty and His judgments, His Son's continual intercession for the elect, their trials, and their victory.

3.

The City of Antichrist.

THE Angel thus interprets to St. John the vision of the Great Harlot, the enchantress, who seduced the inhabitants of the earth. He says, " The woman which thou sawest is that great city, which reigneth over the kings of the earth." The city spoken of in these words is evidently Rome, which was then the seat of empire all over the earth,—which was supreme even in Judæa. We hear of the Romans all through the Gospels and Acts. Our Saviour was born when His mother the Blessed Virgin, and Joseph, were brought up to Bethlehem to be taxed by the Roman governor. He was crucified under Pontius Pilate, the Roman governor. St. Paul was at various times protected by the circumstance of his being a Roman citizen ; on the other hand, when he was seized and imprisoned, it was by the Roman governors, and at last he was sent to Rome itself, to the emperor, and eventually martyred there, together with St. Peter. Thus the sovereignty of Rome, at the time when Christ and His Apostles preached and wrote, which is a matter of historical notoriety, is forced on our notice in the New Testament itself. It is undeniably meant by the Angel when he speaks of "the great city which reigneth over the earth."

The connexion of Rome with the reign and exploits of Antichrist, is so often brought before us in the controversies of this day, that it may be well, after what I have already had occasion to say on the subject of the last enemy of the Church, to consider now what Scripture prophecy says concerning Rome ; which I shall attempt to do, as before, with the guidance of the early Fathers.

I.

Now let us observe what is said concerning Rome, in the passage which the Angel concludes in the words which I have quoted, and what we may deduce from it.

That great city is described under the image of a woman, cruel, profligate, and impious. She is described as arrayed in all worldly splendour and costliness, in purple and scarlet, in gold and precious stones, and pearls, as shedding and drinking the blood of the saints, till she was drunken with it. Moreover she is called by the name of "Babylon the Great," to signify her power, wealth, profaneness, pride, sensuality, and persecuting spirit, after the pattern of that former enemy of the Church. I need not here relate how all this really answered to the character and history of Rome at the time St. John spoke of it. There never was a more ambitious, haughty, hard-hearted, and worldly people than the Romans ; never any, for none else had ever the opportunity, which so persecuted the Church. Christians suffered ten persecutions at their hands, as they are commonly reckoned, and very horrible ones, extending over two hundred and fifty years. The day would fail to go through an account of the tortures they suffered from Rome ; so that the Apostle's description was as signally fulfilled afterwards as a prophecy, as it was accurate at the time as an historical notice.

This guilty city, represented by St. John as an abandoned woman, is said to be seated on " a scarlet-

coloured monster, full of names of blasphemy, having
seven heads and ten horns." Here we are sent back by
the prophetic description to the seventh chapter of
Daniel, in which the four great empires of the world are
shadowed out under the figure of four beasts, a lion, a
bear, a leopard, and a nameless monster, "diverse" from
the rest, "dreadful and terrible, and strong exceedingly;"
"and it had ten horns." This surely is the very same
beast which St. John saw: the ten horns mark it. Now
this fourth beast in Daniel's vision is the Roman Empire;
therefore "the beast," on which the woman sat, is the
Roman Empire. And this agrees very accurately with
the actual position of things in history; for Rome, the
mistress of the world, might well be said to sit upon,
and be carried about triumphantly on that world which
she had subdued and tamed, and made her creature.
Further, the prophet Daniel explains the ten horns of
the monster to be "ten kings that shall arise" out of this
Empire; in which St. John agrees, saying, "The ten
horns which thou sawest are ten kings, which have
received no kingdom as yet, but receive power as kings
one hour with the beast." Moreover in a former vision
Daniel speaks of the Empire as destined to be "divided,"
as "partly strong and partly broken."* Further still,
this Empire, the beast of burden of the woman, was at
length to rise against her and devour her, as some savage
animal might turn upon its keeper; and it was to do
this in the time of its divided or multiplied existence.
"The ten horns which thou sawest upon him, these shall
hate" her, "and shall make her desolate and naked, and
shall eat her flesh and burn her with fire." Such was to
be the end of the great city. Lastly, three of the kings,
perhaps all, are said to be subdued by Antichrist, who

* Dan. ii. 41, 42.

is to come up suddenly while they are in power ; for
such is the course of Daniel's prophecy : "Another shall
rise after them, and he shall be diverse from the first,
and he shall subdue three kings, and he shall speak
great words against the Most High, and shall wear out
the saints of the Most High, and think to change times
and laws ; and they shall be given into his hands until a
time, times, and the dividing of time." This power, who
was to rise upon the kings, is Antichrist; and I would
have you observe how Rome and Antichrist stand towards each other in the prophecy. Rome is to fall before
Antichrist rises ; for the ten kings are to destroy Rome,
and Antichrist is then to appear and supersede the ten
kings. As far as we dare judge from the words, this
seems clear. First, St. John says, " The ten horns shall
hate and devour" the woman ; secondly, Daniel says,
"I considered the horns, and behold, there came up
among them another little horn," viz., Antichrist, "before
whom" or by whom "there were three of the first horns
plucked up by the roots."

2.

Now then, let us consider how far these prophecies have
been fulfilled, and what seems to remain unfulfilled.

In the first place, the Roman Empire did break up, as
foretold. It divided into a number of separate kingdoms,
such as our own, France, and the like ; yet it is difficult
to number ten accurately and exactly. Next, though
Rome certainly has been desolated in the most fearful
and miserable way, yet it has not exactly suffered from
ten parts of its former empire, but from barbarians who
came down upon it from regions external to it ; and, in
the third place, it still exists as a city, whereas it was to
be "desolated, devoured, and burned with fire." And,

fourthly, there is one point in the description of the ungodly city, which has hardly been fulfilled at all in the case of Rome. She had "a golden cup in her hand full of abominations," and made "the inhabitants of the earth drunk with the wine of her fornication;" expressions which imply surely some seduction or delusion which she was enabled to practise upon the world, and which, I say, has not been fulfilled in the case of that great imperial city upon seven hills of which St. John spake. Here then are points which require some consideration.

I say, the Roman Empire has scarcely yet been divided into ten. The Prophet Daniel is conspicuous among the inspired writers for the clearness and exactness of his predictions; so much so, that some unbelievers, overcome by the truth of them, could only take refuge in the unworthy, and, at the same time, unreasonable and untenable supposition, that they were written after the events which they profess to foretell. But we have had no such exact fulfilment in history of the ten kings; therefore we must suppose that it is yet to come. With this accords the ancient notion, that they were to come at the end of the world, and last for but a short time, Antichrist coming upon them. There have, indeed, been approximations to that number, yet, I conceive, nothing more. Now observe how the actual state of things corresponds to the prophecy, and to the primitive interpretation of it. It is difficult to say whether the Roman Empire is gone or not; in one sense, it is gone, for it is divided into kingdoms; in another sense, it is not, for the date cannot be assigned at which it came to an end, and much might be said in various ways to show that it may be considered still existing, though in a mutilated and decayed state. But if this be so, and if it is to end in ten vigorous kings, as Daniel says, then it must one day *revive.* Now observe, I say, how the prophetic description answers to this account of it. "The wild Beast," that is, the Roman Empire, "the Monster that thou sawest, *was and is not,* and *shall* ascend out of the abyss, and go into perdition." Again mention is made of "the Monster that was, and *is not, and yet is.*" Again we are expressly told that the ten kings and the Empire shall rise together; the kings appearing at the time of the monster's resurrection, not during its languid and torpid state. "The ten kings . . . have received no kingdom as yet, but receive power as kings one hour with the beast." If, then, the Roman Empire is still prostrate, the ten kings have not come ; and if the ten kings have not come, the destined destroyers of the woman, the full judgments upon Rome, have not yet come.

3.

Thus the full measure of judgment has not fallen upon Rome ; yet her sufferings, and the sufferings of her Empire, have been very severe. St. Peter seems to predict them, in his First Epistle, as then impending. He seems to imply that our Lord's visitation, which was then just occurring, was no local or momentary vengeance upon one people or city, but a solemn and extended judgment of the whole earth, though beginning at Jerusalem. "The time is come," he says, " when judgment must begin at *the house* of God " (at the sacred city) ; "and, if it first begin at us, what shall the end be of them that obey not the Gospel of God ? And if the righteous scarcely be saved,"—(*i. e.,* the remnant who should go forth of Zion, according to the prophecy, that chosen seed in the Jewish Church which received Christ

when He came, and took the new name of Christians,
and shot forth and grew far and wide into a fresh Church,
or, in other words, the elect whom our Saviour speaks
of as being involved in all the troubles and judgments
of the devoted people, yet safely carried through) ; "if
the righteous scarcely be saved, where shall the ungodly
and the sinner appear,"—the inhabitants of the world at
large ? *

Here is intimation of the presence of a fearful scourge
which was then going over all the ungodly world, beginning at apostate Jerusalem, and punishing it. Such
was the case : vengeance first fell upon the once holy
city, which was destroyed by the Romans : it proceeded
next against the executioners themselves.† The empire
was disorganized, and broken to pieces by dissensions
and insurrections, by plagues, famines, and earthquakes,
while countless hosts of barbarians attacked it from the
north and east, and portioned it out, and burned and
pillaged Rome itself. The judgment, I say, which began
at Jerusalem, steadily tracked its way for centuries round
and round the world, till at length, with unerring aim,
it smote the haughty mistress of the nations herself, the
guilty woman seated upon the fourth monster which
Daniel saw. I will mention one or two of these fearful
inflictions.

Hosts of barbarians came down upon the civilized
world, the Roman empire. One multitude—though
multitude is a feeble word to describe them,—invaded
France, ‡ which was living in peace and prosperity under
the shadow of Rome. They desolated and burned town
and country. Seventeen provinces were made a desert.

* Pet. iv. 17, 18. *Vide* also Jer. xxv. 28, 29. Ezek. ix. 6:
† *Vide* Is. xlvii. 5, 6.
‡ A.D. 407. *Vide* Gibbon, Hist. vol. v. chap. 30.

Eight metropolitan cities were set on fire and destroyed. Multitudes of Christians perished even in the churches.

The fertile coast of Africa was the scene of another of these invasions.* The barbarians gave no quarter to any who opposed them. They tortured their captives, of whatever age, rank, and sex, to force them to discover their wealth. They drove away the inhabitants of the cities to the mountains. They ransacked the churches. They destroyed even the fruit-trees, so complete was the desolation.

Of judgments in the course of nature, I will mention three out of a great number. One, an inundation from the sea in all parts of the Eastern empire. The water overflowed the coast for two miles inland, sweeping away houses and inhabitants along a line of some thousand miles. One great city (Alexandria) lost fifty thousand persons.†

The second, a series of earthquakes ; some of which were felt all over the empire. Constantinople was thus shaken above forty days together. At Antioch 250,000 persons perished in another.

And in the third place a plague, which lasted (languishing and reviving) through the long period of fifty-two years. In Constantinople, during three months, there died daily 5,000, and at length 10,000 persons. I give these facts from a modern writer, who is neither favourable to Christianity, nor credulous in matters of historical testimony. In some countries the population was wasted away altogether, and has not recovered to this day.‡

Such were the scourges by which the fourth monster

---

* A.D. 430.   *Vide* Gibbon, Hist. vol. vi. chap. 33.
† A.D. 365.   Ibid. vol. iv. chap. 26.
‡ A.D. 540.   Ibid. vol. vii. chap. 43.

of Daniel's vision was brought low, "the Lord God's sore judgments, the sword, the famine, and the pestilence." * Such was the process by which "that which withholdeth," (in St. Paul's language) began to be "taken away;" though not altogether removed even now.

And, while the world itself was thus plagued, not less was the offending city which had ruled it. Rome was taken and plundered three several times. The inhabitants were murdered, made captives, or obliged to fly all over Italy. The gold and jewels of the queen of the nations, her precious silk and purple, and her works of art, were carried off or destroyed.

4.

These are great and notable events, and certainly form part of the predicted judgment upon Rome; at the same time they do not adequately fulfil the prophecy, which says expressly, on the one hand, that the ten portions of the Empire itself which had almost been slain, shall rise up against the city, and "make her desolate and burn her with fire," which they have not yet done; and, on the other hand, that the city shall experience a *total* destruction, which has not yet befallen her, for she still exists. St. John's words on the latter point are clear and determinate. "Babylon the great is fallen, is fallen; and is become the habitation of devils, and the hole of every foul spirit, and a cage of every unclean and hateful bird;" † words which would seem to refer us to the curse upon the literal Babylon; and we know how that curse was fulfilled. The prophet Isaiah had said, that in Babylon "wild beasts of the desert should lie there, and their houses be full of doleful creatures, and owls should dwell there, and satyrs," or wild beasts "dance there." ‡

* Ezek. xiv. 21.　　　† Rev. xviii. 2.　　　‡ Isa. xiii. 21.

And we know that all this has in fact happened to Babylon; it is a heap of ruins; no man dwells there; nay, it is difficult to say even where exactly it was placed, so great is the desolation. Such a desolation St. John seems to predict, concerning the guilty persecuting city we are considering; and in spite of what she has suffered, such a desolation has not come upon her yet. Again, "she shall be utterly burnt with fire, for strong is the Lord God, who judgeth her." Surely this implies utter destruction, annihilation. Again, "a mighty Angel took up a stone, like a great millstone, and cast it into the sea, saying, Thus with violence, shall that great city Babylon be thrown down, and *shall be found no more at all.*"

To these passages I would add this reflection. Surely Rome is spoken of in Scripture as a more inveterate enemy of God and His saints even than Babylon, as the great pollution and bane of the earth : if then Babylon has been destroyed wholly, much more, according to all reasonable conjecture, will Rome be destroyed one day.

It may be farther observed that holy men in the early Church certainly thought that the barbarian invasions were not all that Rome was to receive in the way of vengeance, but that God would one day destroy it by the fury of the elements. "Rome," says Pope Gregory, at a time when a barbarian conqueror had possession of the city, and all things seemed to threaten its destruction, " Rome shall not be destroyed by the nations, but shall consume away internally, worn out by storms of lightning, whirlwinds, and earthquakes." * In accordance with this is the prophecy ascribed to St. Malachi of Armagh, a mediæval Archbishop (A.D. 1130), which declares, "In the last persecution of the Holy Church,

* Greg. Dial. ii. 15.

Peter of Rome shall be on the throne, who shall feed his flock in many tribulations. When these are past, *the city upon seven hills shall be* destroyed, and the awful Judge shall judge the people."*

5.

This is what may be said on the one side, but after all something may be said on the other; not indeed to show that the prophecy is already fully accomplished, for it certainly is not, but to show that, granting this, such accomplishment as has to come has reference, not to Rome, but to some other object or objects of divine vengeance. I shall explain my meaning under two heads.

First, why has Rome not been destroyed hitherto? how was it that the barbarians left it? Babylon sank under the avenger brought against it—Rome has not: why is this? for if there has been a something to procrastinate the vengeance due to Rome hitherto, peradventure that obstacle may act again and again, and stay the uplifted hand of divine wrath till the end come. The cause of this unexpected respite seems to be simply this, that when the barbarians came down, God had a people in that city. Babylon was a mere prison of the Church; Rome had received her as a guest. The Church dwelt in Rome, and while her children suffered in the heathen city from the barbarians, so again they were the life and the salt of that city where they suffered.

Christians understood this at the time, and availed themselves of their position. They remembered Abraham's intercession for Sodom, and the gracious announcement made him, that, had there been ten righteous men therein, it would have been saved.

* *Vide* Dr. Burton, Antiq. of Rome, p. 475.

When the city was worsted, threatened, and at length overthrown, the Pagans had cried out that Christianity was the cause of this. They said they had always flourished under their idols, and that these idols or devils (gods as they called them) were displeased with them for the numbers among them who had been converted to the faith of the Gospel, and had in consequence deserted them, given them over to their enemies, and brought vengeance upon them. On the other hand, they scoffed at the Christians, saying in effect, "Where is now your God? Why does He not save you? You are not better off than we;" they said, with the impenitent thief, "If thou be the Christ, save Thyself and us;" or with the multitude, "If He be the Son of God, let Him come down from the Cross." This was during the time of one of the most celebrated bishops and doctors of the Church, St. Augustine, and he replied to their challenge. He replied to them, and to his brethren also, some of whom were offended and shocked that such calamities should have happened to a city which had become Christian.* He pointed to the cities which had already sinned and been visited, and showed that they had altogether perished, whereas Rome was still preserved. Here, then, he said, was the very fulfilment of the promise of God, announced to Abraham ;—for the sake of the Christians in it, Rome was chastised, not overthrown utterly.

Historical facts support St. Augustine's view of things. God provided visibly, not only in His secret counsels, that the Church should be the salvation of the city. The fierce conqueror Alaric, who first came against it, exhorted his troops "to respect the Churches of the Apostles St. Peter and St. Paul, as holy and inviolable sanctuaries ;" and he gave orders that a quantity of plate, consecrated

* August. de Urbis Excidio, vol. vi. p. 622. ed. Ben. et de Civ. Dei, i. 1—7.

to St. Peter, should be removed into his Church from the place where it had been discovered.*

Again, fifty years afterwards, when Attila was advancing against the city, the Bishop of Rome of the day, St. Leo, formed one of a deputation of three, who went out to meet him, and was successful in arresting his purpose.

A few years afterwards, Genseric, the most savage of the barbarian conquerors, appeared before the defenceless city. The same fearless pontiff went out to meet him at the head of his clergy, and though he did not succeed in saving the city from pillage, yet he gained a promise that the unresisting multitude should be spared, the buildings protected from fire, and the captives from torture.†

Thus from the Goth, Hun, and Vandal did the Christian Church shield the guilty city in which she dwelt. What a wonderful rule of God's providence is herein displayed which occurs daily!—the Church sanctifies, yet suffers with, the world,—sharing its sufferings, yet lightening them. In the case before us, she has (if we may humbly say it) suspended, to this day, the vengeance destined to fall upon that city which was drunk with the blood of the martyrs of Jesus. That vengeance has never fallen; it is still suspended ; nor can reason be given *why* Rome has not fallen under the rule of God's general dealings with His rebellious creatures, and suffered (according to the prophecy) the fulness of God's wrath begun in it, except that a Christian Church is still in that city, sanctifying it, interceding for it, saving it. We in England consider that the Christian Church there has in process of time become infected with the sins of Rome itself, and has learned to be ambitious and cruel after the fashion of those who possessed the place aforetimes. Yet, if it were what many would make it, if it were as reprobate as

* *Vide* Gibbon, Hist. vol. v. chap. 31.   Ibid. vol. vi. chap. 35, 36.

heathen Rome itself, what stays the judgment long ago begun? why does not the Avenging Arm, which made its first stroke ages since, deal its second and its third, till the city has fallen? Why is not Rome as Sodom and Gomorrah, if there be no righteous men in it?

This then is the first remark I would make as to that fulfilment of the prophecy which is not yet come; perhaps through divine mercy, it may be procrastinated even to the end, and never be fulfilled. Of this we can know nothing one way or the other.

Secondly, let it be considered, that as Babylon is a type of Rome, and of the world of sin and vanity, so Rome in turn may be a type also, whether of some other city, or of a proud and deceiving world. The woman is said to be Babylon as well as Rome, and as she is something more than Babylon, namely, Rome, so again she may be something more than Rome, which is yet to come. Various great cities in Scripture are made, in their ungodliness and ruin, types of the world itself. Their end is described in figures, which in their fulness apply only to the end of the world; the sun and moon are said to fall, the earth to quake, and the stars to fall from heaven.* The destruction of Jerusalem in our Lord's prophecy is associated with the end of all things. As then their ruin prefigures a greater and wider judgment, so the chapters, on which I have been dwelling, may have a further accomplishment, not in Rome, but in the world itself, or some other great city to which we cannot at present apply them, or to all the great cities of the world together, and to the spirit that rules in them, their avaricious, luxurious, self-dependent, irreligious spirit. And in this sense is already fulfilled a portion of the chapter before us, which does not apply to heathen Rome;—I

* *Vide* Isaiah xiii. 10, etc.

mean the description of the woman as making men
drunk with her sorceries and delusions; for such, surely,
and nothing else than an intoxication, is that arrogant,
ungodly, falsely liberal, and worldly spirit, which great
cities make dominant in a country.

6.

To sum up what I have said. The question asked
was, Is it not true (as is commonly said and believed
among us) that Rome is mentioned in the Apocalypse,
as having especial share in the events which will come
at the end of the world by means, or after the time,
of Antichrist? I answer this, that Rome's judgments
have come on her in great measure, when her Empire
was taken from her; that her persecutions of the Church
have been in great measure avenged, and the Scripture
predictions concerning her fulfilled; that whether or not
she shall be further judged depends on two circumstances, first, whether "the righteous men" in the city
who saved her when her judgment first came, will not,
through God's great mercy, be allowed to save her still;
next, whether the prophecy relates in its fulness to Rome
or to some other object or objects of which Rome is a
type. And further, I say, that if it is in the divine
counsels that Rome should still be judged, this must be
before Antichrist comes, because Antichrist comes upon
and destroys the ten kings, and lasts but a short space,
but it is the ten kings who are to destroy Rome. On
the other hand, so far would seem to be clear, that the
prophecy itself has not been fully accomplished, whatever we decide about Rome's concern in it. The Roman
Empire has not yet been divided into ten heads, nor has
it yet risen against the woman, whomsoever she stands for,
nor has the woman yet received her ultimate judgment.

We are warned against sharing in her sins and in her punishment;—against being found, when the end comes, mere children of this world and of its great cities ; with tastes, opinions, habits, such as are found in its cities ; with a heart dependent on human society, and a reason moulded by it ;—against finding ourselves at the last day, before our Judge, with all the low feelings, principles, and aims which the world encourages; with our thoughts wandering (if that be possible then), wandering after vanities ; with thoughts which rise no higher than the consideration of our own comforts, or our gains ; with a haughty contempt for the Church, her ministers, her lowly people ; a love of rank and station, an admiration of the splendour and the fashions of the world, an affectation of refinement, a dependence upon our powers of reason, an habitual self-esteem, and an utter ignorance of the number and the heinousness of the sins which lie against us.   If we are found thus, when the end comes, where, when the judgment is over, and the saints have gone up to heaven, and there is silence and darkness where all was so full of life and expectation, where shall we find ourselves then?   And what good could the great Babylon do us then, though it were as immortal as we are immortal ourselves ?

4.

The Persecution of Antichrist.

WE have been so accustomed to hear of the persecutions of the Church, both from the New
Testament and from the history of Christianity, that it
is much if we have not at length come to regard the
account of them as words of course, to speak of them
without understanding what we say, and to receive no
practical benefit from having been told of them ; much
less are we likely to take them for what they really are,
a characteristic mark of Christ's Church. They are
not indeed the necessary lot of the Church, but at least
one of her appropriate badges ; so that, on the whole,
looking at the course of history, you might set down
persecution as one of the peculiarities by which you
recognize her. And our Lord seems to intimate how
becoming, how natural persecution is to the Church, by
placing it among His Beatitudes. " Blessed are they
who are persecuted for righteousness' sake, for theirs is
the kingdom of heaven ;" giving it the same high and
honourable rank in the assemblage of evangelical graces,
which the Sabbath holds among the Ten Command-
ments,—I mean, as a sort of sign and token of His
followers, and, as such, placed in the moral code, though
in itself external to it.

He seems to show us this in another way, viz., by in-
timating to us the fact, that in persecution the Church
begins and in persecution she ends. He left her in perse-

cution, and He will find her in persecution. He recognizes her as His own,—He framed, and He will claim her,—as a persecuted Church, bearing His Cross. And that awful relic of Him which He gave her, and which she is found possessed of at the end, she cannot have lost by the way.

The prophet Daniel, who shadows out for us so many things about the last time, speaks of the great persecution yet to come. He says, " There shall be a time of trouble, such as never was, since there was a nation, even to that same time : and at that time thy people shall be delivered, every one that shall be found written in the Book." To these words our Lord seems to refer, in His solemn prophecy before His passion, in which He comprises both series of events, both those which attended His first, and those which will attend at His second coming—both persecutions of His Church, the early and the late. He speaks as follows : " Then shall be great tribulation, such as was not since the beginning of the world to this time, no, nor ever shall be ; and except those days should be shortened, there should no flesh be saved ; but for the elect's sake, those days shall be shortened." *

Now I shall conclude what I have to say about the coming of Antichrist by speaking of the persecution which will attend it. In saying that a persecution will attend it, I do but speak the opinion of the early Church, as I have tried to do all along, and as I shall do in what follows.

I.

First, I will cite some of the principal texts which seem to refer to this last persecution.

* Matt. xxiv. 21 22.

" Another shall rise after them, and . . . he shall speak great words against the Most High, and shall wear out the saints of the Most High, and think to change times and laws ; and they shall be given into his hand until a time, times, and the dividing of time :" * that is, three years and a half.

" They shall pollute the Sanctuary of strength, and shall take away the Daily Sacrifice, and they shall place the Abomination that maketh desolate, and such as do wickedly against the Covenant shall he corrupt by flatteries ; but the people that do know their God shall be strong and do exploits. And they that understand among the people, shall instruct many ; yet they shall fall by the sword, and by flame, by captivity, and by spoil, many days." †

" Many shall be purified, and made white, and tried ; but the wicked shall do wickedly ; . . . . and from the time that the Daily Sacrifice shall be taken away, and the Abomination that maketh desolate set up, there shall be a thousand two hundred and ninety days." ‡

" Then shall be great tribulation, such as was not since the beginning of the world," § and so on, as I just now read it.

" And there was given unto him a mouth speaking great things and blasphemies ; and power was given unto him to continue forty and two months. And he opened his mouth in blasphemy against God, to blaspheme His name, and His tabernacle, and them that dwell in heaven : and it was given unto him to make war with the saints, and to overcome them . . . . and all that dwell upon the earth shall worship him, whose

* Dan. vii. 24, 25.   ‡ Dan. xii. 10, 11.
- Dan. xi. 31—33.   § Matt. xxiv. 21

names are not written in the book of life of the Lamb slain from the foundation of the world ." *

" I saw an Angel come down from heaven, having the key of the bottomless pit, and a great chain in his hand ; and he laid hold on the dragon, that old serpent, which is the devil and Satan, and bound him a thousand years . . . . and after that he must be loosed a little season . . . . and shall go out to deceive the nations which are in the four quarters of the earth, Gog and Magog, to gather them together to battle : the number of whom is as the sand of the sea. And they went up on the breadth of the earth, and compassed the camp of the saints about and the beloved city." †

These passages were understood by the early Christians to relate to the Persecution which was to come in the last times ; and they seem evidently to bear upon them that meaning. Our Lord's words, indeed, about the fierce trial which was coming, might seem at first sight to refer to the early persecutions, those to which the first Christians were exposed ; and doubtless so they do also : yet, violent as these persecutions were, they were not considered by those very men who underwent them to be the proper fulfilment of the prophecy; and this surely is itself a strong reason for thinking they were not so. And we are confirmed by parallel passages, such as the words of Daniel quoted just now, which certainly speak of a persecution still future ; if then our Lord used those very words of Daniel, and was speaking of what Daniel spoke of, therefore, whatever partial accomplishment His prediction had in the history of the early Church, He surely speaks of nothing short of the last persecution, when His words are viewed in their full scope. He says, " There shall be great tribulation, such

* Rev. xiii. 5—8.   † Rev. xx. 1—9.

as was not since the beginning of the world to this time, no, nor ever shall be : and except those days should be shortened, there shall no flesh be saved ; but for the elect's sake those days shall be shortened." And immediately after, " There shall arise false Christs and false prophets, and shall show great signs and wonders ; insomuch that, if it were possible, they shall deceive the very elect." In accordance with this language, Daniel says, " There shall be a time of trouble, such as never was since there was a nation, even to that same time : and at that time thy people shall be delivered, every one that shall be found written in the book." One of the passages I quoted from the Revelation says the same, and as strongly : " It was given him to make war with the Saints, and to overcome them . . . . and all that dwell on the earth shall worship him, whose names are not written in the book of life ." *

2.

Let us then apprehend and realize the idea, thus clearly brought before us, that, sheltered as the Church has been from persecution for 1500 years, yet a persecution awaits it, before the end, fiercer and more perilous than any which occurred at its first rise.

Further, this persecution is to be attended with the cessation of all religious worship. "They shall take away the Daily Sacrifice,"—words which the early Fathers interpret to mean, that Antichrist will suppress for three years and a half all religious worship. St. Augustine questions whether baptism even will be administered to infants during that season.

And further we are told : " They shall place the Abomination that maketh desolate " in the Holy Place

* Rev. xiii 7, 8.

—they shall " set it up : " our Saviour declares the same.
What this means we cannot pronounce.   In the former
fulfilment of this prophecy, it has been the introduction
of heathen idols into God's house.

Moreover the reign of Antichrist will be supported, it
would appear, with a display of miracles, such as the
magicians of Egypt effected against Moses.   On this
subject, of course, we wait for a fuller explanation of the
prophetical language, such as the event alone can give
us.   So far, however, is clear, that whether false miracles
or not, whether pretended, or the result, as some have
conjectured, of discoveries in physical science, they will
produce the same effect as if they were real,—viz., the
overpowering the imaginations of such as have not the
love of God deeply lodged in their hearts,—of all but
the elect."   Scripture is remarkably precise and consistent in this prediction.   " Signs and wonders," says
our Lord, " insomuch that, if it were possible, they shall
deceive the very elect."   St. Paul speaks of Antichrist
as one " whose coming is after the work of Satan, with
all powers and signs, and lying wonders, and with all
deceivableness of unrighteousness in them that perish ;
because they received not the love of the Truth, that they
might be saved.   And for this cause God shall send them
strong delusion, that they should believe a lie."*   And St.
John : " He doeth great wonders, so that He maketh fire
come down from heaven on the earth in the sight of men,
and deceiveth them that dwell on the earth by the means
of those miracles which He had power to do in the sight
of the beast."†

In these four respects, then, not to look for others,
will the last persecution be more awful than any of the
earlier ones : in its being in itself fiercer and more hor-

* 2 Thess. ii. 9—11.   † Rev. xiii. 13, 14.

rible; in its being attended by a cessation of the Ordinances of grace, "the Daily Sacrifice;" and by an open and blasphemous establishment of infidelity, or some such enormity, in the holiest recesses of the Church; lastly, in being supported by a profession of working miracles. Well is it for Christians that the days are shortened!—shortened for the elect's sake, lest they should be overwhelmed,—shortened, as it would seem, to three years and a half.

3.

Much might be said, of course, on each of these four particulars; but I will confine myself to making one remark on the first of them, the sharpness of the persecution.—It is to be worse than any persecution before it. Now, to understand the force of this announcement, we should understand in some degree what those former persecutions were.

This it is very difficult to do in a few words; yet a very slight survey of the history of the Church would convince us that cruelties more shocking than those which the early Christians suffered from their persecutors, it is very difficult to conceive. St. Paul's words, speaking of the persecutions prior to his time, describes but faintly the trial which came upon the Church in his own day and afterwards. He says of the Jewish saints, "They were tortured, not accepting deliverance" . . . they "had trials of cruel mockings and scourgings, yea moreover, of bonds and imprisonment: they were stoned, they were sawn asunder, were tempted, were slain with the sword: they wandered about in sheepskins and goatskins; being destitute, afflicted, tormented." Such were the trials of the Prophets under the Law, who in a measure anticipated the Gospel, as in creed, so in suffering;

yet the Gospel suffering was as much sharper as the
Gospel creed was fuller than their foretaste of either.

Let me take, as a single specimen, a portion of a letter,
giving an account of some details of one of the persecutions in the south of France. It is written by eye-
witnesses.

" . . . The rage of the populace, governor, and soldiers especially lighted on Sanctus, a deacon ; on Maturus, a late convert ;
on Attalus, and on Blandina, a slave, through whom Christ showed
that the things which are lowly esteemed among men have high
account with God. For when we were all in fear, and her own
mistress was in agony for her, lest she should be unable to make
even one bold confession, from the weakness of her body, Blandina
was filled with such strength, that even those who tortured her
by turns, in every possible way, from morning till evening, were
wearied and gave it up, confessing she had conquered them. And
they wondered at her remaining still alive, her whole body being
mangled and pierced in every part. But that blessed woman,
like a brave combatant, renewed her strength in confessing ; and it
was to her a recovery, a rest, and a respite, to say, ' I am a
Christian.' . . Sanctus also endured exceedingly all the cruelties
of men with a noble patience . . and to all questions would
say nothing but ' I am a Christian.' When they had nothing left
to do to him, they fastened red-hot plates of brass on the tenderest
parts of his body. But though his limbs were burning, he remained
upright and unshrinking, steadfast in his confession, bathed and
strengthened from Heaven with that fountain of living water that
springs from the well of Christ. But his body bore witness of what
had been done to it, being one entire wound, and deprived of the
external form of man."

After some days they were taken to the shows where
the wild beasts were, and went through every torture
again, as though they had suffered nothing before. Again
they were scourged, forced into the iron chair (which
was red hot), dragged about by the beasts, and so came
to their end. " But Blandina was hung up upon a cross,
and placed to be devoured by the beasts that were turned

in." Afterwards she was scourged ; at last placed in a basket and thrown to a bull, and died under the tossings of the furious animal.   But the account is far too long and minute, and too dreadful, to allow of my going through it.   I give this merely as a specimen of the sufferings of the early Christians from the malice of the devil.

As another instance, take again the sufferings which the Arian Vandals inflicted at a later time.   Out of four hundred and sixty Bishops in Africa, they sent forty-six out of the country to an unhealthy place, and confined them to hard labour, and three hundred and two to different parts of Africa.   After an interval of ten years they banished two hundred and twenty more. At another time they tore above four thousand Christians, clergy and laity, from their homes, and marched them across the sands till they died either of fatigue or ill-usage.   They lacerated others with scourges, burned them with hot iron, and cut off their limbs.*

Hear how one of the early Fathers, just when the early persecutions were ceasing, meditates on the prospect lying before the Church, looking earnestly at the events of his own day, in order to discover from them, if he could, whether the predicted evil was coming :

"There will be a time of affliction, such as never happened since there was a nation upon the earth till that time.   The fearful monster, the great serpent, the unconquerable enemy of mankind, ready to devour. . . The Lord knowing the greatness of the enemy, in mercy to the religious, says, ' Let those that are in Judea flee to the mountains.'   However, if any feel within him a strong heart to wrestle with Satan, let him remain, (for I do not despair of the Church's strength of nerve,) let him remain, and let him say, ' Who shall separate us from the love of Christ ?' . . . Thanks to God, who limits the greatness of the affliction to a few days ; 'for the elect's sake those days shall be cut short.'   Antichrist shall reign

* Gibbon, Hist., chap. 37.

only three years and a half, a time, times, and the dividing of
times. . . : "Blessed surely he who then shall be a martyr for
Christ! I consider that the martyrs at that season will be greater
than all martyrs; for the former ones wrestled with man only, but
these, in the time of Antichrist, will battle with Satan himself personally. Persecuting emperors slaughtered the former; but they
did not pretend to raise the dead, nor make show of signs and
wonders: but here there will be the persuasion both of force and of
fraud, so as to deceive, if possible, even the elect. Let no one at
that day say in his heart, 'What could Christ do more than this or
that? by what virtue worketh he these things? Unless God willed
it, He would not have permitted it.' No: the Apostle forewarns
you, saying beforehand, 'God shall send them a strong delusion,'—
not that they may be excused, but condemned—viz., those who
believe not in the Truth, that is, the true Christ, but take pleasure
in unrighteousness, that is, in Antichrist. . . . Prepare thyself,
therefore, O man! thou hearest the signs of Antichrist; nor remind
only thyself of them, but communicate them liberally to all around
thee. If thou hast a child according to the flesh, delay not to instruct him. If thou art a teacher, prepare also thy spiritual children,
lest they take the false for the True. 'For the mystery of iniquity
doth already work.' I fear the wars of the nations, I fear the
divisions among Christians, I fear the hatred among brethren.
Enough; but God forbid that it should be fulfilled in our day.
However, let us be prepared."—*Cyr. Catech.* xv. 16, 17.

4.

I have two remarks to add: first, that it is quite certain, that if such a persecution has been foretold, it has
not yet come, and therefore is to come. We may be
wrong in thinking that Scripture foretells it, though it
has been the common belief, I may say, of all ages; but
if there be a persecution, it is still future. So that every
generation of Christians should be on the watch-tower,
looking out,—nay, more and more, as time goes on.

Next, I observe that signs do occur from time to time,
not to enable us to fix the day, for that is hidden, but to
show us it is coming. The world grows old—the earth

is crumbling away—the night is far spent—the day is at hand. The shadows begin to move—the old forms of empire, which have lasted ever since our Lord was with us, heave and tremble before our eyes, and nod to their fall. These it is that keep Him from us—He is behind them. When they go, Antichrist will be released from " that which withholdeth," and after his short but fearful season, Christ will come.

For instance : one sign is the present state of the Roman Empire, if it may be said to exist, though it does exist ; but it is like a man on his death-bed, who after many throes and pangs at last goes off when you least expect, or perhaps you know not when. You watch the sick man, and you say every day will be the last ; yet day after day goes on—you know not when the end will come—he lingers on—gets better—relapses, —yet you are sure after all he must die—it is a mere matter of time, you call it a matter of time : so is it with the Old Roman Empire, which now lies so still and helpless. It is not dead, but it is on its death-bed. We suppose indeed that it will not die without some violence even yet, without convulsions. Antichrist is to head it ; yet in another sense it dies to make way for Antichrist, and this latter form of death is surely hastening on, whether it comes sooner or later. It may outlast our time, and the time of our children ; for we are creatures of a day, and a generation is like the striking of a clock ; but it tends to dissolution, and its hours are numbered.

Again, another anxious sign at the present time is what appears in the approaching destruction of the Mahometan power. This too may outlive our day; still it tends visibly to annihilation, and as it crumbles, perchance the sands of the world's life are running out.

And lastly, not to mention many other tokens which might be observed upon, here is this remarkable one. In one of the passages I just now read from the book of Revelation, it is said that in the last times, and in order to the last persecution, Satan, being loosed from his prison, shall deceive the nations in the extremities of the earth, Gog and Magog, and bring them to battle against the Church. These appellations had been already used by the prophet Ezekiel, who borrows the latter of them from the tenth chapter of Genesis. We read in that chapter, that after the flood the sons of Japheth were "Gomer, and Magog, and Madai, and Javan, and Tubal, and Meshech, and Tiras." Magog is supposed to be the ancestor of the nations in the north, the Tartars or Scythians. Whatever then Gog means, which is not known, here is a prophecy that the northern nations should be stirred up against the Church, and be one of the instruments of its suffering. And it is to be observed, that twice since that prophecy was delivered the northern nations have invaded the Church, and both times they have brought with them, or rather (as the text in the Revelation expresses it) they have been deceived into, an Antichristian delusion,—been deceived into it, not invented it. The first irruption was that of the Goths and Vandals in the early times of the Church, and they were deceived into and fought for the Arian heresy. The next was that of the Turks, and they in like manner were deceived into and fought for Mahometanism. Here then the after history, as in other instances, is in part a comment upon the prophecy Now, I do not mean that as to the present time, we see how this is to be accomplished in its fulness, after the pattern of the Shadows which have gone before. But thus much we see—we see that in matter of fact the nations of the North * are gathering strength, and beginning to frown over the seat of the Roman Empire as they never have done since the time when the Turks came down. Here then we have a sign of Antichrist's appearance—I do not say of his instant coming, or his certain coming, for it may after all be but a type or shadow of things far future ; still, so far as it goes, it is a preparation, a warning, a call to sober thought—just as a cloud in the sky (to use our Lord's instance) warns us about the weather. It is no sure proof that it precedes a storm, but we think it prudent to keep our eye upon it.

5.

This is what I have to say about the last persecution and its signs. And surely it is profitable to think about it, though we be quite mistaken in the detail. For instance, after all perhaps it may not be a persecution of blood and death, but of craft and subtlety only—not of miracles, but of natural wonders and powers of human skill, human acquirements in the hands of the devil. Satan may adopt the more alarming weapons of deceit —he may hide himself—he may attempt to seduce us in little things, and so to move Christians, not all at once, but by little and little from their true position. We know he has done much in this way in the course of the last centuries. It is his policy to split us up and divide us, to dislodge us gradually from off our rock of strength. And if there is to be a persecution, perhaps it will be then ; then, perhaps, when we are all of us in all parts of Christendom so divided, and so reduced, so full of schism, so close upon heresy. When we have cast ourselves upon the world, and depend for protection upon

* [*E. g.*, The Chinese ?]

it, and have given up our independence and our strength, then he may burst upon us in fury, as far as God allows him. Then suddenly the Roman Empire may break up, and Antichrist appear as a persecutor, and the barbarous nations around break in. But all these things are in God's hand and God's knowledge, and there let us leave them.

This alone I will say, in conclusion, as I have already said several times, that such meditations as these may be turned to good account. It will act as a curb upon our self-willed, selfish hearts, to believe that a persecution is in store for the Church, whether or not it comes in our days. Surely, with this prospect before us, we cannot bear to give ourselves up to thoughts of ease and comfort, of making money, settling well, or rising in the world. Surely, with this prospect before us, we cannot but feel that we are, what all Christians really are in the best estate (nay, rather would wish to be, had they their will, if they be Christians in heart), pilgrims, watchers waiting for the morning, waiting for the light, eagerly straining our eyes for the first dawn of day—looking out for our Lord's coming, His glorious advent, when He will end the reign of sin and wickedness, accomplish the number of His elect, and perfect those who at present struggle with infirmity, yet in their hearts love and obey Him.

POSTSCRIPT.

THE above expositions of the teaching of the Fathers on the subject treated, were preached by the Author in the form of Sermons in Advent, 1835, and are illustrated by the following remarkable passage in a letter of Bishop Horsley's, written before the beginning of this century ; vide *British Magazine*, May, 1834.

" The Church of God on earth will be greatly reduced, as we may well imagine, in its apparent numbers, in the times of Antichrist, by the open desertion of the powers of the world. This desertion will begin in a professed indifference to any particular form of Christianity, under the pretence of universal toleration ; which toleration will proceed from no true spirit of charity and forbearance, but from a design to undermine Christianity, by multiplying and encouraging sectaries. The pretended toleration will go far beyond a just toleration, even as it regards the different sects of Christians. For governments will pretend an indifference to all, and will give a protection in preference to none. All establishments will be laid aside. From the toleration of the most pestilent heresies, they will proceed to the toleration of Mahometanism, Atheism, and at last to a positive persecution of the truth of Christianity. In these times the Temple of God will be reduced almost to the Holy Place, that is, to the small number of real Christians who worship the Father in spirit and in truth, and regulate their doctrine and their worship, and their whole conduct, strictly by the word of God. The merely nominal

Christians will all desert the profession of the truth, when the powers of the world desert it. And this tragical event I take to be typified by the order to St. John to measure the Temple and the Altar, and leave the outer court (national Churches) to be trodden under foot by the Gentiles. The property of the clergy will be pillaged, the public worship insulted and vilified by these deserters of the faith they once professed, who are not called apostates because they never were in earnest in their profession. Their profession was nothing more than a compliance with fashion and public authority. In principle they were always, what they now appear to be, Gentiles. When this general desertion of the faith takes place, then will commence the sackcloth ministry of the witnesses. . . . There will be nothing of splendour in the external appearance of their churches ; they will have no support from governments, no honours, no emoluments, no immunities, no authority, but that which no earthly power can take away, which they derived from Him, who commissioned them to be His witnesses."— *B. M.*, vol. v., p. 520.

June, 1838.

III.

HOLY SCRIPTURE IN ITS RELATION TO THE CATHOLIC CREED.

IN EIGHT LECTURES.

I.

Difficulties in the Scripture Proof of the Catholic Creed.

I PROPOSE in the following Lectures to suggest some thoughts by way of answering an objection, which often presses on the mind of those who are inquiring into the claims of the Church, and the truth of that system of doctrine which she especially represents, and which is at once her trust and her charter. They hear much stress laid upon that Church system of doctrine; they see much that is beautiful in it, much that is plausible in the proof advanced for it, much which is agreeable to the analogy of nature—which bespeaks the hand of the Creator, and is suitable to the needs and expectations of the creature,—much that is deep, much that is large and free, fearless in its course, sure in its stepping, and singularly true, consistent, entire, harmonious, in its adjustments; but they seem to ask for more rigid proof in behalf of the simple elementary propositions on which it rests; or, in other words, by way of speaking more clearly, and as a chief illustration of what is meant (though it is not quite the same thing), let me say, they desire more adequate and explicit *Scripture proof* of its truth. They find that the proof is *rested* by us on Scripture, and therefore they require more explicit *Scripture proof*. They say, "All this that you say about the Church is very specious, and very attractive ; but where is it to be found in the inspired Volume?" And that it is *not* found there (that is, I mean not found as fully as it might be), seems to them proved at once by the simple fact, that all persons (I may say all, for the exceptions are very few),—all those who try to form their Creed by Scripture only, fall away from the Church and her doctrines, and join one or other sect or party, as if showing that, whatever is or is not scriptural, at least the Church, by consent of all men, is not so.

I am stating no rare or novel objection : it is one which, I suppose, all of us have felt, or perhaps still feel: it is one which, before now (I do not scruple to say), I have much felt myself, and that without being able satisfactorily to answer : and which I believe to be one of the main difficulties, and (as I think) one of the intended difficulties, which God's providence puts at this day in the path of those who seek Him, for purposes known or unknown, ascertainable or not. Nor am I at all sanguine that I shall be able, in what I have to say, to present anything like a full view of the difficulty itself, even as a phenomenon ; which different minds feel differently, and do not quite recognize as their own when stated by another, and which it is difficult to bring out even according to one's own idea of it. Much less shall I be able to assign it its due place in that great Catholic system which nevertheless I hold to be true, and in which it is *but* a difficulty. I do not profess to be able to account for it, to reconcile the mind to it, and to dismiss it as a thing which was in a man's way, but is henceforth behind him ;—yet, subdued as my hopes may be, I have too great confidence in that glorious Creed, which I believe to have been once delivered to the Saints, to wish in any degree to deny the difficulty, or to be unfair to it, to smooth it over, misrepresent it, or defraud it of its due weight and extent. Though I were to grant that the champions of Israel have not yet rescued this portion of the sacred territory from the Philistine, its usurping occupant, yet was not Jerusalem in the hands of the Jebusites till David's time?—and shall I, seeing with my eyes and enjoying the land of promise, be over-troubled with one objection, which stands unvanquished (supposing it) ; and, like haughty Haman, count the King's favour as nothing till I have all my own way, and nothing to try me ? In plain terms, I conceive I have otherwise most abundant evidence given me of the divine origin of the Church system of doctrine: how then is that evidence which *is* given, *not* given because, *though* given in Scripture, it might be there given more explicitly and fully, and (if I may so say) more consistently ?

One consideration alone must create an anxiety in entering on the subject I propose. It is this :—Those who commonly urge the objection which is now to be considered, viz., the want of adequate Scripture evidence for the Church creed, have, I feel sure, no right to make it ; that is, *they* are *inconsistent* in making it ; inasmuch as they cannot consistently find fault with a person who believes more than they do, unless they cease to believe just so much as they do believe. They ought, on their own principles, to doubt or disown much which happily they do not doubt or disown. This then is the direct, appropriate, polemical answer to them, or (as it is called) *an argumentum ad hominem.* " Look at home, and say,

if you can, *why* you believe this or that, which you do
believe : whatever reasons you give for your own belief
in one point, this or that article, of your Creed, those
parallel reasons we can give for our belief in the articles
of our Creed.   If you are reasonable in believing the
one, we are reasonable in believing the other.   Either
we are reasonable, or you are not so.   You ought not to
stand where you are ; you ought to go further one way
or the other."   Now it is plain that if this be a sound
argument against our assailants, it is a most convincing
one ; and it is obviously very hard and very unfair if we
are to be deprived of the use of it.   And yet a cautious
mind will ever use it with anxiety ; not that it is not
most effective, but because it may be (as it were) too
effective : it may drive the parties in question the wrong
way, and make things worse instead of better.   It only
undertakes to show that they are inconsistent in their
present opinions ; and from this inconsistency it is plain
they can escape, by going further either one way or the
other—by adding to their creed, or by giving it up altogether.   It is then what is familiarly called a kill-or-cure
remedy.   Certainly it is better to be inconsistent, than
to be consistently wrong—to hold some truth amid error,
than to hold nothing but error—to believe than to doubt.
Yet when I show a man that he is inconsistent, I make
him decide whether of the two he loves better, the portion of truth or the portion of error, which he already
holds.   If he loves the truth better, he will abandon the
error ; if the error, he will abandon the truth.   And this
is a fearful and anxious trial to put him under, and one
cannot but feel loth to have recourse to it.   One feels
that perhaps it may be better to keep silence, and to let
him, in shallowness and presumption, assail one's own
position with impunity, than to retort, however justly,

his weapons on himself;—better for oneself to seem a bigot, than to make him a scoffer.

Thus, for instance, a person who denies the Apostolical Succession of the Ministry, because it is not clearly taught in Scripture, ought, I conceive, if consistent, to deny the divinity of the Holy Ghost, which is nowhere literally stated in Scripture. Yet there is something so dreadful in his denying the latter, that one may often feel afraid to show him his inconsistency; lest, rather than admit the Apostolical Succession, he should consent to deny that the Holy Ghost is God. This is one of the great delicacies of disputing on the subject before us: yet, all things considered, I think, it only avails for the cautious use, not the abandonment, of the argument in question. For it is our plain duty to preach and defend the truth in a straightforward way. Those who are to stumble must stumble, rather than the heirs of grace should not hear. While we offend and alienate one man, we secure another; if we drive one man further the wrong way, we drive another further the right way. The cause of truth, the heavenly company of saints, gains on the whole more in one way than in the other. A wavering or shallow mind does perhaps as much harm to others as a mind that is consistent in error, nay, is in no very much better state itself; for if it has not developed into systematic scepticism, merely because it has not had the temptation, its present conscientiousness is not worth much. Whereas he who is at present obeying God under imperfect knowledge has a claim on His Ministers for their doing all in their power towards his obtaining further knowledge. He who admits the doctrine of the Holy Trinity, in spite of feeling its difficulties, whether in itself or in its proof,—who submits to the indirectness of the Scripture evidence as regards that particular doctrine,—has a right to be told those other doctrines, such as the Apostolical Succession, which are as certainly declared in Scripture, yet not more directly and prominently, and which will be as welcome to him, when known, because they are in Scripture, as those which he already knows. It is therefore our duty to do our part, and leave the event to God, begging Him to bless, yet aware that, whenever He visits, He divides.

In saying this, I by no means would imply that the only argument in behalf of our believing more than the generality of men believe at present, is, that else we ought in consistency to believe less—far from it indeed ; but this argument is the one that comes first, and is the most obvious and the most striking. Nor do I mean to say—far from it also—that all on whom it is urged, *will* in fact go one way or the other ; the many will remain pretty much where education and habit have placed them, and at least they will not confess that they are affected by any new argument at all. But of course when one speaks of anxiety about the effect of a certain argument, · one speaks of cases in which it will have effect, not of those in which it will not. Where it *has* effect, I say, that effect may be for good *or* for evil, and that is an anxious thing.

I.

Now then, first, let me state the objection itself, which is to be considered. It may be thrown into one or other of the following forms : that "if Scripture laid such stress, as we do, upon the ordinances of Baptism, Holy Eucharist, Church Union, Ministerial Power, Apostolical Succession, Absolution, and other rites and ceremonies, —upon external, or what is sometimes called formal religion,—it would not in its general tenor make such merely indirect mention of them ;—that it would speak of them as plainly and frequently as we always speak of them now ; whereas every one must allow that there is next to nothing on the surface of Scripture about them, and very little even under the surface of a satisfactory character." Descending into particulars, we shall have it granted us, perhaps, that Baptism is often mentioned in the Epistles, and its spiritual benefits ; but "its peculiarity as the *one plenary* remission of sin," it will be urged, "is not insisted on with such frequency and earnestness as might be expected—chiefly in one or two passages of one Epistle, and there obscurely" (in Heb. vi. and x.) Again, "the doctrine of Absolution is made to rest on but one or two texts (in Matt. xvi. and John xx.), with little or no practical exemplification of it in the Epistles, where it was to be expected. Why," it may be asked, "are not the Apostles continually urging their converts to rid themselves of sin after Baptism, as best they can, by penance, confession, absolution, satisfaction ? Again, why are Christ's ministers nowhere called Priests? or, at most, in one or two obscure passages (as in Rom. xv. 16)? Why is not the Lord's Supper expressly said to be a Sacrifice ? why is the Lord's Table called an Altar but once or twice (Matt. v. and Heb. xiii.), even granting these passages refer to it ? why is consecration of the elements expressly mentioned only in one passage (1 Cor. x.) in addition to our Lord's original institution of them? why is there but once or twice express mention made at all of the Holy Eucharist, all through the Apostolic Epistles, and what there is said, said chiefly in one Epistle ? why is there so little said about Ordination ? about the appointment of a Succession of Ministers ? about the visible Church (as in 1 Tim. iii. 15)? why but one or two passages on the duty of fasting ? "

"In short, is not (it may be asked) the state of the evidence for all these doctrines just this—a few striking texts at most, scattered up and down the inspired Volume, or one or two particular passages of one particular Epistle, or a number of texts which may mean, but need not mean, what they are said by Churchmen to mean, which say something looking like what is needed, but with little strength and point, inadequately and unsatisfactorily? Why then are we thus to be put off? why is our earnest desire of getting at the truth to be trifled with? is it conceivable that, if these doctrines were from God, He would not tell us plainly? why does He make us to doubt? why does 'He keep us in suspense?' *—it is impossible He should do so. Let us, then, have none of these expedients, these makeshift arguments, this patchwork system, these surmises and conjectures, and here a little and there a little, but give us some broad, trustworthy, masterly view of doctrine, give us some plain intelligible interpretation of the sacred Volume, such as will approve itself to all educated minds, as being really gained from the text, and not from previous notions which are merely brought to Scripture, and which seek to find a sanction in it. Such a broad comprehensive view of Holy Scripture is most assuredly fatal to the Church doctrines." "But this (it will be urged) is not all; there are texts in the New Testament actually inconsistent with the Church system of teaching. For example, what can be stronger against the sanctity of particular places, nay of any institutions, persons, or rites at all, than our Lord's declaration, that 'God is a Spirit, and they that worship Him, must worship Him in spirit and in truth'? or against the Eucharistic Sacrifice, than St. Paul's contrast in Heb. x. between the Jewish sacrifices

* John x 24

and the one Christian Atonement? or can Baptism really have the gifts which are attributed to it in the Catholic or Church system, considering how St. Paul says, that all rites are done away; and that faith is all in all?"

Such is the sort of objection which it is proposed now to consider.

2.

My first answer to it is grounded on the *argumentum ad hominem* of which I have already spoken. That is, I shall show that, if the objection proves anything, it proves too much for the purposes of those who use it; that it leads to conclusions beyond those to which they would confine it; and if it tells for them, it tells for those whom they would not hesitate to consider heretical or unbelieving.

Now the argument in question proves too much, first, in this way, that it shows that external religion is not only not important or necessary, but not allowable. If, for instance, when our Saviour said, "Woman, believe Me, the hour cometh, when ye shall neither in this mountain, nor yet at Jerusalem, worship the Father. . . The hour cometh, and now is, when the true worshippers shall worship the Father in spirit and in truth: for the Father seeketh such to worship Him. God is a Spirit, and they that worship Him must worship Him in spirit and in truth," *—if He means that the external local worship of the Jews was so to be abolished that no external local worship should again be enjoined, that the Gospel worship was but mental, stripped of everything material or sensible, and offered in that simple spirit and truth which exists in heaven, if so, it is plain that all external religion *is* not only not imperative under the

* John iv. 21—24.

Gospel, but forbidden. This text, if it avails for any thing against Sacraments and Ordinances, avails entirely; it cuts them away root and branch. It says, not that they are unimportant, but that they are not to be. It does not leave them at our option. Any interpretation which gives an opening to their existing, gives so far an opening to their being important. If the command to worship in spirit and truth is consistent with the permission to worship through certain rites, it is consistent with the duty to worship through them. Why are *we* to have a greater freedom, if I may so speak, than God Himself? why are *we* to choose what rites we please to worship in, and not He choose them?—as if spirituality consisted, not in doing without rites altogether, (a notion which at least is intelligible,) but in our forestalling our Lord and Master in the choice of them. Let us take the text to mean that there shall be no external worship at all, if we will (we shall be wrong, but we shall speak fairly and intelligibly); but, if there may be times, places, ministers, ordinances of worship, although the text speaks of worshipping in spirit and in truth, then, what is there in it to negative the notion of God's having chosen those times places, ministers, and ordinances, so that if *we* attempt to choose, we shall be committing the very fault of the Jews, who were ever setting up golden calves, planting groves, or consecrating ministers, without authority from God?

And what has been observed of this text, holds good of all arguments drawn, whether from the silence of Scripture about, or its supposed positive statements against, the rites and ordinances of the Church. If obscurity of texts, for instance, about the grace of the Eucharist, be taken as a proof that no great benefit is therein given, it is an argument against there being any benefit. On the other hand, when certain passages are once interpreted to refer to it, the emphatic language used in those passages shows that the benefit is not small. We cannot say that the subject is unimportant, without saying that it is not mentioned at all. Either no gift is given in the Eucharist, or a great gift. If only the sixth chapter of St. John, for instance, does allude to it, it shows it is not merely an edifying rite, but an awful communication beyond words. Again, if the phrase, " the communication of the Body of Christ," used by St. Paul, means any gift, it means a great one. You may say, if you will, that it does not mean any gift at all, but means only a representation or figure of the communication ; this I call explaining away, but still it is intelligible ; but I do not see how, if it is to be taken literally as a real *communication* of something, it can be other than a communication of *His Body*. Again, though the Lord's Table be but twice called an Altar in Scripture, yet, granting that it *is* meant in those passages, it is there spoken of so solemnly, that it matters not though it be nowhere else spoken of. " We have an Altar, whereof they have no right to eat which serve the tabernacle." We do not know of the existence of the Ordinance except in the knowledge of its importance ; and in corroboration and explanation of this matter of fact, let it be well observed that St. Paul expressly declares that the Jewish rites are *not* to be practised because they are *not* important.

This is one way in which this argument proves too much ; so that they who for the sake of decency or edification, or from an imaginative turn of mind, delight in Ordinances, yet think they may make them for themselves, in that those ordinances bring no special blessing with them, such men contradict the Gospel as plainly as those who attribute a mystical virtue to them,—nay more so ; for if any truth is clear, it is, that such ordinances as are without virtue are abolished by the Gospel, this being St. Paul's very argument against the use of the Jewish rites.

3.

Now as to the other point of view in which the argument in question proves too much for the purpose of those who use it :—If it be a good argument against the truth of the Apostolical Succession and similar doctrines, that so little is said about them in Scripture, this is quite as good an argument against nearly all the doctrines which are held by any one who is called a Christian in any sense of the word ; as a few instances will show.

(1.) First, as to Ordinances and Precepts. There is not a single text in the Bible enjoining infant baptism : the Scripture warrant on which we baptize infants consists of inferences carefully made from various texts. How is it that St. Paul does not in his Epistles remind parents of so great a duty, if it is a duty ?

Again, there is not a single text telling us to keep holy the first day of the week, and that *instead* of the seventh. God hallowed the seventh day, yet we now observe the first. Why do we do this ? Our Scripture warrant for doing so is such as this : " *since* the Apostles met on the first day of the week, *therefore* the first day is to be hallowed ; and *since* St. Paul says the Sabbath is abolished, *therefore* the seventh day (which is the Sabbath) is not to be hallowed : "—these are true inferences, but very indirect surely. The duty is not on the surface of Scripture. We might infer,—though incorrectly, still we might infer,—that St. Paul meant that the command in the second chapter of Genesis was repealed, and that now there is no sacred day at all in the seven, though meetings for prayer on Sunday are right and proper. There is nothing on the surface of Scripture to prove that the sacredness conferred in the beginning on the seventh day now by transference attaches to the first.

Again, there is scarcely a text enjoining our going to Church for joint worship. St. Paul happens in one place of his Epistle to the Hebrews, to warn us against forgetting to assemble together for prayer. Our Saviour says that where two or three are gathered together, He is in the midst of them; yet this alludes in the first instance not to public worship, but to Church Councils and censures, quite a distinct subject. And in the Acts and Epistles we meet with instances or precepts in favour of joint worship; yet there is nothing express to show that it is necessary for all times,—nothing more express than there is to show that in 1 Cor. vii. St. Paul meant that an unmarried state is better at all times,— nothing which does not need collecting and inferring with minute carefulness from Scripture. The first disciples did pray together, and so in like manner the first disciples did not marry. St. Paul tells those who were in a state of distress to pray together so much the more *as they see the day approaching*—and he says that celibacy is "good *for the present distress.*" The same remarks might be applied to the question of community of goods. On the other hand, our Lord did not use social prayer: even when with His disciples He prayed by Himself; and His directions in Matt. vi. about *private* prayer, with the silence which He observes about *public*, might be as plausibly adduced as an argument against public, as the same kind of silence in Scripture concerning turning to the east, or making the sign of the Cross, or concerning commemorations for the dead in Christ, accompanied with its warnings against formality and ceremonial abuses, is now commonly urged as an argument against these latter usages.

Again:—there is no text in the New Testament which enjoins us to " establish" Religion (as the phrase is), or to make it national, and to give the Church certain honour and power; whereas our Lord's words, "My kingdom is not of this world" (John xviii. 36), may be interpreted to discountenance such a proceeding. We consider that it is right to establish the Church on the ground of mere deductions, though of course true ones, from the sacred text; such as St. Paul's using his rights as a Roman citizen.

There is no text which allows us to take oaths. The words of our Lord and St. James look plainly the other way. Why then do we take them ? We *infer* that it is allowable to do so, from finding that St. Paul uses such expressions as "I call God for a record upon my soul"— " The things which I write unto you, behold, before God, I lie not " (2 Cor. i. 23; Gal. i. 20) ; these we *argue*, and rightly, are equivalent to an oath, and a precedent for us.

Again, considering God has said, " Whoso sheddeth man's blood, by man shall his blood be shed," it seems a very singular power which we give to the Civil Magistrate to take away life. It ought to rest, one might suppose, on some very clear permission given in Scripture. Now, on what does it rest ? on one or two words of an Apostle casually introduced into Scripture, as far as anything is casual,—on St. Paul's saying in a parenthesis, " he (the magistrate) beareth not the *sword* in vain ; " and he is speaking of a *heathen* magistrate, *not* of Christian.

Once more:—On how many texts does the prohibition of polygamy depend, if we set about counting them ?

(2.) So much for ordinances and practices : next, consider how Doctrine will stand, if the said rule of interpretation is to hold.

If the Eucharist is never distinctly called a Sacrifice, or Christian Ministers never called Priests, still, let me ask (as I have already done), is the Holy Ghost ever expressly called God in Scripture ? Nowhere ; we infer it from what is said then ; we compare parallel passages.

If the words Altar, Absolution, or Succession, are not in Scripture (supposing it), neither is the word Trinity.

Again : how do we know that the New Testament is inspired ? does it anywhere declare this of itself ? nowhere ; *how*, then, do we know it ? we infer it from the circumstance that the very office of the Apostles who wrote it was to publish the Christian Revelation, and from the Old Testament being said by St. Paul to be inspired.

Again : whence do Protestants derive their common notion, that every one may gain his knowledge of revealed truth from Scripture for himself ?

Again : consider whether the doctrine of the Atonement may not be explained away by those who explain away the doctrine of the Eucharist : if the expressions used concerning the latter are merely figurative, so may be those used of the former.

Again : on how many texts does the doctrine of Original Sin rest, that is, the doctrine that we are individually born under God's displeasure, in consequence of the sin of Adam ? on one or two.

Again : how do we prove the doctrine of justification by faith only ? it is nowhere declared in Scripture. St. Paul does but speak of justification by faith, not by faith only, and St. James actually denies that it is by faith only. Yet we think right to infer, that there is a correct

sense in which it is by faith only; though an Apostl
has in so many words said just the contrary. Is any of
the special Church doctrines about the power of Absolution, the Christian Priesthood, or the danger of sin after
Baptism, so disadvantageously circumstanced in point of
evidence as this, " articulus," as Luther called it, "stantis
ut cadentis ecclesiæ "?

On the whole, then, I ask, on how many special or
palmary texts do any of the doctrines or rites which we
hold depend ? what doctrines or rites would be left to us,
if we demanded the clearest and fullest evidence, before
we believed anything ? what would the Gospel consist
of? would there be any Revelation at all left ? Some all-
important doctrines indeed at first sight certainly would
remain in the New Testament, such as the divinity of
Christ, the unity of God, the supremacy of divine grace,
our election in Christ, the resurrection of the body, and
eternal life or death to the righteous or sinners ; but little
besides.   Shall we give up the divinity of the Holy Ghost,
original sin, the Atonement, the inspiration of the New
Testament, united worship, the Sacraments, and Infant
Baptism ?   Let us do so.   Well :—I will venture to say,
that then we shall go on to find difficulties as regards
those other doctrines, as the divinity of Christ, which
at first sight seem to be in Scripture certainly ; they are
only *more* clearly there than the others, not so clearly
stated as to be secured from specious objections.   We
shall have difficulties about the *meaning* of the word
" everlasting," as applied to punishment, about the *compatibility* of divine grace with free-will, about the *possibility* of the resurrection of the body, and about the *sense*
in which Christ is God.   The inquirer who rejects a doctrine which has but one text in its favour, on the ground
that if it were important it would have more, may, even

in a case when a doctrine is mentioned often, always find occasion to wonder that still it is not mentioned in this or that particular place, where it might be expected. When he is pressed with such a text as St. Thomas's confession, "My Lord and my God," he will ask, But why did our Lord say but seven days before to St. Mary Magdalen, "I ascend to My Father and your Father, to My God and your God"? When he is pressed with St. Peter's confession, "Lord, Thou knowest all things,—Thou knowest that I love Thee," he will ask, "But why does Christ say of Himself, that He does not know the last day, but only the Father?" Indeed, I may truly say, the more arguments there are for a certain doctrine found in Scripture, the more objections will be found against it; so that, on the whole, after all, the Scripture evidence, even for the divinity of Christ, will be found in fact as little able to satisfy the cautious reasoner, when he is fairly engaged to discuss it, as that for Infant Baptism, great as is the difference of strength in the evidence for the one and for the other. And the history of these last centuries bears out this remark.

I conclude, then, that there must be some fault somewhere in this specious argument; that it does not follow that a doctrine or rite is not divine, because it is not directly stated in Scripture; that there are some wise and unknown reasons for doctrines being, as we find them, not clearly stated there. To be sure, I might take the other alternative, and run the full length of scepticism, and openly deny that any doctrine or duty, whatever it is, is divine, which is not stated in Scripture beyond all contradiction and objection. But for many reasons I cannot get myself to do this, as I shall proceed to show.

2.

The Difficulties of Latitudinarianism.

NO one, I think, will seriously maintain, that any other definite religious *system* is laid down in Scripture at all more clearly than the Church system. It may be maintained, and speciously, that the Church system is not there, or that this or that particular doctrine of some other system seems to be there more plainly than the corresponding Church doctrine ; but that Presbyterianism as a whole, or Independency as a whole, or the religion of Lutherans, Baptists, Wesleyans, or Friends, as a whole, is more clearly laid down in Scripture, and with fewer texts looking the other way— that any of these denominations has less difficulties to encounter than the Creed of the Church,—this I do not think can successfully be maintained. The arguments which are used to prove that the Church system is not in Scripture, may as cogently be used to prove that no system is in Scripture. If silence in Scripture, or apparent contrariety, is an argument against the Church system, it is an argument against system altogether. No system is on the surface of Scripture ; none, but has at times to account for the silence or the apparent opposition of Scripture as to particular portions of it.

I.

This, then, is the choice of conclusions to which we are brought :—*either* Christianity contains no definite mes-

sage, creed, revelation, system, or whatever other name
we give it, nothing which can be made the subject of
belief at all ; *or*, secondly, though there really is a true
creed or system in Scripture, still it is not on the surface
of Scripture, but is found latent and implicit within it,
and to be maintained only by indirect arguments, by
comparison of texts, by inferences from what is said
plainly, and by overcoming or resigning oneself to
difficulties ;—or again, though there is a true creed or
system revealed, it is not revealed in Scripture, but must
be learned collaterally from other sources. I wish in-
quirers to consider this statement steadily. I do not see
that it can be disputed ; and if not, it is very important.
I repeat it ; we have a choice of three conclusions.
Either there is no definite religious information given us
by Christianity at all, or it is given in Scripture in an
indirect and covert way, or it is indeed given, but not in
Scripture. The first is the Latitudinarian view which
has gained ground in this day ; the second is our own
Anglican ground ; the third is the ground of the Roman
Church. If then we will not content ourselves with
merely probable, or (what we may be disposed to call)
insufficient proofs of matters of faith and worship, we
must become either utter Latitudinarians or Roman
Catholics. If we will not submit to the notion of the
doctrines of the Gospel being hidden under the text of
Scripture from the view of the chance reader, we must
submit to believe either that there are no doctrines at all
in Christianity, or that the doctrines are not in Scripture,
but elsewhere, as in Tradition. I know of no other
alternative.

Many men, indeed, will attempt to find a fourth way,
thus : they would fain discern one or two doctrines in
Scripture clearly, and no more ; or some generalized

form, yet not so much as a *body* of doctrine of any character. They consider that a certain message, consisting of one or two great and simple statements, makes up the whole of the Gospel, and that these *are* plainly in Scripture ; accordingly, that he who holds and acts upon these is a Christian, and ought to be acknowledged by all to be such, for in holding these he holds all that is necessary. These statements they sometimes call the essentials, the peculiar doctrines, the vital doctrines, the leading idea, the great truths of the Gospel,—and all this sounds very well ; but when we come to realize what is abstractedly so plausible, we are met by this insurmountable difficulty, that no great number of persons agree together what *are* these great truths, simple views, leading ideas, or peculiar doctrines of the Gospel. Some say that the doctrine of the Atonement is the leading idea ; some, the doctrine of spiritual influence ; some, that both together are the peculiar doctrines ; some, that love is all in all; some, that the acknowledgment that Jesus is the Christ; and some, that the resurrection from the dead ; some, that the announcement of the soul's immortality, is after all the essence of the Gospel, and all that need be believed.

Moreover, since, as all parties must confess, the Catholic doctrine of the Trinity is not brought out in form upon the surface of Scripture, it follows either that it is not included in the leading idea, or that the leading idea is not on the surface. And if the doctrine of the Trinity is not to be accounted as one of the leading or fundamental truths of Revelation, the keystone of the mysterious system is lost ; and, that being lost, mystery will, in matter of fact, be found gradually to fade away from the Creed altogether ; that is, the notion of Christianity as being a revelation of new truths, will gradually fade away, and the Gospel in course of time will be considered scarcely more than the republication of the law of nature. This, I think, will be found to be the historical progress and issue of this line of thought. It is but one shape of Latitudinarianism. If we will have it so, that the doctrines of Scripture should be on the surface of Scripture, though I may have my very definite notion what doctrines *are* on the surface, and you yours, and another his, yet you and he and I, though each of us in appearance competent to judge, though all serious men, earnest, and possessed of due attainments, nevertheless will not agree together *what* those doctrines are ; so that, practically, what I have said will come about in the end, —that (if we are candid) we shall be forced to allow, that there is no system, no creed, no doctrine at all lucidly and explicitly set forth in Scripture ; and thus we are brought to the result, which I have already pointed out : if we will not seek for revealed truth under the surface of Scripture, we must either give up seeking for it, or must seek for it in Tradition,—we must become Latitudinarians or Roman Catholics.

2.

Now of these alternatives, the Roman idea or the Latitudinarian, the latter I do really conceive to be quite out of the question with every serious mind. The Latitudinarian doctrine is this: that every man's view of Revealed Religion is acceptable to God, if he acts up to it ; that no one view is in itself better than another, or at least that we cannot tell which is the better. All that we have to do then is to act consistently with what we hold, and to value others if they act consistently with what they hold ; that to be consistent constitutes sincerity ; that where there is this evident sincerity, it is no matter

9

whether we profess to be Romanists or Protestants, Catholics or Heretics, Calvinists or Arminians, Anglicans or Dissenters, High Churchmen or Puritans, Episcopalians or Independents, Wesleyans or Socinians. Such seems to be the doctrine of Latitude. Now, I can conceive such a view of the subject to be maintainable, supposing God had given us no Revelation,—though even then, (by the way,) and were we even left to the light of nature, belief in His existence and moral government would, one should think, at least be necessary to please Him. "He that cometh to God must believe that He is, and that He is a rewarder of them which diligently seek Him."* But however, not to press this point, one may conceive that, before God had actually spoken to us, He might accept as sufficient a sincere acting on religious opinions of whatever kind ; but that, after a Revelation is given, there is nothing to believe, nothing (to use an expressive Scripture word) to "hold," to "hold fast," that a message comes from God, and contains no subject-matter, or that, containing it (as it must do), it is not important to be received, and is not capable of being learned by any one who takes the proper means of learning it, that there is in it nothing such, that we may depend on our impression of it to be the true impression, may feel we have really gained something, and continue in one and one only opinion about it,—all this is so extravagant, that I really cannot enter into the state of mind of a person maintaining it. I think he is not aware what he is saying. Why should God speak, unless He meant to say something ? Why should He say it, unless He meant us to hear? Why should we be made to hear if it mattered not whether we accepted it or no ? *What* the doctrine is, is another and distinct question ; but

* Heb. xi. 6.

that there is *some* doctrine revealed, and that it is revealed in order that it may be received, and that it
really *is* revealed, (I mean, not so hidden that it is a
mere matter of opinion, a mere chance, what is true and
what is not, and that there are a number of opposite
modes of holding it, one as good as another, but) that it
is plain in one and the same substantial sense to all who
sincerely and suitably seek for it, and that God is better
pleased when we hold it than when we do not,—all this
seems a truism. Again, *where* it is given us, whether
entirely in Scripture, or partly elsewhere,—this too is
another and secondary question; though, if some doctrine or other is really given, that it must be given somewhere, is a proposition which cannot be denied, without some eccentricity or confusion of mind, or without
some defect in seriousness and candour. I say, first, if
there be a Revelation, there must be some essential
doctrine proposed by it to our faith; and, if so, the
question at once follows, *what* is it, and *how much*,
and *where?* and we are forthwith involved in *researches*
of some kind or other, somewhere or other; for the
doctrine is not written on the sun.

For reasons such as the above, I really cannot conceive a serious man, who realized what he was speaking
about, to be a consistent Latitudinarian. He always will
reserve from the general proscription his own favourite
doctrine, whatever it is; and then holding it, he will be
at once forced into the difficulty, which is ours also, but
which he would fain make ours only and not his, that
of stating clearly what this doctrine of his is, and what
are those grounds of it, such, as to enable him to take in
just so much of dogmatic teaching as he does take in,
and nothing more, to hold so much firmly, and to treat
all the rest as comparatively unimportant.

Revelation implies a something revealed, and what is revealed is imperative on our faith, *because* it is revealed. Revelation implies imperativeness; it limits in its very notion our liberty of thought, because it limits our liberty of error, for error is one kind of thought.

If then I am not allowed to hold that Scripture, however implicit in its teaching, is really dogmatic, I shall be led to be, not a Latitudinarian, but a Roman Catholic. You tell me, that "no creed is to be found in Scripture,— *therefore*, Christianity has no creed." Indeed! supposing the fact to be as stated (which I do not grant, but supposing it), is this the necessary conclusion? No: there is another. Such an inference indeed as the above is a clever controversial way of settling the matter; it is the sort of answer which in the schools of disputation or the courts of law may find a place, where men are not in earnest; but it is an answer without a heart. It is an excuse for indolence, love of quiet, or worldliness. There is another answer. I do not adopt it, I do not see I am driven to it, because I do not allow the premisses from which the Latitudinarian argument starts. I do not allow that there *is* no creed at all contained in Scripture, though I grant it is not on the surface. But if there *be* no divine message, gospel, or creed producible from Scripture, this would not lead me one inch toward deciding that there was none at all *anywhere*. No; it would make me look *out* of Scripture for it, that is all. If there is a Revelation, there must be a doctrine; both our reason and our hearts tell us so. If it is not in Scripture, it is somewhere else; it is to be sought elsewhere. Should the fact so turn out, (which I deny,) that Scripture is so obscure that nothing can be made of it, even when the true interpretation is elsewhere given, so obscure that every person will have his own

interpretation of it, and no two alike, this would drive
me, not into Latitudinarianism, but into Romanism.
Yes, and it will drive the multitude of men. It is far
more certain that Revelation must contain a message,
than that that message must be in Scripture. It is a
less violence to one's feelings to say that part of it is
revealed elsewhere, than to say that nothing is revealed
anywhere. There is an overpowering antecedent improbability in Almighty God's announcing that He has
revealed something, and then revealing nothing; there
is no antecedent improbability in His revealing it elsewhere than in an inspired volume.

And, I say, the mass of mankind will feel it so. It
is very well for educated persons, at their ease, with
few cares, or in the joyous time of youth, to argue and
speculate about the impalpableness and versatility of
the divine message, its chameleon-like changeableness, its
adaptation to each fresh mind it meets; but when men
are conscious of sin, are sorrowful, are weighed down,
are desponding, they ask for something to lean on,
something external to themselves. It will not do to
tell them that whatever they at present hold as true,
is enough. They want to be assured that what seems
to them true, is true; they want something to lean on,
holier, diviner, more stable than their own minds. They
have an instinctive feeling that there is an external, eternal truth which is their only stay; and it mocks them,
after being told of a Revelation, to be assured, next, that
that Revelation tells us nothing certain, nothing which we
do not know without it, nothing distinct from our own
impressions concerning it, whatever they may be,—
nothing such, as to exist independently of that shape
and colour into which our own individual mind happens
to throw it. Therefore, practically, those who argue for

the vague character of the Scripture informations, and the harmlessness of all sorts of religious opinions, do not tend to advance Latitudinarianism one step among the many,—they advance Romanism. That truth, which men are told they cannot find in Scripture, they will seek out of Scripture. They will never believe, they will never be content with, a religion without doctrines. The common sense of mankind decides against it. Religion cannot but be dogmatic ; it ever has been. All religions have had doctrines ; all have professed to carry with them benefits which could be enjoyed only on condition of believing the word of a supernatural informant, that is, of embracing some doctrines or other.

And it is a mere idle sophistical theory, to suppose it can be otherwise. Destroy religion, make men give it up, if you can ; but while it exists, it will profess an insight into the next world, it will profess important information about the next world, it will have points of faith, it will have dogmatism, it will have anathemas. Christianity, therefore, ever will be looked on, by the multitude, what it really is, as a rule of faith as well as of conduct. Men may be Presbyterians, or Baptists, or Lutherans, or Calvinists, or Wesleyans ; but something or other they will be ; a creed, a creed necessary to salvation, they will have ; a creed either in Scripture or out of it ; and if in Scripture, I say, it must be, from the nature of the case, only indirectly gained from Scripture. Latitudinarianism, then, is out of the question ; and you have your choice, to be content with inferences from texts *in* Scripture, or with tradition *out of* Scripture. You cannot get beyond this ; *either* you must take up with us, (or with some system not at all better off, whether Presbyterianism or Independency, or the like,) *or* you must go to Rome. Which will you choose ? You may not like us ; you may be impatient and impetuous; you may go forward, but back you cannot go.

3.

But, further, it can scarcely be denied that Scripture, if it does not furnish, at least speaks of, refers to, takes for granted, sanctions, some certain doctrine or message, as is to be believed in order to salvation; and which, accordingly, if not found in Scripture, must be sought for out of it. It says, " He who believeth shall be saved, and he who believeth not shall be damned ;" it speaks of "the doctrine of Christ," of "keeping the faith," of " the faith once *delivered* to the saints," and of " delivering that which has been received," recounting at the same time some of the articles of the Apostles' Creed. And the case is the same as regards discipline; rules of worship and order, whether furnished or not, are at least alluded to again and again, under the title of "traditions." Revelation then will be inconsistent with itself, unless it has provided some Creed somewhere. For it declares in Scripture that it has given us a Creed; therefore some creed exists somewhere, whether in Scripture or out of it.

Nor is this all; from the earliest times, so early that there is no assignable origin to it short of the Apostles, one definite system has in fact existed in the Church both of faith and worship, and that in countries far disjoined from one another, and without any appearance (as far as we can detect) of the existence of any other system anywhere; and (what is very remarkable) a system such, that the portion in it which relates to matters of faith (or its theology), accurately fits in and corresponds to that which relates to matters of worship and order (or its ceremonial) ; as if they were evidently parts of a whole, and not an accidental assemblage of rites on the one hand, and doctrines on the other;—a system moreover which has existed ever since, and exists at the present day, and in its great features, as in other branches of the Church, so among ourselves;—a system moreover which at least professes to be quite consistent with, and to appeal and defer to, the written word, and thus in all respects accurately answers to that to which Scripture seems to be referring in the notices above cited. Now, is it possible, with this very significant phenomenon standing in the threshold of Christian history, that any sensible man can be of opinion that one creed or worship is as good as another? St. Paul speaks of one faith, one baptism, one body; this in itself is a very intelligible hint of his own view of Christianity; but as if to save his words from misinterpretation, here in history is at once a sort of realization of what he seems to have before his mind.

Under these circumstances, what excuse have we for not recognizing, in this system of doctrine and worship existing in history, that very system to which the Apostles refer in Scripture? They evidently did not in Scripture say out all they had to say; this is evident on the face of Scripture, evident from what they do say. St. Paul says, " *The rest* will I set in order when I come." St. John, " I had *many things* to write, but I will not with ink and pen write unto thee; but I trust I shall shortly see thee, and we shall *speak* face to face." This he says in two Epistles. Now supposing, to take the case of profane history, a collection of letters were extant written by the founders or remodellers of the Platonic or Stoic philosophy, and supposing those masters referred in them to their philosophy, and treated of it in some of its parts, yet without drawing it out in an orderly way, and then secondly, supposing there did exist other and more direct historical sources of various kinds, from which a distinct systematic account of their philosophy might be drawn, that is, one account of it and but one from many witnesses, should we not take it for granted that this *was* their system, that system of which their letters spoke? Should not we accept that system conveyed to us by history with (I will not say merely an antecedent disposition in its favour, but with) a confidence and certainty that it *was* their system; and if we found discrepancies between it and their letters, should we at once cast it aside as spurious, or should we not rather try to reconcile the two together, and suspect that *we* were in fault, that *we* had made some mistake; and even if after all we could not reconcile all parts (supposing it), should we not leave the discrepancies *as* difficulties, and believe in the system notwithstanding? The Apostles refer to a large existing fact, their system, —"the whole counsel of God"; history informs us of a system, as far as we can tell, contemporaneous with, and claiming to be theirs;—what other claimant is there?

Whether, then, the system of doctrine and worship, referred to but not brought out in Scripture, be really latent there or not, whether our hypothesis be right or the Roman view, at any rate a system there is; we see it, we have it external to Scripture. There it stands, however we may determine the further question, whether it is also in Scripture. Whether we adopt our Sixth Article or not, we cannot obliterate the fact that a system does substantially exist in history; all the proofs you may bring of the obscurities or of the unsystematic character of Scripture cannot touch this independent fact; were Scripture lost to us, that fact, an existing Catholic system, will remain. You have your choice to say that Scripture does or does not agree with it. If you think it actually disagrees with Scripture, then you have your choice between concluding either that you are mistaken in so thinking, or that, although this system comes to us as it does, on the same evidence with Scripture, yet it is not divine, while Scripture is. If, however, you consider that it merely teaches things additional to Scripture, then you have no excuse for not admitting it in addition to Scripture. And if it teaches things but indirectly taught in Scripture, then you must admit it as an interpreter or comment upon Scripture. But, whether you say it is an accordant or a discordant witness, whether the supplement, or complement, or interpreter of Scripture, there it stands, that consistent harmonious system of faith and worship, as in the beginning; and, if history be allowed any weight in the discussion, it is an effectual refutation of Latitudinarianism. It is a fact concurring with the common sense of mankind and with their wants. Men want a dogmatic system ; and behold, in the beginning of Christianity, and from the beginning to this day, there it stands. This is so remarkable a coincidence that it will always practically weigh against Latitudinarian views. Infidelity is more intelligible, more honest than they are.

Nor does it avail to say, that there were additions made to it in the course of years, or that the feeling of a want may have given rise to it ; for what was added after, whatever it was, could not create that to which it was added ; and I say that first of all, before there was a time for the harmonious uniform expansion of a system, for the experience and supply of human wants, for the inroads of innovation, and the growth of corruption, and with all fair allowance for differences of opinions as to how much is primitive, or when and where this or that particular fact is witnessed, or what interpretation is to be given to particular passages in historical documents,—from the first a system exists. And we have no right to refuse it, merely on the plea that *we* do not see all the parts of it in Scripture, or that we think some parts of it to be inconsistent with Scripture ; for even though some parts were not there, this would not disprove its truth ; and even though some parts seemed contrary to what is there, this appearance might after all be caused simply by our own incompetency to judge of Scripture.

4.

But perhaps it may here be urged, that I have proved too much; that is, it may be asked " If a system of doctrine is so necessary to Revelation, and appears at once in the writings of the Apostles' disciples, as in the Epistles of St. Ignatius, how is it that it is not in the writings of the Apostles themselves ? how does it happen that it does appear in the short Epistles of Ignatius, and does not in the longer Epistles of St. Paul ? so that the tendency of the foregoing argument is to disparage the Apostles' teaching, as showing that it is not adapted, and Ignatius's is adapted, to our wants." But the answer to this is simple : for though the Apostles' writings do not on their surface set forth the Catholic system of doctrine, they certainly do contain (as I have said) a recognition of its existence, and of its principle, and of portions of it. If, then, in spite of this, there is no Apostolic system of faith and worship, all we shall have proved by our argument is, that the Apostles are inconsistent with themselves ; that they recognize the need of such a system, and do not provide one. How it is they do not draw out a system, while they nevertheless both recognize its principle and witness its existence, has often been discussed, and perhaps I may say something incidentally on the subject hereafter. Here, I do but observe, that on the one side of the question we have the human heart expecting, Scripture sanctioning, history providing,—a coincidence of three witnesses ; and on the other side only this, Scripture not actually providing by itself in form and fulness what it sanctions.

Lastly, I would observe, that much as Christians have differed in these latter or in former ages, as to what *is* the true faith and what the true worship and discipline of Christ, yet one and all have held that Christianity is dogmatic and social, that creeds and forms are not to be dispensed with. There has been an uninterrupted maintenance of this belief from the beginning of Christianity down to this day, with exceptions so partial or so ephemeral as not to deserve notice. I conclude, then, either that the notion of forms and creeds, and of unity by means of them, is so natural to the human mind as to be spontaneously produced and cherished in every age ; or that there has been a strong external reason for its having been so cherished, whether in authority, or in argumentative proof, or in the force of tradition. In whatever way we take it, it is a striking evidence in favour of dogmatic religion, and against that unreal form, or rather that mere dream of religion, which pretends that modes of thinking and social conduct are all one and all the same in the eyes of God, supposing each of us to be sincere in his own.

Dismissing, then, Latitudinarianism once for all, as untenable, and taking for granted that there is a system of religion revealed in the Gospel, I come, as I have already stated several times, to one or other of two conclusions : either that it is not all in Scripture, but part in tradition only, as the Romanists say,—or, as the English Church says, that though it is in tradition, yet it can also be gathered from the communications of Scripture. As to the nondescript system of religion now in fashion, viz., that nothing is to be believed but what is clearly stated in Scripture, that all its own doctrines are clearly there and none other, and that, as to history, it is no matter what history says and what it does not say, except so far as it must of course be used to prove the canonicity of Scripture, this will come before us again and again in the following Lectures. Suffice that it has all the external extravagance of Latitudinarianism without any gain in consistency. It is less consistent because it is morally better : Latitudinarianism is less inconsistent because it is intellectually deeper. Both, however, are mere theories in theology, and ought to be discarded by serious men. We must give up our ideal notions, and resign ourselves to facts. We must take things as we find them, as God has given them. We did not make them, we cannot alter them, though we are sometimes tempted to think it very hard that we cannot. We must submit to them, instead of quarrelling with them. We must submit to the indirectness of Scripture,* unless we think it wiser and better to become Romanists : and we must employ our minds rather (if so be) in accounting for the fact, than in excepting against it.

* [It may require explanation, why it was that the author, in this argument against Latitudinarianism, should so earnestly insist on the implicit teaching of Scripture, with history for its explicit interpreter, instead of boldly saying that, not Scripture, but history, is our informant in Christian doctrine. But he was hampered by his belief in the Protestant tenet that *all* revealed doctrine is in Scripture, and, since he could not maintain that it was on the surface of the inspired Word, he was forced upon the (not untrue, but unpractical) theory of the implicit sense, history developing it. *Vide infr.* p. 149.]

3.

On the Structure of the Bible, antecedently considered.

I.

ENOUGH perhaps has now been said by way of opening the subject before us. The state of the case I conceive to be as I have said. The structure of Scripture is such, so irregular and immethodical, that either we must hold that the Gospel doctrine or message is not contained in Scripture (and if so, either that there is no message at all given, or that it is given elsewhere, external to Scripture), or, as the alternative, we must hold that it is but indirectly and covertly recorded there, that is, under the surface. Moreover, since the great bulk of professing Christians in this country, whatever their particular denomination may be, do consider, agreeably with the English Church, that there *are* doctrines revealed (though they differ among themselves as to what), and next that they are *in Scripture*, they must undergo, and resign themselves to an inconvenience which certainly does attach to our Church, and, as they often suppose, to it alone, that of having to infer from Scripture, to prove circuitously, to argue at disadvantage, to leave difficulties unsolved, and to appear to the world weak or fanciful reasoners. They must leave off criticising our proof of our doctrines, because they are not stronger in respect to proof themselves. No matter whether they are Lutherans or Calvinists, Wesleyans or Independents, they have to wind their way through obstacles, in and out, avoiding some things and catching at others, like men making their way in a wood, or over broken ground.

If they believe in consubstantiation with Luther, or in the absolute predestination of individuals, with Calvin, they have very few texts to produce which, in argument, will appear even specious. And still more plainly have these religionists strong texts actually against them, whatever be their sect or persuasion. If they be Lutherans, they have to encounter St. James's declaration, that "by works a man is justified, and not by faith only;"* if Calvinists, God's solemn declaration, that "as He liveth, He willeth not the death of a sinner, but rather that he should live;" if a Wesleyan, St. Paul's precept to "obey them that have the rule over you, and submit yourselves;"† if Independents, the same Apostle's declaration concerning the Church's being "the pillar and ground of the Truth;" if Zuinglians, they have to explain how Baptism is not really and in fact connected with regeneration, considering it is always connected with it in Scripture; if Friends, why they allow women to speak in their assemblies, contrary to St. Paul's plain prohibition; if Erastians, why they forget our Saviour's plain declaration, that His kingdom is not of this world; if maintainers of the ordinary secular Christianity, what they make of the woe denounced against riches, and the praise bestowed on celibacy. Hence, none of these sects and persuasions has any right to ask the question of which they are so fond, "Where in the Bible are the Church doctrines to be found? *Where* in Scripture, for instance, is Apostolical Succes-

* James ii. 24.   † Heb. xiii. 7.

sion, or the Christian Priesthood, or the power of Absolution?" This is with them a favourite mode of dealing
with us ; and I in return ask them, *Where* are we told
that the Bible contains all that is necessary to salvation ?
Where are we told that the New Testament is inspired ?
Where are we told that justification is by faith only ?
Where are we told that every individual who is elected
is saved ? Where are we told that we may leave the
Church, if we think its ministers do not preach the
Gospel ? or, Where are we told that we may make
ministers for ourselves ?

All Protestants, then, in this country,—Churchmen,
Presbyterians, Baptists, Arminians, Calvinists, Lutherans,
Friends, Independents, Wesleyans, Unitarians,—and
whatever other sect claims the Protestant name, all who
consider the Bible as the one standard of faith, and
much more if they think it the standard of morals and
discipline too, are more or less in this difficulty,—the
more so, the larger they consider the contents of Revelation to be, and the less, the scantier they consider them ;
but they cannot escape from the difficulty altogether,
except by falling back into utter scepticism and latitudinarianism, or, on the other hand, by going on to
Rome. Nor does it rid them of their difficulties, as I
have said more than once, to allege, that all points that are
beyond clear Scripture proof are the mere *peculiarities*
of each sect ; so that if all Protestants were to agree to
put out of sight their respective peculiarities, they would
then have a Creed set forth distinctly, clearly, and
adequately, in Scripture. For take that single instance,
which I have referred to in a former Lecture, the doctrine
of the Holy Trinity. Is this to be considered as a mere
peculiarity or no ? Apparently a peculiarity ; for on the
one hand it is not held by all Protestants, and next, it

is not brought out in form in Scripture. First, the word Trinity is not in Scripture. Next I ask, *How* many of the verses of the Athanasian Creed are distinctly set down in Scripture? and further, take particular portions of the doctrine, viz., that Christ is co-eternal with the Father, that the Holy Ghost is God, or that the Holy Ghost proceedeth from the Father and the Son, and consider the kind of texts and the modes of using them, by which the proof is built up. Yet is there a more sacred, a more vital doctrine in the circle of the articles of faith than that of the Holy Trinity? Let no one then take refuge and comfort in the idea that he will be what is commonly called an orthodox Protestant,—I mean, that he will be just this and no more; that he will admit the doctrine of the Trinity, but not that of the Apostolic Succession,—of the Atonement, but not of the Eucharist, —of the influences of grace, but not of Baptism. This is an impossible position : it is shutting one eye, and look- ing with the other. Shut both or open both. Deny that there is any necessary doctrine in Scripture, or consent to infer indirectly from Scripture what you at present disbelieve.

2.

The whole argument, however, depends of course on the certainty of the fact assumed, viz., that Scripture *is* unsystematic and uncertain in its communications to the extent to which I have supposed it to be. To this point, therefore, I shall, in the Lectures which follow, direct attention. Here, however, I shall confine myself to a brief argument with a view of showing that under the circumstances the fact *must* be so. I observe, then, as follows :—

In what way inspiration is compatible with that per-

10

sonal agency on the part of its instruments, which the composition of the Bible evidences, we know not ; but if anything is certain, it is this,—that, though the Bible is inspired, and therefore, in one sense, written by God, yet very large portions of it, if not far the greater part of it, are written in as free and unconstrained a manner, and (apparently) with as little apparent consciousness of a supernatural dictation or restraint, on the part of His earthly instruments, as if He had had no share in the work. As God rules the will, yet the will is free,—as He rules the course of the world, yet men conduct it,— so He has inspired the Bible, yet men have written it. Whatever else is true about it, this is true, that we may speak of the history or the mode of its composition, as truly as of that of other books ; we may speak of its writers having an object in view, being influenced by circumstances, being anxious, taking pains, purposely omitting or introducing matters, leaving things incomplete, or supplying what others had so left. Though the Bible be inspired, it has all such characteristics as might attach to a book uninspired,—the characteristics of dialect and style, the distinct effects of times and places, youth and age, of moral and intellectual character; and I insist on this, lest in what I am going to say, I seem to forget (what I do not forget), that in spite of its human form, it has in it the Spirit and the Mind of God.

I observe, then, that Scripture is not one book ; it is a great number of writings, of various persons, living at different times, put together into one, and assuming its existing form as if casually and by accident. It is as if you were to seize the papers or correspondence of leading men in any school of philosophy or science, which were never designed for publication, and bring them out in one volume. You would find probably in the collection so resulting many papers begun and not finished ; some parts systematic and didactic, but the greater part made up of hints or of notices which assume first principles instead of asserting them, or of discussions upon particular points which happened to require their attention. I say the doctrines, the first principles, the rules, the objects of the school, would be taken for granted, alluded to, implied, not directly stated. You would have some trouble to get at them ; you would have many repetitions, many hiatuses, many things which looked like contradictions ; you would have to work your way through heterogeneous materials, and, after your best efforts, there would be much hopelessly obscure ; and, on the other hand, you might look in vain in such a casual collection for some particular opinions which the writers were known nevertheless to have held, nay to have insisted on.

Such, I conceive, with limitations presently to be noticed, is the structure of the Bible. Parts, indeed, are more regular than others ; parts of the Pentateuch form a regular history. The book of Job is a regular narrative; some Prophecies are regular, one or two Epistles ; but even these portions are for the most part incorporated in or with writings which are not regular in their form or complete ; and we never can be sure beforehand what we shall find in them, or what we shall not find. They are the writings of men who had already been introduced into a knowledge of the unseen world and the society of Angels, and who reported what they had seen and heard ; and they are full of allusions to a system, a course of things, which was ever before their minds, which they felt both too awful and too familiar to them to be described minutely, which we do not know, and which these allusions, such as they are, but partially

disclose to us. Try to make out the history of Rome
from the extant letters of some of its great politicians,
and from the fragments of ancient annals, histories,
laws, inscriptions, and medals, and you will have something like the state of the case, viewed antecedently, as
regards the structure of the Bible, and the task of de-
ducing the true system of religion from it.

This being, as I conceive, really the state of the
case in substance, I own it seems to me, judging antecedently, very improbable indeed, that it *should* contain
the whole of the Revealed Word of God. I own that in
my own mind, at first sight, I am naturally led to look
not only there, but elsewhere, for notices of sacred truth ;
and I consider that they who say that the Bible does
contain the whole Revelation (as I do say myself), that
they and I, that we, have what is called the *onus probandi*, the burden and duty of proving the point, on our
side. Till we prove that Scripture does contain the
whole Revealed Truth, it is natural, from its *prima facie*
appearance, to suppose that it does not. Why, for instance, should a certain number of letters, more or less
private, written by St. Paul and others to particular
persons or bodies, contain the whole of what the Holy
Spirit taught them ? We do not look into Scripture for
a complete history of the secular matters which it mentions ; why should we look for a complete account of
religious truth ? You will say that its writers wrote in
order to communicate religious truth ; true, but not all
religious truth : that is the point. They did not sit
down with a design to commit to paper all they had to
say on the whole subject, all they could say about the
Gospel, " the whole counsel of God " ; but they either
wrote to correct some particular error of a particular
time or place, or to " stir up the pure minds " of their

brethren, or in answer to questions, or to give direction for conduct, or on indifferent matters. For instance, St. Luke says he wrote his Gospel that Christians might know "the certainty of the things in which they had been instructed." Does this imply he told all that was to be told? Anyhow he did *not;* for the other Evangelists add to his narrative. It is then far from being a self-evident truth that Scripture must contain all the revealed counsel of God; rather, the probability at first sight lies the other way.

Nevertheless, at least as regards matters of faith, it *does* (as we in common with all Protestants hold) contain all that is necessary for salvation; it has been overruled to do so by Him who inspired it. By parallel acts of power, He both secretly inspired the books, and secretly formed them into a perfect rule or canon. I shall not prove what we all admit, but I state it, to prevent mis-apprehension. If asked *how* we know this to be the case, I answer, that the early Church thought so, and the early Church must have known. And, if this an-swer does not please the inquirer, he may look out for a better as he can. I know of no other. I require no other. For our own Church it is enough, as the Homi-lies show. It is enough that Scripture has been over-ruled to contain the whole Christian faith, and that the early Church so taught, though the form of Scripture at first sight might lead to an opposite conclusion. And this being once proved, we see in this state of things an analogy to God's providence in other cases. How con-fused is the course of the world, yet it is the working out of a moral system, and is overruled in every point by God's will! Or, take the structure of the earth; man-kind are placed in fertile and good dwelling-places, with hills and valleys, springs and fruitful fields, with metals and marbles, and coal, and other minerals, with seas and forests; yet this beautiful and fully-furnished surface is the result of (humanly speaking) a series of accidents, of gradual influences and sudden convulsions, of a long history of change and chance.

3.

Yet while we admit, or rather maintain, that the Bible is the one standard of faith, there is no reason why we should suppose the overruling hand of God to go further than we are told that it has gone. That He has over-ruled matters so far as to make the apparently casual writings of the Apostles a complete canon of saving faith, is no reason why He should have given them a systematic structure, or a didactic form, or a completeness in their subject-matter. So far as we have no positive proof that the Bible is more than at first sight it seems to be, so far the antecedent probability, which I have been insisting on, tells against its being more. Both the history of its composition and its internal structure are opposed to the notion of its being a complete depository of the Divine Will, unless the early Church says that it is. Now the early Church does not tell us this. It does not seem to have considered that a complete code of *morals*, or of Church *government*, or of *rites*, or of *discipline*, is in Scripture; and therefore so far the original improbability remains in force. Again, this antecedent improbability tells, even in the case of the doctrines of faith, as far as this, viz., it reconciles us to the necessity of gaining them only *indirectly* from Scripture, for it is a near thing (if I may so speak) that they are in Scripture at all; the wonder is, that they are *all* there; humanly judging, they would not be there but for divine interposition; and, therefore, since they are there by a sort of accident, it is not strange they are there only in an implicit shape, and only indirectly producible thence. Providence effects His greatest ends by apparent accidents. As in respect to this earth, we do not find minerals or plants arranged within it as in a cabinet—as we do not find the materials for building laid out in order, stone, timber, and iron—as metal is found in ore, and timber on the tree,—so we must not be surprised, but think it great gain, if we find revealed doctrines scattered about high and low in Scripture, in places expected and unexpected. It could not be otherwise, the same circumstances being supposed. Supposing fire, water, and certain chemical and electrical agents in free operation, the earth's precious contents *could* not be found arranged in order and in the light of day without a miracle ; and so without a miracle (which we are nowhere told to expect) we could not possibly find in Scripture all sacred truths in their place, each set forth clearly and fully, with its suitable prominence, its varied bearings, its developed meaning, supposing Scripture to be, what it is, the work of various independent minds in various times and places, and under various circumstances. And so much on what might reasonably be expected from the nature of the case.

4.

Structure of the Bible in matter of fact.

I HAVE above insisted much upon this point,—that if Scripture contains any religious system at all, it *must* contain it covertly, and teach it obscurely, because it is altogether most immethodical and irregular in its structure ; and therefore, that the indirectness of the Scripture proofs of the Catholic system is not an objection to its cogency, except as it is an objection to the Scripture proofs of every other form of Christianity ; and accordingly that we must take our choice (Romanism being for the time put aside) between utter Latitudinarianism and what may be called the Method of Inferences. Now this argument depends evidently on the fact, that Scripture is thus unsystematic in its structure —a fact which it would not be necessary to dwell upon, so obvious is it, except that examining into it will be found to give us a much more vivid apprehension of it, and to throw light upon the whole subject of Scripture teaching. Something accordingly, I have just been observing about it from antecedent probability, and now I proceed, at some length, to inquire into the matter of fact.

I shall refer to Scripture as a record both of historical events and of general doctrine, with a view of exhibiting the peculiar character of its structure, the unostentatious, indirect, or covert manner, which it adopts, for whatever reason, in its statements of whatever kind. This, I say, will throw light on the subject in hand ; for so it is, as soon as we come to see that anything, which has already attracted our notice in one way, holds good in others, that there is a certain law, according to which it occurs uniformly under various circumstances, we gain a satisfaction from that very coincidence, and seem to find a reason for it in the very circumstance that it does proceed on a rule or law. Even in matters of conduct, with which an external and invariable standard might seem to interfere, the avowal, "It is my way," "I always do so," is often given and accepted as a satisfactory account of a person's mode of acting. Order implies a principle ; order in God's Written Word implies a principle or design in it. If I show that the Bible is written throughout with this absence of method, I seem to find an order in the very disorder, and hence become reconciled to it in particular instances. That it is inartificial and obscure as regards the relation of facts, has the effect of explaining its being obscure in statement of doctrines ; that it is so as regards one set of doctrines, seems naturally to account for its being so as regards another. Thus, the argument from analogy, which starts with the profession of being only of a *negative* character, ends with being *positive*, when drawn out into details ; such being the difference between its abstract pretension and its actual and practical force.

First I propose to mention some instances of the unstudied and therefore perplexed character of Scripture, as regards its relation of *facts;* and to apply them, as I go, to the point under discussion, viz., the objection brought against the Church doctrines from the mode in which they too are stated in Scripture; and I shall begin without further preface.

I.

An illustration occurs in the very beginning of the Bible. However we account for it, with which I am not concerned, you will find that the narrative of the Creation, commenced in the first chapter, ends at the third verse of the second chapter; and then begins a fresh narrative, carrying on the former, but going back a little way. The difference is marked, as is well known, by the use of the word " God " in the former narrative, and of " Lord God " in the latter. According to the former, God is said to create man "in His own image ; *male and female* created He them " on the sixth day. According to the latter, the Lord God created Adam, and placed him in the garden of Eden, to dress and keep it, and gave him the command about the forbidden fruit, and brought the beasts to him ; and *afterwards*, on his finding the want of a helpmeet, caused him to sleep, and took one of his ribs, and thence made woman. This is an instance of the unsolicitous freedom and want of system of the sacred narrative. The second account, which is an expansion of the first, is in the letter opposed to it. Now supposing the narrative contained in the second chapter was *not* in Scripture, but *was* the received Church account of man's creation, it is plain not only would it not be *in*, but it could not even be gathered or proved *from* the first chapter ; which makes the argument all the stronger. Evidently not a pretence could be made of *proving* from the first chapter the account of the dressing the garden, the naming the brutes, the sleep, and the creation of Eve from a rib. And most persons in this day would certainly have disbelieved it. Why ? Because it wanted *authority ?* No. There would be some sense in such a line of argument, but they would not go into the question of authority. Whether or not it had Catholic tradition in its favour, whether Catholic tradition were or were not a sufficient guarantee of its truth, would not even enter into their minds; they would not go so far, they would disbelieve it at once on two grounds: first, they would say Scripture was *silent* about it, nay, that it contradicted it, that it spoke of man and woman being created both together on the sixth day; and, secondly, they would say it was incongruous and highly improbable, and that the account of Adam's rib sounded like an idle tradition. If (I say) they were to set it aside for want of evidence of its truth, that would be a fair ground; but I repeat, their reason for setting it aside (can it be doubted?) would be, that it was *inconsistent* with Scripture in actual statement, and *unlike* it in tone. But it is in Scripture. It seems then that a statement may seem at variance with a certain passage of Scripture, may bear an improbable exterior, and yet come from God. Is it so strange then, so contrary to the Scripture account of the institution, that the Lord's Supper should also be a Sacrifice, when it is no interference at all with the truth of the first chapter of Genesis, that the second chapter also should be true? No one ever professed to deduce the second chapter from the first: all Anglo-Catholics profess to prove the sacrificial character of the Lord's Supper from Scripture. Thus the Catholic doctrine of the Eucharist is not unscriptural, unless the book of Genesis is (what is impossible, God forbid the thought!) self-contradictory.

Again, take the following account, in the beginning of the fifth chapter of Genesis, and say whether, if this passage only had come down to us, and not the chapters before it, we should not, with our present notions, have utterly disallowed any traditional account of Eve's creation, the temptation, the fall, and the history of Cain and Abel:—" This is the book of the generation of Adam. In the day that God created man, in the likeness of God created He him ; male and female created He them ; and blessed them, and called their name Adam, in the day when they were created. *And* Adam lived an hundred and thirty years, and begat a son in his own likeness, after his image, and called his name Seth." If the contrast between God's likeness and Adam's image be insisted on as intentional, then I would have it observed, how indirect and concealed that allusion is.

Again : I believe I am right in saying that we are nowhere told in Scripture, certainly not in the Old Testament, that the Serpent that tempted Eve was the Devil. The nearest approach to an intimation of it is the last book of the Bible, where the devil is called " that old serpent." Can we be surprised that other truths are but obscurely conveyed in Scripture, when this hardly escapes (as I may say) omission ?

Again : we have two accounts of Abraham's denying his wife ; also, one instance of Isaac being betrayed into the same weakness. Now supposing we had only one or two of these in Scripture, and the others by tradition, should we not have utterly rejected these others as perversions and untrustworthy? On the one hand, we should have said it was inconceivable that two such passages should occur in Abraham's life ; or, on the other, that it was most unlikely that both Abraham and Isaac should have gone to Gerar, in the time of a king of the same name, Abimelech. Yet because St. James says, " Confess your faults *one to another,*" if we read that in the early Church there was an usage of secret confession made *to the priest*, we are apt to consider this latter practice, which our Communion Service recognizes, as a mere perversion or corruption of the Scripture command, and that the words of St. James are a positive argument against it.

In Deuteronomy we read that Moses fasted for forty days in the Mount, twice ; in Exodus only one fast is mentioned. Now supposing Deuteronomy were not Scripture, but merely part of the Prayer Book, should we not say the latter was in this instance evidently mistaken? This is what men do as regards Episcopacy. Deacons are spoken of by St. Paul in his Epistles to Timothy and Titus, and Bishops ; but no third order in direct and express terms. The Church considers that there are two kinds of Bishops, or, as the word signifies, overseers ; those who have the oversight of single parishes, or priests, and those who have the oversight of many together, or what are now specially called Bishops. People say, " Here is a contradiction to Scripture, which speaks of two orders, not of three." Yes, just as real a contradiction, as the chapter in Deuteronomy is a contradiction of the chapter in Exodus. But this again is to take far lower ground than we need ; for we all contend that the doctrine of Episcopacy, even granting it goes beyond the teaching of some passages of Scripture, yet is in exact accordance with others.

Again : in the history of Balaam we read, " God came unto Balaam at night, and said unto him, If the men come to call thee, rise up and *go with them ;* but yet the word which I shall say unto thee, that shalt thou speak." *
Presently we read, " And God's anger was kindled, *because* he went ; and the Angel of the Lord stood in the way for an adversary against him." Now supposing the former circumstance (the permission given him to go) was not in Scripture, but was only the received belief of the Church,

* Numb. xxii. 20.

would it not be at once rejected by most men as inconsistent with Scripture ?   And supposing a Churchman were to entreat objectors to consider the strong evidence in Catholic tradition for its truth, would not the answer be, " Do not tell us of evidence ; we cannot give you a hearing ; your statement is in plain contradiction to the inspired text, which says that God's *anger* was kindled. How then can He have told Balaam to go with the men ? The matter stands to reason ; we leave it to the private judgment of any unbiassed person.   Sophistry indeed may try to reconcile the tradition with Scripture ; but after all you are unscriptural, and we uphold the pure word of truth without glosses and refinements."   Now, is not this just what is done in matters of doctrine ? Thus, because our Lord represents the Father saying, in the parable of the Prodigal Son, " Bring forth the best robe, and put it on him ; and put a ring on his hand, and shoes on his feet," * it is argued that this is inconsistent with the Church's usage (even supposing for argument's sake it has no Scripture sanction) of doing penance for sin.

Again : the book of Deuteronomy, being a recapitulation of the foregoing Books, in an address to the Israelites, is in the position of the Apostolic Epistles.   Exodus‘ Leviticus, and Numbers, being a very orderly and systematic account of events, are somewhat in the position of Catholic tradition.   Now Deuteronomy differs in some minute points from the former books.   For example : in Exodus, the fourth commandment contains a reference to the creation of the world on the seventh day, as the reason of the institution of the Sabbath: in Deuteronomy, the same commandment refers it to the deliverance of the Israelites out of Egypt on that day.   Supposing we had

* Luke xv. 22.

only the latter statement in Scripture, and supposing the former to be only the received doctrine of the Church, would not this former, that is, the statement contained in Exodus, that the Sabbatical rest was in memory of God's resting after the Creation, have seemed at once fanciful and unfounded ?   Would it not have been said, " Why do you have recourse to the mysticism of types ? here is a plain intelligible reason for keeping the Sabbath holy, viz., the deliverance from Egypt.   Be content with this : —besides, your view is grossly carnal and anthropomorphic.   How can Almighty God be said to rest ?   And it is unscriptural ; for Christ says, ' My Father worketh hitherto, and I work.' "   Now is it not a similar procedure to argue, that *since* the Holy Eucharist is a " communication of the body and blood of Christ," *therefore* it is not also a mysterious representation of His meritorious Sacrifice in the sight of Almighty God ?

2.

Let us proceed to the history of the Monarchy, as contained in the Books of Samuel and Kings, and compare them with the Chronicles.   Out of many instances in point, I will select a few.   For instance :—

In 2 Kings xv. we read of the reign of Azariah, or Uzziah, king of Judah.   It is said, " he did that which was right in the sight of the Lord, according to all that his father Amaziah had done ; " and then that "the Lord smote the king, so that he was a leper unto the day of his death ; " and we are referred for " the rest of the acts of Azariah, and all that he did," to "the book of the Chronicles of the kings of Judah."   We turn to the Chronicles, and find an account of the cause of the visitation which came upon him.   " When he was strong, his heart was lifted up to his destruction ; for he transgressed against the Lord his God, and went into the temple of the Lord to burn incense upon the altar of incense. And Azariah the priest went in after him, and with him fourscore priests of the Lord that were valiant men. And they withstood Uzziah the king, and said unto him, It appertaineth not unto thee, Uzziah, to burn incense unto the Lord, but to the priests, the sons of Aaron, that are consecrated to burn incense : go out of the sanctuary, for thou hast trespassed ; neither shall it be for thine honour from the Lord God. Then Uzziah was wroth, and had a censer in his hand to burn incense ; and while he was wroth with the priests, the leprosy even rose up in his forehead, before the priests in the house of the Lord, from beside the incense altar. And Azariah, the chief priest, and all the priests, looked upon him, and behold he was leprous in his forehead, and they thrust him out from thence ; yea, himself hasted also to go out because the Lord had smitten him. And Uzziah the king was a leper unto the day of his death, and dwelt in a several house, being a leper." *

Now nothing can be more natural than this joint narrative. The one is brief, but refers to the other for the details ; and the other gives them. Suppose, then, a captious mind were to dwell upon the remarkable *silence* of the former narrative,—magnify it as an objection,—and on the other hand should allude to the tendency of the second narrative to uphold the priesthood, and should attribute it to such a design. Should we think such an argument valid, or merely ingenious, clever, amusing, yet not trustworthy ? I suppose the latter ; yet this instance is very near a parallel to the case as it stands, between the New Testament and the doctrine of the Church. For instance, after St. Paul

* 2 Chron. xxvi. 16—21.

has declared some plain truths to the Corinthians, he says, "Be ye followers of me : *for this cause* have I sent unto you Timotheus, who is my beloved son, and faithful in the Lord, *who shall bring you into remembrance of my ways*, which be in Christ, as I *teach* everywhere in every Church." * He refers them to an authority beyond and beside his epistle,—to Timothy, nay to his doctrine *as* he had taught in every Church. If then we can ascertain, for that I here assume, what was that doctrine taught everywhere in the Church, we have ascertained that to which St. Paul refers us ; and if that doctrine, so ascertained, adds many things in detail to what he has written, develops one thing, and gives a different impression of others, it is no more than such a reference might lead us to expect,—it is the very thing he prepares us for. It as little, therefore, contradicts what is written, as the books of Chronicles contradict the books of Kings; and if it appears to favour the priesthood more than St. Paul does, this is no more than can be objected to the Chronicles compared with the Kings.

Again, after, not teaching, but reminding them about the Lord's Supper, he adds, "*the rest* will I set in order when I come." When then we find the Church has always considered that Holy Sacrament to be not only a feast or supper, but in its fulness to contain a sacrifice, and to require a certain liturgical form, how does this contradict the inspired text, which plainly signifies that something else *is* to come besides what it has said itself ? So far from its being strange that the Church brings out and fills up St. Paul's outline, it would be very strange if it did not. Yet it is not unusual to ascribe these additional details to priestcraft, and without proof to call them corruptions and innovations, in the very spirit

* 1 Cor. iv. 17.

in which freethinkers have before now attributed the books of Chronicles to the Jewish priests, and accused them of bigotry and intolerance.

It is remarkable how frequent are the allusions in the Epistles to *other* Apostolic teaching beyond themselves, that is, besides the written authority. For instance ; in the same chapter, " I *praise* you, brethren, that ye *remember* me in all things, and *keep the traditions*, as I delivered them to you." Again, " I have also received," or had by tradition, " of the Lord that which also I delivered unto you," that is, which I gave by tradition unto you. This giving and receiving was not in writing. Again, " If any man seem to be contentious, we have nc such custom, neither the churches of God : " he appeals to the received custom of the Church. Again, " I declare unto you the Gospel which I preached unto you, which also ye have received, and wherein ye stand, . . . for I delivered unto you (gave by tradition) first of all that which I also received" (by tradition). Again, " Stand fast, and hold the traditions which ye have been taught, whether by word or our epistle."* Such passages prove, as all will grant, that at the time there were means of gaining knowledge distinct from Scripture, and sources of information in addition to it. When, then, we actually do find in the existing Church system of those times, as historically recorded, such additional information, that information may be Apostolic or it may be not ; but however this is, the mere circumstance that it is in addition, is no proof against its being Apostolic ; that it is extra-scriptural is no proof that it is unscriptural, for St. Paul himself tells us in Scripture, that there are truths not in Scripture, and we may as fairly object to the books of Chronicles, that they are an addition

* 1 Cor. xi. 2, 16, 23 ; ɪ v. 1—3 ; 1 Thess. ii. 15.

to the books of Kings. In saying this, I am not entering into the question which lies between us and the
Romanists, whether these further truths are substantive
additions or simply developments, whether in faith or in
conduct and discipline.

Further : the Chronicles pass over David's great sin,
and Solomon's fall ; and they insert Manasseh's repentance. The account of Manasseh's reign is given at
length in the second book of Kings ; it is too long of
course to cite, but the following are some of its particulars. Manasseh * "used enchantments and dealt
with familiar spirits and wizards ; " he "seduced them
to do more evil than did the nations whom the Lord
destroyed before the children of Israel." "Moreover
Manasseh shed innocent blood very much, till he had
filled Jerusalem from one end to another." Afterwards,
when Josiah had made his reforms, the sacred writer
adds,† "Notwithstanding the Lord turned from the
fierceness of His great wrath, wherewith His anger was
kindled against Judah, *because* of all the provocations
that *Manasseh* had provoked him withal." And again
in Jehoiakim's time,‡ "Surely, at the commandment of
the Lord came this upon Judah, to remove them out of
His sight for the sins of Manasseh, according to all that
he did ; and also for the innocent blood, that he shed ;
for he filled Jerusalem with innocent blood, *which the
Lord would not pardon.*" And again in the book of Jere-
miah,§ "I will cause them to be removed into all the
kingdoms of the earth, *because of Manasseh,* the son of
Hezekiah, king of Judah, for that which he did in Jerusalem." Who would conjecture, with such passages of
Scripture before him, that Manasseh repented before his
death, and was forgiven ? but to complete the *illusion* (as

* 2 Kings xxi. † 2 Kings xxiii. 26. ‡ 2 Kings xxiv. 3, 4. § Jer. xv. 4.

it may be called), the account of his reign in the book
of Kings ends thus :* "Now the rest of the acts of
Manasseh, and all that he did, and *his sin that he sinned,*
are they not *written in the book of the Chronicles* of the
kings of Judah ?"—not a word about his repentance.
Might it not then be plausibly argued that the books of
Kings precisely limited and defined *what* the Chronicles
were to relate, " *the sin that he sinned ;*" that this was to
be the theme of the history, its outline and ground plan,
and that the absolute silence of the books of Kings about
his repentance was a cogent, positive argument that he
did not repent? How little do they prepare one for
the following most touching record of him : "When he
was in affliction, he besought the Lord his God, and
humbled himself greatly before the God of his fathers,
and prayed unto Him. And He was entreated of him,
and heard his supplication, and brought him again to
Jerusalem into his kingdom. Then Manasseh knew
that the Lord He was God. . . . And he took away the
strange gods, and the idol out of the house of the Lord,
and the altars that he had built in the mount of the
house of the Lord, and in Jerusalem, and cast them out
of the city," etc. . . . "Now the rest of the acts of
Manasseh, and his prayer unto his God, and the words
of the seers that spake to him in the name of the Lord
God of Israel, behold they are written in the book of
the kings of Israel. . . . So Manasseh slept with his
fathers." † If then the books of Kings were the only
canonical account, and the book of Chronicles part of the
Apocrypha, would not the latter be pronounced an
unscriptural record, a legend and a tradition of men,
not because the evidence for their truth was insufficient, but on the allegation that they contradicted the

* 2 Kings xxi.   † 2 Chron. xxxiii. 12—20.

books of Kings?—at least, is not this what is done as regards the Church system of doctrine, as if it must be at variance with the New Testament, because it views the Gospel from a somewhat distinct point of view, and in a distinct light?

Again; the account given of Jehoash in the Kings is as follows : * "Jehoash did that which was right in the sight of the Lord *all his days, wherein* Jehoiada the priest instructed him." And it ends thus : "His servants arose and made a conspiracy, and slew Joash in the house of Millo :" there is no hint of any great defection or miserable ingratitude on his part, though, as it turns out on referring to Chronicles, the words "all his days, wherein," etc., are significant. In the Chronicles we learn that *after* good Jehoiada's death, whose wife had saved him from Athaliah, and who preserved for him his throne, he went and served groves and idols, and killed Zechariah the son of Jehoiada, when he was raised up by the Spirit of God to protest. Judgments followed,—the Syrians, and then "great diseases," and then assassination. Now, if the apparently simple words, "all the days wherein," etc., are emphatic, why may not our Saviour's words, "If thou bring thy gifts to the *altar*," be emphatic, or "If thou wouldst be *perfect*," suggest a doctrine which it does not exhibit?

3.

Now let us proceed to the Gospels ; a few instances must suffice.

Considering how great a miracle the raising of Lazarus is in itself, and how connected with our Lord's death, how is it that the three first Gospels do not mention it? They speak of the chief priests taking counsel to put Him

* 2 Kings xii.

to death, but they give no reason; rather they seem to
assign other reasons,—for instance, the parables He
spoke against them.* At length St. John mentions the
miracle and its consequences. Things important then
may be true, though particular inspired documents do
not mention them. As the raising of Lazarus is true,
though not contained at all in the first three Gospels, so
the gift of consecrating the Eucharist may have been
committed by Christ to the priesthood, though this
is only indirectly stated in any of the four. Will you
say I am arguing against our own Church, which says
that Scripture "contains all things necessary to be believed to salvation"? Doubtless, Scripture *contains* all
things necessary to be *believed;* but there may be things
contained in it, which are not *on the surface,* and things
which belong to the *ritual* and not to *belief.* Points of
faith may lie *under* the surface, points of observance need
not be in Scripture *at all.* The rule for consecrating is
a point of ritual; yet it *is* indirectly taught in Scripture,
though not brought out, when Christ said, "Do this,"
for He spoke to the Apostles who were priests, not to
His disciples generally.

Again: I just now mentioned the apparent repetition
in Genesis of the account of Abraham's denying his
wife; a remark which applies to the parallel miracles
which occur in the histories of Elijah and Elisha, as the
raising of the dead child and the multiplication of the
oil. Were only the first of these parallel instances in
Scripture, and the second in tradition, we should call
the second a corruption or distorted account; and not
without some plausibility, till other and contrary reasons
were brought. And in like manner, as regards the
Gospels, did the account of the feeding of the 4,000

* Matt. xxi. 45.

with seven loaves rest on the testimony of Antiquity, most of us would have said, " You see how little you can trust the Fathers ; it was not 4,000 with seven loaves, but 5,000 with five." Again, should we not have pronounced that the discourses in Luke vi., xi., and xii., if they came to us through the Fathers, were the same, only in a corrupt form, as the Sermon on the Mount in Matt. v.—vii. and as chapter xxiii. ? Nay, we should have seized on Luke xi. 41, " But rather give alms of such things as ye have, and behold *all things are clean* unto you," as a symptom of incipient Popery, a mystery already working. Yes, our Saviour's own sacred words (I fear too truly) would have been seized on by some of us as the signs of the dawn of Antichrist. This is a most miserable thought.

Again : St. Matthew, St. Mark, and St. Luke say, that Simon of Cyrene bore Christ's cross ; St. John, that Christ Himself bore it. Both might be true, and both of course were true. He bore it part of the way, and Simon part. Yet I conceive, did we find it was the tradition of the Church that Simon bore it, we should decide, without going into the evidence, that this was a gloss upon the pure scriptural statement. So, in like manner, even supposing that, when St. Paul says, " Ye do *shew forth* the Lord's death till He come," he meant, which I do not grant, by " shew forth," preach, remind each other of, or commemorate among yourselves, and nothing more, (which I repeat I do not grant,) even then it may be that the Holy Eucharist is also a remembrance in God's sight, a pleading before Him the merits of Christ's death, and, so far, a propitiatory offering, even though this view of it were only contained in the immemorial usage of the Church, and were no point of necessary faith contained in Scripture.

Again : Judas is represented as hanging himself in St. Matthew, yet in the Acts as falling headlong, and his bowels gushing out. I do not mean to say, of course, that these accounts are irreconcilable even by us ; but they certainly differ from each other : do not they differ as much as the explicit Scripture statement that Confirmation imparts miraculous gifts, differs from the Church view, not clearly brought out in Scripture, that it is also an ordinary rite conferring ordinary gifts ?

We know how difficult it is to reconcile the distinct accounts of the occurrences which took place at the Resurrection with each other, and our Lord's appearances to His disciples. For instance :—according to Matt. xxviii., it might seem that Christ did not appear to His disciples, till He met them on the mountain in Galilee ; but in St. Luke and St. John His first appearance was on the evening of the day of Resurrection. Again : in the Gospel according to St. Mark and St. Luke, the Ascension seems to follow immediately on the Resurrection ; but in the Acts our Lord is declared to have shown Himself to His disciples for forty days. These forty days are a blank in two Gospels. And in like manner, even though Scripture be considered to be altogether silent as to the intermediate state, and to pass from the mention of death to that of the Judgment, there is nothing in this circumstance to disprove the Church's doctrine, (if there be other grounds for it,) that there *is* an intermediate state, and that it has an important place in the scheme of salvation, that in it the souls of the faithful are purified and grow in grace, that they pray for us, and that our prayers benefit them.

Moreover, there is on the face of the New Testament plain evidence, that often the sacred writers are but *referring* to the circumstances it relates, *as* known, and not narrating them. Thus St. Luke, after describing our Lord's consecration of the bread at supper time, adds immediately, *"Likewise* also the cup after supper, saying,"* etc. ; he does not narrate it in its place ; he does but allude to it as a thing well known, in the way of a note or memorandum. Again: St. Mark, in giving an account of St. John Baptist's martyrdom, says, " When his disciples heard of it, they came and took up his corpse and laid it in *the* tomb."† He is evidently speaking of an occurrence, and of a tomb, which were well known to those for whom he wrote. If historical facts be thus merely alluded to, not taught, why may not doctrines also ? Here again it will be replied, that Scripture was written to teach doctrine, not history ; but such an answer will not hold good for many reasons. First, is it true that the Gospels were *not* written to teach us the facts of Christ's life ? Next, is it true that the account of the institution of the Lord's Supper is a mere abstract historical narrative, and not recorded to direct our practice ? Further, where is the proof that Scripture *was* intended to teach doctrine ? This is one of the main points in dispute. But enough in answer to a gratuitous proposition ; and enough indeed in exemplification of the characteristic of Scripture, which I proposed to consider.

* Luke xxii. 20.

† Mark vi. 29. [In the revised Version of 1881, it is translated "in a tomb ;" but μνημεῖον is more than a tomb, it implies a place of *remembrance*.]

5.

The Impression made on the Reader by the Statements of Scripture.

THE characteristics then, of the narrative portion of Scripture are such as I have described; it is unsystematic and unstudied;—from which I would infer, that as Scripture relates *facts* without aiming at completeness or consistency, so it relates *doctrines* also; so that, if it does after all include in its teaching the whole Catholic Creed, (as we of the English Church hold,) this does not happen from any purpose in its writers so to do, but from the overruling providence of God, overruling just so far as this: to secure a certain result, not a certain mode of attaining it,—not so as to interfere with their free and natural manner of writing, but by imperceptibly guiding it; in other words, not securing their teaching against indirectness and disorder, but against eventual incompleteness. From which it follows, that we must not be surprised to find in Scripture doctrines of the Gospel, however momentous, nevertheless taught obliquely, and capable only of circuitous proof;—such, for instance, as that of the Blessed Trinity,—and, among them, the especial Church doctrines, such as the Apostolical Succession, the efficacy of the Holy Eucharist, and the essentials of the Ritual.

The argument, stated in a few words, stands thus:—Since distinct portions of Scripture itself are apparently inconsistent with one another, yet are not really so, therefore it does not follow that Scripture and Catholic doctrine are at variance with each other, even though there may be sometimes a difficulty in adjusting the one with the other.

Now I propose to go over the ground again in somewhat a different way, not confining myself to illustrations from Scripture narrative, but taking others from Scripture teaching also, and that with a view of answering another form which the objection is likely to take.

I.

The objection then may be put thus: "We are told, it seems, in the Prayer Book, of a certain large and influential portion of doctrine, as constituting one great part of the Christian Revelation, that is, of Sacraments, of Ministers, of Rites, of Observances; we are told that these are the appointed means through which Christ's gifts are conveyed to us. Now when we turn to Scripture, we see much indeed of those gifts, viz., we read much of what He has done for us, by atoning for our sins, and much of what He does in us, that is, much about holiness, faith, peace, love, joy, hope, and obedience; but of those intermediate provisions of the Revelation coming between Him and us, of which the Church speaks, we read very little. Passages, indeed, are pointed out to us as if containing notices of them, but they are in our judgment singularly deficient and unsatisfactory; and that, either because the meaning assigned to them is not obvious and natural, but (as we think) strained, unexpected, recondite, and at best but possible, or because they are conceived in such plain, unpretending words, that we cannot imagine the writers meant to say any great thing in introducing them. On the other hand, a silence is observed in certain places, where one might expect the doctrines in question to be mentioned. Moreover, the general tone of the New Testament is to our apprehension a full disproof of them ; that is, it is moral, rational, elevated, impassioned, but there is nothing of what may be called a sacramental, ecclesiastical, mysterious tone in it.

"For instance, let Acts xx. be considered : ' Upon the first day of the week, when the disciples came together to break bread '—who would imagine, from such a mode of speaking, that this was a solemn, mysterious rite ?   The words 'break bread' are quite a familiar expression.

"Or again: 'Christ our Passover is sacrificed for us, therefore let us keep the feast, not with old leaven, neither with the leaven of malice and wickedness, but with the unleavened bread of sincerity and truth.'   Here, if the Church system were true, one might have expected that in mentioning 'keeping the feast,' a reference would be made to the Eucharist, as being the great feast of Christ's sacrifice; whereas, instead of the notion of any literal feast occuring to the sacred writer, a mental feast is the only one he proceeds to mention ; and the unleavened bread of the Passover, instead of suggesting to his mind the sacred elements in the Eucharist, is to him but typical of something moral, 'sincerity and truth.'

"Or again : ' Lo, I am with you alway, even unto the end of the world.' *   This means, we are told, that Christ is with the present Church : *for* when Christ said ' with you,' He meant with you and your descendants ; and the Church, at present so called, is descended from the Apostles and first disciples.   How very covert, indirect, and unlikely a meaning !

* Matt. xxviii. 20.

" Or, to take another instance : How is it proved that the Lord's Supper is generally necessary to salvation ? By no part of Scripture except the sixth chapter of St. John. Now, suppose that a person denies that this passage belongs to that Sacrament, how shall we prove it ? And is it any very strong step to deny it ? Do not many most excellent men now alive deny it ? have not many now dead denied it ? "

This is the objection now to be considered, which lies it would seem in this : that after considering what I have been saying about the statement of facts in Scripture, after all allowances on the score of its unstudied character, there is still a serious difficulty remaining,—that the circumstance that its books were written at different times and places, by different persons, without concert, explains indeed much,—explains indeed why there is no system in it, why so much is out of place, why great truths come in by-the-bye, nay, would explain why others were left out, were there any such ; but it does not explain the case as it stands, it does not explain why a doctrine is not introduced when there is an actual call for it, why a sacred writer should come close up to it, as it were, and yet pass by it ; why, when he does introduce it, he should mention it so obscurely, as not at all to suggest it to an ordinary reader ; why, in short, the tone and character of his writing should be just contrary to his real meaning. This is the difficulty,—strongly, nay almost extravagantly put, but still plausible,—on which I shall now attempt some remarks.

2.

Now there are two attributes of the Bible throughout, which, taken together, seem to meet this difficulty,— attributes which, while at first sight in contrast, have

a sort of necessary connexion, and set off each other—
simplicity and depth. Simplicity leads a writer to say
things without display; and depth obliges him to use
inadequate words. Scripture then, treating of invisible
things, at best must use words less than those things;
and, as if from a feeling that no words can be worthy of
them, it does not condescend to use even the strongest
that exist, but often takes the plainest. The deeper the
thought, the plainer the word; the word and thought
diverge from each other. Again, it is a property of
depth to lead a writer into verbal contradictions; and
it is a property of simplicity not to care to avoid them.
Again, when a writer is deep, his half sentences, paren-
theses, clauses, nay his words, have a meaning in them
independent of the context, and admit of exposition.
There is nothing put in for ornament's sake, or for
rhetoric; nothing put in for the mere sake of anything
else, but all for its own sake; all as the expressions and
shadows of great things, as seeds of thought, and with
corresponding realities. Moreover, when a writer is deep,
or again when he is simple, he does not set about exhausting his subject in his remarks upon it; he says so
much as is in point, no more; he does not go out of
his way to complete a view or to catch at collateral
thoughts; he has something before him which he aims
at, and, while he cannot help including much in his
meaning which he does not aim at, he does aim at one
thing, not at another. Now to illustrate these remarks,
and to apply them.

One of the most remarkable characteristics of Scripture narrative, which I suppose all readers must have
noticed, is the absence of expressions by which the
reader can judge whether the events recorded are presented for praise or blame. A plain bare series of facts

is drawn out ; and whether for imitation or warning, often cannot be decided except by the context, or by the event, or by our general notions of propriety—often not at all. The bearing and drift of the narrative are not given.

For instance, when the prophet Isaiah told Ahaz to ask a sign, he said, " I will not ask, neither *will I tempt* the Lord." Was this right or wrong ?

When Elisha said to Joash, " Smite on the ground," the king " smote thrice and stayed." What was the fault of this ? We should not know it was faulty but by the event, viz., that "the man of God was wroth with him, and said, Thou shouldest have smitten five or six times." *

What was David's sin in numbering the people ? Or take the account of Moses striking the rock : " And Moses took the rod from before the Lord, as He commanded him. And Moses and Aaron gathered the congregation together before the rock, and he said unto them, Hear now, ye rebels ; must we fetch you water out of this rock ? And Moses lifted up his hand, and with his rod he smote the rock twice : and the water came out abundantly, and the congregation drank, and their beasts also."† I really do not think we should have discovered that there was anything wrong in this, but for the comment that follows : " Because ye believed Me not, to sanctify Me," etc. ; though, of course, when we are told, we are able to point out where their fault lay.

And in that earlier passage in the history of Moses, when his zeal led him to smite the Egyptian, we are entirely left by the sacred narrative to determine for ourselves whether his action was good or bad, or how far one, how far the other. We are left to a comment, the comment of our own judgment, external to the inspired volume.

* 2 Kings xiii. 18, 19. † Numb. xx. 9—11.

Or consider the account of Jeroboam's conduct from first to last in the revolt of the ten tribes ; or that of the old prophet who dwelt in Samaria. Is it not plain that Scripture does not interpret itself?

Or consider the terms in which an exceeding great impiety of Ahaz and the high priest is spoken of; and say, if we knew not the Mosaic law, or if we were not told in the beginning of the chapter what the character of Ahaz was, whether we should be able to determine, from the narrative itself, whether he was doing a right or a wrong, or an indifferent action. There is no epithet, no turn of sentence, which betrays the divine judgment of his deed. It passes in the Scripture narrative, as in God's daily providence, silently. I allude to the following passage : " And king Ahaz went to Damascus to meet Tiglath-pileser, king of Assyria, and saw an altar that was at Damascus : and king Ahaz sent to Urijah the priest the fashion of the altar, and the pattern of it, according to all the workmanship thereof. And Urijah the priest built an altar according to all that king Ahaz had sent from Damascus : so Urijah the priest made it against king Ahaz came from Damascus. And when the king was come from Damascus, the king saw the altar ; and the king approached to the altar, and offered thereon. And he burned his burnt-offering, and his meat-offering, and poured his drink-offering, and sprinkled the blood of his peace-offerings upon the altar. And he brought also the brasen altar, which was before the Lord, from the fore-front of the house, from between the altar and the house of the Lord, and put it on the north side of the altar. And king Ahaz commanded Urijah the priest, saying, Upon the great altar burn the morning burnt-offering . . . and the brasen altar shall be for me to inquire by. Thus did

Urijah the priest, according to all that king Ahaz commanded." *

Or, again, how simple and unadorned is the account of St. John Baptist's martyrdom! "Herod had laid hold of John, and bound him and put him in prison for Herodias' sake, his brother Philip's wife; for John said unto him, It is not lawful for thee to have her. And when he would have put him to death, he feared the multitude, because they counted him as a prophet. But when Herod's birthday was kept, the daughter of Herodias danced before them, and pleased Herod. Whereupon, he promised with an oath, to give her whatsoever she would ask. And she, being before instructed of her mother, said, Give me here John Baptist's head in a charger. And the king was sorry: nevertheless for the oath's sake, and them which sat with him at meat, he commanded it to be given her. And he sent, and beheaded John in the prison. And his head was brought in a charger, and given to the damsel; and she brought it to her mother. And his disciples came, and took up the body, and buried it, and went and told Jesus." † Not a word of indignation, of lament, or of triumph! Such is the style of Scripture, singularly contrasted to the uninspired style, most beautiful but still human, of the ancient Martyrologies; for instance, that of the persecution at Lyons and Vienne.

St. Paul's journey to Jerusalem, against the warnings of the prophets, is the last instance of this character of Scripture narrative which shall be given. The facts of it are related so nakedly, that there has been room for maintaining that he was wrong in going thither. That he was right would seem certain, from the way in which he speaks of these warnings: "Behold, I go *bound in the*

---

* 2 Kings xvi. 10—16.   † Matt. xiv.

Spirit unto Jerusalem, not knowing the things that shall befall me there, save that the Holy Ghost witnesseth in every city, saying, that bonds and afflictions abide me ;"* and also from Christ's words in the vision : " Be of good cheer, Paul; for as thou *hast testified of Me* in Jerusalem,"† etc. Yet though this be abundantly enough to convince us, nevertheless, the impression conveyed by the warning of the disciples at Tyre saying, " through the Spirit, that he should not go up to Jerusalem,"‡ and by that of Agabus at Cæsarea, and, when he got to Jerusalem, by his attempt to soften the Jews by means of a conformity to the Law, and by his strong words, seemingly retracted, to Ananias, and by his cleverly dividing the Jewish council by proclaiming himself a Pharisee,—the impression, I say, conveyed by all this would *in itself* be (a very false one,) that there was something human in his conduct.

3.

Thus the style of Scripture is plain and colourless, as regards the relation of facts ; so that we are continually perplexed what to think about them and about the parties concerned in them. They need a comment,—they are evidently but a text *for* a comment,—they have no comment ; and as they stand, may be turned this way or that way, according to the accidental tone of mind in the reader. And often the true comment, when given us in other parts of Scripture, is startling. I think it startling at first sight that Lot, being such as he is represented to be on the whole in the Old Testament, should be called by St. Peter " a just man." I think Ehud's assassination of Eglon a startling act,—the praise given to Jael for killing Sisera, startling. It is evident that the letter of the sacred history conveys to the ordinary

* Acts xx. 22, 23.   † Ib. xxiii. 11.   ‡ Ib. xxi. 4.

reader a very inadequate idea of the facts recorded in it, considered as bodily, substantial, and (as it were) living and breathing transactions.

Equal simplicity is observed in the relation of great and awful events. For instance, consider the words in which is described the vision of God vouchsafed to the elders of Israel. " Then went up Moses and Aaron, and Nadab and Abihu, and seventy of the elders of Israel ; and they saw the God of Israel : and there was under His feet as it were a paved work of a sapphire stone, and as it were the body of heaven in his clearness. And upon the nobles of the children of Israel He laid not His hand: also they saw God, and did eat and did drink." * Or consider the account of Jacob's wrestling with the Angel. Or the plain, unadorned way in which the conversations, if I may dare use the word, between Almighty God and Moses are recorded, and His gracious laments, purposes of wrath, appeasement, repentance. Or between the Almighty and Satan, in the first chapter of Job. Or how simply and abruptly the narrative runs, " And [the Serpent] said unto the woman . . . and the woman said unto the serpent ; " or, " And the Lord opened the mouth of the ass, and she said to Balaam. . . . and Balaam said unto the ass."† Minds familiarized to supernatural things, minds set upon definite great objects, have no disposition, no time to indulge in embellishment, or to aim at impressiveness, or to consult for the weakness or ignorance of the hearer.

And so in like manner the words in which the celebration of the holy Eucharist is spoken of by St. Luke and St. Paul, viz., " breaking bread," are very simple : they are applicable to a common meal quite as well as to the Sacrament, and they only do not exclude, they in no

* Exod. xxiv. 9—11.   † Numb. xxii. 28—29.

respect introduce that full and awful meaning which the Church has ever put on them. " As He sat at meat with them, He took bread, and blessed it, and brake, and gave to them ; and their eyes were opened."* "They continued stedfastly in the breaking of bread, and in prayers."† " The first day of the week, when the disciples came together to break bread. . . . When he therefore was come up again and had broken bread, and eaten, and talked a long while even till break of day, so he departed."‡ " When he had thus spoken, he took bread, and gave thanks to God in the presence of them all ; and when he had broken it, he began to eat."§ " The bread which we break, is it not the communion of the Body of Christ ? "‖ " The Lord Jesus, the same night in which He was betrayed, took bread ; and when He had given thanks, He brake it."¶ Now no words can be simpler than these. What *is* remarkable is the repeated mention of the very same acts in the same order—taking, blessing or giving thanks, and breaking. Certainly the constant use of the word " break" is very remarkable. For instance, in the ship, why should it be said, " And when He had thus spoken, He took bread, and gave thanks ; and when He had *broken* it, He began to eat," since he *alone* ate it, and did not divide it among his fellow-passengers ? But supposing the passages had been a little less frequent, so as not to attract attention by their similarity, what could be more simple than the words,—what less adapted to force on the mind any high meaning ? Yet these simple words, *blessing, breaking, eating, giving,* have a very high meaning put on them in our Prayer Book, put on them by the Church from the first ; and a person may be tempted to say

---

* Luke xxiv. 30, 31.   ‡ Acts xx. 7—11.   ‖ 1 Cor. x. 16.

† Acts ii. 42.   § Ib. xxvii. 35.   ¶ Ib. xi. 23, 24.

that the Church's meaning is not borne out by such simple words. I ask, are they more bare and colourless than the narrative of many a miraculous transaction in the Old Testament?

Such is the plain and (as it were) unconscious way in which great things are recorded in Scripture. However, it may be objected that there is no allusion to Catholic doctrines, even where one would think there must have been, had they been in the inspired writer's mind; that is, supposing them part of the Divine Revelation. For instance, if Baptism is so indispensable for the evangelical blessings, why do we hear nothing of the baptism of the Apostles? If Ordinances are so imperative now, why does not our Lord say so, when He says, " Neither in this mountain, nor yet at Jerusalem, shall ye worship the Father " ? That is, the tone of the New Testament is unsacramental; and the impression it leaves on the mind is not that of a Priesthood and its attendant system. This may be objected: yet I conceive that a series of Scripture parallels to this, as regards other matters, might easily be drawn out, all depending on this principle, and illustrating it in the case before us ; viz., that when the sacred writers were aiming at one thing, they did not go out of their way ever so little to introduce another. The fashion of this day, indeed, is ever to speak about all religious things at once, and never to introduce one, but to introduce all, and never to maintain reserve about any ; and those who are imbued with the spirit which this implies, doubtless will find it difficult to understand how the sacred writers could help speaking of what was very near their subject, when it was not their subject. Still we must submit to facts, which abundantly evidence that they could. This omission of the Sacraments in St. Paul and St. John, so

far as distinct mention is omitted (for in fact they are frequently mentioned), as little proves that those Apostles
were not aware and thinking of them, as St. James's
Epistle is an evidence that he did not hold the doctrine
of the Atonement, which is not there mentioned. Or
consider how many passages there are in the history, in
which some circumstance is omitted which one would
expect to be inserted. For instance : St. Peter struck
off the ear of Malchus when our Lord was seized. St.
John gives the names ; St. Matthew and St. Mark relate the occurrence without the names. This is commonly explained on the ground that St. John, writing
later than his brother Evangelists, and when all parties
were dead, might give the names without exposing St.
Peter, if indeed he was still alive, to any civil inconve-
niences. True, this is an explanation so far ; but what
explains their omitting, and St. John omitting, our
Lord's miracle in healing the ear, while St. Luke relates it ? Was not this to deliver a half account ? is it
not what would be called unnatural, if it were a question, not of history, but of doctrine ?

4.

Now let us review cases in which matters of doctrine,
or the doctrinal tone of the composition, is in question.
Is the tone of Scripture more unfavourable to the doctrine
of a Priesthood than it is to the idea of Christianity, such
as we have been brought up to regard it,—I mean of an
established, endowed, dignified Church ; and, if its establishment is not inconsistent (as it is not) with the New
Testament, why should its mysticalness be ? Certainly,
if anything is plain, it is that Scripture represents the
very portion of Christians, one and all, to be tribulation,
want, contempt, persecution. I do not,—of course not,

far from it,—I do not say that the actual present state of
the Church Catholic and the text of the New Testament,
are not reconcilable ; but is it not a fact, that the first
impression from Scripture of what the Church should be,
is not fulfilled in what we see around us ?

Again : I suppose another impression which would be
left on an unbiassed reader by the New Testament would
be, that the world was soon to come to an end. Yet it
has not. As, then, we submit to facts in one case, and
do not exercise our so-called right of private judgment
to quarrel with our own consciousness that we do live,
and that the world does still go on, why should we not
submit to facts in the other instance ? and if there be
good proof that what the Church teaches is true, and is
comformable to given texts of Scripture, in spite of this
vague impression from its surface to the contrary, why
should we not reconcile ourselves to the conclusion that
that impression of its being opposed to a Sacramental or
Priestly system is a false impression, is private and personal, or peculiar to a particular age, untrustworthy, in
fact false, just as the impression of its teaching that the
world was soon to come to an end is false, because it has
not been fulfilled ?

Again : I suppose any one reading our Lord's discourses, would, with the Apostles, consider that the
Gentiles, even if they were to be converted, yet were
not to be on a level with the Jews. The impression
His words convey is certainly such. But of this more
presently.

Again : it is objected that little is said in the New
Testament of the danger of sin after baptism, or of the
penitential exercises by which it is to be remedied.
Well : supposing it for argument's sake : yet let me ask
the previous question. Is there much said in the New

Testament of the chance of sin after baptism at all ?
Are not all Christians described as if in all important
respects sinless ?   Of course, falling away is spoken of,
and excommunication ; but grievous sin has no distinct
habitat among those who are "called to be saints" and
members of the Church in the Epistles of St. Paul and
St. John.   Till we examine Scripture on the subject,
perhaps we have no adequate notion how little those
Apostles contemplate recurring sin in the baptized.   The
argument then proves too much : for if silence proves
anything, it will prove either that Christians who now
live do not fall into gross sin, or that those who have so
fallen have forfeited their Christianity.

   Again : the first three Gospels contain no declaration
of our Lord's divinity, and there are passages which tend
at first sight the other way.   Now, is there one doctrine
more than another the essential and characteristic of a
Christian mind ?   Is it possible that the Evangelists
could write any one particle of their records of His
life, without having the great and solemn truth stead-
fastly before them, that He was their God ?   Yet they
do not show this.   It follows, that truths may be in the
mind of the inspired writers, which are not discoverable
to ordinary readers in the tone of their composition.   I
by no means deny that, now we know the doctrine,
we can gather proofs of it from the three Gospels in
question, and can discern in them a feeling of reverence
towards our Lord, which fully implies it ; but no one will
say it is on the surface, and such as to strike a reader.
I conceive the impression left on an ordinary mind would
be, that our Saviour was a superhuman being, intimately
possessed of God's confidence, but still a creature ; an
impression infinitely removed from the truth as really
contained and intended in those Gospels.

Again: is the tone of the Epistle of St. James the same as the tone of St. Paul's Epistle to the Ephesians? or that of St. Paul's Epistle to the Romans as that of the same Apostle's Epistle to the Hebrews? Might they not be as plausibly put in opposition with each other, as the Church system is made contrary to Scripture?

Again: consider what the texts are from which Calvinists are accustomed to argue, viz., such as speak of God's sovereign grace, without happening to make mention of man's responsibility. Thus: "He who has begun a good work in you will perform it unto the day of the Lord Jesus," and, "Who are kept by the power of God through faith unto salvation," are taken as irrefragable arguments for final perseverance. If mention in Scripture of God's electing mercy need not exclude man's moral freedom, why need the stress laid in Scripture upon faith and love exclude the necessity of sacraments as instruments of grace?

Again: if silence implies denial or ignorance of the things passed over; if nothing is the sense of Scripture but what is openly declared; if first impressions are everything, what are we to say to the Book of Canticles, which nowhere hints, (nor Scripture afterwards anywhere hints either,) that it has a spiritual meaning? Either, then, the apparent tone of passages of Scripture is not the real tone, or the Canticles is not a sacred book.

Again: is not the apparent tone of the Prophecies concerning Christ of a similarly twofold character, as is shown by the Jewish notion that there were to be two Messiahs, one suffering and one triumphant?

Another illustration which deserves attention, lies in the impression which David's history in the Books of Samuel conveys, compared with that derived from the Chronicles and the Psalms. I am not speaking of verbal discrepan-

cies or difficulties to be reconciled,—the subject which
I have already discussed,—but of the tone of the narrative, and the impression thence made upon the reader;
and I think that it must be allowed that the idea which
we have of David's character from the one document, is
very different from that gained from the other two. In
the Books of Samuel we have the picture of a monarch,
bold, brave, generous, loyal, accomplished, attractive, and
duly attached to the cause, and promoting the establishment, of the Mosaic law, but with apparently little permanent and consistent personal religion; his character
is sullied with many sins, and clouded with many sus-
picions. But in the First Book of Chronicles, and in
the Psalms, we are presented with the picture of a
humble, tender, devotional, and deeply spiritual mind,
detached from this world, and living on the thought and
in the love of God. Is the impression derived from the
New Testament more unfavourable to the Church
system (admitting that it is unfavourable), than that of
the Books of Samuel to David's personal holiness?

5.

I just now reserved the doctrine of the admission of
the Gentiles into the Church, for separate consideration;
let us now turn to it. Their call, certainly their equality
with the Jews, was but covertly signified in our Lord's
teaching. I think it is plainly there signified, though
covertly; but, if covertly, then the state of the evidence
for the Catholicity of the Christian Church will lie in the
same disadvantage in the Gospels as the state of the
evidence for its ritual character in the Epistles; and
we may as well deny that the Church is Gentile, on the
ground that our Lord but indirectly teaches it, as that
it is sacramental on the ground that His Apostles indi-

rectly teach it. It is objected that the Church system, the great Episcopal, Priestly, Sacramental system, was an after-thought, a corruption coming upon the simplicity of the primitive and Apostolic religion. The primitive religion, it is said was more simple. More simple! Did objectors never hear that there have been unbelievers who have written to prove that Christ's religion was more simple than St. Paul's—that St. Paul's Epistles are a second system coming upon the three Gospels and changing their doctrine? Have we never heard that some have considered the doctrine of our Lord's Divinity to be an addition upon the "simplicity" of the Gospels? Yes : this has been the belief not only of heretics, as the Socinians, but of infidels, such as the historian Gibbon, who looked at things with less of prejudice than heretics, as having no point to maintain. I think it will be found quite as easy to maintain that the Divinity of Christ was an after-thought, brought in by the Greek Platonists and other philosophers, upon the simple and primitive creed of the Galilean fishermen, as infidels say, as that the Sacramental system came in from the same source as rationalists say.—But to return to the point before us. Let it be considered whether a very plausible case might not be made out by way of proving that our Blessed Lord did not contemplate the evangelizing of the heathen at all, but that it was an after-thought, when His Apostles began to succeed, and their ambitious hopes to rise.

If texts from the Gospels are brought to show that it was no after-thought, such as the mustard-seed, or the labourers of the vineyard, which imply the calling and conversion of the Gentiles, and the implication contained in His discourse at Nazareth concerning the miracles of Elijah and Elisha wrought upon Gentiles, and His signi-

ficant acts, such as His complying with the prayer of the
Canaanitish woman, and His condescension towards the
centurion, and, above all, His final command to go into all
the world and preach the Gospel to every creature, " and
to go teach all nations, baptizing them ;" still it may be
asked, Did not the Apostles hear our Lord, and what
was *their* impression from what they heard ? Is it not
certain that the Apostles did not gather this command
from His teaching ? So far is certain : and it is certain
that none of us will deny that nevertheless that command
comes from Him. Well then, it is plain, that important
things may be in Scripture, yet not brought out : is
there then any reason why *we* should be more clear-
sighted as regards another point of doctrine, than the
Apostles were as regards this ? I ask this again : Is
there any reason that we, who have not heard Christ
speak, should have a clearer apprehension of the meaning
of His recorded discourses on a given point, than the
Apostles who did ? and if it be said that we have now
the gift of the Holy Spirit, which the Apostles had not
during our Lord's earthly ministry, then I ask again, where
is there any promise that we, as individuals, should be
brought by His gracious influences into the perfect truth
by merely employing ourselves on the text of Scripture
by ourselves ? However, so far is plain, that a doctrine
which we see to be plainly contained, nay necessarily
presupposed, in our Lord's teaching, did not so impress
itself on the Apostles.

These thoughts deserve consideration ; but what I was
coming to in particular is this ; I wish you to turn in
your mind such texts as the following : " Ye shall be
witnesses unto Me both in Jerusalem and in all Judæa
and in Samaria, and unto *the uttermost part of the earth*."
An objector would say that " the uttermost part of the

earth" ought to be translated "uttermost part of the *land*"—that is, the Holy Land. And he would give this reason to confirm it. "How very unlikely that the whole of the world, except Judæa, should be *straitened up into one clause!* Jerusalem, Judæa, Samaria, mentioned distinctly, and the whole world brought under one word!" And I suppose the Apostles did at the time understand the sentence to mean only the Holy Land. Certainly they did not understand it to imply the absolute and immediate call of the Gentiles as mere Gentiles.

You will say that such texts as Luke xxiv. 47, are decisive : "that repentance and remission of sins should be preached in His Name *among all nations,* beginning at Jerusalem." Far from it ; as men nowadays argue, they would say it was not *safe* to rely on such texts. *Among* all nations :" "*into* or *to* all nations," this need not mean more than that the Jews in those nations should be converted. The Jews were scattered about in those days ; the Messiah was to collect them together. This text speaks of His doing so, according to the prophecies, wherever they were scattered. To this, the question of the populace relates, "Whither will He go that we shall not find Him ? will He go unto the dispersed among the Gentiles, and teach the Gentiles "* or Greek Jews ? And St. John's announcement also, that He died "not for that nation only, but that also He should gather together in one the children of God that were scattered abroad."† And St. Peter's address "to the strangers scattered throughout Pontus, Galatia, Cappadocia, Asia, and Bithynia." And especially on the day of Pentecost, when the same Apostle addressed the Jews, devout men dwelling at Jerusalem, out of every nation under heaven."‡

* John vi. 35.   † Ib. xi. 51. 52.   ‡ Acts ii. 5.

Again : if the words "preach the Gospel to every creature," were insisted on, an objector might say that creature or creation does not mean all men any more than it includes all animals or all Angels, but one part of the creation, the elect, the Jews.*

Here then are instances of that same concise and indirect mode of stating important doctrine in half sentences, or even words, which is supposed to be an objection to the peculiar Church doctrines only. For instance, it is objected that the sacred truth of the procession of the Holy Ghost from the Father, is only contained in the words, " the Spirit of Truth, which *proceedeth rom* the Father :"† the co-equality of the Son to the Father, in the phrase, " who being in the form of God, thought it not robbery *to be equal with* God," and in the Jews' inference from our Lord's words, " He said that God was His Father, making Himself equal with God."‡ The doctrine of original sin depends on a few implications such as this, " *As* in Adam all die, even so in Christ shall all be made alive." § And in like manner the necessity of the Holy Eucharist for salvation, upon the sixth chapter of St. John, in which the subject of Christ's flesh and blood is mentioned, but not a word expressly concerning that Sacrament, which as yet was future. So also, 1 Cor. x. 16, " The cup of blessing," etc., is almost a parenthesis : and the ministerial power of Absolution depends on our Lord's words to His Apostles, " Whosesoever sins ye remit," ‖ etc. ; and the doctrine of the Christian Altar, upon such words as, " If thou bring thy gift to the Altar," etc. Now I say all these are paralleled by the mode in which our Lord taught the call of the Gentiles : He said, "Preach the Gospel to every crea-

* *Vide* Rom. viii. 19.   § 1 Cor. xv. 22.
† John xv. 26.   ‖ John xx. 23.
‡ Philip. ii. 6 ; John v. 18.

ture." These words need have only meant, " Bring all men to Christianity through Judaism :" make them Jews, that they may enjoy Christ's privileges, which are lodged in Judaism ; teach them those rites and cere- monies, circumcision and the like, which hereto have been dead ordinances, and now are living : and so the Apostles seem to have understood them. Yet they meant much more than this ; that Jews were to have no precedence of the Gentiles, but the one and the other to be on a level. It is quite plain that our Saviour must have had this truth before His mind, if we may so speak, when He said, " Preach to every creature." Yet the words did not on the surface mean all this. As then they meant more than they need have been taken to mean, so the words, " I am with you alway," or, " Re- ceive ye the Holy Ghost," may mean much more than they need mean ; and the early Church may, in God's providence, be as really intended to bring out and settle the meaning of the latter, as St. Peter at Joppa, and St. Paul on his journeys, to bring out the meaning of the former.

To this there are other parallels. For instance : who would have conceived that the doctrine of the Resur- rection of the Dead lay hid in the words, " I am the God of Abraham," etc. ? Why may not the doctrines con- cerning the Church lie hid in repositories which certainly are less recondite ? Why may not the Church herself, who is called the pillar and ground of the Truth, be the appointed interpreter of the doctrines about herself ?

Again : consider how much is contained, and how covertly, in our Saviour's words, " But ye are clean, but not all ;"—or in His riding on an ass, and not saying why ; or in His saying " Destroy this Temple," when " He spoke of the Temple of His Body." Let it be borne in mind, that a figurative, or, what may be called a sacramental style, was the very characteristic of oriental teaching ; so that it would have been a wilful disrespect in any hearer who took the words of a great prophet in their mere literal and outside sense.

Here, too, the whole subject of prophecy might be brought in.   What doctrine is more important than that of the miraculous conception of our Lord ?   Yet how is it declared in prophecy ?   Isaiah said to Ahaz, " Behold, a Virgin shall conceive, and bear a Son, and shall call His Name Immanuel."   The first meaning of these words seems not at all to allude to Christ, but to an event of the day.   The great Gospel doctrine is glanced at (as we may say) through this minor event.

6.

These remarks surely suffice on this subject, viz., to show that the impression we gain from Scripture need not be any criterion or any measure of its true and full sense ; that solemn and important truths may be silently taken for granted, or alluded to in a half sentence, or spoken of indeed, yet in such unadorned language that we may fancy we see through it, and see nothing ;—peculiarities of Scripture which result from what is the peculiar character of its teaching, simplicity and depth.   Yet even without taking into account these peculiarities, it is obvious, from what meets us daily in the course of life, how insufficient a test is the surface of any one composition, conversation, or transaction, of the full circle of opinions of its author.   How different persons are, when we know them, from what they appeared to us in their writings ! how many opinions do they hold, which we did not expect in them ! how many practices and ways have they, how many peculiarities, how many tastes, which we did not imagine! I will give an illustration ;—that great philosopher, Bp. Butler, has written a book, as we know, on the Analogy of Religion. It is distinguished by a grave, profound, and severe style ; and apparently is not the work of a man of lively or susceptible mind. Now we know from his history, that, when Bishop, he put up a Cross in his chapel at Bristol. Could a reader have conjectured this from that work ? At first sight would it not have startled one who knew nothing of him but from that work? I do not ask whether, on consideration, he would not find it fell in with his work ; of course it would, if his philosophy were consistent with itself ; but certainly it is not on the surface of his work. Now might not we say that his work contained the *whole* of his philosophy, and yet say that the use of the Cross was one of his *usages ?* In like manner we may say that the Bible is the *whole* of the Divine Revelation, and yet the use of the Cross a divine usage.

But this is not all. Some small private books of his are extant, containing a number of every-day matters, such as of course one could not expect to be able to con-jecture from his great work ; I mean, matters of ordinary and almost household life. Yet those who have seen these papers are likely to feel a surprise that they should be Butler's. I do not say that they can give any reason why they should not be so ; but the notion we form of any one whom we have not seen, will ever be in its details very different from the true one.

Another series of illustrations might be drawn from the writings of the ancients. Those who are acquainted with the Greek historians know well that they, and par-ticularly the gravest and severest of them, relate events so simply, calmly, unostentatiously, that an ordinary reader does not recognize what events are great and

what little ; and on turning to some modern history
in which they are commented on, will find to his surprise that a battle or a treaty, which was despatched in
half a line by the Greek author, is perhaps the turning-
point of the whole history, and was certainly known by
him to be so.   Here is the case of the gospels, with
this difference, that they are unsystematic compositions,
whereas the Greek historians profess to be methodical.

Again : instances might easily be given of the silence
of contemporary writers, Greek or Roman, as to great
events of their time, when they might be expected to
notice them ; a silence which has even been objected
against the fact of those events having occurred, yet, in
the judgment of the mass of well-informed men, without
any real cogency.

Again : as to Greek poetry, philosophy, and oratory,
how severe and unexceptionable is it for the most part ;
yet how impure and disgraceful was the Greek daily
life !   Who shows a more sober and refined majesty
than Sophocles ? yet to him Pericles addressed the
rebuke recorded in the first book of Cicero's Offices.*

7.

I conclude with two additional remarks.   I have been
arguing that Scripture is a deep book, and that the peculiar doctrines concerning the Church, contained in the
Prayer Book, are in its depths.   Now let it be remarked
in corroboration, first, that the early Church always did
consider Scripture to be what I have been arguing that
it is from its structure,—viz., a book with very recondite
meanings ; this they considered, not merely with reference to its teaching the particular class of doctrines in
question, but as regards its entire teaching.   They con-

* i. 40.

sidered that it was full of mysteries. Therefore, saying that Scripture has deep meanings, is not an hypothesis invented to meet this particular difficulty, that the Church doctrines are not on its surface, but is an acknowledged principle of interpretation independent of it.

Secondly, it is also certain that the early Church did herself conceal these same Church doctrines. I am not determining whether or not all her writers did so, or all her teachers, or at all times, but merely that, viewing that early period as a whole, there is on the whole a great secrecy observed in it concerning such doctrines (for instance) as the Trinity and the Eucharist ; that is, the early Church did the very thing which I have been supposing Scripture does,—conceal high truths. To suppose that Scripture conceals them, is not an hypothesis invented to meet the difficulty arising from the fact that they are not on the surface; for the early Church, independent of that alleged difficulty, did herself in her own teaching conceal them. This is a second very curious coincidence. If the early Church had reasons for concealment, it may be that Scripture has the same ; especially if we suppose,—what at the very least is no very improbable idea,—that the system of the early Church is a continuation of the system of those inspired men who wrote the New Testament,

6.

External Difficulties of the Canon and the Catholic Creed, compared.

I AM now proceeding to a subject which will in some little degree take me beyond the bounds which I had proposed to myself when I began, but which, being closely connected with that subject, and (as I think) important, has a claim on our attention. The argument which has been last engaging us is this : Objection is made to the indirectness of the evidence from Scripture on which the peculiar Church doctrines are proved ;—I have answered, that sacred *history* is for the most part marked by as much apparent inconsistency, as recorded in one part of Scripture and another, as there is inconsistency as regards *doctrine* in the respective informations of Scripture and the Church ; one event being told us here, another there ; so that we have to compare, compile, reconcile, adjust. As then we do not complain of the history being conveyed in distinct, and at times conflicting, documents, so too we have no fair reason for complaining of the obscurities and intricacies under which doctrine is revealed through its two channels.

I then went on to answer in a similar way the objection, that Scripture was contrary to the teaching of the Church (*i. e.*, to our Prayer Book), not only in specific statements, but in tone ; for I showed that what we call the tone of Scripture, or the impression it makes on the reader, varies so very much according to the reader, that little stress can be laid upon it, and that its tone and the impression it makes would tell against a variety of other points undeniably true and firmly held by us, quite as much as against the peculiar Church doctrines.

In a word, it is as easy to show that Scripture has no contents at all, or next to none, as that it does not contain the special Church doctrines—I mean, the objection which is brought against the Apostolical Succession or the Priesthood being in Scripture, tells against the instruction and information conveyed in Scripture generally. But now I am going to a further point, which has been incidentally touched on, that this same objection is prejudicial not only to the Revelation, whatever it is, contained in Scripture, but to the text of Scripture itself, to the books of Scripture, to their canonicity, to their authority. I have said, the line of reasoning entered on in this objection may be carried forward, and, if it reaches one point, may be made to reach others also. For, first, if the want of method and verbal consistency in Scripture be an objection to the "teaching of the Prayer Book," it is also an objection equally to what is called "Orthodox Protestantism." Further, I have shown that it tells also against the trustworthiness of the sacred history, to the statement of facts contained in any part of Scripture, which is in great measure indirect. And now, lastly, I shall show that it is an objection to the Bible itself, both because that Book cannot be a Revelation which contains neither definite doctrine nor unequivocal matter of fact, and next because the evidence, on which its portions are received, is not clearer or fuller than its own evidence for the facts and doctrines which our Article says it "contains." This is the legitimate consequence of the attempt to invalidate the scripturalness of Catholic doctrine, on the allegation of its want of Scripture proof—an invalidating of Scripture itself; this is the conclusion to which both the argument itself, and the temper of mind which belongs to it, will assuredly lead those who use it, at least in the long run.

There is another objection which is sometimes attempted against Church doctrines, which may be met in the same way. It is sometimes strangely maintained, not only that Scripture does not clearly teach them, but that the Fathers do not clearly teach them ; that nothing can be drawn for certain from the Fathers ; that their evidence leaves matters pretty much as it found them, as being inconsistent with itself, or of doubtful authority. This part of the subject has not yet been considered, and will come into prominence as we proceed with the present argument.

I purpose, then, now to enlarge on this point ; that is, to show that those who object to Church doctrines, whether from deficiency of Scripture proof or of Patristical proof, ought, if they acted consistently on their principles, to object to the canonicity and authority of Scripture ; a melancholy truth, if it be a truth; and I fear it is but too true. Too true, I fear, it is *in fact*,— not only that men ought, if consistent, to proceed from opposing Church doctrine to oppose the authority of Scripture, but that the leaven which at present makes the mind oppose Church doctrine, *does* set it, or *will* soon set it, against Scripture. I wish to declare what I think will be found really to be the case, viz., that a battle for the Canon of Scripture is but the next step after a battle for the Creed,—that the Creed comes first in the assault, that is all ; and that if we were not defending the Creed, we should at this moment be defending the Canon. Nay, I would predict as a coming event, that minds *are to be* unsettled as to what is Scripture and what is not; and I predict it that, as far as the voice of one person in one place can do, I may defeat my own prediction by making it. Now to consider the subject.

I.

How do we know that the whole Bible is the word of God? Happily at present we are content to believe this, because we have been so taught. It is our great blessedness to receive it on faith. A believing spirit is in all cases a more blessed spirit than an unbelieving. The testimony of unbelievers declares it : they often say, " I wish I *could* believe ; I should be happier, if I could ; but my *reason* is unconvinced." And then they go on to speak as if they were in a more exalted, though less happy state of mind. Now I am not here to enter into the question of the grounds on which the duty and blessedness of believing rest ; but I would observe, that Nature certainly does give sentence against scepticism, against doubt, nay, against a habit (I say a *habit*) of inquiry, against a critical, cold, investigating temper, the temper of what are called shrewd, clear-headed, hard-headed, men, in that, by the confession of all, happiness is attached, not to *their* temper, but rather to confiding, unreasoning faith. I do not say that inquiry may not under circumstances be a duty, as going into the cold and rain may be a duty, instead of stopping at home,— as serving in war may be a duty ; but it does seem to me preposterous to confess, that free inquiry leads to scepticism, and scepticism makes one less happy than faith, and yet, that such free inquiry is a merit. What is right and what is happy cannot in the long run and on a large scale be disjoined. To follow after truth can never be a subject of regret ; free inquiry does lead a man to regret

the days of his childlike faith ; therefore it is not following after truth. Those who measure everything by utility,
should on their own principles embrace the obedience of
faith for its very expedience; and they should cease
this kind of seeking, which begins in doubt.

I say, then, that never to have been troubled with a
doubt about the truth of what has been taught us, is the
happiest state of mind; and if any one says, that to
maintain this is to admit that heretics ought to remain
heretics, and pagans pagans, I deny it.   For I have not
said that it is a happy thing never to *add* to what you
have, but that it is not happier to *take away*.   Now true
religion is the summit and perfection of false religions :
it combines in one whatever there is of good and true,
severally remaining in each.   And in like manner the
Catholic Creed is for the most part the combination of
separate truths which heretics have divided among themselves, and err in dividing.   So that, in matter of fact, if
a religious mind were educated in and sincerely attached
to some form of heathenism or heresy, and then were
brought under the light of truth, it would be drawn off
from error into the truth, not by losing what it had, but
by gaining what it had not,—not by being unclothed,
but by being " clothed upon," " that mortality may be
swallowed up of life."   That same principle of faith
which attaches it to its original human teaching, would
attach it to the truth ; and that portion of its original
teaching which was to be cast off as absolutely false,
would not be directly rejected, but indirectly rejected
in the reception of the truth which is its opposite.   True
conversion is of a positive, not a negative character.
This was St. Paul's method of controversy at Athens ;
and, if Apologists after him were wont to ridicule the
heathen idolatries, it must be considered that belief in

the popular mythology was then dying out, and was ridiculed by the people themselves.

All this is a digression : but before returning to my subject, I will just add, that it must not be supposed from my expressing such sentiments, that I have any fear of argument for the cause of Christian truth, as if reason were dangerous to it, as if it could not stand before a scrutinizing inquiry. Nothing is more out of place, though it is too common, than such a charge against the defenders of Church doctrines. They may be right or they may be wrong in their arguments, but argue they do ; they are ready to argue ; they believe they have reason on their side ; but they remind others, they remind themselves, that though argument on the whole will but advance the cause of truth, though so far from dreading it, they are conscious it is a great weapon in their hands ; yet that, after all, if a man does nothing more than argue, if he has nothing deeper at bottom, if he does not seek God by some truer means, by obedi- ence, by faith prior to demonstration, he will either not attain truth, or attain a shallow, unreal view of it, and have a weak grasp of it. Reason will prepare for the reception, will spread the news, and secure the outward recognition of the truth ; but in all we do we ought to seek edification, not mere knowledge. Now to return.

I say, it is our blessedness, if we have no doubts about the Canon of Scripture, as it is our blessedness to have no doubts about the Catholic Creed. And this *is* at present actually our blessedness as regards the Canon ; we have no doubts. Even those persons who unhappily have doubts about the Church system, have no doubts about the Canon,—by a happy inconsistency, *I* say. They ought to have doubts on their principles ; this I shall now show, in the confidence that their belief in the

Canon is so much stronger than their disbelief of the Church system, that if they must change their position, they will rather go on and believe the Church system, than go back to disbelieve the Canon.

2.

Now there are two chief heads of objection made against the Catholic or Church system of doctrine and worship,— external and internal. It is said, on the one hand, to be uncertain, not only what is in Scripture, but what is in Antiquity, and what not ; for the early Fathers, it is objected, who are supposed to convey the information, contradict each other ; and the most valuable and voluminous of them did not live till two or three hundred years after St. John's death, while the earlier records are scanty ; and moreover that their view of doctrine was from the first corrupted from assignable external sources, pagan, philosophical, or Jewish. And on the other hand, the system itself may be accused of being contrary to reason and incredible. Here I shall consider the former of these two objections.

Objectors, then, speak thus : " We are far from denying," they say, "that there is truth and value in the ancient Catholic system, as reported by the Fathers ; but we deny that it is *unmixed* truth. We consider it is truth and error mixed together : we do not see why the system of doctrine must be taken together as a whole, so that if one part is true, all is true. We consider that we have a right to take it piecemeal, and examine each part by itself ; that so far as it is true, it is true not as belonging to the ancient system, but for other reasons, as being agreeable to our reason, or to our understanding of Scripture, not because stated by the Fathers ; and, after all, the Church system in question (that is, such doctrines as the mystical power of the Sacraments, the power of the keys, the grace of Ordination, the gifts of the Church, and the Apostolical Succession), has very little authority really primitive. The Fathers whose works we have, not only ought to be of an earlier date, in order to be of authority, but they contradict each other; they declare what is incredible and absurd, and what can reasonably be ascribed to Platonism, or Judaism, or Paganism."

Be it so: well, how will the same captious spirit treat the sacred Canon? in just the same way. It will begin thus :—" These many writings are put together in one book ; what makes them one ? who put them together ? the printer. The books of Scripture have been printed together for many centuries. But that does not make them one ; what authority had those who put them together to do so ? what authority to put just so many books, neither more nor less ? when were they first so put together ? on what authority do we leave out the Wisdom, or the Son of Sirach, and insert the book of Esther ? Catalogues certainly are given of these books in early times : but not exactly the same books are enumerated in all. The language of St. Austin is favourable to the admission of the Apocrypha.* The Latin Church anciently left out the Epistle to the Hebrews, and the Eastern Church left out the book of Revelation. This so-called Canon did not exist at earliest till the fourth century, between two and three hundred years after St. John's death. Let us then see into the matter with our own eyes. Why should not we be as good judges as the Church of the fourth century, on whose authority we receive it ? Why should one book be divine, because another is ? " This is what objectors would say. Now to follow them into particulars

* De Doctr. Christ., ii. 13.

as far as the first head; viz., as to the evidence itself, which is offered in behalf of the divinity and inspiration of the separate books.

For instance; the first Father who expressly mentions Commemorations for the Dead in Christ (such as we still have in substance at the end of the prayer for the Church Militant, where it was happily restored in 1662, having been omitted a century earlier), is Tertullian, about a hundred years after St. John's death. This, it is said, is not authority early enough to prove that that Ordinance is Apostolical, though succeeding Fathers, Origen, St. Cyprian, Eusebius, St. Cyril of Jerusalem, etc., bear witness to it ever so strongly. " Errors might have crept in by that time; mistakes might have been made; Tertullian is but one man, and confessedly not sound in many of his opinions; we ought to have clearer and more decisive evidence." Well, supposing it: suppose Tertullian, a hundred years after St. John, is the first that mentions it, yet Tertullian is also the first who refers to St. Paul's Epistle to Philemon, and even he without quoting or naming it. He is followed by two writers; one of Rome, Caius, whose work is not extant, but is referred to by Eusebius, who, speaking of *thirteen* Epistles of St. Paul, and as excluding the Hebrews, by implication includes that to Philemon; and the other, Origen, who quotes the fourteenth verse of the Epistle, and elsewhere speaks of *fourteen* Epistles of St. Paul. Next, at the end of the third century, follows Eusebius. Further, St. Jerome observes, that in his time some persons doubted whether it was St. Paul's (just as Aerius about that time questioned the Commemorations for the Dead), or at least whether it was canonical, and that from internal evidence; to which he opposes the general consent of external testimony as a sufficient answer. Now, I ask, why do we receive the Epistle to Philemon as St. Paul's, and not the Commemorations for the faithful departed as Apostolical also? Ever after indeed the date of St. Jerome, the Epistle to Philemon was accounted St. Paul's, and so too ever after the same date the Commemorations which I have spoken of are acknowledged on all hands to have been observed as a religious duty, down to three hundred years ago. If it be said that from historical records we have good reasons for thinking that the Epistle of St. Paul to Philemon, with his other Epistles, was read from time immemorial in Church, which is a witness independent of particular testimonies in the Fathers, I answer, no evidence can be more satisfactory and conclusive to a well-judging mind; but then it is a moral evidence, resting on very little formal and producible proof; and quite as much evidence can be given for the solemn Commemorations of the Dead in the Holy Eucharist which I speak of. They too were in use in the Church from time immemorial. Persons, then, who have the heart to give up and annul the Ordinance, will not, if they are consistent, scruple much at the Epistle. If in the sixteenth century the innovators on religion had struck the Epistle to Philemon out of Scripture, they would have had just as much right to do it as to abolish these Commemorations; and those who wished to defend such innovation as regards the Epistle to Philemon, would have had just as much to say in its behalf as those had who put an end to the Commemorations.

If it be said they found nothing on the subject of such Commemorations in Scripture, even granting this for argument's sake, yet I wonder where they found in Scripture that the Epistle to Philemon was written by St. Paul, except indeed in the Epistle itself. Nowhere; yet they kept the one, they abolished the other—as far, that is, as human tyranny could abolish it. Let us be thankful that they did not also say, "The Epistle to Philemon is of a private nature, and has no marks of inspiration about it. It is not mentioned by name or quoted by any writer till Origen, who flourished at a time when mistakes had begun, in the third century, and who actually thinks St. Barnabas wrote the Epistle which goes under his name ; and he too, after all, just mentions it once, but not as inspired or canonical, and also just happens to speak elsewhere of St. Paul's fourteen Epistles. In the beginning of the fourth century, Eusebius, without anywhere naming this Epistle," (as far as I can discover,) "also speaks of fourteen Epistles, and speaks of a writer one hundred years earlier, who in like manner enumerated thirteen besides the Hebrews. All this is very unsatisfactory. We will have nothing but the pure word of God ; we will only admit what has the clearest proof. It is impossible that God should require us to believe a book to come from Him without authenticating it with the highest and most cogent evidence."

Again : the early Church with one voice testifies in favour of Episcopacy, as an ordinance especially pleasing to God. Ignatius, the very disciple of the Apostles, speaks in the clearest and strongest terms ; and those who follow fully corroborate his statements for three or four hundred years. And besides this, we know the fact, that a succession of Bishops from the Apostles did exist in all the Churches all that time. At the end of that time, one Father, St. Jerome, in writing controversially, had some strong expressions against the divine origin of the ordinance. And this is all that can be said in favour of any other regimen. Now, on the other hand, what is the case as regards the Epistle to the Hebrews ? Though received in the East, it was not received in the Latin Churches, till that same St. Jerome's time. St. Irenæus either does not affirm or actually denies that it is St. Paul's. Tertullian ascribes it to St. Barnabas. Caius excluded it from his list. St. Hippolytus does not receive it. St. Cyprian is silent about it. It is doubtful whether St. Optatus received it. Now, that this important Epistle is part of the inspired word of God, there is no doubt. But why? Because the testimony of the fourth and fifth centuries, when Christians were at leisure to examine the question thoroughly, is altogether in its favour. I know of no other reason, and I consider this to be quite sufficient: but with what consistency do persons receive this Epistle as inspired, yet deny that Episcopacy is a divinely ordained means of grace?

Again: the Epistles to the Thessalonians are quoted by six writers in the first two hundred years from St. John's death; first, at the end of the first hundred, by three Fathers, Irenæus, Clement, and Tertullian; and are by implication acknowledged in the lost work of Caius, at the same time, and are in Origen's list some years after. On the other hand, the Lord's table is always called an Altar, and is called a Table only in one single passage of a single Father, during the first three centuries. It is called Altar in four out of the seven Epistles of St. Ignatius. It is called Altar by St. Clement of Rome, by St. Irenæus, Tertullian, St. Cyprian, Origen, Eusebius, St. Athanasius, St. Ambrose, St. Gregory Nazianzen, St. Optatus, St. Jerome, St. Chrysostom, and St. Austin.* It is once called Table by St. Diony-

---

* It is perhaps unnecessary to say that the sense of the word Altar (θυσια- στήριον) in some of these passages has been contested; as it has been contested whether the Fathers' works are genuine, or the Books of Scripture genuine, or its text free from interpolations. There is no one spot in the

sius of Alexandria. (Johnson's U. S., vol. i., p. 306.) I do not know on what ground we admit the Epistles to the Thessalonians to be the writing of St. Paul, yet deny that the use of Altars is Apostolic.

Again : that the Eucharist is a Sacrifice is declared or implied by St. Clement of Rome, St. Paul's companion, by St. Justin, by St. Irenæus, by Tertullian, by St. Cyprian, and others. On the other hand, the Acts of the Apostles are perhaps alluded to by St. Polycarp, but are first distinctly noticed by St. Irenæus, then by three writers who came soon after (St. Clement of Alexandria, Tertullian, and the Letter from the Church of Lyons), and then not till the end of the two hundred years from St. John's death. Which has the best evidence, the Book of Acts, or the doctrine of the Eucharistic Sacrifice?

Again : much stress, as I have said, is laid by objectors on the fact that there is so little evidence concerning Catholic doctrine in the very first years of Christianity. Now, how does this objection stand, as regards the Canon of the New Testament ? The New Testament consists of twenty-seven books in all, though of varying import- ance. Of these, fourteen are not mentioned at all till from eighty to one hundred years after St. John's death, in which number are the Acts, the Second to the Co- rinthians, the Galatians, the Colossians, the Two to the

---

territory of theology but has been the scene of a battle. Anything has been ventured and believed in the heat of controversy ; but the ultimate appeal in such cases is the common sense of mankind. Ignatius says, " Be diligent to use one Eucharist, for there is one Flesh of our Lord Jesus Christ, and one cup for the union of His Blood ; one Altar, as one Bishop, together with the Presbytery and deacons, my fellow-servants."—*Ad Phil.* 4. Would it have entered into any one's mind, were it not for the necessities of his theory, to take Eucharist, Flesh, Cup, Blood, Bishop, Presbytery, Deacon, in their ecclesiastical meaning, as belonging to the Visible Church, and the one word Altar figuratively ?

Thessalonians, and St. James. Of the other thirteen, five, viz., St. John's Gospel, the Philippians, the First of Timothy, the Hebrews, and the First of John, are quoted but by one writer during the same period. Lastly, St. Irenæus, at the close of the second century, quotes all the books of the New Testament but five, and deservedly stands very high as a witness. Now, why may not so learned and holy a man, and so close on the Apostles, stand also as a witness of some doctrines which he takes for granted, as the invisible but real Presence in the Holy Eucharist, the use of Catholic tradition in ascertaining revealed truth, and the powers committed to the Church?

If men then will indulge that eclectic spirit which chooses part and rejects part of the primitive Church system, I do not see what is to keep them from choosing part and rejecting part of the Canon of Scripture.

3.

There are books, which sin as it would be in us to reject, I think any candid person would grant are presented to us under circumstances less promising than those which attend upon the Church doctrines. Take, for instance, the Book of Esther. This book is not quoted once in the New Testament. It was not admitted as canonical by two considerable Fathers, Melito and Gregory Nazianzen. It contains no prophecy; it has nothing on the surface to distinguish it from a mere ordinary history; nay, it has no mark on the surface of its even being a religious history. Not once does it mention the name of God or Lord, or any other name by which the God of Israel is designated. Again, when we inspect its contents, it cannot be denied that there are things in it which at first sight startle us, and make de-

mands on our faith. Why then do we receive it ? Because we have good reason from tradition to believe it to
be one of those which our Lord intended, when He spoke
of " the prophets." *

In like manner the Book of Ecclesiastes contains no
prophecy, is referred to in no part of the New Testament,
and contains passages which at first sight are startling.
Again : that most sacred Book, called the Song of Songs,
or Canticles, is a continued type from beginning to end.
Nowhere in Scripture, as I have already observed, are
we told that it is a type ; nowhere is it hinted that it is
not to be understood literally. Yet it is only as having
a deeper and hidden sense, that we are accustomed to
see a religious purpose in it. Moreover, it is not quoted
or alluded to once all through the New Testament. It
contains no prophecies. Why do we consider it divine ?
For the same reason ; because tradition informs us that
in our Saviour's time it was included under the title of
" the Psalms " : and our Saviour, in St. Luke's Gospel,
refers to "the Law, the Prophets, and *the Psalms*."

Objections as plausible, though different, might be
urged against the Epistles of St. James, St. Jude, the
Second of St. Peter, the Second and Third of St. John,
and the Book of Revelation.

Again : we are told that the doctrine of the mystical
efficacy of the Sacraments comes from the Platonic
philosophers, the ritual from the Pagans, and the Church
polity from the Jews. So they do ; that is, in a sense
in which much more also comes from the same sources.
Traces also of the doctrines of the Trinity, Incarnation,
and Atonement, may be found among heathens, Jews,
and philosophers; for the Almighty scattered through the
world, before His Son came, vestiges and gleams of His

* Luke xxiv. 44.

true Religion, and collected all the separated rays together, when He set Him on His holy hill to rule the day, and the Church, as the moon, to govern the night. In the sense in which the doctrine of the Trinity is Platonic, doubtless the doctrine of mysteries generally is Platonic also. But this by the way. What I have here to notice is, that the same supposed objection can be and has been made against the books of Scripture too viz., that they borrow from external sources. Unbelievers have accused Moses of borrowing his law from the Egyptians or other Pagans ; and elaborate comparisons have been instituted, on the part of believers also, by way of proving it ; though even if proved, and so far as proved, it would show nothing more than this,—that God, who gave His law to Israel absolutely and openly, had already given some portions of it to the heathen.

Again : an infidel historian accuses St. John of borrowing the doctrine of the Eternal Logos or Word from the Alexandrian Platonists.

Again : a theory has been advocated,—by whom I will not say,—to the effect that the doctrine of apostate angels, Satan and his hosts, was a Babylonian tenet, introduced into the Old Testament after the Jews' return from the Captivity ; that no allusion is made to Satan, as the head of the malignant angels, and as having set up a kingdom for himself against God, in any book written before the Captivity ; from which circumstance it may easily be made to follow, that those books of the Old Testament which were written after the Captivity are not plenarily inspired, and not to be trusted as canonical. Now, I own I am not at all solicitous to deny that this doctrine of an apostate Angel and his host was gained from Babylon : it might still be divine, neverthe-less. God who made the prophet's ass speak, and thereby instructed the prophet, might instruct His Churcn by means of heathen Babylon. *

In like manner, is no lesson intended to be conveyed to us by the remarkable words of the governor of the feast, upon the miracle of the water changed to wine ? " Every man at the beginning doth set forth good wine, and when men have well drunk, then that which is worse ; but Thou hast kept the good wine until now." † Yet at first sight they have not a very serious meaning. It does not therefore seem to me difficult, nay, nor even unlikely, that the prophets of Israel should, in the course of God's providence, have gained new truths from the heathen, among whom those truths lay corrupted. The Church of God in every age has been, as it were, on visitation through the earth, surveying, judging, sifting, selecting, and refining all matters of thoughts and practice; detecting what was precious amid what is ruined and refuse, and putting her seal upon it. There is no reason, then, why Daniel and Zechariah should not have been taught by the instrumentality of the Chaldeans. However, this is insisted on, and as if to the disparagement of the Jewish Dispensation by some persons ; and under the notion that its system was not only enlarged but altered at the era of the Captivity. And I certainly think it may be insisted on as plausibly as pagan customs are brought to illustrate and thereby to invalidate the ordinances of the Catholic Church ; though the proper explanation in the two cases is not exactly the same.

The objection I have mentioned is applied, in the quarter to which I allude, to the Books of Chronicles. These, it has already been observed, have before now been ascribed by sceptics to (what is called) priestly influence : here then is a second exceptional influence, a

* [This principle seems here too broadly enunciated.]   † John ii. 10.

second superstition. In the Second Book of Samuel it
is said, "the anger of the Lord was kindled against
Israel : and He moved David against them to say, Go,
number Israel and Judah." * On the other hand, in
Chronicles it is said, " *Satan* stood up against Israel, and
provoked David to number Israel."† On this a writer,
not of the English Church, says, " The author of the
Book of Chronicles . . . *availing himself* of the learning which he had acquired in the East, and *influenced* by
a suitable tenderness for the harmony of the Divine
Attributes, refers the act of temptation to the malignity
of the evil principle." You see in this way a blow is
also struck against the more ancient parts of the Old
Testament, as well as the more modern. The books
written before the Captivity are represented, as the whole
discussion would show, as containing a ruder, simpler,
less artificial theology ; those after the Captivity, a more
learned and refined : God's inspiration is excluded in
both cases.

The same consideration has been applied to determine
the date and importance of the Book of Job, which has
been considered, from various circumstances, external
and internal, not to contain a real history, but an Eastern
story.

But enough has been said on this part of the subject.

4.

It seems, then, that the objections which can be made
to the evidence for the Church doctrines are such as also
lie against the Canon of Scripture ; so that if they avail
against the one, they avail against both. If they avail
against both, we are brought to this strange conclusion,
that God has given us a Revelation, yet has revealed

* 2 Sam. xxxiv. 1. † 1 Chron. xxi. 1.

nothing,—that at great cost, and with much preparation, He has miraculously declared His will, that multitudes have accordingly considered they possessed it, yet that, after all, He has said nothing so clearly as to recommend itself as His to a cautious mind ; that nothing is so revealed as to be an essential part of the Revelation nothing plain enough to act upon, nothing so certain that we dare assert that the contrary is very much less certain.

Such a conclusion is a practical refutation of the objection which leads to it. It surely cannot be meant that we should be undecided all our days. We were made for action, and for right action,—for thought, and for true thought. Let us live while we live ; let us be alive and doing ; let us act on what we have, since we have not what we wish. Let us believe what we do not see and know. Let us forestall knowledge by faith. Let us maintain before we have demonstrated. This seeming paradox is the secret of happiness. Why should we be unwilling to go by faith ? We do all things in this world by faith in the word of others. By faith only we know our position in the world, our circumstances, our rights and privileges, our fortunes, our parents, our brothers and sisters, our age, our mortality. Why should Religion be an exception ? Why should we be unwilling to use for heavenly objects what we daily use for earthly ? Why will we not discern, what it is so much our interest to discern, that trust, in the first instance, in what Providence sets before us in religious matters, is His will and our duty ; that thus it is He leads us into all truth, not by doubting, but by believing ; that thus He speaks to us, by the instrumentality of what seems accidental ; that He sanctifies what He sets before us, shallow or weak as it may be in itself, for His high purposes ; that

most systems have enough of truth in them, to make
it better for us, when we have no choice besides, and
cannot discriminate, to begin by taking all (that is not
plainly immoral) than by rejecting all ; that He will not
deceive us if we thus trust in Him.   Though the received
system of religion in which we are born were as unsafe
as the sea when St. Peter began to walk on it, yet " be
not afraid."   He who could make St. Peter walk the
waves, could make even a corrupt or defective creed a
mode and way of leading us into truth, even were ours
such ; much more can He teach us by the witness of the
Church Catholic.   It is far more probable that her witness should be true, whether about the Canon or the
Creed, than that God should have left us without any
witness at all.

7.

Internal Difficulties of the Canon and the Catholic Creed, compared.

I SHALL now finish the subject I have commenced, the parallel between the objections adducible against the Catholic system, and those against the Canon of Scripture. It will be easily understood, that I am not attempting any formal and full discussion of the subject, but offering under various general heads such suggestions as may be followed out by those who will. The objections to the evidence for the Canon have been noticed; now let us consider objections that may be made to its contents.

I.

Perhaps the main objection taken to the Church system, is the dislike which men feel of its doctrines. They call them the work of priestcraft, and in that word is summed up all that they hate in them. Priestcraft is the art of gaining power over men by appeals to their consciences; its instrument is mystery; its subject-matter, superstitious feeling. "Now the Church doctrines," it is urged, "invest a certain number of indifferent things with a new and extraordinary power, beyond sense, beyond reason, beyond nature, a power over the soul; and they put the exclusive possessions and use of the things thus distinguished into the hands of the Clergy. Such, for instance, is the Creed; some mysterious benefit is supposed to result from holding it, even though with but a partial comprehension, and the Clergy are practically its sole expounders. Such still more are the Sacraments, which the Clergy only administer, and which are supposed to effect some supernatural change in the soul, and to convey some supernatural gift." This then is the antecedent exception taken against the Catholic doctrines, that they are mysterious, tending to superstition, and to dependence on a particular set of men. And this object is urged, not merely as a reason for demanding fair proof of what is advanced, but as a reason for refusing to listen to any proof whatever, as if it fairly created an insurmountable presumption against the said doctrines.

Now I say, in like manner, were it not for our happy reverence for the Canon of Scripture, we should take like exception to many things in Scripture ; and, since we do not, neither ought we, consistently, to take this exception to the Catholic system ; but if we do take such grounds against that system, there is nothing but the strength of habit, good feeling, and our Lord's controlling grace, to keep us from using them against Scripture also. This I shall now attempt to show, and with that view, shall cite various passages in Scripture which, to most men of this generation, will appear at first sight strange, superstitious, incredible, and extreme. If then, in spite of these, Scripture is nevertheless from God, so again, in spite of similar apparent difficulties, the Catholic system may be from Him also ; and what the argument comes to is this, that the minds of none of us are in such a true state, as to warrant us in judging peremptorily in every case what is from God and what is not. We shrink from the utterances of His providence with offence, as if they were not His, in consequence of our inward ears being attuned to false harmonies. Now for some instances of what I mean.

2.

1. I conceive, were we not used to the Scripture narrative, that we should be startled at the accounts there given us of demoniacs.—For instance : " And He asked him, What is thy name ?   And He answered, *My name is Legion,* for we are many."*—Again, consider the passage, " When the unclean spirit is gone out of a man, he walketh through dry places, seeking rest, and findeth none," † etc. ; and in like manner, the account of the damsel who was " possessed of a spirit of divination," or " Python," that is, of a heathen god, in Acts xvi. ; and in connexion with this, St. Paul's assertion " that the things which the Gentiles sacrifice, they sacrifice to devils and not to God,"‡ and this as being so literally true that he deduces a practical conclusion from it, " I would not that ye should have fellowship with devils."   But, as regards this instance, we are not at all driven to conjecture, but we know it is really the case, that they who allow themselves to treat the inspired text freely, do at once explain away, or refuse to admit its accounts of this mysterious interference of evil spirits in the affairs of men.   Let those then see to it, who call the Fathers credulous for recording similar narratives.   If they find fault with the evidence, that is an intelligible objection ; but the common way with objectors is at once and before examination to charge on the narrators of such accounts childish superstition and credulity.

2. If we were not used to the narrative, I conceive we should be very unwilling to receive the account of the serpent speaking to Eve, or its being inhabited by an

* Mark v. 9.   † Matt. xii. 43.   ‡ 1 Cor. x. 20.

evil spirit ; or, again, of the devils being sent into the swine. We should scoff at such narratives, as fanciful and extravagant. Let us only suppose that, instead of being found in Scripture, they were found in some legend of the middle ages ; should we merely ask for evidence, or simply assume that there was none ? Should we think that it was a case for evidence one way or the other ? Should we not rather say, " This is intrinsically incredible ?—it supersedes the necessity of examining into evidence, it decides the case." Should we allow the strangeness of the narrative merely to act as suspending our belief, and throwing the burden of proof on the other side, or should we not rather suffer it to settle the question for us ? Again, should we have felt less distrust in the history of Balaam's ass speaking ? Should we have been reconciled to the account of the Holy Ghost appearing in a bodily shape, and that apparently the shape of an irrational animal, a dove ? And, again, though we might bear the figure of calling our Saviour a lamb, if it occurred once, as if to show that He was the antitype of the Jewish sacrifices, yet, unless we were used to it, would there not be something repugnant to our present habits of mind in calling again and again our Saviour by the name of a brute animal ? Unless we were used to it, I conceive it would hurt and offend us much to read of " glory and honour " being ascribed to Him that sitteth upon the Throne and to the Lamb, as being a sort of idolatry, or at least an unadvised way of speaking. It seems to do too much honour to an inferior creature, and to dishonour Christ. You will see this, by trying to substitute any other animal, however mild and gentle. It is said that one difficulty in translating the New Testament into some of the oriental languages actually is this, that the word in them for Lamb does not carry with it the associations which it does in languages which have had their birth in Christianity. Now we have a remarkable parallel to this in the impression produced by another figure, which was in use in primitive times, when expressed in our own language. The ancients formed an acrostic upon our Lord's Greek titles as the Son of God, the Saviour of men, and in consequence called Him from the first letters ἰχθὺς, or "fish." Hear how a late English writer speaks of it. "This contemptible and disgusting quibble originated in certain verses of one of the pseudo-sibyls. . . . I know of no figure which so revoltingly degrades the person of the Son of God." Such as this is the nature of the comment made in the farther east on the sacred image of the Lamb.

But without reference to such peculiar associations, which vary with place and person, there is in the light of reason a strangeness, perhaps, in God's allowing material symbols of Himself at all; and, again, a greater strangeness in His vouchsafing to take a brute animal as the name of His Son, and bidding us ascribe praise to it. Now it does not matter whether we take all these instances separate or together. Separate, they are strange enough; put them together, you have a law of God's dealings, which accounts indeed for each separate instance, yet does not make it less strange that the brute creation should have so close a connexion with God's spiritual and heavenly kingdom. Here, moreover, it is in place to make mention of the "four beasts" spoken of in the Apocalypse as being before God's throne. Translate the word "living thing," as you may do, yet the circumstance is not less startling. They were respectively like a lion, calf, man, and eagle. To this may be added the figure of the Cherubim in the

Jewish law, which is said to have been a symbol made up of limbs of the same animals. Is it not strange that Angels should be represented under brute images? Consider, then, if God has thus made use of brutes in His supernatural acts and in His teaching, as real instruments and as symbols of spiritual things, what is there strange antecedently in supposing He makes use of the inanimate creation also? If Balaam's ass instructed Balaam, what is there fairly to startle us in the Church's doctrine, that the water of Baptism cleanses from sin, that eating the consecrated Bread is eating His Body, or that oil may be blessed for spiritual purposes, as is still done in our Church in the case of a coronation? Of this I feel sure, that those who consider the doctrines of the Church incredible, will soon, if they turn their thoughts steadily that way, feel a difficulty in the serpent that tempted Eve, and the ass that admonished Balaam.

3.

3. We cannot, it seems, believe that water applied to the body really is God's instrument in cleansing the soul from sin; do we believe that, at Bethesda, an Angel gave the pool a miraculous power? What God has done once, He may do again; that is, there is no antecedent improbability in His connecting real personal benefits to us with arbitrary outward means. Again, what should we say, unless we were familarized with it, to the story of Naaman bathing seven times in the Jordan? or rather to the whole system of mystical signs :—the tree which Moses cast into the waters to sweeten them ; Elisha's throwing meal into the pot of poisonous herbs ; and our Saviour's breathing, making clay, and the like ? Indeed, is not the whole of the Bible, Old and New Testament, engaged in a system of outward signs with

hidden realities under them, which in the Church's
teaching is only continued? Is it not certain, then, that
those who stumble at the latter as incredible, will
stumble at the former too, as soon as they learn just so
much irreverence as to originate objections as well as to
be susceptible of them? I cannot doubt that, unless we
were used to the Sacraments, we should be objecting,
not only to the notion of their conveying virtue, but to
their observance altogether, viewed as mere badges and
memorials. They would be called Oriental, suited to
a people of warm imagination, suited to the religion of
other times, but too symbolical, poetical, or (as some
might presume to say) theatrical for us ; as if there
were something far more plain, solid, sensible, practical,
and edifying in a sermon, or an open profession, or a
prayer.

4. Consider the accounts of virtue going out of our
Lord, and that, in the case of the woman with the issue
of blood, as it were by a natural law, without a distinct
application on His part ;—of all who touched the hem
of His garment being made whole ; and further, of
handkerchiefs and aprons being impregnated with healing
virtue by touching St. Paul's body, and of St. Peter's
shadow being earnestly sought out,—in the age when
religion was purest, and the Church's condition most like
a heaven upon earth. Can we hope that these passages
will not afford matter of objection to the mind, when
once it has brought itself steadily to scrutinize the evidence for the inspiration of the Gospels and Acts? Will
it not be obvious to say, " St. Luke was not an Apostle ;
and I do not believe this account of the handkerchiefs
and aprons, though I believe the Book of Acts as a whole."
Next, when the mind gets bolder, it will address itself to
the consideration of the account of the woman with the

issue of blood. Now it is not wonderful that she, poor ignorant woman (as men speak), in deplorable ignorance of spiritual religion (alas! that words should be so misused), dark, and superstitious,—it is not wonderful, I say, that she should expect a virtue from touching our Lord's garment ; but that she should obtain it by means of this *opus operatum* of merely touching, and again that He should even commend her faith, will be judged impossible. The notion of virtue going out of Him will be considered as Jewish, pagan, or philosophical.

Yes ; the outline of the story will be believed,—the main fact, the leading idea,—not the details. Indeed, if persons have already thought it inherently incredible that the hands of Bishop or priest should impart a power, or grace, or privilege, if they have learned to call it profane, and (as they speak) blasphemous to teach this with the early Church, how can it be less so, to consider that God gave virtue to a handkerchief, or apron, or garment, though our Lord's ? What was it, after all, but a mere earthly substance, made of vegetable or animal material ? How was it more holy because He wore it ? *He* was holy, not *it ;* it did not gain holiness by being near Him. Nay : do they not already lay this down as a general principle, that, to suppose He diffuses from His Person heavenly virtue, is a superstition ? do not they, on this ground, object to the Catholic doctrine of the Eucharist ; and on what other ground do they deny that the Blessed Virgin, whom all but heretics have ever called the Mother of God, was most holy in soul and body, from her ineffable proximity to God ? He who gave to the perishing and senseless substances of wool or cotton that grace of which it was capable, should not He rather communicate of His higher spiritual perfections to her in whose bosom He lay, or to those

who now possess Him through the Sacramental means
He has appointed?

5. I conceive that, if men indulge themselves in criticizing, they will begin to be offended at the passage in
the Apocalyse, which speaks of the "number of the
beast." Indeed, it is probable that they will reject that
book of Scripture altogether, not sympathizing with the
severe tone of doctrine which runs through it. Again:
there is something very surprising in the importance
attached to the Name of God and Christ in Scripture.
The Name of Jesus is said to work cures and frighten
away devils. I anticipate that this doctrine will become
a stone of stumbling to those who set themselves to inquire into the trustworthiness of the separate parts of
Scripture. For instance, the narrative of St. Peter's
cure of the impotent man, in the early chapters of the
Acts:—first, "Silver and gold," he says, "have I none;
but such as I have, give I thee; In the Name of Jesus
Christ of Nazareth, rise up and walk." Then, "And
His Name, through faith in His Name, hath made this
man strong." Then the question "By what power, or by
what *name*, have ye done this?" Then the answer, "By
the Name of Jesus Christ of Nazareth . . . even by it
doth this man now stand here before you whole . . .
there is none other name under heaven given among men
whereby we must be saved." Then the threat, that the
Apostles should not "speak at all, nor teach in the Name
of Jesus." Lastly, their prayer that God would grant
"that signs and wonders might be done by the Name of
His Holy Child Jesus." In connexion with which must
be considered, St. Paul's declaration, "that in the Name
of Jesus every knee should bow." * Again: I conceive
that the circumstances of the visitation of the Blessed

* Acts iii. 4   Phil. ii 10

Virgin to Elizabeth would startle us considerably if we lost our faith in Scripture. Again : can we doubt that the account of Christ's ascending into heaven will not be received by the science of this age, when it is carefully considered what is implied in it ? Where is heaven ? Beyond all the stars ? If so, it would take years for any natural body to get there. We say, that with God all things are possible. But this age, wise in its own eyes, has already decided the contrary, in main-taining, as it does, that He who virtually annihilated the distance between earth and heaven, on His Son's ascen-sion, cannot annihilate it in the celebration of the Holy Communion, so as to make us present with Him, though He be on God's right hand in heaven.

4.

6. Further, unless we were used to the passage, I cannot but think that we should stumble greatly at the account of our Lord's temptation by Satan. Putting aside other considerations, dwell awhile on the thought of Satan showing " *all* the kingdoms of the world in a moment of time." * What is meant by this ? How did he show all, and in a moment ? and if by a mere illusion, why from the top of a high mountain ?

Or again : consider the account of our Saviour's bidding St. Peter catch a fish in order to find money in it, to pay tribute with. What should we say if this narrative occurred in the Apocrypha ? Should we not speak of it as an evident fiction ? and are we likely to do less, whenever we have arrived at a proper pitch of unscru-pulousness, and what is nowadays called critical acumen, in analyzing and disposing of what we have hitherto re-ceived as divine ? Again : I conceive that the blood and

* Luke iv. 5:

₊

water which issued from our Saviour's side, particularly
taken with the remarkable comment upon it in St. John's
Epistle, would be disbelieved, if men were but consistent
in their belief and disbelief. The miracle would have
been likened to many which occur in Martyrologies, and
the inspired comment would have been called obscure
and fanciful, as on a par with various doctrinal interpretations in the Fathers, which carry forsooth their own
condemnation with them.   Again : the occurrence mentioned by St. John, "Then came there a voice from
heaven, saying, I have both glorified it (My Name), and
will glorify it again. The people, therefore, that stood
by, and heard it, said that it thundered ; others said,
An Angel spake to him : " * this, I conceive, would soon
be looked upon as suspicious, did men once begin to
examine the claims of the Canon upon our faith.

Or again : to refer to the Old Testament.   I conceive
that the history of the Deluge, the ark, and its inhabitants, will appear to men of modern tempers more and
more incredible, the longer and more minutely it is
dwelt upon.   Or, again, the narrative of Jonah and the
whale.   Once more, the following narrative will surely
be condemned also, as bearing on its face evident marks
of being legendary : "And the sons of the prophets said
unto Elisha, Behold now, the place where we dwell with
thee is too strait for us.   Let us go, we pray thee, unto
Jordan, and take thence every man a beam, and let us
make us a place there, where we may dwell.   And he answered, Go ye.   And one said, Be content, I pray thee,
and go with thy servants.   And he answered, I will go.
So he went with them.   And when they came to Jordan, they cut down wood.   But as one was felling a
beam, the axe-head fell into the water ; and he cried,

* 2 John xii. 28, 29.

and said, Alas, master! for it was borrowed. And the man of God said, Where fell it? And he showed him the place. And he cut down a stick, and cast it in thither; and the iron did swim. Therefore said he, Take it up to thee. And he put out his hand, and took it."*

5.

7. Having mentioned Elisha, I am led to say a word or two upon his character. Men of this age are full of their dread of priestcraft and priestly ambition; and they speak and feel as if the very circumstance of a person claiming obedience upon a divine authority was priestcraft and full of evil. They speak as if it was against the religious rights of man (for some such rights are supposed to be possessed by sinners, even by those who disown the doctrine of the political rights of man), as if it were essentially an usurpation for one man to claim spiritual power over another. They do not ask for the voucher of his claim, for his commission, but think the claim absurd. They so speak, that any one who heard them, without knowing the Bible, would think that Almighty God had never "given such power unto men." Now, what would such persons say to Elisha's character and conduct? Let me recount some few passages in his history, in the Second Book of Kings, and let us bear in mind what has been already observed of the character of the Books of Chronicles. When the little children out of Bethel mocked him, "he cursed them in the name of the Lord."† This was his first act after entering on his office. Again: Jehoram, the son of Ahab, put away Baal, and walked not in the sins of his father and his mother; but because he did not put away

* 2 Kings vi. 1—7.　　　　　† 2 Kings ii. 23.

the false worship of Jeroboam, but kept to his calves, his self-appointed priests, altars, and holy days, which he probably thought a little sin, when he was in distress, and called upon Elisha, Elisha said, " What have I to do with thee ? Get thee to the prophets of thy father, and to the prophets of thy mother : " * and went on to say, that, but for the presence of good Jehoshaphat, " I would not look toward thee nor see thee." This was taking (what would now be called) a high tone. Again: the Shunammite was a great woman; he was poor. She got her husband's leave to furnish a " little chamber" for him, not in royal style, but as for a poor minister of God. It had "a bed and a table and a stool and a candlestick," and when he came that way he availed himself of it. The world would think that she was the patron, and he ought to be humble, and to know his place.   But observe his language on one occasion of his lodging there. He said to his servant, " Call this Shunammite." When she came, she, the mistress of the house, " stood before him." He did not speak to her, but bade his servant speak, and then she retired ; then he held a consultation with his servant, and then he called her again, and she " stood in the door ; " then he pro- mised her a son. Again : Naaman was angered that Elisha did not show him due respect : he only sent him a message, and bade him wash and be clean. After- wards we find the prophet interposing in political matters in Israel and Syria.

Now, it is not to the purpose to account for all this, by saying he worked miracles. Are miracles necessary for being a minister of God ? Are miracles the only way in which a claim can be recognized ? Is a man the higher minister, the more miracles he does ? Are we to

* Ib. iii. **13.**

honour only those who minister temporal miracles, and to be content to eat and be filled with the loaves and fishes ? Are there no higher miracles than visible ones ? John the Baptist did no miracles, yet he too claimed, and gained, the obedience of the Jews. Miracles prove a man to be God's minister ; they do not make him God's minister. No matter how a man is proved to come from God, if he is known to come from God. If Christ is with His ministers, according to His promise, even to the end of the world, so that he that despiseth them despiseth Him, then, though they do no miracles, they are in office as great as Elisha. And if Baptism be the cleansing and quickening of the dead soul, to say nothing of Holy Eucharist, they do work miracles. If God's ministers are then only to be honoured when we see that they work miracles, where is place for faith ? Are we not under a dispensation of faith, not of sight ? Was Elisha great because he was seen to work miracles, or because he could, and did, work them ? Is God's minister a proud priest now, for acting as if he came from God, if he does come from Him ? Yet men of this generation, without inquiring into his claims, would most undoubtedly call him impostor and tyrant, proud, arrogant, profane, and Antichristian, nay, Antichrist himself, if he, a Christian minister, assume one-tenth part of Elisha's state. Yes, Antichrist ;—" If they have called the Master of the house Beelzebub, how much more shall they call them of His household ? "*

8. St. John the Baptist's character, I am persuaded, would startle most people, if they were not used to Scripture ; and when men begin to doubt about the integrity of Scripture, it will be turned against the authenticity or the authority of the particular passages which

* Matt. x. 25.

relate to it.   Let us realize to ourselves a man living on locusts and wild honey, and with a hair shirt on, bound by a leathern girdle.   Our Lord indeed bids us avoid outward show, and therefore the ostentation of such austerity would be wrong now, of course; but what is there to show that the thing itself would be wrong, if a person were moved to do it?   Does not our Saviour expressly say, with reference to the austerities of St. John's disciples, that after His departure His own disciples shall resemble them,—"then shall they fast"?   Yet, I suppose, most persons would cry out now against the very semblance of the Baptist's life ; and why?   Those who gave a reason would perhaps call it Jewish.   Yet what had St. John to do with the Jews, whose religion was one, not of austerity, but of joyousness and feasting, and that by divine permission?   Surely the same feeling which would make men condemn an austere life now, if individuals attempted it, which makes them, when they read of such instances in the early Church, condemn it, would lead the same parties to condemn it in St. John, were they not bound by religious considerations ; and, therefore, I say, if ever the time comes that men begin to inquire into the divinity of the separate parts of Scripture, as they do now scrutinize the separate parts of the Church system, they will no longer be able to acquiesce in St. John's character and conduct as simply right and religious.

6.

9. Lastly, I will mention together a number of doctrinal passages, which, though in Scripture, they who deny that the Fathers contain the pure Gospel, hardly would consider parts of it, if they were but consistent in their free speculations.   Such are St. Paul's spiritualizing

the history of Sarah and Hagar; his statement of the
fire trying every man's work in the day of judgment;
his declaring that women must have their heads covered
in church, "because of the Angels;" his charging
Timothy "before the elect Angels;" his calling the
Church "the pillar and ground of the Truth;" the tone
of his observations on celibacy, which certainly, if written
by any of the Fathers, would in this day have been cited
in proof of "the mystery of iniquity" (by which they
mean Romanism) "already working" in an early age;
St. John's remarkable agreement of tone with him in a
passage in the Apocalypse, not to say our Lord's; our
Lord's account of the sin against the Holy Ghost, viewed
in connexion with St. Paul's warning against falling
away, after being enlightened, and St. John's notice of
a sin which is unto death—(this would be considered
opposed to the free grace of the Gospel); our Lord's
strong words about the arduousness of a rich man's getting to heaven; what He says about binding and loosing; about a certain kind of evil spirit going out only by
fasting and prayer; His command to turn the left cheek
to him who smites the right; St. Peter's saying that we
are partakers of a divine nature; and what he says
about Christ's "going and preaching to the spirits in
prison;" St. Matthew's account of the star which guided
the wise men to Bethlehem; St. Paul's statement, that
a woman is saved through childbearing; St. John's
directions how to treat those who hold not "the doctrine
of Christ;"—these and a multitude of other passages
would be adduced, not to prove that Christianity was
not true, or that Christ was not the Son of God, or the
Bible not inspired, or not on *the whole* genuine and
authentic, but that every part of it was not *equally*
divine; that portions, books, particularly of the Old

Testament, were not so; that we must use our own
judgment. Nay, as time went on, perhaps it would be
said that the Old Testament altogether was not inspired,
only the New—nay, perhaps only parts of the New, not
certain books which were for a time doubted in some
ancient Churches, or not the Gospels according to St.
Mark and St. Luke, nor the Acts, because not the
writing of Apostles, or not St. Paul's reasonings, only his
conclusions. Next, it would be said, that no reliance
can safely be placed on single texts; and so men would
proceed, giving up first one thing, then another, till it
would become a question what they gained of any kind,
what they considered they gained, from Christianity as a
definite revelation or a direct benefit. They would come
to consider its publication mainly as an historical event
occurring eighteen hundred years since, which modified
or altered the course of human thought and society, and
thereby altered what would otherwise have been our
state; as something infused into an existing mass, and
influencing us in the improved tone of the institutions
in which we find ourselves, rather than as independent,
substantive, and one, specially divine in its origin, and
directly acting upon us.

This is what the Age is coming to, and I wish it observed. We know it denies the existence of the Church
as a divine institution: it denies that Christianity has
been cast into any particular social mould. Well: but
this, I say, is not all; it is rapidly tending to deny the
existence of any system of Christianity either; any creed,
doctrine, philosophy, or by whatever other name we de-
signate it. Hitherto it has been usual, indeed, to give
up the Church, and to speak only of the covenant, religion, creed, matter, or system of the Gospel; to consider
the Gospel as a sort of literature or philosophy, open for

all to take and appropriate, not confined to any set of men, yet still a real, existing system of religion. This has been the approved line of opinion in our part of the world for the last hundred and fifty years ; but now a further step is about to be taken. The view henceforth is to be, that Christianity does not exist in documents, any more than in institutions ; in other words, the Bible will be given up as well as the Church. It will be said that the benefit which Christianity has done to the world, and which its Divine Author meant it should do, was to give an impulse to society, to infuse a spirit, to direct, control, purify, enlighten the mass of human thought and action, but not to be a separate and definite something, whether doctrine or association, existing ob-jectively, integral, and with an identity, and for ever, and with a claim upon our homage and obedience. And all this fearfully coincides with the symptoms in other directions of the spread of a Pantheistic spirit, that is, the religion of beauty, imagination, and philosophy, without constraint moral or intellectual, a religion speculative and self-indulgent. Pantheism, indeed, is the great deceit which awaits the Age to come.

7.

Let us then look carefully, lest we fall in with the evil tendencies of the times in which our lot is cast. God has revealed Himself to us that we might believe : surely His Revelation is something great and important. He who made it, meant it to be a blessing even to the end of the world : this is true, if any part of Scripture is true. From beginning to end, Scripture implies that God has spoken, and that it is right, our duty, our interest, our safety to believe. Whether, then, we have in our hands the means of exactly proving this or that part of Scripture to be genuine or not, whether we have in our hands the complete proofs of all the Church doctrines, we are more sure that hearty belief in something is our duty, than that it is not our duty to believe those doctrines and that Scripture as we have received them. If our choice lies between accepting all and rejecting all, which I consider it does when persons are consistent, no man can hesitate which alternative is to be taken.

So far then every one of us may say,—Our Heavenly Father gave the world a Revelation in Christ; we are baptized into His Name. He wills us to believe, *because* He has given us a Revelation. He who wills us to believe *must* have given us an object to believe. Whether I can prove this or that part to my satisfaction, yet, since I can prove all in a certain way, and cannot separate part from part satisfactorily, I cannot be wrong in taking the whole. I am sure that, if there be error, which I have yet to learn, it must be, not in principles, but in mere matters of detail. If there be corruption or human addition in what comes to me, it must be in little matters, not in great. On the whole, I cannot but have God's Revelation, and that, in what I see before me, with whatever incidental errors. I am sure, on the other hand, that the way which the Age follows cannot be right, for it tends to destroy Revelation altogether. Whether this or that doctrine, this or that book of Scripture is fully provable or not, that line of objection to it cannot be right, which, when pursued, destroys Church, Creed, Bible altogether,—which obliterates the very Name of Christ from the world. It is then God's will, under my circumstances, that I should believe what, in the way of Providence, He has put before me to believe. God will not deceive me. I can trust Him. Either every part of the system is pure truth, or, if this or that be an addition, He will (I humbly trust and believe) make such addition harmless to my soul, if I thus throw myself on His mercy with a free and confiding spirit. Doubt is misery and sin, but belief has received Christ's blessing.

This is the reflection which I recommend to all, so far as they have not the means of examining the Evidences for the Church, Creed, and Canon of Scripture; but I must not be supposed to imply, because I have so put the matter, that those who have the means, will not find abundant evidence for the divinity of all three.

8.

Difficulties of Jewish and of Christian Faith compared.

I HAVE been engaged for some time in showing that the Canon of Scripture rests on no other foundation than the Catholic doctrines rest; that those who dispute the latter should, if they were consistent,—will, when they learn to be consistent,—dispute the former; that in both cases we believe, mainly, because the Church of the fourth and fifth centuries unanimously believed, and that we have at this moment to defend our belief in the Catholic doctrines merely because they come first, are the first object of attack; and that if we were not defending our belief in them, we should at this very time be defending our belief in the Canon. Let no one then hope for peace in this day; let no one attempt to purchase it by concession;—vain indeed would be that concession. Give up the Catholic doctrines, and what do you gain? an attack upon the Canon, with (to say the least) the same disadvantages on your part, or rather, in fact, with much greater; for the circumstance that you have already given up the Doctrines as if insufficiently evidenced in primitive times, will be an urgent call on you, in consistency, to give up the Canon too. And besides, the Church doctrines may also be proved from Scripture, but no one can say that the Canon of Scripture itself can be proved from Scripture to be a Canon; no one can say, that Scripture anywhere enumerates all the books of which it is composed, and puts its seal upon them ever so indirectly, even if it might allowably bear witness to itself.

I.

But here, before proceeding to make some reflections on the state of the case, I will make one explanation, and notice one objection.

In the first place, then, I must explain myself, when I say that we depend for the Canon and Creed upon the fourth and fifth centuries. We depend upon them thus : As to Scripture, former centuries certainly do not speak distinctly, frequently, or unanimously, except of some chief books, as the Gospels : but still we see in them, as we believe, an ever-growing tendency and approximation to that full agreement which we find in the fifth. The testimony given at the latter date is the limit to which all that has been before given converges. For instance, it is commonly said, *Exceptio probat regulam ;* when we have reason to think, that a writer or an age *would* have witnessed so and so, but for this or that, and this or that were mere accidents of his position, then he or it may be said to tend towards such testimony. In this way the first centuries tend towards the fifth. Viewing the matter as one of moral evidence, we seem to see in the testimony of the fifth the very testimony which every preceding century gave, accidents excepted, such as the present loss of documents once extant, or the then existing misconceptions, which want of intercourse between the Churches occasioned. The fifth century acts as a comment on the obscure text of the centuries before it, and brings out a meaning which, with the help of that comment, any candid person sees really to belong to them.

And in the same way as regards the Catholic Creed,

though there is not so much to explain and account for. Not so much, for no one, I suppose, will deny that in the Fathers of the fourth century it is as fully developed, and as unanimously adopted, as it is in the fifth century; and, again, there had been no considerable doubts about any of its doctrines previously, as there were about the Epistle to the Hebrews or the Apocalypse : or if any, they were started by individuals, as Origen's about eternal punishment, not by Churches,—or they were at once condemned by the general Church, as in the case of heresies,—or they were not about any primary doctrine, for instance, the Incarnation or Atonement ; and all this, in spite of that want of free intercourse which did occasion doubts about portions of the Canon. Yet, in both cases, we have at first an inequality of evidence as regards the constituent parts of what was afterwards universally received as a whole,—the doctrine of the Holy Trinity, for instance, and, on the other hand, the four Gospels being generally witnessed from the first ; but certain other doctrines, (as the necessity of infant baptism,) being at first rather practised and assumed, than insisted on, and certain books, (as the Epistle to the Hebrews and the Apocalypse,) doubted, or not admitted, in particular countries. And as the unanimity of the fifth century as regards the Canon, clears up and overcomes all previous differences, so the abundance of the fourth as to the Creed interprets, develops, and combines all that is recondite or partial, in previous centuries, as to doctrine, acting in a parallel way as a comment, not, indeed, as in the case of the Canon, upon a perplexed and disordered, but upon a concise text. In both cases, the after centuries contain but the termination and summing up of the testimony of the foregoing.

2.

So much as to the explanation which I proposed to give; the objection I have to notice is this. It is said, that the Fathers might indeed bear witness to a document such as the books of Scripture are, and yet not be good witnesses to a doctrine, which is, after all, but an opinion. A document or book is something external to the mind; it is an object that any one can point at, and if a person about two or three hundred years after Christ, said, "This book of the New Testament has been accounted sacred ever since it was written," we could be as sure of what he said, as we are at the present day, that the particular church we now use was built at a certain date, or that the date in the title-page of a certain printed book is trustworthy. On the other hand, it is urged, a doctrine does not exist, except in the mind of this or that person, it is not a thing you can point at, it is not a something which two persons see at once,—it is an opinion; and every one has his own opinion. I have an opinion, you have an opinion;—if on comparing notes we think we agree, we call it the same opinion, but it is not the same really, only called the same, because similar; and, in fact, probably no two such opinions really do coincide in all points. Every one describes and colours from his own mind. No one then can bear witness to a doctrine being ancient. Strictly speaking, that which he contemplates, witnesses, speaks about, began with himself; it is a birth of his own mind. He may, indeed, have caught it from another, but it is not the same as another man's doctrine, unless one flame is the same as a second kindled from it; and as flame communicated from spirit to sulphur, from sulphur to wood, from wood to coal, from coal to charcoal, burns variously, so, true as it may be that certain doctrines originated in the Apostles, it does not follow that the particular form in which we possess them, originated with the Apostles also. Such is the objection ; that the Fathers, if honest men, may be credible witnesses of facts, but not, however honest, witnesses to doctrines.

It admits of many answers :—I will mention two.

1. It does not rescue the Canon from the difficulties of its own evidence, which is its professed object ; for it is undeniable that there are books of Scripture, which in the first centuries particular Fathers, nay, particular Churches did not receive. What is the good of contrasting testimony to facts with testimony to opinions, when we have not in the case of the Canon that clear testimony to the facts in dispute, which the objection supposes ? Lower, as you will, the evidence for the Creed ; you do nothing thereby towards raising the evidence for the Canon. The first Fathers, in the midst of the persecutions, had not, as I have said, time and opportunity to ascertain always what was inspired and what was not ; and, since nothing but an agreement of many, of different countries, will prove to us what the Canon is, we must betake ourselves of necessity to the fourth and fifth centuries, to those centuries which did hold those very doctrines, which, it seems, are to be rejected as superstitions and corruptions. But if the Church then was in that miserable state of superstition, which belief in those doctrines is supposed to imply, then I must contend, that blind bigotry and ignorance were not fit judges of what was inspired and what was not. I will not trust the judgment of a worldly-minded partizan, or a crafty hypocrite, or a credulous fanatic in this matter. Unless then you allow those centuries to be tolerably free from doctrinal corruptions, I conceive, you cannot use them as witnesses of the canonicity of the Old and

New Testament, as we now have them; but, if you do consider the fourth and fifth centuries enlightened enough to decide on the Canon, then I want to know why you call them not enlightened in point of doctrine. The only reason commonly given is, that their Christianity contains many notions and many usages and rites not *in* Scripture, and which, because not *in* Scripture, are to be considered, it seems, as if *against* Scripture. But this surely is no sound argument, unless it is true also that the canonicity itself of the Old and New Testament, not being declared *in* Scripture, is therefore unscriptural. I consider then that the man, whether we call him cautious or sceptical, who quarrels with the testimony for Catholic doctrine, because a doctrine is a mere opinion, and not an objective fact, ought also in consistency to quarrel with the testimony for the Canon, as being that of an age which is superstitious as a teacher and uncritical as a judge.

2. But again: the doctrines of the Church are after all not mere matters of opinion; they were not in early times mere ideas in the mind to which no one could appeal, each individual having his own, but they were external facts, quite as much as the books of Scripture; —how so? Because they were embodied in rites and ceremonies. A usage, custom, or monument, has the same kind of identity, is in the same sense common property, and admits of a common appeal, as a book. When a writer appeals to the custom of the Sign of the Cross, or the Baptism of infants, or the Sacrifice or the Consecration of the Eucharist, or Episcopal Ordination, he is not speaking of an opinion in his mind, but of something external to it, and is as trustworthy as when he says that the Acts of the Apostles is written by St. Luke. Now such usages are symbols of common,

not individual opinions, and more or less involve the doctrines they symbolize. Is it not implied, for instance, in the fact of priests only consecrating the Eucharist, that it is a gift which others have not? in the Eucharist being offered to God, that it *is* an offering? in penance being exacted of offenders, that it is right to impose it? in children being exorcised, that they are by nature children of wrath, and inhabited by Satan? On the other hand, when the Fathers witness to the inspiration of Scripture, they are surely as much witnessing to a mere doctrine,—not to the book itself, but to an opinion,—as when they bear witness to the grace of Baptism.

Again, the Creed is a document the same in kind as Scripture, though its wording be not fixed and invariable, or its language. It admits of being appealed to, and is appealed to by the early Fathers, as Scripture is. If Scripture was written by the Apostles, (as it is,) because the Fathers say so, why was not the Creed taught by the Apostles, because the Fathers say so? The Creed is no opinion in the mind, but a form of words pronounced many times a day, at every baptism, at every communion, by every member of the Church:— is it not common property as much as Scripture?

Once more; if Church doctrine is but a hazy opinion, how is it there can be such a thing at all as Catholic consent about it? If, in spite of its being subjective to the mind, Europe, Asia, and Africa could agree together in doctrine in the fourth and fifth centuries (to say nothing of earlier times), why should its subjective character be an antecedent objection to a similar agreement in it between the fourth century and the first? And does not this agreement show that we are able to tell when we agree together, and when we do not? Is it a mere accident, and perhaps a mistake, that Christians

then felt sure that they agreed together in creed, and we
now feel sure that we do not agree together?

Granting, then, that external facts can be discriminated
n a way in which opinions cannot be, yet the Church
doctrines are not mere opinions, but ordinances also: and
though the books of Scripture themselves are an
external fact, yet they are not all of them witnessed by
all writers till a late age, and their canonicity and inspiration are but doctrines, not facts, and open to the
objections, whatever they are, to which doctrines lie
open.

3.

And now, having said as much as is necessary on
these subjects, I will make some remarks on the state of
the case as I have represented it, and thus shall bring
to an end the train of thought upon which I have been
engaged. Let us suppose it proved, then, as I consider
it has been proved, that many difficulties are connected
with the evidence for the Canon, that we might have
clearer evidence for it than we have; and again, let us
grant that there are many difficulties connected with
the evidence for the Church doctrines, that they might
be more clearly contained in Scripture, nay, in the extant writings of the first three centuries, than they are.
This being assumed, I observe as follows :—

1. There is something very arresting and impressive
in the fact, that there should be these difficulties attending those two great instruments of religious truth which
we possess. We are all of us taught from the Bible, and
from the Creed or the Prayer Book: it is from these that we
get our knowledge of God. We are sure they contain a doctrine which is from Him. We are sure of it ; but *how* do
we know it ? We are sure the doctrine is from Him, and

(I hesitate not to say) by a supernatural divinely inspired assurance; but *how* do we know the doctrine is from Him? When we go to inquire into the reasons in argument, we find that the Creed or the Prayer Book with its various doctrines rests for its authority upon the Bible, and that these might be more clearly stated in the Bible than they are; and that the Bible, with its various books, rests for its authority on ancient testimony, and that its books might have been more largely and strongly attested than they are. I say, there is something very subduing to a Christian in this remarkable coincidence, which cannot be accidental. We have reason to believe that God, our Maker and Governor, has spoken to us by Revelation; yet why has He not spoken more distinctly? He has given us doctrines which are but obscurely gathered from Scripture, and a Scripture which is but obscurely gathered from history. It is not a single fact, but a double fact; it is a coincidence. We have two informants, and both leave room, if we choose, for doubt. God's ways surely are not as our ways.

2. This is the first reflection which rises in the mind on the state of the case. The second is this : that, most remarkable it is, the Jews were left in the same uncertainty about Christ, in which we are about His doctrine. The precept, " *Search* the Scriptures," and the commendation of the Berœans, who " *searched* the Scriptures daily," surely implies that divine truth was not on the surface of the Old Testament. We do not search for things which are before us, but for what we have lost or have to find. The whole system of the prophecies left the Jews (even after Christ came) where we are—in uncertainty. The Sun of Righteousness did not at once clear up the mists from the Prophetic Word. It was a dark saying to the many, after He came, as well as

before. It is not to be denied that there were and are many real difficulties in the way of the Jews admitting that Jesus Christ is their Messiah. The Old Testament certainly does speak of the Messiah as a temporal monarch, and a conqueror of this world. *We* are accustomed to say that the prophecies must be taken spiritually ; and rightly do we say so. True : yet does not this look like an evasion, to a Jew ? Is it not much more like an evasion, though it be not, than to say (what the Church does say and rightly) that rites remain, *though* Jewish rites are done away, because *our* rites are not Jewish, but spiritual, gifted with the Spirit, channels of grace ? The Old Testament certainly spoke as if, when the Church expanded into all nations, still those nations were to be inferior to the Jews, even if admitted into the Church ; and so St. Peter understood it till he had the vision. Yet when the Jews complained, instead of being soothed and consoled, they were met with language such as this : " Friend, I do thee no wrong. . . . Is it not lawful for Me to do what I will with Mine own ? Is thine eye evil because I am good ? " And, " Nay but, O man, who art thou that repliest against God ? Shall the thing formed say to Him that formed it, Why hast Thou made me thus ? " *

Again ; why were the Jews discarded from God's election ? for *keeping* to their Law. Why, this was the very thing they were *told* to do, the very thing which, if *not* done, was to be their ruin. Consider Moses' words : " If thou wilt not observe to do all the words of this law that are written in this book, that thou mayest fear this glorious and fearful Name, The Lord thy God ; then the Lord will make thy plagues wonderful, and the plagues of thy seed, even great plagues, and of

* Matt xx. 13—15. Rom. ix. 20.

long continuance, and sore sicknesses, and of long continuance." * Might they not, or rather did they not, bring passages like this as an irrefragable argument against Christianity, that they were told to give up their Law, that Law which was the charter of their religious prosperity? Might not their case seem a hard one, judging by the surface of things, and without reference to "the hidden man of the heart"? *We* know how to answer this objection; we say, Christianity lay *beneath* the letter; that the letter slew those who for whatever cause went by it; that when Christ came, He shed a light on the sacred text and brought out its secret meaning. Now, is not this just the case I have been stating, as regards Catholic doctrines, or rather a more difficult case? The doctrines of the Church are not hidden so deep in the New Testament, as the Gospel doctrines are hidden in the Old; but they are hidden; and I am persuaded that were men but consistent, who oppose the Church doctrines as being unscriptural, they would vindicate the Jews for rejecting the Gospel.

Much might be said on this subject: I will but add, by way of specimen, how such interpretations as our Lord's of "I am the God of Abraham," etc., would, were we not accustomed to them, startle and offend reasoning men. Is it not much further from the literal force of the words, than the doctrine of the Apostolical Succession is from the words, "I am with you alway, even unto the end of the world"? In the one case we argue, "Therefore, the Apostles are in one sense *now* on earth, because Christ says 'with *you alway;*'" in the other, Christ Himself argues, "therefore in one sense the bodies of the patriarchs are still alive; for God calls Himself '*their* God.'" We say, "therefore the Apostles

* Deut. xxviii. 58, 59.

live in their successors." Christ implies, "therefore the body never died, and therefore it will rise again." His own divine mouth hereby shows us that doctrines may be in Scripture, though they require a multitude of links to draw them thence. It must be added that the Sadducees *did* profess (what they would call) a plain and simple creed ; they recurred to Moses and went by Moses, and rejected all additions to what was on the surface of the Mosaic writings, and thus they rejected what really was in the mind of Moses, though not on his lips. They denied the Resurrection ; they had no idea that it was contained in the books of Moses.

Here, then, is another singular instance of the same procedure on the part of Divine Providence. That Gospel which was to be "the glory of His people Israel,"* was a stumblingblock to them, as for other reasons, so especially *because* it was not on the *surface* of the Old Testament. And all the compassion (if I may use the word) that they received from the Apostles in their perplexity was, "because they *knew* Him not, nor yet the *voice* of the Prophets which are read every Sabbath day, they have fulfilled them in condemning Him."† Or again : "Well spake the Holy Ghost by Esaias the prophet unto our fathers, saying, Go unto this people, and say, Hearing, ye shall hear, and shall not understand,"‡ etc. Or when the Apostles are mildest : "I have great heaviness and continual sorrow in my heart. For I could wish that myself were accursed from Christ for my brethren, my kinsman according to the flesh ; " or "I bear them record that they have a zeal of God, but not according to knowledge." § Moreover, it is observable that the record of their anxiety is preserved

* Luke ii. 32.   ‡ Ib. xxviii. 25, 26.
† Acts xiii. 27.   § Rom. ix. 2, 3 : x. 2.

to us ; an anxiety which many of us would call just and
rational, many would pity, but which the inspired writers
treat with a sort of indignation and severity. " Then
came the Jews round about Him, and said unto Him,
How long dost Thou make us to doubt?"* or more
literally, " How long dost Thou keep our soul in suspense ? If thou be the Christ, *tell us plainly.*" Christ
answers by referring to His works, and by declaring that
His sheep do hear and know Him, and follow Him.   If
any one will seriously consider the intercourse between
our Lord and the Pharisees, he will see that, not denying
their immorality and miserable pride, still they had
reason for complaining (as men now speak) that " the
Gospel was not preached to them,"—that the Truth was
not placed before them clearly, and fully, and uncom-
promisingly, and intelligibly, and logically,—that they
were bid to believe on weak arguments and fanciful deductions. †

This then, I say, is certainly a most striking coincidence
in addition. Whatever perplexity any of us may feel
about the evidence of Scripture or the evidence of Church
doctrine, we see that such perplexity is represented in
Scripture as the lot of the Jews too ; and this circumstance, while it shows that it is a sort of law of God's
providence, and thereby affords an additional evidence of
the truth of the Revealed System by showing its harmony,
also serves to quiet and console, and moreover to awe
and warn us.   Doubt and difficulty, as regards evidence,
seems our lot; the simple question is, What is our duty
under it ?   Difficulty is our lot, as far as we take on ourselves to inquire ; the multitude are not able to inquire,
and so escape the trial ; but when men inquire, this trial
at once comes upon them.   And surely we may use the

* John x. 24.   † [This is too strongly worded.]

parable of the Talents to discover what our duty is under the trial. Do not those who refuse to go by the hints and probable meaning of Scripture hide their talent in a napkin ? and will they be excused ?

3. Now in connexion with what has been said, observe the singular coincidence, or rather appositeness, of what Scripture enjoins, as to the duty of going by *faith* in religious matters. The difficulties which exist in the evidence give a deep meaning to that characteristic enunciation. Scripture is quite aware of those difficulties. Objections can be brought against its own inspiration, its canonicity, its doctrines in our case, as in the case of the Jews against the Messiahship of Jesus Christ. It knows them all : it has provided against them, by recognizing them. It says, "Believe," because it knows that, unless we believe, there is no means of our arriving at a knowledge of divine things. If we will doubt, that is, if we will not allow evidence to be sufficient for us which mainly results, considered in its details, in a balance preponderating on the side of Revelation ; if we will determine that no evidence is enough to prove revealed doctrine but what is simply overpowering ; if we will not go by evidence in which there are (so to say) a score of reasons for Revelation, yet one or two against it, we cannot be Christians ; we shall miss Christ either in His inspired Scriptures, or in His doctrines, or in His ordinances.

4

To conclude : our difficulty and its religious solution are contained in the sixth chapter of St. John. After our Lord had declared what all who heard seemed to feel to be a hard doctrine, some in surprise and offence left Him. Our Lord said to the Twelve most tenderly, "Will ye also go away ?" St. Peter promptly answered,

No : but observe on what ground he put it : " Lord, *to whom* shall we go ? " He did not bring forward evidences of our Lord's mission, though he knew of such. He knew of such in abundance, in the miracles which our Lord wrought : but, still, questions might be raised about the so-called miracles of others, such as of Simon the sorcerer, or of vagabond Jews, or about the force of the evidence from miracles itself. This was not the evidence on which he rested personally, but this,—that if Christ were not to be trusted, there was nothing in the world to be trusted ; and this was a conclusion repugnant both to his reason and to his heart. He had within him ideas of greatness and goodness, holiness and eternity, —he had a love of them—he had an instinctive hope and longing after their possession. Nothing could convince him that this unknown good was a dream. Divine life, eternal life was the object which his soul, as far as it had learned to realize and express its wishes, supremely longed for. In Christ he found what he wanted. He says, " Lord, to whom *shall* we go ? " implying he must go somewhere. Christ had asked, " Will ye also go *away ?* " He only asked about Peter's leaving *Himself ;* but in Peter's thought to leave Him was to go somewhere else. He only thought of leaving Him *by* taking another god. That negative state of neither believing nor disbelieving, neither acting this way nor that, which is so much in esteem now, did not occur to his mind as possible. The fervent Apostle ignored the existence of scepticism. With him, his course was at best but a *choice of difficulties*—of difficulties perhaps, but still a choice. He knew of no course without a choice,—choice he must make. Somewhither he must go : whither else ? If Christ could deceive him, to whom should he go ? Christ's ways might be dark, His words often perplexing, but still he found in Him what he found nowhere else,—amid difficulties, a realization of his inward longings. " Thou hast the words of eternal life."

So far he saw. He might have misgivings at times ; he might have permanent and in themselves insuperable objections ; still, in spite of such objections, in spite of the assaults of unbelief, on the whole, he saw that in Christ which was positive, real, and satisfying. He saw it nowhere else. " Thou," he says, " hast the words of eternal life ; and we *have believed* and *have known* that thou art the Christ, the Son of the Living God." As if he said, " We will stand by what we believed and knew yesterday,—what we believed and knew the day before. A sudden gust of new doctrines, a sudden inroad of new perplexities, shall not unsettle us. We *have* believed, we *have* known : we cannot collect together all the evidence, but this is the abiding deep conviction of our minds. We feel that it is better, safer, truer, pleasanter, more blessed to cling to Thy feet, O merciful Saviour, than to leave Thee. Thou *canst not* deceive us : it is impossible. We will hope in Thee against hope, and believe in Thee against doubt, and obey Thee in spite of gloom."

Now what are the feelings I have described but the love of Christ ? Thus love is the parent of faith.* We

* [To say that " love is the parent of faith " is true, if by " love " is meant, not evangelical charity, the theological virtue, but that desire for the knowledge and drawing towards the service of our Maker, which precedes religious conversion. Such is the main outline, personally and historically, of the inward acceptance of Revelation on the part of individuals, and does not at all exclude, but actually requires, the exercise of Reason, and the presence of grounds for believing, as an incidental and necessary part of the process. The preliminary, called in the text "love," but more exactly, a "pia affectio," or "bona voluntas," does not stand in antagonism or in contrast to Reason, but is a sovereign condition without which Reason cannot be brought to bear upon the great work in hand.—*Vid.* Univ. Serm. xii., 20.]

believe in things we see not from love of them : if we
did not love, we should not believe.   Faith is reliance on
the word of another ; the word of another is in itself a
faint evidence compared with that of sight or reason.
It is influential only when we cannot do without it.   We
cannot do without it when it is our informant about
things which we cannot do without.   Things we cannot
do without, are things which we desire.   They who feel
they cannot do without the next world, go by faith (not
that sight would not be better), but because they have no
other means of knowledge to go by.   " To whom shall
they go ? "   If they will not believe the word preached
to them, what other access have they to the next world ?
Love of God led St. Peter to follow Christ, and love of
Christ leads men now to love and follow the Church, as
His representative and voice.

Let us then say, If we give up the Gospel, as we have
received it in the Church, to whom shall we go ?   It has
the words of eternal life in it : where else are they to be
found ? Is there any other Religion to choose but that of
the Church ?   Shall we go to Mahometanism or Paganism ?   But we may seek some heresy or sect : true, we
may ; but why are they more sure ? are they not a part,
while the Church is the whole ?   Why is the part true, if
the whole is not ?   Why is not that evidence trustworthy
for the whole, which is trustworthy for a part ?   Sectaries
commonly give up the Church doctrines, and go by the
Church's Bible ; but if the doctrines cannot be proved
true, neither can the Bible ; they stand or fall together.
If we begin, we must soon make an end.   On what consistent principle can I give up part and keep the rest ?
No : I see a work before me, which professes to be the
work of that God whose being and attributes I feel within me to be real.   Why should not this great sight be,—

what it professes to be—His presence ? Why should not
the Church be divine ? The burden of proof surely is on
the other side. I will accept her doctrines, and her rites,
and her Bible,—not one, and not the other, but all,—till
I have clear proof, which is an impossibility, that she is
mistaken. It is, I feel, God's will that I should do so ;
and besides, I love all that belong to her,—I love her
Bible, her doctrines, her rites, and therefore I believe.

September, 1838.

IV.

THE TAMWORTH READING ROOM.

(Addressed to the Editor of the TIMES. *By Catholicus.)*

I.

Secular Knowledge in contrast with Religion.

SIR,—Sir Robert Peel's position in the country, and his high character, render it impossible that his words and deeds should be other than public property. This alone would furnish an apology for my calling the attention of your readers to the startling language, which many of them doubtless have already observed, in the Address which this most excellent and distinguished man has lately delivered upon the establishment of a Library and Reading-room at Tamworth ; but he has superseded the need of apology altogether, by proceeding to present it to the public in the form of a pamphlet. His speech, then, becomes important, both from the name and the express act of its author. At the same time, I must allow that he has not published it in the fulness in which it was spoken. Still it seems to me right and fair, or rather imperative, to animadvert upon it as it has appeared in your columns, since in that shape it will have the widest circulation. A public man must not claim to harangue the whole world in newspapers, and then to offer his second thoughts to such as choose to buy them at a bookseller's.

I shall surprise no one who has carefully read Sir Robert's Address, and perhaps all who have not, by stating my conviction, that, did a person take it up without looking at the heading, he would to a certainty set it down as a production of the years 1827 and 1828, —the scene Gower Street, the speaker Mr. Brougham or Dr. Lushington, and the occasion, the laying the first stone, or the inauguration, of the then-called London University. I profess myself quite unable to draw any satisfactory line of difference between the Gower Street and the Tamworth Exhibition, except, of course, that Sir Robert's personal religious feeling breaks out in his Address across his assumed philosophy. I say assumed, I might say affected ;—for I think too well of him to believe it genuine.

On the occasion in question, Sir Robert gave expression to a theory of morals and religion, which of course, in a popular speech, was not put out in a very dogmatic form, but which, when analyzed and fitted together, reads somewhat as follows :—

Human nature, he seems to say, if left to itself, becomes sensual and degraded. Uneducated men live in the indulgence of their passions; or, if they are merely taught to read, they dissipate and debase their minds by trifling or vicious publications. Education is the cultivation of the intellect and heart, and Useful Knowledge is the great instrument of education. It is the parent of virtue, the nurse of religion; it exalts man to his highest perfection, and is the sufficient scope of his most earnest exertions.

Physical and moral science rouses, transports, exalts, enlarges, tranquillizes, and satisfies the mind. Its attractiveness obtains a hold over us ; the excitement attending it supersedes grosser excitements ; it makes

us know our duty, and thereby enables us to do it ; by
taking the mind off itself, it destroys anxiety ; and by
providing objects of admiration, it soothes and subdues
us.

And, in addition, it is a kind of neutral ground, on
which men of every shade of politics and religion may
meet together, disabuse each other of their prejudices,
form intimacies, and secure co-operation.

This, it is almost needless to say, is the very theory,
expressed temperately, on which Mr. Brougham once
expatiated in the Glasgow and London Universities.
Sir R. Peel, indeed, has spoken with somewhat of his
characteristic moderation ; but for his closeness in sentiment to the Brougham of other days, a few parallels
from their respective Discourses will be a sufficient
voucher.

For instance, Mr. Brougham, in his Discourses upon
Science, and in his Pursuit of Knowledge under Difficulties,* wrote about the "pure delight" of physical
knowledge, of its "pure gratification," of its "tendency
to purify and elevate man's nature," of its "elevating
and refining it," of its "giving a dignity and *importance*
to the enjoyment of life." Sir Robert, pursuing the
idea, shows us its importance even in death, observing,
that physical knowledge supplied the thoughts from
which "a great experimentalist professed *in his last
illness* to derive some pleasure and some consolation,
when most other sources of consolation and pleasure
were closed to him."

Mr. Brougham talked much and eloquently of "the
sweetness of knowledge," and "the *charms* of philosophy,"
of students "smitten with the love of knowledge," of

---

* [This latter work is wrongly ascribed to Lord Brougham in this passage.
It is, however, of the Brougham school.]

" *wooing* truth with the unwearied ardour of a *lover*," of "keen and overpowering *emotion*, of *ecstasy*," of "the absorbing *passion* of knowledge," of "the *strength* of the passion, and the exquisite pleasure of its *gratification*." And Sir Robert, in less glowing language, but even in a more tender strain than Mr. Brougham, exclaims, "If I can only persuade you to enter upon that delightful path, I am sanguine enough to believe that there *will be opened to you gradual charms and temptations* which will induce you to persevere."

Mr. Brougham naturally went on to enlarge upon "bold and successful adventures in the pursuit ;"—such, perhaps, as in the story of Paris and Helen, or Hero and Leander ; of daring ambition in its course to greatness," of "enterprising spirits," and their "brilliant feats," of "adventurers of the world of intellect," and of "the illustrious vanquishers of fortune." And Sir Robert, not to be outdone, echoes back "aspirations for knowledge and distinction," "simple determination of overcoming difficulties," "premiums on skill and intelligence," "mental activity," "steamboats and railroads," "producer and consumer," "spirit of inquiry afloat ; " and at length he breaks out into almost conventical eloquence, crying, " Every newspaper *teems with notices* of publications written upon *popular principles*, detailing all the recent discoveries of science, and their connexion with improvements in arts and manufactures. *Let me earnestly entreat you* not to neglect the *opportunity* which we are now willing to afford you ! *It will not be our fault* if the ample page of knowledge, rich with the spoils of time, is not unrolled to you ! *We tell you*," etc., etc.

Mr. Brougham pronounces that a man by "learning truths wholly new to him," and by "satisfying himself of the grounds on which known truths rest," "will enjoy a *proud consciousness* of having, by his own exertions become a *wiser,* and *therefore* a more *exalted* creature." Sir Robert runs abreast of this great sentiment. He tells us, in words which he adopts as his own, that a man "in becoming *wiser* will become *better :*" he will "rise *at once* in the scale of intellectual and moral existence, and by being accustomed to such contemplations, he will feel the *moral dignity* of his nature *exalted.*"

Mr. Brougham, on his inauguration at Glasgow, spoke to the ingenuous youth assembled on the occasion, of "the benefactors of mankind, when they rest from their pious labours, looking down upon the blessings with which their toils and sufferings have clothed the scene of their former existence ; " and in his Discourse upon Science declared it to be "no mean reward of our labour to become acquainted with the prodigious genius of those who have almost exalted the nature of man above his destined sphere; " and who "hold a station apart, rising over *all* the great teachers of mankind, and spoken of reverently, as if Newton and La Place were not the names of mortal men." Sir Robert cannot, of course, equal this sublime flight ; but he succeeds in calling Newton and others "those mighty spirits which have made the *greatest* (though imperfect) advances towards the understanding of 'the Divine Nature and Power.' "

Mr. Brougham talked at Glasgow about putting to flight the "evil spirits of *tyranny and persecution* which haunted the long night now gone down the sky," and about men "no longer suffering themselves to be led *blindfold in ignorance ;* " and in his Pursuit of Knowledge he speaks of Pascal having, "under the influence of certain religious views, during a period of

depression, conceived scientific pursuits " to be little
better than abuse of his time and faculties." Sir Robert,
fainter in tone, but true to the key, warns his hearers,—
" Do not be deceived by the sneers that you hear against
knowledge, which are uttered by men who *want to
depress you*, and keep you depressed to the level of their
own contented ignorance."

Mr. Brougham laid down at Glasgow the infidel
principle, or, as he styles it, " the great truth," which
" has gone forth to all the ends of the earth, that man
shall no more render account to man for his belief, over
which he has himself no control." And Dr. Lushington
applied it in Gower Street to the College then and there
rising, by asking, " Will any one argue for establishing
a *monopoly* to be enjoyed by the few who are of one
denomination of the Christian Church only ? " And he
went on to speak of the association and union of all
without exclusion or restriction, of "friendships cementing
the bond of charity, and softening the asperities which
ignorance and separation have fostered." Long may it be
before Sir Robert Peel professes the great principle itself !
even though, as the following passages show, he is
inconsistent enough to think highly of its application
in the culture of the mind. He speaks, for instance, of
" this preliminary and fundamental rule, that no works
of *controversial divinity* shall enter into the library
(applause),"—of " the institution being open to all persons of all descriptions, without reference to political
opinions, or *religious creed*,"—and of " an edifice in which
men of all political opinions and *all religious feelings*
may unite in the furtherance of knowledge, without the
asperities of party feeling." Now, that British society
should consist of persons of different religions, is this a
positive standing evil, to be endured at best as unavoid-

able, or a topic of exultation ?   Of exultation, answers Sir Robert ; the greater differences the better, the more the merrier.   So we must interpret his tone.

It is reserved for few to witness the triumph of their own opinions ; much less to witness it in the instance of their own direct and personal opponents.   Whether the Lord Brougham of this day feels all that satisfaction and inward peace which he attributes to success of whatever kind in intellectual efforts, it is not for me to decide ; but that he has achieved, to speak in his own style, a mighty victory, and is leading in chains behind his chariot-wheels, a great captive, is a fact beyond question.

Such is the reward in 1841 for unpopularity in 1827.

What, however, is a boast to Lord Brougham, is in the same proportion a slur upon the fair fame of Sir Robert Peel, at least in the judgment of those who have hitherto thought well of him.   Were there no other reason against the doctrine propounded in the Address which has been the subject of these remarks, (but I hope to be allowed an opportunity of assigning others,) its parentage would be a grave *primâ facie* difficulty in receiving it.   It is, indeed, most melancholy to see so sober and experienced a man practising the antics of one of the wildest performers of this wild age ; and taking off the tone, manner, and gestures of the versatile ex-Chancellor, with a versatility almost equal to his own.

Yet let him be assured that the task of rivalling such a man is hopeless, as well as unprofitable.   No one can equal the great sophist.   Lord Brougham is inimitable in his own line.

2.

Secular Knowledge not the Principle of Moral Improvement.

A DISTINGUISHED Conservative statesman tells us from the town-hall of Tamworth that "in becoming wiser a man will become better;" meaning by wiser more conversant with the facts and theories of physical science; and that such a man will "rise *at once* in the scale of intellectual and *moral* existence." "That," he adds, "is my belief." He avows, also, that the fortunate individual whom he is describing, by being "accustomed to such contemplations, will feel the *moral dignity of his nature exalted.*" He speaks also of physical knowledge as "being the means of useful occupation and rational recreation;" of "the pleasures of knowledge" superseding "the indulgence of sensual appetite," and of its "contributing to the intellectual and *moral improvement* of the community." Accordingly, he very consistently wishes it to be set before "the female as well as the male portion of the population;" otherwise, as he truly observes, "great injustice would be done to the well-educated and virtuous women" of the place. They are to "have equal power and equal influence with others." It will be difficult to exhaust the reflections which rise in the mind on reading avowals of this nature.

The first question which obviously suggests itself is *how* these wonderful moral effects are to be wrought under the instrumentality of the physical sciences. Can the process be analyzed and drawn out, or does it act like a dose or a charm which comes into general use empirically ? Does Sir Robert Peel mean to say, that whatever be the occult reasons for the result, so it is ; you have but to drench the popular mind with physics, and moral and religious advancement follows on the whole, in spite of individual failures ? Yet where has the experiment been tried on so large a scale as to justify such anticipations ? Or rather, does he mean, that, from the nature of the case, he who is imbued with science and literature, unless adverse influences interfere, cannot but be a better man ? It is natural and becoming to seek for some clear idea of the meaning of so dark an oracle. To know is one thing, to do is another ; the two things are altogether distinct. A man knows he should get up in the morning,—he lies a-bed ; he knows he should not lose his temper, yet he cannot keep it. A labouring man knows he should not go to the ale-house, and his wife knows she should not filch when she goes out charing ; but, nevertheless, in these cases, the consciousness of a duty is not all one with the performance of it. There are, then, large families of instances, to say the least, in which men may become wiser, without becoming better ; what, then, is the meaning of this great maxim in the mouth of its promulgators ?

Mr. Bentham would answer, that the knowledge which carries virtue along with it, is the knowledge how to take care of number one—a clear appreciation of what is pleasurable, what painful, and what promotes the one and prevents the other. An uneducated man is ever mistaking his own interest, and standing in the way of his own true enjoyments. Useful Knowledge is that which tends to make us more useful to ourselves ;—a most definite and intelligible account of the matter, and needing no explanation. But it would be a great injustice, both to Lord Brougham and to Sir Robert, to suppose, when they talk of Knowledge being Virtue, that they are Benthamizing. Bentham had not a spark of poetry in him ; on the contrary, there is much of high aspiration, generous sentiment, and impassioned feeling in the tone of Lord Brougham and Sir Robert. They speak of knowledge as something "pulchrum," fair and glorious, exalted above the range of ordinary humanity, and so little connected with the personal interest of its votaries, that, though Sir Robert does *obiter* talk of improved modes of draining, and the chemical properties of manure, yet he must not be supposed to come short of the lofty enthusiasm of Lord Brougham, who expressly panegyrizes certain ancient philosophers who gave up riches, retired into solitude, or embraced a life of travel, smit with a sacred curiosity about physical or mathematical truth.

Here Mr. Bentham, did it fall to him to offer a criticism, doubtless would take leave to inquire whether such language was anything better than a fine set of words " signifying nothing,"—flowers of rhetoric, which bloom, smell sweet, and die. But it is impossible to suspect so grave and practical a man as Sir Robert Peel of using words literally without any meaning at all ; and though I think at best they have not a very profound meaning, yet, such as it is, we ought to attempt to draw it out.

Now, without using exact theological language, we may surely take it for granted, from the experience of facts, that the human mind is at best in a very unformed or disordered state ; passions and conscience, likings and reason, conflicting,—might rising against right, with the prospect of things getting worse. Under these circum-

stances, what is it that the School of philosophy in which
Sir Robert has enrolled himself proposes to accomplish ?
Not a victory of the mind over itself—not the supremacy
of the law—not the reduction of the rebels—not the
unity of our complex nature—not an harmonizing of the
chaos—but the mere lulling of the passions to rest by
turning the course of thought ; not a change of character,
but a mere removal of temptation.   This should be
carefully observed.   When a husband is gloomy, or an
old woman peevish and fretful, those who are about them
do all they can to keep dangerous topics and causes of
offence out of the way, and think themselves lucky, if,
by such skilful management, they get through the day
without an outbreak.   When a child cries, the nurserymaid
dances it about, or points to the pretty black horses out
of window, or shows how ashamed poll-parrot or poor puss
must be of its tantarums.   Such is the sort of prescrip-
tion which Sir Robert Peel offers to the good people of
Tamworth.   He makes no pretence of subduing the
giant nature, in which we were born, of smiting the loins
of the domestic enemies of our peace, of overthrowing
passion and fortifying reason ; he does but offer to bribe
the foe for the nonce with gifts which will avail for that
purpose just so long as they *will* avail, and no longer.

This was mainly the philosophy of the great Tully,
except when it pleased him to speak as a disciple of the
Porch.   Cicero handed the recipe to Brougham, and
Brougham has passed it on to Peel.   If we examine the
old Roman's meaning in "*O philosophia, vitæ dux,*" it was
neither more nor less than this ;—that, *while* we were
thinking of philosophy, we were not thinking of anything
else ; we did not feel grief, or anxiety, or passion, or
ambition, or hatred all that time, and the only point was
to keep thinking of it.   How to keep thinking of it was

extra artem. If a man was in grief, he was to be amused ;
if disappointed, to be excited; if in a rage, to be soothed ;
if in love, to be roused to the pursuit of glory. No
inward change was contemplated, but a change of external objects ; as if we were all White Ladies or Undines,
our moral life being one of impulse and emotion, not
subjected to laws, not consisting in habits, not capable
of growth. When Cicero was outwitted by Cæsar, he
solaced himself with Plato ; when he lost his daughter,
he wrote a treatise on Consolation. Such, too, was the
philosophy of that Lydian city, mentioned by the historian, who in a famine played at dice to stay their
stomachs.

And such is the rule of life advocated by Lord
Brougham; and though, of course, he protests that knowledge "must invigorate the mind as well as entertain it,
and refine and elevate the character, while it gives listlessness and weariness their most agreeable excitement and
relaxation," yet his notions of vigour and elevation, when
analyzed, will be found to resolve themselves into a mere
preternatural excitement under the influence of some
stimulating object, or the peace which is attained by
there being nothing to quarrel with. He speaks of philosophers leaving the care of their estates, or declining
public honours, from the greater desirableness of Knowledge ; envies the shelter enjoyed in the University of
Glasgow from the noise and bustle of the world ; and,
apropos of Pascal and Cowper, " so mighty," says he, " is
the power of intellectual occupation, to make the heart
forget, *for the time,* its most prevailing griefs, and to
change its deepest gloom to sunshine."

Whether Sir Robert Peel meant all this, which others
before him have meant, it is impossible to say ; but I will
be bound, if he did not mean this, he meant nothing

else, and his words will certainly insinuate this meaning, wherever a reader is not content to go without any meaning at all. They will countenance, with his high authority, what in one form or other is a chief error of the day, in very distinct schools of opinion,—that our true excellence comes not from within, but from without; not wrought out through personal struggles and sufferings, but following upon a passive exposure to influences over which we have no control. They will countenance the theory that diversion is the instrument of improvement, and excitement the condition of right action ; and whereas diversions cease to be diversions if they are constant, and excitements by their very nature have a crisis and run through a course, they will tend to make novelty ever in request, and will set the great teachers of morals upon the incessant search after stimulants and sedatives, by which unruly nature may, *pro re natâ,* be kept in order.

Hence, be it observed, Lord Brougham, in the last quoted sentence, tells us, with much accuracy of statement, that "intellectual occupation made the heart" of Pascal or Cowper "*for the time* forget its griefs." He frankly offers us a philosophy of expedients : he shows us how to live by medicine. Digestive pills half an hour before dinner, and a posset at bedtime at the best ; and at the worst, dram-drinking and opium,—the very remedy against broken hearts, or remorse of conscience, which is in request among the many, in gin-palaces *not* intellectual.

And if these remedies be but of temporary effect at the utmost, more commonly they will have no effect at all. Strong liquors, indeed, do for a time succeed in their object ; but who was ever consoled in real trouble by the small beer of literature or science ? " Sir," said Rasselas, to the philosopher who had lost his daughter,

" mortality is an event by which a wise man can never be surprised." "Young man," answered the mourner, " you speak like one that hath never felt the pangs of separation. What comfort can truth or reason afford me ? of what effect are they now but to tell me that my daughter will not be restored ?" Or who was ever made more humble or more benevolent by being told, as the same practical moralist words it, " to concur with the great and unchangeable scheme of universal felicity, and co-operate with the general dispensation and tendency of the present system of things" ? Or who was made to do any secret act of self-denial, or was steeled against pain, or peril, by all the lore of the infidel La Place, or those other "mighty spirits " which Lord Brougham and Sir Robert eulogize ? Or when was a choleric tempera-ment ever brought under by a scientific King Canute planting his professor's chair before the rising waves ? And as to the "keen" and "ecstatic" pleasures which Lord Brougham, not to say Sir Robert, ascribes to in-tellectual pursuit and conquest, I cannot help thinking that in that line they will find themselves outbid in the market by gratifications much closer at hand, and on a level with the meanest capacity. Sir Robert makes it a boast that women are to be members of his institution ; it is hardly necessary to remind so accomplished a classic, that Aspasia and other learned ladies in Greece are no very encouraging precedents in favour of the purifying effects of science. But the strangest and most painful topic which he urges, is one which Lord Brougham has had the good taste altogether to avoid,—the power, not of religion, but of scientific knowledge, on a death-bed ; a subject which Sir Robert treats in language which it is far better to believe is mere oratory than is said in earnest.

Such is this new art of living, offered to the labouring classes,—we will say, for instance, in a severe winter, snow on the ground, glass falling, bread rising, coal at 20d. the cwt., and no work.

It does not require many words, then, to determine that, taking human nature as it is actually found, and assuming that there is an Art of life, to say that it con-sists, or in any essential manner is placed, in the cultiva-tion of Knowledge, that the mind is changed by a dis-covery, or saved by a diversion, and can thus be amused into immortality,—that grief, anger, cowardice, self-conceit, pride, or passion, can be subdued by an ex-amination of shells or grasses, or inhaling of gases, or chipping of rocks, or calculating the longitude, is the veriest of pretences which sophist or mountebank ever professed to a gaping auditory. If virtue be a mastery over the mind, if its end be action, if its perfection be inward order, harmony, and peace, we must seek it in graver and holier places than in Libraries and Reading-rooms.

3.

Secular Knowledge not a direct Means of Moral Improvement.

THERE are two Schools of philosophy, in high esteem, at this day, as at other times, neither of them accepting Christian principles as the guide of life, yet both of them unhappily patronized by many whom it would be the worst and most cruel uncharitableness to suspect of unbelief. Mr. Bentham is the master of the one ; and Sir Robert Peel is a disciple of the other.

Mr. Bentham's system has nothing ideal about it ; he is a stern realist, and he limits his realism to things which he can see, hear, taste, touch, and handle. He does not acknowledge the existence of anything which he cannot ascertain for himself. Exist it may nevertheless, but till it makes itself felt, to him it exists not ; till it comes down right before him, and he is very short-sighted, it is not recognized by him as having a co-existence with himself, any more than the Emperor of China is received into the European family of Kings. With him a being out of sight is a being simply out of mind ; nay, he does not allow the traces or glimpses of facts to have any claim on his regard, but with him to have a little and not much, is to have nothing at all. With him to speak truth is to be ready with a definition, and to imagine, to guess, to doubt, or to falter, is much the same as to lie. What opinion will such an iron thinker entertain of Cicero's "glory," or Lord Brougham's "truth," or Sir

Robert's "scientific consolations," and all those other airy nothings which are my proper subject of remark, and which I have in view when, by way of contrast, I make mention of the philosophy of Bentham ? And yet the doctrine of the three eminent orators, whom I have ventured to criticise, has in it much that is far nobler than Benthamism ; their misfortune being, not that they look for an excellence above the beaten path of life, but that whereas Christianity has told us what that excellence is, Cicero lived before it was given to the world, and Lord Brougham and Sir Robert Peel prefer his involuntary error to their own inherited truth. Surely, there is something unearthly and superhuman in spite of Bentham ; but it is not glory, or knowledge, or any abstract idea of virtue, but great and good tidings which need not here be particularly mentioned, and the pity is, that these Christian statesmen cannot be content with what is divine without as a supplement hankering after what was heathen.

Now, independent of all other considerations, the great difference, in a practical light, between the object of Christianity and of heathen belief, is this—that glory, science, knowledge, and whatever other fine names we use, never healed a wounded heart, nor changed a sinful one ; but the Divine Word is with power. The ideas which Christianity brings before us are in themselves full of influence, and they are attended with a supernatural gift over and above themselves, in order to meet the special exigencies of our nature. Knowledge is not " power," nor is glory " the first and only fair ; " but " Grace," or the " Word," by whichever name we call it, has been from the first a quickening, renovating, organizing principle. It has new created the individual, and transferred and knit him into a social body, composed of members each similarly created. It has cleansed man of his moral diseases, raised him to hope and energy, given him to pro-pagate a brotherhood among his fellows, and to found a family or rather a kingdom of saints all over the earth ; —it introduced a new force into the world, and the im-pulse which it gave continues in its original vigour down to this day. Each one of us has lit his lamp from his neighbour, or received it from his fathers, and the lights thus transmitted are at this time as strong and as clear as if 1800 years had not passed since the kindling of the sacred flame. What has glory or knowledge been able to do like this ? Can it raise the dead ? can it create a polity? can it do more than testify man's need and typify God's remedy?

And yet, in spite of this, when we have an instrument given us, capable of changing the whole man, great orators and statesmen are busy, forsooth, with their heathen charms and nostrums, their sedatives, correc-tives, or restoratives ; as preposterously as if we were to build our men-of-war, or conduct our iron-works, on the principles approved in Cicero's day. The utmost that Lord Brougham seems to propose to himself in the edu-cation of the mind, is to keep out bad thoughts by means of good—a great object, doubtless, but not so great in philosophical conception, as is the destruction of the bad in Christian fact. "If it can be a pleasure," he says, in his Discourse upon the Objects and Advan-tages of Science, "if it can be a *pleasure to gratify curiosity*, to know what we were ignorant of, to have our *feelings of wonder* called forth, *how pure a delight of this very kind* does natural science hold out to its students ! How wonderful are the laws that regulate the motions of fluids ! Is there anything in all the idle books of tales and horrors, more truly astonish-

ing that the fact, that a few pounds of water may, by
mere pressure, without any machinery, by merely being
placed in one particular way, produce very irresistible
force ?   What can be more strange, than that an ounce
weight should balance hundreds of pounds by the intervention of a few bars of thin iron ? Can anything surprise us more than to find that the colour white is a
mixture of all others ? that water should be chiefly composed of an inflammable substance ?   Akin to this
pleasure of contemplating new and extraordinary truths
is the *gratification of a more learned curiosity*, by tracing
resemblances and relations between things which to common apprehension seem widely different," etc., etc.   And
in the same way Sir Robert tells us even of a *devout*
curiosity.   In all cases *curiosity* is the means, *diversion*
of mind the highest end ; and though of course I will
not assert that Lord Brougham, and certainly not that
Sir Robert Peel, denies any higher kind of morality,
yet when the former rises above Benthamism, in which
he often indulges, into what may be called *Broughamism
proper*, he commonly grasps at nothing more real and
substantial than these Ciceronian ethics.

In morals, as in physics, the stream cannot rise higher
than its source.   Christianity raises men from earth, for
it comes from heaven ; but human morality creeps,
struts, or frets upon the earth's level, without wings to
rise.   The Knowledge School does not contemplate raising man above himself; it merely aims at disposing of
his existing powers and tastes, as is most convenient, or
is practicable under circumstances.   It finds him, like the
victims of the French Tyrant, doubled up in a cage in
which he can neither lie, stand, sit, nor kneel, and its
highest desire is to find an attitude in which his unrest
may be least.   Or it finds him like some musical instru-

ment, of great power and compass, but imperfect ; from
its very structure some keys must ever be out of tune,
and its object, when ambition is highest, is to throw the
fault of its nature where least it will be observed. It leaves
man where it found him—man, and not an Angel—a
sinner, not a Saint; but it tries to make him look as
much like what he is not as ever it can. The poor indulge in low pleasures; they use bad language, swear
loudly and recklessly, laugh at coarse jests, and are rude
and boorish. Sir Robert would open on them a wider
range of thought and more intellectual objects, by teaching
them science ; but what warrant will he give us that, if
his object could be achieved, what they would gain in
decency they would not lose in natural humility and
faith ? If so, he has exchanged a gross fault for a more
subtle one. " Temperance topics" stop drinking ; let
us suppose it ; but will much be gained, if those who
give up spirits take to opium ? *Naturam expellas furcâ,
tamen usque recurret,* is at least a heathen truth, and
universities and libraries which recur to heathenism may
reclaim it from the heathen for their motto.

Nay, everywhere, so far as human nature remains
hardly or partially Christianized, the heathen law remains
in force ; as is felt in a measure even in the most religious places and societies. Even there, where Christianity has power, the venom of the old Adam is not
subdued. Those who have to do with our Colleges give
us their experience, that in the case of the young committed to their care, external discipline may change the
fashionable excess, but cannot allay the principle of sin-
ning. Stop cigars, they will take to drinking parties ;
stop drinking, they gamble ; stop gambling, and a worse
license follows. You do not get rid of vice by human
expedients ; you can but use them according to circum-
* *
 *
18

stances, and in their place, as making the best of a bad matter. You must go to a higher source for renovation of the heart and of the will. You do but play a sort of " hunt the slipper " with the fault of our nature, till you go to Christianity.

I say, you must use human methods *in their place*, and there they are useful ; but they are worse than useless out of their place. I have no fanatical wish to deny to any whatever subject of thought or method of reason a place altogether, if it chooses to claim it, in the cultivation of the mind. Mr. Bentham may despise verse-making, or Mr. Dugald Stewart logic, but the great and true maxim is to sacrifice none—to combine, and therefore to adjust, all. All cannot be first, and therefore each has its place, and the problem is to find it. It is at least not a lighter mistake to make what is secondary first, than to leave it out altogether. Here then it is that the Knowledge Society, Gower Street College, Tamworth Reading-room, Lord Brougham and Sir Robert Peel, are all so deplorably mistaken. Christianity, and nothing short of it, must be made the element and principle of all education. Where it has been laid as the first stone, and acknowledged as the governing spirit, it will take up into itself, assimilate, and give a character to literature and science. Where Revealed Truth has given the aim and direction to Knowledge, Knowledge of all kinds will minister to Revealed Truth. The evidences of Religion, natural theology, metaphysics,—or, again, poetry, history, and the classics,—or physics and mathematics, may all be grafted into the mind of a Christian, and give and take by the grafting. But if in education we begin with nature before grace, with evidences before faith, with science before conscience, with poetry before practice, we shall be doing much the same as if we were to indulge the appetites and passions, and turn a deaf ear to the reason. In each case we misplace what in its place is a divine gift. If we attempt to effect a moral improvement by means of poetry, we shall but mature into a mawkish, frivolous, and fastidious sentimentalism; —if by means of argument, into a dry, unamiable long-headedness;—if by good society, into a polished outside, with hollowness within, in which vice has lost its grossness, and perhaps increased its malignity;—if by experimental science, into an uppish, supercilious temper, much inclined to scepticism. But reverse the order of things: put Faith first and Knowledge second; let the University minister to the Church, and then classical poetry becomes the type of Gospel truth, and physical science a comment on Genesis or Job, and Aristotle changes into Butler, and Arcesilas into Berkeley.*

Far from recognizing this principle, the teachers of the Knowledge School would educate from Natural Theology up to Christianity, and would amend the heart through literature and philosophy. Lord Brougham, as if faith came from science, gives out that "henceforth nothing shall prevail over us to praise or to blame any one for" his belief, "which he can no more change than he can the hue of his skin, or the height of his stature." And Sir Robert, whose profession and life give the lie to his philosophy, founds a library into which "no works of controversial divinity shall enter," that is, no Christian doctrine at all; and he tells us that "an increased sagacity will make men not merely believe in the cold doctrines of Natural Religion, but that it will *so prepare*

* [On the supremacy of each science in its own field of thought, and the encroachments upon it of other sciences, *vide* the author's "University Teaching," Disc. 3, and "University Subjects," No. 7 and 10.]

and temper the spirit and understanding that they will be better *qualified to comprehend the great scheme of human redemption.*" And again, Lord Brougham considers that " the pleasures of science tend not only to make our lives more agreeable, but better ;" and Sir Robert responds, that " he entertains the hope that there will be the means afforded of useful occupation and rational recreation; that men will prefer the pleasures of knowledge above the indulgence of sensual appetite, and that there is a prospect of contributing to the intellectual and moral improvement of the neighbourhood."

Can the nineteenth century produce no more robust and creative philosophy than this ?

4.

Secular Knowledge not the Antecedent of Moral Improvement.

HUMAN nature wants recasting, but Lord Brougham is all for tinkering it. He does not despair of making something of it yet. He is not, indeed, of those who think that reason, passion, and whatever else is in us, are made right and tight by the principle of self-interest. He understands that something more is necessary for man's happiness than self-love; he feels that man has affections and aspirations which Bentham does not take account of, and he looks about for their legitimate objects. Christianity has provided these; but, unhappily, he passes them by. He libels them with the name of dogmatism, and conjures up instead the phantoms of Glory and Knowledge; *idola theatri,* as his famous predecessor calls them. " There are idols," says Lord Bacon, "which have got into the human mind, from the different tenets of philosophers, and the perverted laws of demonstration. And these we denominate idols of the theatre ; because all the philosophies that have been hitherto invented or received, are but so many stage plays, written or acted, as having shown nothing but fictitious and theatrical worlds. Idols of the theatre, or theories, are many, and will probably grow much more numerous ; for if men had not, through many ages, *been prepossessed with religion and theology,*

and *if civil governments,* but particularly monarchies,"
(and, I suppose, their ministers, counsellors, functionaries,
inclusive,) " *had not been averse to innovations of this kind,*
though but intended, so as to make it dangerous and
prejudicial to the private fortunes of such as take the
bent of innovating, not only by depriving them of
advantages, but also of exposing them to contempt
and hatred, there would doubtless have been *numerous
other sects* of philosophies and theories, introduced, of kin
to those that in great variety formerly flourished among
the Greeks.   And these theatrical fables have this in
common with dramatic pieces, that the fictitious narrative
is neater, more elegant and pleasing, than the true
history."

I suppose we may readily grant that the science of
the day is attended by more lively interest, and issues in
more entertaining knowledge, than the study of the New
Testament.   Accordingly, Lord Brougham fixes upon
such science as the great desideratum of human nature,
and puts aside faith under the nickname of opinion.   I
wish Sir Robert Peel had not fallen into the snare, insulting doctrine by giving it the name of " controversial
divinity."

However, it will be said that Sir Robert, in spite of
such forms of speech, differs essentially from Lord
Brougham : for he goes on, in the latter part of the
Address which has occasioned these remarks, to speak
of Science as leading to Christianity.   " I can never
think it possible," he says, " that a mind can be so
constituted, that after being familiarized with the great
truth of observing in every object of contemplation that
nature presents the manifest proofs of a Divine Intelligence, if you range even from the organization of the
meanest weed you trample upon, or of the insect that

lives but for an hour, up to the magnificent structure of the heavens, and the still more wonderful phenomena of the soul, reason, and conscience of man ; I cannot believe that any man, accustomed to such contemplations, can return from them with any other feelings than those of enlarged conceptions of the Divine Power, and greater reverence for the name of the Almighty Creator of the universe." A long and complicated sentence, and no unfitting emblem of the demonstration it promises. It sets before us a process and deduction. Depend on it, it is not so safe a road and so expeditious a journey from premiss and conclusion as Sir Robert anticipates. The way is long, and there are not a few half-way houses and traveller's rests along it; and who is to warrant that the members of the Reading-room and Library will go steadily on to the goal he would set before them ? And when at length they come to " Christianity," pray how do the roads lay between it and "controversial divinity" ? Or, grant the Tamworth readers to *begin* with "Christianity" as well as science, the same question suggests itself, What *is* Christianity ? Universal benevolence ? Exalted morality ? Supremacy of law ? Conservatism ? An age of light ? An age of reason ?— Which of them all ?

Most cheerfully do I render to so religious a man as Sir Robert Peel the justice of disclaiming any insinuation on my part, that he has any intention at all to put aside Religion ; yet his words either mean nothing, or they do, both on their surface, and when carried into effect, mean something very irreligious.

And now for one plain proof of this.

It is certain, then, that the multitude of men have neither time nor capacity for attending to many subjects. If they attend to one, they will not attend to the other ;

if they give their leisure and curiosity to this world, they will have none left for the next. We cannot be everything; as the poet says, "*non omnia possumus omnes.*" We must make up our minds to be ignorant of much, if we would know anything. And we must make our choice between risking Science, and risking Religion. Sir Robert indeed says, "Do not believe that you have not time for rational recreation. It is the idle man who wants time for everything." However, this seems to me rhetoric; and what I have said to be the matter of fact, for the truth of which I appeal, not to argument, but to the proper judges of facts,—common sense and practical experience; and if they pronounce it to be a fact, then Sir Robert Peel, little as he means it, does unite with Lord Brougham in taking from Christianity what he gives to Science.

I will make this fair offer to both of them. Every member of the Church Established shall be eligible to the Tamworth Library on one condition—that he brings from the "public minister of religion," to use Sir Robert's phrase, a ticket in witness of his proficiency in Christian knowledge. We will have no "controversial divinity" in the Library, but a little out of it. If the gentlemen of the Knowledge School will but agree to teach town and country Religion first, they shall have a *carte blanche* from me to teach anything or everything else second. Not a word has been uttered or intended in these Letters against Science; I would treat it, as they do *not* treat "controversial divinity," with respect and gratitude. They caricature doctrine under the name of controversy. I do not nickname science infidelity. I call it by their own name, "useful and entertaining knowledge;" and I call doctrine "Christian knowledge:" and, as thinking Christianity something more than useful and entertaining, I want faith to come first, and utility and amusement to follow.

That persons indeed are found in all classes, high and low, busy and idle, capable of proceeding from sacred to profane knowledge, is undeniable ; and it is desirable they should do so. It is desirable that talent for particular departments in literature and science should be fostered and turned to account, wherever it is found. But what has this to do with this general canvass of "*all* persons of all descriptions without refer-ence to religious creed, who shall have attained *the age of fourteen*" ? Why solicit "the working classes, without distinction of party, political opinion, or religious profession ; " that is, whether they have heard of a God or no ? Whence these cries rising on our ears, of " Let me entreat you ! " " Neglect not the opportunity ! " " It will not be our fault ! " " Here is an access for you!" very like the tones of a street preacher, or the cad of an omnibus,—little worthy of a great statesman and a religious philosopher ?

However, the Tamworth Reading-room admits of one restriction, which is not a little curious, and has no very liberal sound. It seems that all "*virtuous* women" may be members of the Library ; that "great injustice would be done to the *well-educated and virtuous* women of the town and neighbourhood " had they been excluded. A very emphatic silence is maintained about women not virtuous. What does this mean ? Does it mean to exclude them, while bad *men* are admitted ? Is this accident, or design, sinister and insidious, against a portion of the community ? What has virtue to do with a Reading-room ? It is to *make* its members virtuous ; it is to "exalt the *moral dignity* of their nature ; " it is to provide " charms and temptations" to allure them from sensuality and riot. To whom but to the vicious ought Sir Robert to discourse about "opportunities," and "access," and "moral improvement;" and who else would prove a fitter experiment, and a more glorious triumph, of scientific influences? And yet he shuts out all but the well-educated and virtuous.

Alas, that bigotry should have left the mark of its hoof on the great "fundamental principle of the Tamworth Institution"! Sir Robert Peel is bound in consistency to attempt its obliteration. But if that is impossible, as many will anticipate, why, O why, while he is about it, why will he not give us just a little more of it? *Cannot* we prevail on him to modify his principle, and to admit into his library none but "well-educated and virtuous" *men?*

5.

Secular Knowledge not a Principle of Social Unity.

SIR ROBERT PEEL proposes to establish a Library which "shall be open to all persons of all descriptions, without reference to political opinions or to religious creed." He invites those who are concerned in manufactories, or who have many workmen, "without distinction of party, political opinions, *or* religious profession." He promises that "in the selection of subjects for public lectures everything calculated to excite religious *or* political animosity shall be excluded." Nor is any "discussion on matters connected with religion, politics, *or* local party differences" to be permitted in the reading-room. And he congratulates himself that he has "laid the foundation of an edifice in which men of all political opinions *and* of all religious feelings may unite in furtherance of Knowledge, without the asperities of "party feeling." In these statements religious difference are made synonymous with "party feeling;" and, whereas the tree is "known by its fruit," their characteristic symptoms are felicitously described as "asperities," and "animosities." And, in order to teach us more precisely what these differences are worth, they are compared to differences between Whig and Tory—nay, even to "*local* party differences;" such, I suppose, as about a municipal election, or a hole-and-corner meeting, or a parish job, or a bill in Parliament for a railway.

But, to give him the advantage of the more honour-

able parallel of the two, are religious principles to be put
upon a level even with political ?   Is it as bad to be a
republican as an unbeliever ?   Is it as magnanimous to
humour a scoffer as to spare an opponent in the House ?
Is a difference about the Reform Bill all one with a
difference about the Creed ?   Is it as polluting to hear
arguments for Lord Melbourne as to hear a scoff against
the Apostles ?   To a statesman, indeed, like Sir Robert,
to abandon one's party is a far greater sacrifice than to
unparliamentary men ; and it would be uncandid to
doubt that he is rather magnifying politics than degrading Religion in throwing them together ; but still, when
he advocates concessions in theology *and* politics, he
must be plainly told to make presents of things that
belong to him, nor seek to be generous with other
people's substance.   There are entails in more matters
than parks and old places.   He made his politics for
himself, but Another made theology.

Christianity is faith, faith implies a doctrine ; a doctrine
propositions ; propositions yes or no, yes or no differences.
Differences, then, are the natural attendants on Christianity, and you cannot have Christianity, and not have
differences.   When, then, Sir Robert Peel calls such
differences points of " party feeling," what is this but to
insult Christianity ?   Yet so cautious, so correct a man,
cannot have made such a sacrifice for nothing ; nor does
he long leave us in doubt what is his inducement.   He
tells us that his great aim is the peace and good order of
the community, and the easy working of the national
machine.   With this in view, any price is cheap, everything is marketable ; all impediments are a nuisance.
He does not undo for undoing's sake ; he gains more
than an equivalent.   It is a mistake, too, to say that he
considers all differences of opinion as equal in import-

ance; no, they are only equally in the way. He only compares them together where they *are* comparable,— in their common inconvenience to a minister of State. They may be as little homogeneous as chalk is to cheese, or Macedon to Monmouth, but they agree in interfering with social harmony; and, since that harmony is the first of goods and the end of life, what is left us but to discard all that disunites us, and to cultivate all that may amalgamate?

Could Sir Robert have set a more remarkable example of self-sacrifice than in thus becoming the disciple of his political foe, accepting from Lord Brougham his new principle of combination, rejecting Faith for the fulcrum of Society, and proceeding to rest it upon Knowledge?

"I cannot help thinking," he exclaims at Tamworth, "that *by bringing together in an institution of this kind* intelligent men of all classes and conditions of life, by uniting together, in the committee of this institution, the gentleman of ancient family and great landed possessions with the skilful mechanic and artificer of good character, I cannot help believing that we are *harmonizing* the gradations of society, and binding men together by a *new* bond, which will have *more than ordinary* strength on account of the object which unites us." The old bond, he seems to say, was Religion; Lord Brougham's is Knowledge. Faith, once the soul of social union, is now but the spirit of division. Not a single doctrine but is "controversial divinity;" not an abstraction can be imagined (could abstractions constrain), not a comprehension projected (could comprehensions connect), but will leave out one or other portion or element of the social fabric. We must abandon Religion, if we aspire to be statesmen. Once, indeed, it was a living power, kindling hearts, leavening them with one idea, moulding them on one model, developing them into one polity. Ere now it has been the life of morality: it has given birth to heroes; it has wielded empire. But another age has come in, and Faith is effete; let us submit to what we cannot change; let us not hang over our dead, but bury it out of sight. Seek we out some young and vigorous principle, rich in sap, and fierce in life, to give form to elements which are fast resolving into their inorganic chaos; and where shall we find such a principle but in Knowledge?

Accordingly, though Sir Robert somewhat chivalrously battles for the appointment upon the Book Committee of what he calls two "public ministers of religion, holding prominent and responsible offices, endowed by the State," and that *ex officio*, yet he is untrue to his new principle only in appearance: for he couples his concession with explanations, restrictions, and safeguards quite sufficient to prevent old Faith becoming insurgent against young Knowledge. First he takes his Vicar and Curate as "conversant with literary subjects and with literary works," and then as having duties "immediately con-nected with the moral condition and improvement" of the place. Further he admits "it is perfectly right to be *jealous* of all power held by such a tenure:" and he insists on the "fundamental" condition that these sacred functionaries shall permit no doctrinal works to be in-troduced or lectures to be delivered. Lastly, he reserves in the general body the power of withdrawing this in-dulgence "if the existing checks be not sufficient, and the power be *abused*,"—abused, that is, by the vicar and curate; also he desires to secure Knowledge from being *perverted* to "*evil* or *immoral* purposes"—such perversion of course, if attempted, being the natural

antithesis, or *pendant*, to the vicar's contraband intro-
troduction of the doctrines of Faith.

Lord Brougham will make all this clearer to us. A
work of high interest and varied information, to which
I have already referred, is attributed to him, and at
least is of his school, in which the ingenious author, whoever he is, shows how Knowledge can do for Society
what has hitherto been supposed the prerogative of Faith.
As to Faith and its preachers, he had already compli-
mented them at Glasgow, as "the evil spirits of tyranny
and persecution," and had bid them good morning as
the scared and dazzled creatures of the " long night now
gone down the sky."

"The great truth," he proclaimed in language borrowed
from the records of faith (for after parsons no men quote
Scripture more familiarly than Liberals and Whigs), has
finally *gone forth to all the ends of the earth*, that man
shall no more render account to man for his belief, over
which he has himself no control. Henceforth nothing
shall prevail on us to *praise or to blame* any one for that
which he can no more change than he can the hue of
his skin or the height of his stature." And then he or
his scholar proceeds to his new *Vitæ Sanctorum*, or, as
he calls it, "Illustrations of the Pursuit of Knowledge ; "
and, whereas the badge of Christian saintliness is conflict, he writes of the " Pursuit of Knowledge *under difficulties ;* " and, whereas this Knowledge is to stand in the
place of Religion, he assumes a hortatory tone, a species
of eloquence in which decidedly he has no rival but Sir
Robert. "Knowledge," he says, " is happiness, as well
as power and virtue;" and he demands "the dedication
of our faculties" to it. " The *struggle*," he gravely
observes, which its disciple " has to wage may be a

protracted, but it ought not to be a *cheerless* one : **for,** if he do not *relax his exertions*, every movement he makes is necessarily a *step forward*, if not towards that distinction which intellectual attainments sometimes confer, at least to that *inward satisfaction and enjoyment* which is always their reward. No one stands in the way of another, or can deprive him of any part of his chance, we should rather say of his certainty, of success ; on the contrary, they are all *fellow-workers*, and may materially *help each other* forward." And he enumerates in various places the virtues which adorn the children of Knowledge— ardour united to humility, childlike alacrity, teachable- ness, truthfulness, patience, concentration of attention, husbandry of time, self-denial, self-command, and heroism.

Faith, viewed in its history through past ages, presents us with the fulfilment of one great idea in particular— that, namely, of an aristocracy of exalted spirits, drawn together out of all countries, ranks, and ages, raised above the condition of humanity, specimens of the capa- bilities of our race, incentives to rivalry and patterns for imitation. This Christian idea Lord Brougham has borrowed for his new Pantheon, which is equally various in all attributes and appendages of mind, with this one characteristic in all its specimens,—the pursuit of Know- ledge. Some of his worthies are low born, others of high degree ; some are in Europe, others in the Anti- podes ; some in the dark ages, others in the ages of light ; some exercise a voluntary, others an involuntary toil ; some give up riches, and others gain them ; some are fixtures, and others adventure much ; some are pro- fligate, and others ascetic ; and some are believers, and others are infidels.

Alfred, severely good and Christian, takes his place in

this new hagiology beside the gay and graceful Lorenzo de Medicis ; for did not the one " import civilization into England," and was not the other " the wealthy and munificent patron of all the liberal arts " ? Edward VI. and Haroun al Raschid, Dr. Johnson and Dr. Franklin, Newton and Protagoras, Pascal and Julian the Apostate, Joseph Milner and Lord Byron, Cromwell and Ovid, Bayle and Boyle, Adrian pope and Adrian emperor, Lady Jane Grey and Madame Roland,—human beings who agreed in nothing but in their humanity and in their love of Knowledge, are all admitted by this writer to one beatification, in proof of the Catholic character of his substitute for Faith.

The persecuting Marcus is a " good and enlightened emperor," and a "delightful" spectacle, when "mixing in the religious processions and ceremonies" of Athens, " re-building and re-endowing the schools," whence St. Paul was driven in derision.   The royal Alphery, on the contrary, "preferred his humble parsonage" to the throne of the Czars.   West was "nurtured among the quiet and gentle affections of a Quaker family."   Kirke White's "feelings became ardently devotional, and he determined to give up his life to the preaching of Christianity."   Roger Bacon was "a brother of the Franciscan Order, at that time the great support and ornament of both Universities."   Belzoni seized "the opportunity" of Bonaparte's arrival in Italy to "throw off his monastic habit," " its idleness and obscurity," and to engage himself as a performer at Astley's.   Duval, "a very able antiquarian of the last century," began his studies as a peasant boy, and finished them in a Jesuits' College.   Mr. Davy, "having written a system of divinity," effected the printing of it in thirteen years "with a press of his own construction," and the assistance of his female servant, working off page by page for twenty-six volumes 8vo, of nearly 500 pages each. Raleigh, in spite of "immoderate ambition," was "one of the very chief glories of an age crowded with towering spirits."

Nothing comes amiss to this author; saints and sinners, the precious and the vile, are torn from their proper homes and recklessly thrown together under the category of Knowledge. 'Tis a pity he did not extend his view, as Christianity has done, to beings out of sight of man. Milton could have helped him to some angelic personages, as patrons and guardians of his intellectual temple, who of old time, before faith had birth,

> " Apart sat on a hill retired
> In thoughts more elevate, and reasoned high
> Of providence, foreknowledge, will, and fate,
> Passion and apathy, and glory, and shame,—
> Vain wisdom all, and false philosophy."

And, indeed, he does make some guesses that way, speaking most catholically of being "admitted to a fellowship with those loftier minds" who "by universal consent *held a station apart*," and are "spoken of *reverently*," as if their names were not those "of mortal men;" and he speaks of these "benefactors of mankind, when they *rest* from their *pious* labours, looking down" upon the blessings with which their "*toils and sufferings* have clothed the scene of their former existence."

Such is the oratory which has fascinated Sir Robert; yet we must recollect that in the year 1832, even the venerable Society for Promoting Christian Knowledge herself, catching its sound, and hearing something about sublimity, and universality, and brotherhood, and effort, and felicity, was beguiled into an admission of this singularly irreligious work into the list of publications which she had delegated to a Committee to select *in usum laicorum.*

That a Venerable Society should be caught by the vision of a Church Catholic is not wonderful ; but what could possess philosophers and statesmen to dazzle her with it, but man's need of some such support, and the divine excellence and sovereign virtue of that which Faith once created ?

6.

Secular Knowledge not a Principle of Action.

PEOPLE say to me, that it is but a dream to suppose
that Christianity should regain the organic power in
human society which once it possessed. I cannot help
that ; I never said it could. I am not a politician ; I
am proposing no measures, but exposing a fallacy, and
resisting a pretence. Let Benthamism reign, if men have
no aspirations ; but do not tell them to be romantic,
and then solace them with glory ; do not attempt by
philosophy what once was done by religion. The
ascendency of Faith may be impracticable, but the
reign of Knowledge is incomprehensible. The problem
for statesmen of this age is how to educate the masses,
and literature and science cannot give the solution.

Not so deems Sir Robert Peel ; his firm belief and
hope is, "that an increased sagacity will administer to
an exalted faith ; that it will make men not merely
believe in the cold doctrines of Natural Religion, but that
it will so prepare and temper the spirit and understanding, that they will be better qualified to comprehend the
great scheme of human redemption." He certainly
thinks that scientific pursuits have some considerable
power of impressing religion upon the mind of the multitude. I think not, and will now say why.

Science gives us the grounds or premises from which
religious truths are to be inferred ; but it does not set about
inferring them, much less does it reach the inference ;—that

is not its province. It brings before us phenomena, and it
leaves us, if we will, to call them works of design, wisdom,
or benevolence; and further still, if we will, to proceed
to confess an Intelligent Creator. We have to take its
facts, and to give them a meaning, and to draw our own
conclusions from them. First comes Knowledge, then
a view, then reasoning, and then belief. This is why
Science has so little of a religious tendency; deductions
have no power of persuasion. The heart is commonly
reached, not through the reason, but through the imagination, by means of direct impressions, by the testimony
of facts and events, by history, by description. Persons
influence us, voices melt us, looks subdue us, deeds
inflame us. Many a man will live and die upon a
dogma: no man will be a martyr for a conclusion. A
conclusion is but an opinion; it is not a thing which *is*,
but which *we are "certain about;"* and it has often been
observed, that we never say we are certain without
implying that we doubt. To say that a thing *must* be,
is to admit that it *may not* be. No one, I say, will die
for his own calculations; he dies for realities. This is
why a literary religion is so little to be depended upon;
it looks well in fair weather, but its doctrines are opinions,
and, when called to suffer for them, it slips them between
its folios, or burns them at its hearth. And this again is
the secret of the distrust and raillery with which moralists have been so commonly visited. They say and do
not. Why? Because they are contemplating the fitness
of things, and they live by the square, when they should
be realizing their high maxims in the concrete. Now Sir
Robert thinks better of natural history, chemistry, and
astronomy, than of such ethics; but they too, what are
they more than divinity *in posse?* He protests against
"controversial divinity:" is *inferential* much better?

I have no confidence, then, in philosophers who cannot help being religious, and are Christians by implication. They sit at home, and reach forward to distances which astonish us; but they hit without grasping, and are sometimes as confident about shadows as about realities. They have worked out by a calculation the lie of a country which they never saw, and mapped it by means of a gazetteer; and like blind men, though they can put a stranger on his way, they cannot walk straight themselves, and do not feel it quite their business to walk at all.

Logic makes but a sorry rhetoric with the multitude; first shoot round corners, and you may not despair of converting by a syllogism. Tell men to gain notions of a Creator from His works, and, if they were to set about it (which nobody does), they would be jaded and wearied by the labyrinth they were tracing. Their minds would be gorged and surfeited by the logical operation. Logicians are more set upon concluding rightly, than on right conclusions. They cannot see the end for the process. Few men have that power of mind which may hold fast and firmly a variety of thoughts. We ridicule "men of one idea;" but a great many of us are born to be such, and we should be happier if we knew it. To most men argument makes the point in hand only more doubtful, and considerably less impressive. After all, man is *not* a reasoning animal; he is a seeing, feeling, contemplating, acting animal. He is influenced by what is direct and precise. It is very well to freshen our impressions and convictions from physics, but to create them we must go elsewhere. Sir Robert Peel " never can think it possible that a mind can be so constituted, that, after being familiarized with the wonderful discoveries which have been made in every part of experimental science, it can

retire from such contemplations without more enlarged
conceptions of God's providence, and a higher reverence
for His name." If he speaks of religious minds, he
perpetrates a truism ; if of irreligious, he insinuates a
paradox.

Life is not long enough for a religion of inferences ; we
shall never have done beginning, if we determine to begin
with proof. We shall ever be laying our foundations ;
we shall turn theology into evidences, and divines into
textuaries. We shall never get at our first principles.
Resolve to believe nothing, and you must prove your
proofs and analyze your elements, sinking further and
further, and finding "in the lowest depth a lower deep,"
till you come to the broad bosom of scepticism. I would
rather be bound to defend the reasonableness of assuming
that Christianity is true, than to demonstrate a moral
governance from the physical world. Life is for action.
If we insist on proofs for everything, we shall never
come to action : to act you must assume, and that
assumption is faith.

Let no one suppose that in saying this I am maintaining that all proofs are equally difficult, and all propositions equally debatable. Some assumptions are greater
than others, and some doctrines involve postulates larger
than others, and more numerous. I only say that impressions lead to action, and that reasonings lead from
it. Knowledge of premisses, and inferences upon them,
—this is not to *live*. It is very well as a matter of liberal
curiosity and of philosophy to analyze our modes of
thought ; but let this come second, and when there is
leisure for it, and then our examinations will in many
ways even be subservient to action. But if we commence
with scientific knowledge and argumentative proof, or
lay any great stress upon it as the basis of personal

Christianity, or attempt to make man moral and religious by Libraries and Museums, let us in consistency take chemists for our cooks, and mineralogists for our masons.

Now I wish to state all this as matter of fact, to be judged by the candid testimony of any persons whatever. Why we are so constituted that Faith, not Knowledge or Argument, is our principle of action, is a question with which I have nothing to do ; but I think it is a fact, and if it be such, we must resign ourselves to it as best we may, unless we take refuge in the intolerable paradox, that the mass of men are created for nothing, and are meant to leave life as they entered it. So well has this practically been understood in all ages of the world, that no Religion has yet been a Religion of physics or of philosophy. It has ever been synonymous with Revelation. It never has been a deduction from what we know : it has ever been an assertion of what we are to believe. It has never lived in a conclusion ; it has ever been a message, or a history, or a vision. No legislator or priest ever dreamed of educating our moral nature by science or by argument. There is no difference here between true Religions and pretended. Moses was instructed, not to reason from the creation, but to work miracles. Christianity is a history supernatural, and almost scenic : it tells us what its Author is, by telling us what He has done. I have no wish at all to speak otherwise than respectfully of conscientious Dissenters, but I have heard it said by those who were not their enemies, and who had known much of their preaching, that they had often heard narrow-minded and bigoted clergymen, and often Dissenting ministers of a far more intellectual cast; but that Dissenting teaching came to nothing,—that it was dissipated in thoughts which had no point, and inquiries which converged to no centre, that it ended as it began, and sent away its hearers as it found them ;— whereas the instruction in the Church, with all its defects and mistakes, comes to some end, for it started from some beginning. Such is the difference between the dogmatism of faith and the speculations of logic.

Lord Brougham himself, as we have already seen, has recognized the force of this principle. He has not left his philosophical religion to argument; he has committed it to the keeping of the imagination. Why should he depict a great republic of letters, and an intellectual Pantheon, but that he feels that instances and patterns, not logical reasonings, are the living conclusions which alone have a hold over the affections, or can form the character?

7.

Secular Knowledge without Personal Religion tends to Unbelief.

WHEN Sir Robert Peel assures us from the Town-hall at Tamworth that physical science must lead to religion, it is no bad compliment to him to say that he is unreal. He speaks of what he knows nothing about. To a religious man like him, Science has ever suggested religious thoughts ; he colours the phenomena of physics with the hues of his own mind, and mistakes an interpretation for a deduction. " I am sanguine enough to believe," he says, " that that superior sagacity which is most conversant with the course and constitution of Nature will be first to turn a deaf ear to objections and presumptions against Revealed Religion, and to acknowledge the complete harmony of the Christian Dispensation with all that Reason, assisted by Revelation, tells us of the course and constitution of Nature." Now, considering that we are all of us educated as Christians from infancy, it is not easy to decide at this day whether Science creates Faith, or only confirms it ; but we have this remarkable fact in the history of heathen Greece against the former supposition, that her most eminent empirical philosophers were atheists, and that it was their atheism which was the cause of their eminence. " The natural philosophies of Democritus and others," says Lord Bacon, " *who allow no God or mind* in the frame of things, but attribute the structure of the uuiverse to infinite essays and trials of nature, or what they call fate or fortune, and assigned the causes of particular things to the necessity of matter, *without any intermixture of final causes,* seem, as far as we can judge from the remains of their philosophy, *much more solid,* and to have *gone deeper into nature,* with regard to physical causes, than the philosophies of Aristotle or Plato: and this only because they *never meddled with final causes,* which the others were perpetually inculcating."

Lord Bacon gives us both the fact and the reason for it. Physical philosophers are ever inquiring *whence* things are, not *why;* referring them to nature, not to mind; and thus they tend to make a system a substitute for a God. Each pursuit or calling has its own dangers, and each numbers among its professors men who rise superior to them. As the soldier is tempted to dissipation, and the merchant to acquisitiveness, and the lawyer to the sophistical, and the statesman to the expedient, and the country clergyman to ease and comfort, yet there are good clergymen, statesmen, lawyers, merchants, and soldiers, notwithstanding; so there are religious experimentalists, though physics, taken by themselves, tend to infidelity; but to have recourse to physics to *make* men religious is like recommending a canonry as a cure for the gout, or giving a youngster a commission as a penance for irregularities.

The whole framework of Nature is confessedly a tissue of antecedents and consequents; we may refer all things forwards to design, or backwards on a physical cause. La Place is said to have considered he had a formula which solved all the motions of the solar system; shall we say that those motions came from this formula or from a Divine Fiat? Shall we have recourse for our theory to physics or to theology? Shall we assume

Matter and its necessary properties to be eternal, or Mind with its divine attributes? Does the sun shine to warm the earth, or is the earth warmed because the sun shines? The one hypothesis will solve the phenomena as well as the other. Say not it is but a puzzle in argument, and that no one ever felt it in fact. So far from it, I believe that the study of Nature, when religious feeling is away, leads the mind, rightly or wrongly, to acquiesce in the atheistic theory, as the simplest and easiest. It is but parallel to that tendency in anatomical studies, which no one will deny, to solve all the phenomena of the human frame into material elements and powers, and to dispense with the soul. To those who are conscious of matter, but not conscious of mind, it seems more rational to refer all things to one origin, such as they know, than to assume the existence of a second origin such as they know not. It is Religion, then, which suggests to Science its true conclusions; the facts come from Knowledge, but the principles come of Faith.*

There are two ways, then, of reading Nature—as a machine and as a work. If we come to it with the assumption that it is a creation, we shall study it with awe; if assuming it to be a system, with mere curiosity. Sir Robert does not make this distinction. He subscribes to the belief that the man " accustomed to such contemplations, *struck with awe* by the manifold proofs of infinite power and infinite wisdom, will yield more ready and hearty assent—yes, the assent of the heart, and not only of the understanding, to the pious ex-

---

* [This is too absolute, if it is to be taken to mean that the legitimate, and what may be called the objective, conclusion from the fact of Nature viewed in the concrete is not in favour of the being and providence of God. —*Vide* " Essay on Assent," pp. 336, 345, 369, and "Univ. Serm." p. 194.]

clamation, 'O Lord, how glorious are Thy works!'"
He considers that greater insight into Nature will lead
a man to say, "How great and wise is the Creator, who
has done this!" True : but it is possible that his
thoughts may take the form of "How clever is the
creature who has discovered it!" and self-conceit may
stand proxy for adoration. This is no idle apprehension.
Sir Robert himself, religious as he is, gives cause for it ;
for the first reflection that rises in his mind, as expressed
in the above passage, *before* his notice of Divine Power
and Wisdom, is, that "the man accustomed to such
contemplations will feel the *moral dignity of his nature
exalted.*" But Lord Brougham speaks out. "The
delight," he says, "is inexpressible of *being able to follow*,
as it were, with our eyes, the marvellous works of the
Great Architect of Nature." And more clearly still :
"One of the most *gratifying treats* which science affords
us is *the knowledge of the extraordinary powers* with
which the human mind is endowed. No man, until he
has studied philosophy, can have a just idea of the great
things for which Providence has fitted his understanding,
the extraordinary disproportion which there is between
his natural strength and the powers of his mind, and the
force which he derives from these powers. When we
survey the marvellous truths of astronomy, we are first
of all lost in the feeling of immense space, and of the
comparative insignificance of this globe and its inhabitants. But there soon arises a *sense of gratification and
of new wonder* at perceiving how so insignificant a
creature has been *able to reach such a knowledge* of the
unbounded system of the universe." So, this is the
religion we are to gain from the study of Nature ; how
miserable ! The god we attain is our own mind ; our
veneration is even professedly the worship of self.

The truth is that the system of Nature is just as much connected with Religion, where minds are not religious, as a watch or a steam-carriage. The material world, indeed, is infinitely more wonderful than any human contrivance; but wonder is not religion, or we should be worshipping our railroads. What the physical creation presents to us in itself is a piece of machinery, and when men speak of a Divine Intelligence as its Author, this god of theirs is not the Living and True, unless the spring is the god of a watch, or steam the creator of the engine. Their idol, taken at advantage (though it is *not* an idol, for they do not worship it), is the animating principle of a vast and complicated system; it is subjected to laws, and it is connatural and co-extensive with matter. Well does Lord Brougham call it "the great architect of nature;" it is an instinct, or a soul of the world, or a vital power; it is not the Almighty God.*

It is observable that Lord Brougham does not allude to any *relation* as existing between his *god* and ourselves. He is filled with awe, it seems, at the powers of the human mind, as displayed in their analysis of the vast creation. Is not this a fitting time to say a word about gratitude towards Him who gave them? Not a syllable. What we gain from his contemplation of Nature is "a gratifying treat," the knowledge of the "great things for which Providence has fitted man's understanding;" our admiration terminates in man; it passes on to no prototype.† I am not quarrelling with his result as illogical or unfair; it is but consistent with the principles with which he started. Take the system of Nature by itself, detached from the axioms of Religion, and I am willing to confess—nay, I have been expressly urging—that it

* [*Vide* "University Teaching," Disc. 2.]
† [*Vide* "Essays," vol. i. p. 37, etc.]

does not force us to take it for *more* than a system ; but why, then, persist in calling the study of it religious, when it can be treated, and is treated, thus atheistically ? Say that Religion hallows the study, and not that the study creates Religion. The essence of Religion is the idea of a Moral Governor and a particular Providence ; now let me ask, is the doctrine of moral governance and a particular providence conveyed to us through the physical sciences at all ? Would they be physical sciences if they treated of morals ? Can physics teach moral matters without ceasing to be physics ? But are not virtue and vice, and responsibility, and reward and punishment, anything else than moral matters, and are *they* not of the essence of Religion ? In what department, then, of physics are they to be found ? Can the problems and principles they involve be expressed in the differential calculus ? Is the galvanic battery a whit more akin to conscience and will, than the mechanical powers ? What we seek is what concerns us, the traces of a Moral Governor ; even religious minds cannot discern these in the physical sciences ; astronomy witnesses divine power, and physics divine skill ; and all of them divine beneficence ; but which teaches of divine holiness, truth, justice, or mercy? Is that much of a Religion which is silent about duty, sin, and its remedies ? Was there ever a Religion which was without the idea of an expiation ?

Sir Robert Peel tells us, that physical science imparts " pleasure and *consolation* " on a death-bed. Lord Brougham confines himself to the "gratifying treat ; " but Sir Robert ventures to speak of " consolation." Now, if we are on trial in this life, and if death be the time when our account is gathered in, is it at all serious or real to be talking of " consoling " ourselves at such a time with scientific subjects? Are these topics to suggest to us the thought of the Creator or not? If not, are they better than story books, to beguile the mind from what lies before it? But, if they are to speak of Him, can a dying man find rest in the mere notion of his Creator, when he knows Him also so awfully as His Moral Governor and his Judge? Meditate indeed on the wonders of Nature on a death-bed! Rather stay your hunger with corn grown in Jupiter, and warm yourself by the Moon.

But enough on this most painful portion of Sir Robert's Address. As I am coming to an end, I suppose I ought to sum up in a few words what I have been saying. I consider, then, that intrinsically excellent and noble as are scientific pursuits, and worthy of a place in a liberal education, and fruitful in temporal benefits to the community, still they are not, and cannot be, *the instrument* of an ethical training; that physics do not supply a basis, but only materials for religious sentiment; that knowledge does but occupy, does not form the mind; that apprehension of the unseen is the only known principle capable of subduing moral evil, educating the multitude, and organizing society; and that, whereas man is born for action, action flows not from inferences, but from impressions,—not from reasonings, but from Faith.

That Sir Robert would deny these propositions I am far from contending; I do not even contend that he has asserted the contrary at Tamworth. It matters little to me whether he spoke boldly and intelligibly, as the newspapers represent, or guarded his strong sayings with the contradictory matter with which they are intercalated in his own report. In either case the drift and the effect of his Address are the same. He has given his respected name to a sophistical School, and condescended to mimic the gestures and tones of Lord Brougham. How melancholy is it that a man of such exemplary life, such cultivated tastes, such political distinction, such Parliamentary tact, and such varied experience, should have so little confidence in himself, so little faith in his own principles, so little hope of sympathy in others, so little heart for a great venture, so little of romantic aspiration, and of firm resolve, and stern dutifulness to the Unseen ! How sad that he who might have had the affections of many, should have thought, in a day like this, that a Statesman's praise lay in preserving the mean, not in aiming at the high ; that to be safe was his first merit, and to kindle enthusiasm his most disgraceful blunder ! How pitiable that such a man should not have understood that a body without a soul has no life, and a political party without an idea, no unity !

February, 1841.

V.

WHO'S TO BLAME?

(*Addressed to the Editor of* THE CATHOLIC STANDARD. *By Catholicus.*)

I.

The British Constitution on its Trial.

SIR,—I have been much shocked, as I suppose has been the case with most of your readers, at the weekly extracts you have made from the correspondents of the daily prints, descriptive of the state of the British army in the Crimea; and a conviction has been steadily growing, or rather has been formed, in my mind, which the running comments of the Press continually strengthen, that we must go very deep indeed to get at the root of the evil, which lies, not in the men in authority, nor in systems of administration simply in themselves, but in nothing short of the British Constitution itself. I do not expect I shall get others to agree with me in this conclusion at once; I do not ask you, Mr. Editor, to assent to it, but to be patient with me, if, in order to do justice to my own ideas on the subject, I ask for a long hearing—if I even ask to be diffuse, roundabout, discursive, nay, perhaps, prosy, in support of what, at first sight, readers may call my paradox,—for I have no chance of establishing it in any other way.

Nor have I embraced it with any satisfaction to my feelings, certainly not to my Catholic feelings. Indeed, I have a decided view that Catholicism is safer and more free under a constitutional *regime*, such as our own, than under any other. I have no wish for "reforms"; and should be sorry to create in the minds of your readers any sentiment favourable either to democracy or to absolutism. I have no liking for the tyranny whether of autocrat or mob; no taste for being whirled off to Siberia, or tarred and feathered in the far West, by the enemies of my religion. May I live and die under the mild sway of a polity which certainly represses and dilutes the blind fanaticism of a certain portion of my country-men,— a fanaticism which, except for it, would sweep us off these broad lands, and lodge us, with little delay or compunction, in the German Sea! Still, we cannot alter facts; and, if the British Constitution is admirably adapted for peace, but not for war, which is the proposi-tion I shall support, and which seems dawning on the public mind, there is a lesson contained in that circum-stance which demands our attention. The lesson is this —that we were not wise to go to war, if we could possibly have avoided it, at a time when, by a lucky accident, the Duke of Wellington had gained for the nation a military prestige which it had little chance of preserving; and the sooner we know our capabilities and our true mission among the nations of the earth, and get back into a state of peace, in which we are really and truly great, the better for us.

It is not that I am doubting the heroic bravery and fortitude of the British soldier. I am not speaking of the individual soldier, whose great qualities I revere and marvel at, and whom I have been following with my anxieties and prayers ever since he set out on his foreign campaign. I am as little concerned here with the valour of our soldiers, as with the bigotry of our middle class ; with the heights of Inkerman, as with the depths of Exeter Hall. I am to speak of our Constitution and of Constitutional Government ; and I say that this said Constitutional Government of ours shows to extreme advantage in a state of peace, but not so in a state of war ; and that it cannot be otherwise from the nature of things. Surely it is not paradoxical to say as much as this ; for no one in this world can secure all things at once, but in every human work there is a maximum of good, short of the best possible. The wonder and the paradox rather would be, if the institutions of England were equally admirable for all contingencies, for war as well as for peace. Certainly martial law and constitutional freedom, the soldier's bayonet and the staff of the police-man, belong to antagonistic classes of ideas, and are not likely to co-operate happily with each other.

Nor, again, do I therefore say that we must never go to war, or that we shall always get the worst off, if we do. I only mean, it is not our strong point. I suppose, if we had no fowling-pieces, we might still manage, like Philoctetes, to knock off our game with bow and arrows. There are always ways of doing things, where there is the will. I am not denying that, with great exertion, we are able to hoist up our complex Constitution, to ease it into position, and fire it off with uncommon effect ; but to do so is a most inconvenient, expensive, tedious process ; it takes much time, much money, many men, and many lives. We ought in consequence to think twice before we set it to work for a purpose for which it was never made ; and this I think we did not do a year ago. We hardly thought once about the matter. With intense self-conceit, we despised our foe.

We treated him as we treated the Pope four years before, and we have caught it. The *Times* put out feelers,
this time last year, as to the possibility of the British
Lion being persuaded into a more good-humoured, as
well as a more prudent course ; but that sagacious journal was soon obliged to draw them in again, and to
swim down the stream with the boldest. For the saiu
Lion was bent on puffing the Muscovite into space with
the mere breath of his growl ; and it did not occur to
him at the moment, that perhaps it was his own wisdom,
and not the Muscovite's merely, to let well alone, and to
live upon the capital which a great military genius had
made for him in the last war. And so, without reflection,
the Lion did what, I am firmly persuaded, neither the
Duke nor Sir Robert Peel would have let him do, had
they been alive. He believed those counsellors who
had the madness to tell him that it was a little war
which he was beginning, and he stood rampant forthwith
both in the Baltic and in the Black Sea.

But there is a further view of the matter, and it suggests another unpleasant consideration. No one likes to
use a cumbrous, clumsy instrument; and, if at war we
are, and with institutions not fitted for war, it is just
possible we may alter our institutions, under the immediate pressure, in order to make them work easier for
the object of war ; and then what becomes of King,
Lords, and Commons ? There are abundant symptoms,
on all sides of us, of the presence of a strong temptation to
some such temerarious proceeding. Any one, then, who,
like myself, is thankful that he is born under the British
Constitution,—any Catholic who dreads the knout and
the tar-barrel, will, for that very reason, look with great
ealousy on a state of things which not only doubles
prices and taxes, but which may bring about a sudden

infringement and an irreparable injury of that remarkable polity, which the world never saw before, or elsewhere, and which it is so pleasant to live under. I do not mean to say that anything serious will be sensibly experienced in our time, at least in the time of those who are gliding rapidly along to the evening of life ; but it would be no consolation to me to be told that the Constitution will last my day, if I know that the next generation, whom I am watching as they come into active life, would fall under a form of government less favourable to the Church. And I do not think that the Catholics of England, who have shown no little exultation at the war, would gain much by rescuing Turkey from the Russo-Greeks, if, after planting Protestant Liberalism there instead, they found on looking homeward that despotism or democracy had mounted in these islands on the ruins of the aristocracy.

However, it is not my business to prophesy, but to attempt to lay down principles, which I hope to be allowed to do in my next letter.

2.

States and Constitutions.

THE proposition I have undertaken to maintain is this :
—That the British Constitution is made for a state of
peace, and not for a state of war ; and that war tries it
in the same way, to use a homely illustration, that it tries
a spoon to use it for a knife, or a scythe or hay-fork to
make it do the work of a spade. I expressed myself thus
generally, in order to give to those who should do me
the honour of reading me the most expeditious insight
into the view which I wished to set before them. But,
if I must speak accurately, my meaning is this,—that,
whereas a Nation has two aspects, internal and external,
one as regards its own members, and one as regards
foreigners, and whereas its government has two duties,
one towards its subjects, and one towards its allies or
enemies, the British State is great in its home department,
which is its primary object, foreign affairs being its
secondary ; while France or Russia, Prussia or Austria,
contemplates in the first place foreign affairs, and is great
in their management, and makes the home department
only its second object. And further, that, if England be
great abroad, as she is, it is not so much the State, as
the People or Nation, which is the cause of her greatness, and that not by means but in spite of the Constitution, or, if by means of it in any measure, clumsily so
and circuitously; on the other hand, that, if foreign powers
are ever great in the management of their own people,

and make men of them, this they do in spite of their polity, and rather by the accidental qualifications of the individual ruler ; or if by their polity, still with inconvenience and effort. Other explanations I may add to the above as I proceed, but this is sufficient for the present.

Now I hope you will have patience with me, if I begin by setting down what I mean by a State, and by a Constitution.

First of all, it is plain that every one has a power of his own to act this way or that, as he pleases. And, as not one or two, but every one has it, it is equally plain, that, if all exercised it to the full, at least the stronger part of mankind would always be in conflict with each other, and no one would enjoy the benefit of it ; so that it is the interest of every one to give up some portion of his birth-freedom in this or that direction, in order to secure more freedom on the whole ; exchanging a freedom which is now large and now narrow, according as the accidents of his conflicts with others are more or less favourable to himself, for a certain definite range of freedom prescribed and guaranteed by settled engagements or laws. In other words, Society is necessary for the well-being of human nature. The result, aimed at and effected by these mutual arrangements, is called a State or Standing; that is, in contrast with the appearance presented by a people before and apart from such arrangements, which is not a standing, but a chronic condition of commotion and disorder.

And next, as this State or settlement of a people, is brought about by mutual arrangements, that is, by laws or rules, there is need, from the nature of the case, of some power over and above the People itself to maintain and enforce them. This living guardian of the laws is called the Government, and a governing power is thus involved in the very notion of Society. Let the Government be suspended, and at once the State is threatened with dissolution, which at best is only a matter of time.

A lively illustration in point is furnished us by a classical historian. When the great Assyrian Empire broke up, a time of anarchy succeeded; and, little as its late subjects liked its sway, they liked its absence less. The historian thus proceeds : " There was a wise man among the Medes, called Deioces. This Deioces, aspiring to be tyrant, did thus. He was already a man of reputation in his own country, and he now, more than ever, practised justice. The Medes, accordingly, in his neighbourhood, seeing his ways, made him their umpire in disputes. He, on the other hand, having empire in his eye, was upright and just. As he proceeded thus, the dwellers in other towns, who had suffered from unjust decisions, were glad to go to him and to plead their causes, till at length they went to no one else. Deioces now had the matter in his own hands. Accordingly he would no longer proceed to the judgment-seat ; for it was not worth his while, he said, to neglect his private affairs for the sake of the affairs of others. When rapine and lawlessness returned, his friends said, ' We must appoint a king over us;' and then they debated who it should be, and Deioces was praised by every one. So they made him their king ; and he, upon this, bade them to build him a house worthy of his kingly power, and protect him with guards ; and the Medes did so."

Now I have quoted this passage from history, because it carries us a step further in our investigation. It is for the good of the many that the one man, Deioces, is set up ; but who is to keep him in his proper work ? He puts down all little tyrants, but what is to hinder his becoming a greater tyrant than them all? This was actually the case; first the Assyrian tyranny, then anarchy, then the tyranny of Deioces. Thus the unfortunate masses oscillate between two opposite evils,—that of having no governor, and that of having too much of one; and which is the lesser of the two? This was the dilemma which beset the Horse in the fable. He was in feud with the Stag, by whose horns he was driven from his pasture. The Man promised him an easy victory, if he would let him mount him. On his assenting, the Man bridled him, and vaulted on him, and pursued and killed his enemy; but, this done, he would not get off him. Now, then, the Horse was even worse off than before, because he had a master to serve, instead of a foe to combat.

Here then is the problem : the social state is necessary for man, but it seems to contain in itself the elements of its own undoing. It requires a power to enforce the laws, and to rule the unruly ; but what law is to control that power, and to rule the ruler? According to the common adage, "Quis custodiat ipsos custodes?" Who is to hinder the governor dispensing with the law in his own favour? History shows us that this problem is as ordinary as it is perplexing.

The expedient, by which the State is kept *in statu* and its ruler is ruled, is called its Constitution ; and this has next to be explained. Now a Constitution really is not a mere code of laws, as is plain at once ; for the very problem is how to confine power within the law, and in order to the maintenance of law. The ruling power can, and may, overturn law and law-makers, as Cromwell did, by the same sword with which he protects them. Acts of Parliament, Magna Charta, the Bill of Rights, the Reform Bill, none of these are the British Constitution.

What then is conveyed in that word? I would answer as follows :—

As individuals have characters of their own, so have races. Most men have their strong and their weak points, and points neither good nor bad, but idiosyncratic. And so of races : one is brave and sensitive of its honour ; another romantic; another industrious, or long-headed, or religious. One is barbarous, another civilized. Moreover, growing out of these varieties or idiosyncrasies, and corresponding to them, will be found in these several races, and proper to each, a certain assemblage of beliefs, convictions, rules, usages, traditions, proverbs, and principles; some political, some social, some moral; and these tending to some definite form of government and *modus vivendi*, or polity, as their natural scope. And this being the case, when a given race has that polity which is intended for it by nature, it is in the same state of repose and contentment which an individual enjoys who has the food, or the comforts, the stimulants, sedatives, or restoratives, which are suited to his *diathesis* and his need. This then is the Constitution of a State : securing, as it does, the national unity by at once strengthening and controlling its governing power. It is something more than law ; it is the embodiment of special ideas, ideas perhaps which have been held by a race for ages, which are of immemorial usage, which have fixed themselves in its innermost heart, which are in its eyes sacred to it, and have practically the force of eternal truths, whether they be such or not. These ideas are sometimes trivial, and, at first sight, even absurd : sometimes they are superstitious, sometimes they are great or beautiful ; but to those to whom they belong they are first principles, watch-words, common property, natural ties, a cause to fight for, an occasion of self-sacrifice. They are the expres-

sions of some or other sentiment,—of loyalty, of order, of
duty, of honour, of faith, of justice, of glory.   They are
the creative and conservative influences of Society ; they
erect nations into States, and invest States with Constitutions.   They inspire and sway, as well as restrain, the
ruler of a people, for he himself is but one of that people
to which they belong.

3.

Constitutional Principles and their Varieties.

IT is a common saying that political power is founded on opinion; this is true, if the word "opinion" be understood in the widest sense of which it is capable. A State depends and rests, not simply on force of arms, not on logic, not on anything short of the sentiment and will of those who are governed. This doctrine does not imply instability and change as inherent characteristics of a body politic. Since no one can put off his opinions in a moment, or by willing it, since those opinions may be instincts, principles, beliefs, convictions, since they may be self-evident, since they may be religious truths, it may be easily understood how a national polity, as being the creation and development of a multitude of men having all the same opinions, may stand of itself, and be most firmly established, and may be practically secure against reverse. And thus it is that countries become settled, with a definite form of social union, and an ascendancy of law and order; not as if that particular settlement, union, form, order, and law were self-sanctioned and self-supported, but because it is founded in the national mind, and maintained by the force of a living tradition. This, then, is what I mean by a State; and, being the production and outcome of a people, it is necessarily for the good of the people, and it has two main elements, power and liberty,—for without power there is no protection, and without liberty there is nothing to protect. The seat of power is the Government ; the seat of liberty is the Constitution.

You will say that this implies that every State must have a Constitution; so I think it has, in the sense in which I have explained the word. As the governing power may be feeble and unready, so the check upon its arbitrary exercise may be partial and uncertain ; it may be rude, circuitous, abrupt, or violent; it need not be scientifically recognized and defined ; but there never has been, there never can be, in any political body, an instance of unmitigated absolutism. Human nature does not allow of it. In pure despotisms, the practical limitation of the ruler's power lies in his personal fears, in the use of the dagger or the bowstring. These expedients have been brought into exercise before now, both by our foes, the Russians, and, still more so, by our friends, the Turks. Nay, when the present war began, some of our self-made politicians put forward the pleasant suggestion that the Czar's assassination at the hands of his subjects, maddened by taxes and blockades, was a possible path to the triumph of the allies.

Such is the lawless remedy which nature finds for a lawless tyranny ; and no one will deny that such a savage justice is national in certain states of Society, and has a traditional authority, and may in a certain sense be called Constitutional. As society becomes civilized, the checks on arbitrary power assume a form in accordance with a more cultivated morality. We have one curious specimen of a Constitutional principle, preserved to us in the Medo-Persian Empire. It was a wholesome and subtle provision, adopting the semblance of an abject servility suitable to the idea of a despotism, which proclaimed the judgment of the despot infallible, and his word irrevocable. Alexander felt what it was to do irrevocable acts in the physical order, when, in the plenitude of his sovereignty, he actually killed his friend in the banquet; and, as to the vulgar multitude, this same natural result, the remedy or penalty of reckless power, is expressed in the unpolite proverb, "Give a rogue rope enough, and he will hang himself." With a parallel significance, then, it was made a sacred principle among the Medo-Persians, which awed and sobered the monarch himself, from its surpassing inconvenience, that what he once had uttered had the force of fate. It was the punishment of his greatness, that, when Darius would have saved the prophet Daniel from the operation of a law, which the king had been flattered into promulgating, he could not do so.

A similar check upon the tyranny of power, assuming the character of veneration and homage, is the form and etiquette which is so commonly thrown round a monarch. By irresistible custom, a ceremonial more or less stringent has been made almost to enter into his essential idea, for we know majesty without its externals is a jest; and, while to lay it aside is to relinquish the discriminating badge which is his claim upon the homage of his subjects, to observe it is to surrender himself manicled and fettered into their hands. It is said a king of Spain was roasted to death because the proper official was not found in time to wheel away his royal person from the fire. If etiquette hindered him from saving his own life, etiquette might also interpose an obstacle to his taking the life of another. If it was so necessary for Sancho Panza, governor of Barataria, to eat his dinner with the sanction of the court physician on every dish, other great functionaries of State might possibly be conditions of other indulgences on his part which were less reasonable and less imperative. As for our own most gracious Sovereign, she is honoured with the Constitutional prerogative that "the king can do no wrong;" that is, he can do no political act of his own mere will at all.

It is, then, no paradox to say that every State has in some sense a Constitution; that is, a set of traditions, depending, not on formal enactment, but on national acceptance, in one way or other restrictive of the ruler's power; though in one country more scientifically developed than another, or more distinctly recognized, or more skilfully and fully adapted to their end. There is a sort of analogy between the political and the physical sense of the word. A man of good constitution is one who has something more than life,—viz., a bodily soundness, organic and functional, which will bring him safely through hardships, or illnesses, or dissipations. On the other hand, no one is altogether without a constitution : to say he has nothing to fall back upon, when his health is tried, is almost to pronounce that his life is an accident, and that he may at any moment be carried off. And, in like manner, that must be pronounced no State, but a mere fortuitous collection of individuals, which has no unity stronger than despotism, or deeper than law.

I am not sure how far it bears upon the main proposition to which these remarks are meant to conduct us, but at least it will illustrate the general subject, if I ask your leave to specify, as regards the depository of political power, four Constitutional principles, distinct in kind from each other, which, among other parallel ones, have had an historical existence. If they must have names given them, they may be called respectively the principles of co-ordination, subordination, delegation, and participation.

1. As all political power implies unity, the word *co-ordination* may seem inconsistent with its essential idea :

and yet there is a state of society, in which the limitation of despotism is by the voice of the people so un-
equivocally committed to an external authority, that we
must speak of it as the Constitution of such a State, in
spite of the seeming anomaly. Such is the recognition
of the authority of Religion, as existing in its own substantive institutions, external to the strictly political
framework, which even in pagan countries has been at
times successfully used to curb the extravagances of
absolute power. Putting paganism aside, we find in the
history both of Israel and of Judah the tyranny of kings
brought within due limits by the priests and prophets,
as by legitimate and self-independent authorities. The
same has been the case in Christian times. The Church
is essentially a popular institution, defending the cause
and encouraging the talents of the lower classes, and
interposing an external barrier in favour of high or low
against the ambition and the rapacity of the temporal
power. " If the Christian Church had not existed," says
M. Guizot, " the whole world would have been abandoned
to unmitigated material force." However, as the cor-
rective principle is in this instance external to the State,
though having its root internally in national opinion, it
cannot, except improperly, be termed Constitutional.

2. Next I come to the principle of *subordination*, which
has been commonly found in young, semi-barbarous
states both in Europe and Asia, and has attained its
most perfect form in what is called the Feudal System.
It has had a military origin ; and, after the pattern of an
army, is carried out in an hierarchy of chiefs, one under
the other, each of whom in consequence had direct jurisdiction only over a few. First came the *suzerain*, or lord
paramount, who had the allegiance of a certain number
of princes, dukes, counts, or even kings. These were his

⁎

feudatories,—that is, they owed him certain military services, and held their respective territories of him. Their vassals, in turn, were the barons, each under his own prince or duke, and owing him a similar service. Under the barons were the soldiers, each settled down on his own portion of land, with the peasants of the soil as his serfs, and with similar feudal duties to his own baron. A system like this furnished a most perfect expedient against absolutism. Power was distributed among many persons, without confusion or the chance of collision ; and, while the paucity of vassals under one and the same rule gave less scope to tyrannical excesses, it created an effective public opinion, which is strongest when the relation between governor and governed is most intimate. Moreover, if any one were disposed to play the tyrant, there were several distinct parties in a condition to unite against him ; the barons and lower class against the king, the king and the lower classs' against the barons. The barbarities of the middle ages have been associated in men's minds with this system ; but, whatever they were, they surely took place in spite of it, not through it,—just as the anti-Catholic virulence of the present race of Englishmen is mitigated, not caused, by the British Constitution.

3. By the principle of *delegation*, I mean that according to which power is committed for a certain time to individuals, with a commensurate responsibility, to be met whenever that time has expired. Thus the Roman Dictator, elected on great emergencies, was autocrat during the term of his rule. Thus a commander of an army has unfettered powers to do what he will, while his command continues ; or the captain of a ship ; but afterwards his acts are open to inquiry, and, if so be, to animadversion. There are great

advantages to a system like this ; it is the mode of bringing out great men, and of working great measures. You choose the fittest man for each department ; you frankly trust him, you heap powers upon him, you generously support him with your authority, you let him have his own way, you let him do his best. Afterwards you review his proceedings ; you reward or censure him. Such, again, in fact, is with us the liberty of the press, censorship being simply unconstitutional, and the courts of law, the remedy against seditious, libellous, or de-moralizing publications. Here, too, your advantage is great ; you form public opinion, and you ascertain the national mind.

4. The very opposite to this is the principle of *participation*. It is that by which a People would leave nothing to its rulers, but has itself, or by its immediate instruments, a concurrent part in everything that is done. Acting on the notion that no one is to be trusted, even for a time, and that every act of its officials is to be jealously watched, it never commits power without embarrassing its exercise. Instead of making a venture for the transcendent, it keeps fast by a safe mediocrity. It rather trusts a dozen persons than one to do its work. This is the great principle of boards and officers, engaged in checking each other, with a second apparatus to check the first apparatus, and other functionaries to keep an eye on both of them,—Tom helping Jack, and Jack waiting for Bill, till the end is lost in the means. Such seems to have been the principle of the military duties performed by the Aulic Council in Germany, which virtually co-operated with Napoleon in his victories in that country. Such is the great principle of committees of taste, which have covered this fair land with architec-tural monstrosities. And as being closely allied to the

principle of comprehension and compromise (a principle, necessary indeed, in some shape, but admitting of ruinous excess), it has had an influence on our national action in matters more serious than architecture or sculpture. And it has told directly upon our political efficiency.

4

Characteristics of the Athenians.

Now at length I am drawing near the subject which I have undertaken to treat, though Athens is both in leagues and in centuries a great way off England after all. But first to recapitulate :—a State or polity implies two things, Power on the one hand, Liberty on the other; a Rule and a Constitution. Power, when freely developed, results in contralization ; Liberty in self-government. The two principles are in antagonism from their very nature ; so far forth as you have rule, you have not liberty ; so far forth as you have liberty, you have not rule. If a People gives up nothing at all, it remains a mere People, and does not rise to be a State. If it gives up everything, it could not be worse off, though it gave up nothing. Accordingly, it always must give up something; it never can give up everything ; and in every case the problem to be decided is, what is the most advisable compromise, what point is the *maximum* of at once protection and independence.

Those political institutions are the best which subtract as little as possible from a people's natural independence as the price of their protection. The stronger you make the Ruler, the more he can do for you, *but* the more he also can do against you; the weaker you make him, the less he can do against you, *but* the less also he can do for you. The Man promised to kill the Stag ; but he fairly owned that he must be first allowed to mount the Horse.

Put a sword into the Ruler's hands, it is at his option to use or not use it against you; reclaim it, and who is to use it for you? Thus, if States are free, they are feeble; if they are vigorous, they are high-handed. I am not speaking of a nation or a people, but of a State as such; and I say, the more a State secures to itself or rule and centralization, the more it can do for its subjects externally; and the more it grants to them of liberty and self-government, the less it can do against them internally : and thus a despotic government is the best for war, and a popular government the best for peace.

Now this may seem a paradox so far as this ;—that I have said a State cannot be at once free and strong, whereas the combination of these advantages is the very boast which we make about our own island in one of our national songs, which runs,—

> " Britannia, *rule* the waves !
> Britons never shall be *slaves.*"

I acknowledge the force of this authority; but I must recall the reader's attention to the distinction which I have just been making between a Nation and a State. Britons are free, considered as a State; they are strong, considered as a Nation;—and, as a good deal depends on this distinction, I will illustrate it, before I come to the consideration of our own country, by the instance of that ancient and famous people whose name I have prefixed to this portion of my inquiry,—a people who, in most respects, are as unlike us, as beauty is unlike utility, but who are in this respect, strange to say, not dissimilar to the Briton.

So pure a democracy was Athens, that, if any of its citizens was eminent, he might be banished by the rest for this simple offence of greatness. Self-government was developed there in the fullest measure, as if provision was not at all needed against any foe. Nor indeed, in the earlier period of Athens, was it required; for the poverty of the soil, and the extent of seaboard as its boundary, secured it against both the cupidity and the successful enterprise of invaders. The chief object, then, of its polity was the maintenance of internal order; but even in this respect solicitude was superfluous, according to its citizens themselves, who were accustomed to boast that they were attracted, one and all, in one and the same way, and moulded into a body politic, by an innate perception of the beautiful and true, and that the genius and cultivation of mind, which were their characteristics, served them better for the observance of the rules of good fellowship and for carrying on the intercourse of life, than the most stringent laws and the best appointed officers of police.

Here then was the extreme of self-government carried out; and the State was intensely free. That in proportion to that internal freedom was its weakness in its external relations, its uncertainty, caprice, injustice, and untrustworthiness, history, I think, abundantly shows. It may be thought unfair to appeal to the age of Philip and Demosthenes, when no Greek State could oppose a military organization worthy of such a foe as Macedon; but at no anterior period had it shown a vigour and perseverance similar to the political force of the barbaric monarchy, which extinguished its liberties. It was simply unable to defend and perpetuate that democratical license which it so inordinately prized.

Had Athens then no influence on the world outside of it, because its political influence was so baseless and fluctuating? Has she gained no conquests, exercised no rule, affected no changes, left no traces of herself upon the nations? On the contrary, never was country able to do so much ; never has country so impressed its image upon the history of the world, except always that similarly small strip of land in Syria. And moreover,—for this I wish to insist upon, rather than merely concede,—this influence of hers was in consequence, though not by means, of her democratical *regime.* That democratical polity formed a *People*, who could do what democracy itself could not do. Feeble all together, the Athenians were superlatively energetic one by one. It was their very keenness of intellect individually which made them collectively so inefficient. This point of character, insisted on both by friendly and hostile orators in the pages of her great historian, is a feature in which Athens resembles England. Englishmen, indeed, do not go to work with the grace and poetry which, if Pericles is to be believed, characterized an Athenian ; but Athens may boast of her children as having the self-reliance, the spirit, and the unflagging industry of the individual Englishman.

It was this individualism which was the secret of the power of Athens in her day, and remains as the instrument of her influence now. What was her trade, or her colonies, or her literature, but private, not public achievments, the triumph, not of State policy, but of personal effort ? Rome sent out her colonies, as Russia now, with political foresight ; modern Europe has its State Universities, its Royal Academies, its periodical scientific Associations ; it was otherwise with Athens. There, great things were done by citizens working in their private capacity ; working, it must be added, not so much from patriotism as for their personal advantage ; or, if with patriotism, still with little chance of State encouragement or reward. Socrates, the greatest of her moralists, and since his day one of her chief glories, lived unrecognized and unrewarded, and died under a judicial sentence. Xenophon conducted his memorable retreat across Asia Minor, not as an Athenian, but as the mercenary or volunteer of a Persian Prince. Miltiades was of a family of adventurers, who by their private energy had founded a colony, and secured a lordship in the Chersonese; and he met his death while prosecuting his private interests with his country's vessels. Themistocles had a double drift, patriotic and traitorous, in the very acts by which he secured to the Greeks the victory of Salamis, having in mind that those acts should profit him at the Persian court, if they did not turn to his account at home. Perhaps we are not so accurately informed of what took place at Rome, when Hannibal threatened the city; but certainly Rome presents us with the picture of a strong State at that crisis, whereas, in the parallel trial, the Athens of Miltiades and Themistocles shows like the clever, dashing population of a large town.

We have another sample of the genius of her citizens in their conduct at Pylos. Neither they, nor their officers, would obey the orders of the elder Demosthenes, who was sent out to direct the movements of the fleet. In vain did he urge them to fortify the place; they did nothing; till, the bad weather detaining them on shore, and inaction becoming tedious, suddenly they fell upon the work with a will; and, having neither tools nor carriages, hunted up stones where they could find them ready in the soil, made clay do the office of mortar, carried the materials on their backs, supporting them with their clasped hands, and thus finished the necessary works in the course of a few days.

By this personal enterprise and daring the Athenians were distinguished from the rest of Greece. "They are fond of change," say their Corinthian opponents in the

Lacedemonian Council; "quick to plan and to perform, venturing beyond their power, hazarding beyond their judgment, and always sanguine in whatever difficulties. They are alive, while you, O Lacedemonians, dawdle; and they love locomotion, while you are especially a home-people. They think to gain a point, even when they withdraw; but with you, even to advance is to surrender what you have attained. When they defeat their foe, they rush on; when they are beaten, they hardly fall back. What they plan and do not follow up, they deem an actual loss; what they set about and gain, they count a mere instalment of the future; what they attempt and fail in here, in anticipation they make up for there. Such is their labour and their risk from youth to age; no men enjoy so little what they have, for they are always getting, and their best holiday is to do a stroke of needful work; and it is a misfortune to them to have to undergo, not the toil of business, but the listlessness of repose."

I do not mean to say that I trace the Englishman in every clause of this passage; but he is so far portrayed in it as a whole, as to suggest to us that perhaps he too, as well as the Athenian, has that inward spring of restless independence, which makes a State weak, and a Nation great.

5.

Parallel Characteristics of Englishmen.

I HOPE I have now made it clear, that, in saying that a free State will not be strong, I am far indeed from saying that a People with what is called a free Constitution will not be active, powerful, influential, and successful. I am only saying that it will do its great deeds, not through the medium of its government, or *politically*, but through the medium of its individual members, or *nationally*. Self-government, which is another name for political weakness, may really be the means or the token of national greatness. Athens, as a State, was wanting in the elements of integrity, firmness, and consistency; but perhaps that political deficiency was the very condition and a result of her intellectual activity.

I will allow more than this readily. Not only in cases such as that of Athens, is the State's loss the Nation's gain, but further, most of those very functions which in despotisms are undertaken by the State may be performed in free countries by the Nation. For instance, roads, the posts, railways, bridges, aqueducts, and the like, in absolute monarchies, are governmental matters; but they may be left to private energy, where self-government prevails. Letter-carriage indeed involves an extent of system and a punctuality in work, which is too much for any combination of individuals; but the care of Religion, which is a governmental work in Russia, and partly so in England, is left to private competition in the United States. Education, in like manner, is sometimes provided by the State, sometimes left to religious denominations, sometimes to private zeal and charity. The Fine Arts sometimes depend on the patronage of Court or Government; sometimes are given in charge to Academies; sometimes to committees or vestries.

I do not say that a Nation will manage all these departments equally well, or so well as a despotic government; and some departments it will not be able to manage at all. Did I think it could manage all, I should have nothing to write about. I am distinctly maintaining that the war department it cannot manage; that is my very point. It cannot conduct a war; but not from any fault in the nation, or with any resulting disparagement to popular governments and Constitutional States, but merely because we cannot have all things at once in this world, however big we are, and because, in the nature of things, one thing cannot be another. I do not say that a Constitutional State never must risk war, never must engage in war, never will conquer in war; but that its strong point lies in the other direction. If we would see what liberty, independence, self-government, a popular Constitution, can do, we must look to times of tranquillity. In peace a self-governing nation is prosperous in itself, and influential in the wide world. Its special works, the sciences, the useful arts, literature, the interests of knowledge generally, material comfort, the means and appliances of a happy life, thrive especially in peace. And thus such a nation spreads abroad, and subdues the world, and reigns in the admiration and gratitude and deference of men, by the use of weapons which war shivers to pieces. Alas! that mortals do not know themselves, and will not (according to the proverb) cut their coat according to their cloth! "*Optat ephippia bos.*" John Bull, like other free, self-governing nations, would undertake a little war just now, as if it were his *forte*,—as great lawyers have cared for nothing but a reputation for dancing gracefully, and literary men have bought a complex coat-of-arms at the Heralds' College. Why will we not content to be human? why not content with the well-grounded consciousness that no polity in the world is so wonderful, so good to its subjects, so favourable to individual energy, so pleasant to live under, as our own? I do not say, why will we go to war? but, why will we not think *twice* first? why do we not ascertain our actual position, our strength, our weakness, before we do so?

For centuries upon centuries England has been, like Attica, a secluded land; so remote from the highway of the world, so protected from the flood of Eastern and Northern barbarism, that her children have grown into a magnanimous contempt of external danger. They have had "a cheap defence" in the stormy sea which surrounds them; and, from time immemorial, they have had such skill in weathering it, that their wooden walls, to use the Athenian term, became a second rampart against the foe, whom wind and water did not overwhelm. So secure have they felt in those defences, that they have habitually neglected others; so that, in spite of their valour, when a foe once gained the shore, be he Dane, or Norman, or Dutch, he was encountered by no sustained action or organized resistance, and became their king. These, however, were rare occurrences, and made no lasting impression; they were not sufficient to divert them from pursuing, or to thwart them in attaining, the amplest measures of liberty. Whom had the people to fear? not even their ships, which could not, like military, become a paid force encircling a tyrant, and securing him against their resistance.

To these outward circumstances of England, determining the direction of its political growth, must be added the character of the people themselves. There are races to whom consanguinity itself is not concord and unanimity, but the reverse. They fight with each other, for lack of better company. Imaginative, fierce, vindictive, with their clans, their pedigrees, and their feuds, snorting war, spurning trade or tillage, the old Highlanders, if placed on the broad plains of England, would have in time run through their national existence, and died the death of the sons of Œdipus. But, if you wish to see the sketch of a veritable Englishman in strong relief, refresh your recollection of Walter Scott's "Two Drovers." He is indeed rough, surly, a bully and a bigot ; these are his weak points : but if ever there was a generous, good, tender heart, it beats within his breast. Most placable, he forgives and forgets : forgets, not only the wrongs he has received, but the insults he has inflicted. Such he is commonly ; for doubtless there are times and circumstances in his dealings with foreigners in which, whether when in despair or from pride, he becomes truculent and simply hateful ; but at home his bark is worse than his bite. He has qualities, excellent for the purposes of neighbourhood and intercourse ;—and he has, besides, a shrewd sense, and a sobriety of judgment, and a practical logic, which passion does not cloud, and which makes him understand that good-fellowship is not only commendable, but expedient too. And he has within him a spring of energy, pertenacity, and perseverance, which makes him as busy and effective in a colony as he is companionable at home. Some races do not move at all ; others are ever jostling

against each other ; the Englishman is ever stirring, yet
never treads too hard upon his fellow-countryman's toes.
He does his work neatly, silently, in his own place ; he
looks to himself, and can take care of himself ; and he
has that instinctive veneration for the law, that he can
worship it even in the abstract, and thus is fitted to go
shares with others all around him in that political
sovereignty, which other races are obliged to concen-
trate in one ruler.

There was a time when England was divided into
seven principalities, formed out of the wild warriors
whom the elder race had called in to their own exter-
mination. What would have been the history of
those kingdoms if the invaders had been Highlanders
instead of Saxons? But the Saxon Heptarchy went
on, without any very desperate wars of kingdom with
kingdom, pretty much as the nation goes on now. Indeed, I much question, supposing Englishmen rose one
morning and found themselves in a Heptarchy again,
whether its seven portions would not jog on together,
much as they do now under Queen Victoria, the union
in both cases depending, not so much on the government
and the governed, but on the people, viewed in themselves, to whom peaceableness, justice, and non-inter-
ference are natural.

It is an invaluable national quality to be keen, yet to
be fair to others ; to be inquisitive, acquisitive, enterprising, aspiring, progressive, without encroaching upon
his next neighbour's right to be the same. Such a
people hardly need a Ruler, as being mainly free from
the infirmities which make a ruler necessary. Law,
like medicine, is only called for to assist nature ; and,
when nature does so much for a people, the wisest policy
is, as far as possible, to leave them to themselves. This,

then, is the science of government with English Statesmen, to leave the people alone; a free action, a clear
stage, and they will do the rest for themselves. The
more a Ruler meddles, the less he succeeds; the less he
initiates, the more he accomplishes; his duty is that of
overseeing, facilitating, encouraging, guiding, interposing
on emergencies. Some races are like children, and
require a despot to nurse, and feed, and dress them, to
give them pocket money, and take them out for airings.
Others, more manly, prefer to be rid of the trouble of
their affairs, and use their Ruler as their mere manager
and man of business. Now an Englishman likes to take
his own matters into his own hands. He stands on his
own ground, and does as much work as half a dozen men
of certain other races. He can join too with others, and
has a turn for organizing, but he insists on its being voluntary. He is jealous of no one, except kings and governments, and offensive to no one except their partisans
and creatures.

This, then, is the people for private enterprise; and
of private enterprise alone have I been speaking all
along. What a place is London in its extent, its com-
plexity, its myriads of dwellings, its subterraneous works!
It is the production, for the most part, of individual
enterprise. Waterloo Bridge was the greatest architec-
tural achievement of the generation before this; it was
built by shares. New regions, with streets of palaces
and shops innumerable, each shop a sort of shrine or
temple of this or that trade, and each a treasure-house
of its own merchandize, grow silently into existence, the
creation of private spirit and speculation. The gigantic
system of railroads rises and asks for its legal *status:*
prudent statesmen decide that it must be left to private
companies, to the exclusion of Government. Trade is to

be encouraged : the best encouragement is, that it should
be free. A famine threatens; one thing must be avoided,
—any meddling on the part of Government with the
export and import of provisions.

Emigration is in vogue : out go swarms of colonists,
not, as in ancient times, from the Prytaneum, under
State guidance and with religious rites, but each by
himself, and at his own arbitrary and sudden will. The
ship is wrecked ; the passengers are cast upon a rock,—
or make the hazard of a raft. In the extremest peril, in
the most delicate and most anxious of operations, every
one seems to find his place, as if by magic, and does his
work, and subserves the rest with coolness, cheerfulness,
gentleness, and without a master. Or they have a fair
passage, and gain their new country ; each takes his
allotted place there, and works in it in his own way.
Each acts irrespectively of the rest, takes care of number
one, with a kind word and deed for his neighbour, but
still as fully understanding that he must depend for
his own welfare on himself. Pass a few years, and a
town has risen on the desert beach, and houses of business are extending their connexions and influence up the
country. At length, a company of merchants make the
place their homestead, and they protect themselves from
their enemies with a fort. They need a better defence than
they have provided, for a numerous host is advancing
upon them, and they are likely to be driven into the
sea. Suddenly a youth, the castaway of his family,
half-clerk, half-soldier, puts himself at the head of a few
troops, defends posts, gains battles, and ends in founding
a mighty empire over the graves of Mahmood and
Aurungzebe.

It is the deed of one man ; and so, wherever we go
all over the earth, it is the solitary Briton, the London,

⁎⁎
⁎

agent, or the *Milordos*, who is walking restlessly about, abusing the natives, and raising a colossus, or setting the Thames on fire, in the East or the West.   He is on the top of the Andes, or in a diving-bell in the Pacific, or taking notes at Timbuctoo, or grubbing at the Pyramids, or scouring over the Pampas, or acting as prime minister to the king of Dahomey, or smoking the pipe of friendship with the Red Indians, or hutting at the Pole. No one can say beforehand what will come of these various specimens of the independent, self-governing, self-reliant Englishman.   Sometimes failure, sometimes openings for trade, scientific discoveries, or political aggrandizements.   His country and his government have the gain ; but it is he who is the instrument of it, and not political organization, centralization, systematic plans, authoritative acts.   The polity of England is what it was before,— the Government weak, the Nation strong,—strong in the strength of its multitudinous enterprise, which gives to its Government a position in the world, which that Government could not claim for itself by any prowess or device of its own.

6.

Reverse of the Picture.

THE social union promises two great and contrary advantages, Protection and Liberty,—such protection as shall not interfere with liberty, and such liberty as shall not interfere with protection. How much a given nation can secure of the one, and how much of the other, depends on its peculiar circumstances. As there are small frontier territories, which find it their interest to throw themselves into the hands of some great neighbour, sacrificing their liberties as the price of purchasing safety from barbarians or rivals, so too there are countries which, in the absence of external danger, have abandoned themselves to the secure indulgence of freedom, to the jealous exercise of self-government, and to the scientific formation of a Constitution. And as, when liberty has to be surrendered for protection, the Horse must not be surprised if the Man whips or spurs him, so, when protection is neglected for the sake of liberty, he must not be surprised if he suffers from the horns of the Stag.

Protected by the sea, and gifted with a rare energy, self-possession, and imperturbability, the English people have been able to carry out self-government to its limits, and to absorb into its constitutional action many of those functions which are necessary for the protection of any country, and commonly belong to the Executive ; and triumphing in their marvellous success they have thought no task too hard for them, and have from time to time attempted more than even England could accomplish. Such a crisis has come upon us now, and the Constitution has not been equal to the occasion. For a year past we have been conducting a great war on our Constitutional *routine*, and have not succeeded in it. If we continue that *routine*, we shall have more failures, with France or Russia (whichever you please) to profit by it : —if we change it, we change what after all is Constitutional. It is this dilemma which makes me wish for peace,—or else some *Deus è machinâ*, some one greater even than Wellington, to carry us through. We cannot depend upon Constitutional *routine*.

People abuse *routine*, and say that all the mischief which happens is the fault of *routine ;*—but can they get out of *routine*, without getting out of the Constitution ? That is the question. The fault of a *routine* Executive, I suppose, is not that the Executive always goes on in one way,—else, system is in fault,—but that it goes on in a bad way, or on a bad system. We must either change the system, then,—our Constitutional system ; or not find fault with its *routine*, which is according to it. The present Parliamentary Committee of Inquiry, for instance, is either a function and instrument of the *routine* system,—and therefore is making bad worse,—or is not, —and then perhaps it is only the beginning of an infringement of the Constitution. There may be Constitutional failures which have no Constitutional remedies, unwilling as we may be to allow it. They may be necessarily incidental to a free self-governing people.

The Executive of a nation is the same all over the world, being, in other words, the administration of the nation's affairs ; it differs in different countries, not in its nature and office, nor in its ends, acts, or functions, but in its characteristics, as being prompt, direct, effective, or the contrary ; that is, as being strong or feeble. If it pursues its ends earnestly, performs its acts vigorously and discharges its functions successfully, then it is a strong Executive ; if otherwise, it is feeble. Now, it is obvious, the more it is concentrated, that is, the fewer are its springs, and the simpler its mechanism, the stronger it is, because it has least friction and loss of power ; on the other hand, the more numerous and widely dispersed its centres of action are, and the more complex and circuitous their inter-action, the more feeble it is. It is strongest, then, when it is lodged in one man out of the whole nation ; it is feeblest, when it is lodged, by participation or conjointly, in every man in it. How can we help what is self-evident ? If the English people lodge power in the many, not in the few, what wonder that its operation is roundabout, clumsy, slow, intermittent, and disappointing ? And what is the good of finding fault with the *routine,* if it is after all the principle of the *routine,* or the system, or the Constitution, which causes the hitch ? You cannot eat your cake and have it ; you cannot be at once a self-governing nation and have a strong government. Recollect Wellington's question in opposition to the Reform Bill, " How is the King's Government to be carried on ? " We are beginning to experience its full meaning.

A people so alive, so curious, so busy as the English, will be a power in themselves, independently of political arrangements ; and will be on that very ground jealous of a rival, impatient of a master, and strong enough to cope with the one and to withstand the other. A government is their natural foe ; they cannot do without it altogether, but they will have of it as little as they can. They will forbid the concentration of power; they will multiply its seats, complicate its acts, and make it safe by making it inefficient. They will take care that it is the worst-worked of all the many organizations which are found in their country. As despotisms keep their subjects in ignorance, lest they should rebel, so will a free people maim and cripple their government, lest it should tyrannize.

This is human nature; the more powerful a man is, the more jealous is he of other powers. Little men endure little men; but great men aim at a solitary grandeur. The English nation is intensely conscious of itself; it has seen, inspected, recognized, appreciated, and warranted itself. It has erected itself into a personality, under the style and title of John Bull. Most neighbourly is he when let alone; but irritable, when commanded or coerced. He wishes to form his own judgment in all matters, and to have everything proved to him; he dislikes the thought of generously placing his interests in the hands of others, he grudges to give up what he cannot really keep himself, and stickles for being at least a sleeping partner in transactions which are beyond him. He pays his people for their work, and is as proud of them, if they do it well, as a rich man of his tall footmen.

Policy might teach him a different course. If you want your work done well, which you cannot do yourself, find the best man, put it into his hand, and trust him implicitly. An Englishman is too sensible not to understand this in private matters; but in matters of State he is afraid of such a policy. He prefers the system of checks and counter-checks, the division of power, the imperative concurrence of disconnected officials, and his own supervision and revision,—the method of hitches, cross-purposes, collisions, dead-locks, to the experiment of treating his public servants as gentlemen. I am not quarelling with what is inevitable in his system of self-government ; I only say that he cannot expect his work done in the best style, if this is his mode of providing for it. Duplicate functionaries do but merge responsibility ; and a jealous master is paid with formal, heartless service. Do your footmen love you across the gulf which you have fixed between them and you ? and can you expect your store-keepers and harbour-masters at Balaklava not to serve you by rule and precedent, not to be rigid in their interpretation of your orders, and to commit themselves as little as they can, when you show no belief in their zeal, and have no mercy on their failures ?

England, surely, is the paradise of little men, and the purgatory of great ones. May I never be a Minister of State or a Field-Marshal! I'd be an individual, self-respecting Briton, in my own private castle, with the *Times* to see the world by, and pen and paper to scribble off withal to some public print, and set the world right. Public men are only my *employés* ; I use them as I think fit, and turn them off without warning. Aberdeen, Gladstone, Sidney Herbert, Newcastle, what are they muttering about services and ingratitude ? were they not paid ? hadn't they their regular quarter-day ? Raglan, Burgoyne, Dundas,—I cannot recollect all the fellows' names,—can they merit aught ? can they be profitable to me their lord and master ? And so, having no tenderness or respect for their persons, their antecedents, or their age,—not caring that in fact they are serving me with all their strength, not asking whether, if they manage ill, it be not, perchance, because they are in the fetters of Constitutional red tape, which have weighed on their hearts and deadened their energies, till the hazard of failure and the fear of censure have quenched

the spirit of daring, I think it becoming and generous,—
during, not after their work, not when it is ended, but in
the very agony of conflict,—to institute a formal process
of inquiry into their demerits, not secret, not indulgent to
their sense of honour, but in the hearing of all Europe, and
amid the scorn of the world,—hitting down, knocking
over, my workhouse apprentices, in order that they
may get up again, and do my matters for me better.

How far these ways of managing a crisis can be amended
in a self-governing Nation, it is most difficult to say. They
are doubly deplorable, as being both unjust and impolitic.
They are kind, neither to ourselves, nor to our public
servants ; and they so unpleasantly remind one of certain passages of Athenian history, as to suggest that
perhaps they must ever more or less exist, except where
a despotism, by simply extinguishing liberty, effectually
prevents its abuse.

7.

English Jealousy of Law Courts.

PEOPLE account for the mismanagement existing in the
department of the military service, on the ground that
war is a novelty in this generation, and that it will be
corrected after the successive failures of a few years. This
doubtless has something to do with our failure, but it is
not a full explanation of it ; else, there would be no mismanagements in time of peace. But, if mismanagements
exist in peace as well as in war, then we may conclude
that they are some defect in our talent for organization ;
a defect, the more unaccountable, because Englishmen are
far from wanting in this faculty, as is shown by the great
undertakings of our master builders and civil engineers.
Yet all the time that private men have been directing
matters and men on a large scale to definite ends, there has
been a general feeling in the community that a government proceeding is a blunder or a job. From the Irish
famines of 1822 to that of 1845 and following years, I
think I recollect instances in point, though I have got no
·ist to produce. As to the latter occasion, it is commonly
said that to this day the Irish will not believe, in spite
of the many millions voted to them by Parliament, that
their population has not been deliberately murdered by
the Government. This was a far larger instance of mismanagement than that which the present Parliamentary
Committee will bring to light. How then shall we account for the phenomenon of the incapable Executive of

a capable people better than by saying, that, for the very reason the people is capable, its Executive is incapable, as I have been urging all along? It is true, there are public departments of acknowledged efficiency, as the Post Office and the Police ; but these only show what the Executive could be, if the Nation gave it fair play.

And thus I might end my remarks on the subject, which have already been discursive and excursive, beyond the patience of most readers ; and yet I think it worth while, Mr. Editor, to try it a little more, if I gain your consent to my doing so. For I have not yet brought out so clearly as I wish, the relation of the Nation to the Executive, as it exists in this corner of the earth.

The functions of the Executive are such as police, judicature, religion, education, finance, foreign transactions, war. The acts of the Executive are such as the appointment, instruction, supervision, punishment, and removal of its functionaries. The end of the Executive is to perform those functions by means of those acts with despatch and success; that is, so to appoint, instruct, superintend, and support its functionaries, as effectually to protect person and property, to dispense justice, to uphold religion, to provide for the country's expenses, to promote and extend its trade, to maintain its place in the political world, and to make it victorious and formidable. These things, and such as these, are the end,—the direct, intelligible end,—of the Executive ; and to secure their accomplishment, and to secure men to accomplish them, one would suppose would be the one and only object of all Executive government; but it is not the only object of the English.

A very few words will explain what I mean. John, Duke of Marlborough, obtained for the town of Witney a monopoly of blanket-making : accordingly, I believe, Witney at one time supplied the whole nation with blankets of such size and quality as the men of Witney chose. Looking at this as a national act, one would say, that the object of the nation was, not to provide itself with best blankets, but with Witney blankets ; and, did a foreigner object that the blankets were not good, he would speak beside the mark, and be open to the retort, "Nobody said they were good; what we maintain is that they come from Witney." Now, applying this illustration to our present circumstances, I humbly submit that, though the end of every Executive, as such, is to do its work well, cheaply, and promptly, yet, were the French in the Crimea to judge us by this principle, and to marvel at our choosing neither means or men in accordance with it, they would be simply criticising what they did not understand. The Nation's object never was that the Executive should be worked in the best possible way, but that the Nation should work it. It is altogether a family concern on a very large scale : the Executive is more or less in commission, and the commission is the Nation itself. It vests in itself, as represented by its different classes, in perpetuity, the prerogative of jobbing the Executive. Nor is this so absurd as it seems :—the Nation has two ends in view, quite distinct from the proper end of the Executive itself ; — first, that the Government should not do too much, and next, that itself should have a real share in the Government. The balance of power, which has been the mainspring of our foreign politics, is the problem of our home affairs also. The great State Commission must be distributed in shares, in correspondence with the respective pretensions of its various expectants. Some States are cemented by loyalty, others by religion; but ours by self-interest, in a large sense of the word. Each element of the political structure demands its special retainer; and power is committed, not to the highest capacity, but to the largest possible constituency. The general public, the constituency, the press, the aristocracy, the capital of the country, the mercantile interest, the Crown, the Court, the great Constitutional parties, Whig and Tory, the great religious parties, Church and Dissent, the country gentlemen, the professions—all must have their part and their proportion in the administration. Such is the will of the Nation, which had rather that its institutions should be firm and stable, than that they should be effective.

But the Sovereign, perhaps it will be said, is the source of all jurisdiction in the English body political, as Tudor monarchs asserted, and Constitutional lawyers have handed down to us ;—yes, as the Merovingian king, not the Mayor of the Palace, was ruler of France, and as the Great Mogul, not the Company, is the supreme power in Hindostan. Could Victoria resume at her will that power which the Tudors exercised, but which slipped out of the hands of the Stuarts? The Pope, too, leaves his jurisdiction in the hands of numberless subordinate authorities, patriarchs, metropolitans, bishops, sacred congregations, religious orders; he, however, can, if he pleases, recall what he has given, and sometimes, in fact, he does put them all aside. I think it would astonish the public if, to take a parallel case, our gracious Sovereign, *motu proprio*, were to resume the management of the Crown lands, or re-distribute the dioceses without an Act of Parliament. Let us dismiss from our minds the fictions of antiquarians; the British people divide among themselves the executive powers of the Crown :—and now to give some illustrations in point.

The end of the Judicature is justice. The functionaries

are commonly a jury, made up of men, not specially prepared for their occasional office, but chosen for it as representatives of a class, and performing it under the direction
of a properly educated and experienced dignitary, called
by courtesy the Judge. When I was young, I recollect
being shocked at hearing an eminent man inveigh against
this time-honoured institution, as if absurdly unfitted to
promote the ends of the Law. He was answered by an
able lawyer, who has since occupied the judicial bench ;
and he, instead of denying that precise allegation, argued
that the institution had a beneficial *political* effect on the
classes who were liable to serve as jurymen, as associating
them with the established order of things, and investing
them with salutary responsibilities. There is a good
deal in this reason :—a still more plausible defence, I
think, may be found in the consideration of the inexpe-
diency of suffering the tradition of Law to flow separate
from that of popular feeling, whereas there ought to be
a continual influx of the national mind into the judicial
conscience; and, unless there was this careful adjustment
between law and politics, the standards of right and
wrong, set up at Westminster, would diverge from those
received by the community at large, and the Nation
might some day find itself condemned and baffled by its
own supreme oracle of truth. This would be gravely
inconvenient ; accordingly, as the Star Chamber recognized the royal decisions as precedents in law, and
formed a tradition of the Court, so it is imperative, in our
better state of things, that Public Opinion should give
the law to Law, and should rule those questions which
directly bear upon any matter of national concern. By
the expedient, then, of a Jury, the good of the country is
made to take the lead of private interest ; for better far is
it that injustice should be done to a pack of individuals,

than that the maxims of the Nation should at any time incur the animadversion of its own paid officials, and a deadlock in State matters should be the result of so unfortunate an antagonism.

What makes me think that this is the real meaning of a jury, is what has lately taken place in a parallel way in the Committee of Privy Council on the baptismal controversy. My lords refused to go into the question of the truth of the doctrine in dispute, or into the meaning of the language used in the Prayer Book ; they merely asserted that a certain neutral reading of that language, by which it would bear contrary senses, was more congenial with the existing and traditional sentiments of the English people. They felt profoundly that it would never do to have the Church of the Nation at variance in opinion with the Nation itself. In other words, neither does English law seek justice, nor English religion seek truth, as ultimate and simple ends, but such a justice and such a truth as may not be inconsistent with the interests of large conservatism.

Again, I have been told by an eminent lawyer, that, in another ecclesiastical dispute which came before the Queen's Bench, a Chief Justice, now no more, rather than commit the Court to an unpopular decision, reversed the precedents of several centuries. No one could suspect that upright Judge of cowardice, time-serving, or party prejudice. The circumstances explained the act. Those precedents were out of keeping with the present national mind, which must be the perpetual standard and authoritative interpreter of the law ; and, as the Minister for Foreign Affairs instructs the Queen's representative at a Congress, what to think and say, so it is the Nation's right to impose upon the Judges the duty of expounding certain points of law in a sense agreeable to its high and mighty self. Accordingly the Chief Justice's decision on the occasion in question resulted in giving the public (as Lord John Russell expressed it as regards the Baptismal question) " great satisfaction." For satisfaction, peace, liberty, conservative interests, were the supreme end of the law, and not mere raw justice, as such. It is another illustration of the same spirit, though it does not strictly fall under our subject, that, at the public meeting held to thank that earnest and energetic man, Mr. Maurice, for the particular complexion of one portion of his theology, a speaker congratulated him on having, in questioning or denying eternal punishment, given (not a more correct, but) a "more genial" interpretation to the declarations of Holy Scripture.

Much, again, might be said upon the Constitutional rights of wealth, as tending to the weakening of the Executive. Wealth does not indeed purchase the higher appointments in the Law, but it can purchase situations, not only in the clerical, but in the military and civil services, and in the legislature. It is difficult to draw the line between such recognized transactions, and what is invidiously called corruption. As to parliamentary matters, I can easily understand the danger of that mode of proceeding, which I have called Constitutional, being carried too far. I can do justice to the feeling which, on a late occasion, if I recollect rightly, caused a will to be set aside, which provided for the purchase of a peerage. We must, of course, draw the line somewhere ; but if you take your stand on principle, as it is the fashion to do, then I cannot go along with you, and have never been able to see the specific wickedness (where oaths are not broken or evaded) of buying a seat in Parliament, as contrasted with the purchase of an eligible incumbency. It must not be forgotten, that, from the time of Sir

Robert Walpole, bribes, to use an uncivil word, have been necessary to our Constitutional *regime ;*—visions of a higher but impracticable system having died away with Bolingbroke's " Patriot King."

This is but one instance of what is seen in so many various ways, that our Executive is on principle subordinate to class interests; we consider it better that it should work badly, than work to the inconvenience and danger of our national liberties. Such is self-government. Ideal standards, generous motives, pure principles, precise aims, scientific methods, must be excluded, and national utility must be the rule of administration. It is not a high system, but no human system is such. The knout and the tar-barrel aforementioned are not more defensible modes of proceeding, and are less pleasant than ours. Under ours, the individual is consulted for far more carefully than under despotism or democracy. Injustice is the exception; a free and easy mode of living is the rule. It is a venal *régime ; que voulez-vous ?* improvement may make things worse. It succeeds in making things pleasant at home; whether it succeeds in war is another question.

8.

English Jealousy of Church and Army.

IN spite of the administrative weakness, characteristic of the English Constitution, from its defects in organization, from the interference of traditional principles and extraneous influences in its working, and from the corruption and jobbing incident to it, still so vast are its benefits in the security which it offers to person and property, in the freedom of speech, locomotion, and action, in the religious toleration, and in the general tranquillity and comfort, which go with it ; and again, so numerous and various are the material and mechanical advantages which the energy of the people has associated with it, that, I suppose, England is, in a political and national point of view, the best country to live in in the world. It has not the climate, it has not the faith, it has not the grace and sweetness, the festive cheerfulness, the social radiance, of some foreign cities and people ; but nowhere else surely can you have so much your own way, nowhere can you find ready to your hand so many of your wants and wishes. Take things as a whole, and the Executive and Nation work well, viewed in their results. What is it to the average Englishman that a jury sometimes gives an unjust verdict, that seats in Parliament are virtually bought, that the prizes of the Establishment are attained by interest, not merit, that political parties and great families monopolize the government, and share among themselves its places and appointments, or that the public press is every now and then both cowardly and tyrannical,—what is all this compared with the upshot of the whole national and political system?

Look at things as a philosopher, and you will learn resignation, or rather thankful content, by perceiving that they all so hang together, that on the whole you cannot make them much better, nor can gain much more without losing much. No idea or principle of political society includes in its operation all conceivable good, or excludes all evil; that is the best form of society which has most of the good, and least of the bad. In the English ideal, the Nation is the centre,—"l'Etat c'est moi:" and everything else is dependent and subservient. We are carried back in our thoughts to the fable of Menenius Agrippa, though with a changed adaptation. The Nation is the sacred seat of vital heat and nourishment, the original element, and the first principle, and the number one of the State framework, and in its various members we find, not what is most effective or exquisite of its kind, but accessories compatible with the supremacy of that digestive and nutritive apparatus. The whole body politic is in unity: "cujus participatio ejus in id ipsum." The kingly office does not give scope for the best of conceivable kings, but for the chief of a self-governing people ; the ministers of state, the members of Parliament, the judges, are not intended to be perfect in their own kind respectively, but national statesmen, councillors and lawyers; the bishops and commanders of the forces, the squires and the justices of the peace, belong to a Constitutional clergy, soldiery, and magistracy. I will not say that nothing admits of improvement, or what is called "reform," in such a society; I will not attempt to determine the limits of improvement; still a limit there is, and things must remain in substance what they are, or "Old England" will cease to be. Let us be merciful to ourselves; as in our own persons, one by one, we consult for our particular constitution of mind and body, and avoid efforts and aims, modes of exercise and diet, which are unsuitable to it, so in like manner those who appreciate the British Constitution aright will show their satisfaction at what it does well, resignation as to what it cannot do, and prudence in steering clear of those problems which are difficult or dangerous in respect to it. Such men will not make it dance on its lame leg. They will not go to war, if they can help it, for the conduct of war is not among its *chef-d'œuvres*, as I now, for positively the last time, will explain.

Material force is the *ultima ratio* of political society everywhere. Arms alone can keep the peace; and, as all other professions are reducible to system and rule, there is of course a science and an art of war. This art is learned like other arts by study and practice ; it supposes the existence of expounders and instructors, an experimental process, a circulation of ideas, a traditionary teaching, and an aggregation of members,—in a word, a school. Continuity, establishment, organization, are necessary to the idea of a school and a craft. In other words, if war be an art, and not a matter of haphazard and pell-mell fighting, as under the walls of Troy, it requires what is appropriately called a standing army, that is, an army which has a *status*. Unless we are in a happy valley, or on a sea-protected island, we must have a standing army, or we are open to hostile attack.

But, when you have got your standing army, how are you to keep it from taking the wrong side, and turning upon you, like elephants in Eastern fights, instead of repelling your foe? Thus it was that the Pretorians, the Gothic mercenaries, the medieval Turks, and later Janizzaries, became the masters and upsetters of the Emperors, Caliphs, and Sultans who employed them. This formidable difficulty has been fatal to the military profession in popular governments, who in alarm have thrown the national defence upon the Nation, aided, as it might happen, by foreign mercenaries paid by the job. In such governments, the war department has not been the science of arms, but a political institution. An army has been raised for the occasion from off the estates and homesteads of the land, being soldiers of the soil, as rude as they were patriotic. When a danger threatened, they were summoned from plough or farm-yard, formed into a force, marched against the enemy, with whatever success in combat, and then marched home again. Which of the two would be the greater,—the inconvenience or the insufficiency of such a mode of waging war ? Thus we have got round again to the original dilemma of the Horse, the Stag, and the Man; the Horse destined to feel at his flanks the Man's spurs, or the Stag's horns,—a Standing Army, or no profession of arms. In this difficulty, we must strike a balance and a compromise, and then get on as well as we can with a conditional Standing Army and a smattering in military science. Such has been the course adopted by England ; and her insular situation, hitherto impregnable, has asked for nothing more.

Every sovereign State will naturally feel a jealousy of the semblance of an *imperium in imperio;* though not every State is in a condition to give expression to it. England has indulged that jealousy to the full, and has assumed a bearing towards the military profession much the same as she shows towards the ecclesiastical. There is indeed a close analogy between these two powers, both in them-

selves and in their relation to the State ; and, in order
to explain the position of the army in England, I cannot do better than refer to the position which in this
country has been assigned to the Church. The Church
and the Army are respectively the instruments of moral
and material force ; and are real powers in their own
respective fields of operation. They necessarily have
common sympathies, and an intense *esprit de corps*.
They are in consequence the strongest supports or the
most formidable opponents of the State to which they
belong, and require to be subjected, beyond any mistake,
to its sovereignty. In England, sensitively suspicious
of combination and system, three precautions have been
taken in dealing with the soldier and the parson,—(I
hope I may be familiar without offence),—precautions
borrowed from the necessary treatment of wild animals,
—(1) to tie him up, (2) to pare his claws, and (3) to keep
him low ; then he will be both safe and useful ;—the
result is a National Church, and a Constitutional Army.

1. In the first place, we tie both parson and soldier up,
by forbidding each to form one large organization. We
prohibit an organized religion and an organized force.
Instead of one corporation in religion, we only allow of
a multitude of small ones, as chapters and rectories,
while we ignore the Establishment as a whole, deny it
any legal *status*, and recognize the Dissenting bodies.
For Universities we substitute Colleges, with rival interests, that the intellect may not be too strong for us, as is
the case with some other countries ; but we freely multiply
local schools, for they have no political significance.
And, in like manner, we are willing to perfect the discipline and appointment of regiments, but we instinc-
tively recoil from the idea of an Army. We toast indeed
" The Army," but as an abstraction, as we used to drink to

"The Church," before the present substitution of "The Clergy of all denominations," which has much more of reality in it. Moreover, while, we have a real reason for sending our troops all over the world, shifting them about, using them for garrison duty, and for the defence of dependencies, we are thereby able also to divide and to hide them from each other. Nor is this all : if any organization requires a directing mind at the head of it, it is an army ; but, faithful to our Constitutional instincts, we have committed its command, *ex abundanti cautelâ*, to as many, I believe, as five independent boards, whose concurrence is necessary for a practical result. Nay, as late occurrences have shown, we have thought it a lesser evil, that our troops should be starved in the Crimea for want of the proper officer to land the stores, and that clothing and fuel shall oscillate to and fro between Balaklava and Malta, than that there should be the chance of the smallest opening for the introduction into our political system of a power formidable to nationalism. Thus we tie up both parson and soldier.

2. Next, in all great systems and agencies of any kind, there are certain accessories, absolutely necessary for their efficiency, yet hardly included in their essential idea. Such, to take a very small matter, is the use of the bag in making a pudding. Material edifices are no part of religion ; but you cannot have religious services without them ; nor can you move field-pieces without horses, nor get together horses without markets and transports. The greater part of these supplemental articles the English Constitution denies to its religious Establishment altogether, and to its Army, when not on active service. Fabrics of worship it encourages ; but it gives no countenance to such ecclesiastical belongings as the ritual and ceremonial of religion, synods, religious orders, sisters of

charity, missions, and the like, necessary instruments of
Christian faith, which zealous Churchmen, in times of
spiritual danger, decay, or promise, make vain endea-
vours to restore. And such in military matters are the
commissariat, transport, and medical departments, which
are jealously suppressed in time of peace, and hastily
and grudgingly restored on the commencement of hos-
tilities. The Constitutional spirit allows to the troops
arms and ammunition, as it allows to the clergy Ordination and two sacraments, neither being really dangerous,
while the supplements, which I have spoken of, are
withheld. Thus it cuts their claws.

3. And lastly, it keeps them low. Though lawyers
are educated for the law, and physicians for medicine,
it is felt among us to be dangerous to the Constitution to
have real education either in the clerical or military profession. Neither theology nor the science of war is
compatible with a national *regime*. Military and naval
science is, in the ordinary Englishman's notion, the
bayonet and the broadside. Religious knowledge comes
by nature; and so far is true, that Anglican divines
thump away in exhortation or in controversy, with a
manliness, good sense, and good will as thoroughly John
Bullish as the stubbornness of the Guards at Inkerman.
Not that they are forbidden to cultivate theology in private as a personal accomplishment, but that they must
not bring too much of it into the pulpit, for then they
become "extreme men," Calvinists or Papists, as it may
be. A general good education, a public school, and a
knowledge of the classics, make a parson ; and he is
chosen for a benefice or a dignity, not on any abstract
ground of merit, but by the great officers of State, by
members of the aristocracy, and by country gentlemen,
or their nominees, men who by their position are a suffi-

cient guarantee that the nation will continually flow into the Establishment, and give it its own colour. And so of the army ; it is not so many days ago that a gentleman in office assured the House of Commons (if he was correctly reported) that the best officers were those who had a University education ; and I doubt not it is far better for the troops to be disciplined and commanded by good scholars than by incapables and dunces. But in each department professional education is eschewed, and it is thought enough for the functionary to be a gentleman. A clergyman is the " resident gentleman " in his parish ; and no soldier must rise from the ranks, because he is not " company for gentlemen."

Let no man call this satire, for it is most seriously said ; nor have I intentionally coloured any one sentence in the parallel which I have been drawing out ; nor do I speak as grumbling at things as they are ;—I merely want to look facts in the face. I have been exposing what I consider the weak side of our Constitution, not exactly because I want it altered, but because people should not consider it the strong side. I think it a necessary weakness ; I do not see how it can be satisfactorily set right without dangerous innovations. We cannot in this world have all things as we should like to have them. Not that we should not try for the best, but we should be quite sure that we do not, like the dog in the fable, lose what we have, in attempting what we cannot have. Not that I deny that, even with a Constitution adapted for peace, British energy and pluck may not, as it has done before, win a battle, or carry through a war. But after all, reforms are but the first steps in revolution, as medicine is often a diluted poison. Enthusiasts have from time to time thought otherwise. There was Dr. Whately in 1826, who maintained that the Establishment was in degrading servitude, that it had a dog's collar round its neck, that the position of Bishops was intolerable, and that it was imperative to throw off State control, keeping the endowments.* And there is the *Times* newspaper in 1855, which would re-organize the Army, and put it on a scientific basis, satisfactory indeed to the military critic, startling to the Constitutional politician.

Mr. Macaulay gives us a warning from history. " The Constitution of England," he says, " was only one of a large family. In the fifteenth century, the government of Castile seems to have been as free as that of our own country. That of Arragon was, beyond all question, more so even than France ; the States-General alone could impose taxes. Sweden and Denmark had Constitutions of a different description. Let us overleap two or three hundred years, and contemplate Europe at the commencement of the eighteenth century. Every free Constitution, save one, had gone down. That of England had weathered the danger, and was riding in full security. What, then, made us to differ ? The progress of civilization introduced a great change. War became a science, and, as a necessary consequence, a trade. The great body of the people grew every day more reluctant to undergo the inconvenience of military service, and thought it better to pay others for undergoing them. That physical force which in the dark ages had belonged to the nobles and the commons, and had, far more than any charter or any assembly, been the safeguard of their privileges, was transferred entire to the king. The great mass of the population, destitute of all military discipline and organization, ceased to exercise any influence by force on political transactions. Thus absolute monarchy

* [I am informed that Dr. Whately never acknowledged the work here referred to as his own.]

was established on the Continent; England escaped, but she escaped very narrowly. If Charles had played the part of Gustavus Adolphus, if he had carried on a popular war for the defence of the Protestant cause in Germany, if he had gratified the national pride by a series of victories, if he had formed an army of 40,000 or 50,000 devoted soldiers, we do not see what chance the nation would have had of escaping from despotism."

These are very different times ; but, however steady and self-righting is John Bull, however elastic his step, and vigorous his arm, I do not see how the strongest and healthiest build can overcome difficulties which lie in the very nature of things.

And now, however circuitously, I have answered my question, "Who's to blame for the untoward events in the Crimea ?" They are to blame, the ignorant, intemperate public, who clamour for an unwise war, and then, when it turns out otherwise than they expected, instead of acknowledging their fault, proceed to beat their zealous servants in the midst of the fight for not doing impossibilities.

March, 1855.

VI.

AN INTERNAL ARGUMENT FOR CHRISTIANITY.

THE word " remarkable " has been so hacked of late in theological criticism—nearly as much so as " earnest " and " thoughtful "—that we do not like to apply it without an apology to the instance of a recent work, called "Ecce Homo," which we propose now to bring before the reader. In truth, it presents itself as a very convenient epithet, whenever we do not like to commit ourselves to any definite judgment on any subject before us, and prefer to spread over it a broad neutral tint to painting it distinctly white, red, or black. A man, or his work, or his deed, is " remarkable" when he produces an effect; be he effective for good or for evil, for truth or for falsehood—a point which, as far as that expression goes, we by adopting it, leave it for others or for the future to determine. Accordingly it is just the word to use in the instance of a Volume in which what is trite and what is novel, what is striking and what is startling, what is sound and what is untrustworthy, what is deep and what is shallow, are so mixed up together, or at least so vaguely suggested, or so perplexingly confessed, —which has so much of occasional force and circumambient glitter, of pretence and of seriousness,—as to make it impossible either with a good conscience to praise it, or without harshness and unfairness to condemn. Such a book is at least likely to be effective, whatever else it is or is not ; it may be safely called remarkable ; and therefore ·we apply the epithet "remarkable" to this *Ecce Homo*.

It is remarkable, then, on account of the sensation which it has made in religious circles. In the course of a few months it has reached a third edition, though it is a fair-sized octavo, and not an over-cheap one. And it has received the praise of critics and reviewers of very distinct shades of opinion. Such a reception must be owing either to the book itself, or to the circumstances of the day in which it has appeared, or to both of these causes together. Or, as seems to be the case, the needs of the day have become a call for some such work ; and the work, on its appearance, has been thankfully welcomed, on account of its professed object, by those whose needs called for it. The author includes himself in the number of these ; and while providing for his own wants he has ministered to theirs. This is what we especially mean by calling his book "remarkable." It deserves remark, because it has excited it.

I.

Disputants may maintain, if they please, that religious doubt is our appropriate, our normal state ; that to cherish doubts is our duty ; that to complain of them is impatience ; that to dread them is cowardice ; that to overcome them is inveracity ; that it is even a happy state, a state of calm philosophic enjoyment, to be conscious of them ;—but after all, unavoidable or not, such a state is not natural, and not happy, if the voice of mankind is to decide the question. English minds, in particular, have too much of a religious temper in them, as a natural gift, to acquiesce for any long time in positive, active doubt. For doubt and devotion are incompatible with each other ; every doubt, be it greater or less, stronger or weaker, involuntary as well as voluntary, acts upon devotion, so far forth, as water sprinkled, or dashed, or poured out upon a flame. Real and proper doubt kills faith, and devotion with it ; and even involuntary or half-deliberate doubt, though it does not actually kill faith, goes far to kill devotion ; and religion without devotion is little better than a burden, and soon becomes a superstition. Since, then, this is a day of objection and of doubt about the intellectual basis of Revealed Truth, it follows that there is a great deal of secret discomfort and distress in the religious portion of the community, the result of that general curiosity in speculation and inquiry which has been the growth among us of the last twenty or thirty years.

The people of this country, being Protestants, appeal to Scripture, when a religious question arises, as their ultimate informant and decisive authority in all such matters ; but who is to decide for them the previous question, that Scripture is really such an authority ? When, then, as at this time, its divine authority is the very point to be determined, that is, the character and extent of its inspiration and its component parts, then they find themselves at sea, without the means of directing their course. Doubting about the authority of Scripture, they doubt about its substantial truth ; doubting about its truth, they have doubts concerning the Object which it sets before their faith, about the historical accuracy and objective reality of the picture which it presents to us of our Lord. We are not speaking of wilful doubting, but of those painful misgivings, greater or less, to which we have already referred. Religious Protestants, when they think calmly on the subject, can hardly conceal from themselves that they have a house without logical foundations, which contrives indeed for the present to stand, but which may go any day,—and where are they then?

Of course Catholics will bid them receive the canon of Scripture on the authority of the Church, in the spirit of St. Augustine's well-known words: "I should not believe the Gospel, were I not moved by the authority of the Catholic Church." But who, they ask, is to be voucher in turn for the Church, and for St. Augustine?—is it not as difficult to prove the authority of the Church and her doctors as the authority of the Scriptures? We Catholics answer, and with reason, in the negative; but, since they cannot be brought to agree with us here, what argumentative ground is open to them? Thus they seem drifting, slowly perhaps, but surely, in the direction of scepticism.

2.

It is under these circumstances that they are invited, in the Volume of which we have spoken, to betake themselves to the contemplation of our Lord's character, as it is recorded by the Evangelists, as carrying with it its own evidence, dispensing with extrinsic proof, and claiming authoritatively by itself the faith and devotion of all to whom it is presented. Such an argument, of course, is as old as Christianity itself; the young man in the Gospel calls our Lord "Good Master," and St. Peter introduces Him to the first Gentile converts as one who "went about doing good;" and in these last times we can refer to the testimony even of unbelievers in behalf of an argument which is as simple as it is constraining. "Si la vie et la mort de Socrate sont d'un sage," says Rousseau, "la vie et la mort de Jésus sont d'un Dieu." And he clenches the argument by observing, that were the picture a mere conception of the sacred writers, "l'inventeur en serait plus étonnant que le héros." The force of this argument lies in its directness; it comes to the point at once, and concentrates in itself evidence, doctrine, and devotion. In theological language, it is the *motivum credibilitatis*, the *objectum materiale*, and the *formale*, all in one; it unites human reason and supernatural faith in one complex act; and it comes home to all men, educated and ignorant, young and old. And it is the point to which, after all and in fact, all religious minds tend, and in which they ultimately rest, even if they do not start from it. Without an intimate apprehension of the personal character of our Saviour, what professes to be faith is little more than an act of ratiocination. If faith is to live, it must love; it must lovingly live in the Author of faith as a true and living Being, *in Deo vivo et vero;* according to the saying of the Samaritans to their townswoman: "We now believe, not for thy saying, for we ourselves have heard Him." Many doctrines may be held implicitly; but to see Him as if intuitively is the very promise and gift of Him who is the object of the intuition. We are constrained to believe when it is He that speaks to us about Himself.

Such undeniably is the characteristic of divine faith viewed in itself: but here we are concerned, not simply with faith, but with its logical antecedents; and the question returns on which we have already touched, as a difficulty with Protestants,—how can our Lord's Life, as recorded in the Gospels, be a logical ground of faith, unless we set out with assuming the truth of those Gospels; that is, without assuming, as proved, the original matter of doubt? And Protestant apologists, it may be urged—Paley, for instance—show their sense of this difficulty when they place the argument drawn from our Lord's character only among the auxiliary Evidences of

Christianity. Now the following answer may fairly be made to this objection; nor need we grudge Protestants the use of it, for, as will appear in the sequel, it proves too much for their purpose, as being an argument for the divinity not only of Christ's mission, but of that of His Church also. However, we say this by the way.

It may be maintained then, that, making as large an allowance as the most sceptical mind, when pressed to state its demands in full, would desire, we are at least safe in asserting that the books of the New Testament, taken as a whole, were existing about the middle of the second century, and were then received by Christians, or were in the way of being received, and nothing else but they were received, as the authoritative record of the origin and rise of their Religion. In that first age they were the only account of the mode in which Christianity was introduced to the world. Internal as well as external evidence sanctions us in so speaking. Four Gospels, the book of the Acts of the Apostles, various Apostolic writings, made up then, as now, our sacred books. Whether there was a book more or less, say even an important book, does not affect the general character of the Religion as those books set it forth. Omit one or other of the Gospels, and three or four Epistles, and the outline and nature of its objects and its teaching remain what they were before the omission. The moral peculiarities, in particular, of its Founder are, on the whole, identical, whether we learn them from St. Matthew, St. John, St. Peter, or St. Paul. He is not in one book a Socrates, in another a Zeno, and in a third an Epicurus. Much less is the religion changed or obscured by the loss of particular chapters or verses, or even by inaccuracy in fact, or by error in opinion, (supposing *per impossibile* such a charge could be made good,) in particular portions of a book. For argument's sake, suppose that the three first Gospels are an accidental collection of traditions or legends, for which no one is responsible, and in which Christians had faith because there was nothing else to put faith in. This is the limit to which extreme scepticism can proceed, and we are willing to commence our argument by granting it. Still, starting at this disadvantage, we should be prepared to argue, that if, in spite of this, and after all, there be shadowed out in these anonymous and fortuitous documents a Teacher *sui generis*, distinct, consistent, and original, then does that picture, thus accidentally resulting, for the very reason of its accidental composition, only become more marvellous ; then is He an historical fact, and again a supernatural or divine fact ;—historical from the consistency of the representation, and because the time cannot be assigned when it was not received as a reality ; and supernatural, in proportion as the qualities with which He is invested in those writings are incompatible with what it is reasonable or possible to ascribe to human nature viewed simply in itself. Let these writings be as open to criticism, whether as to their origin or their text, as sceptics can maintain; nevertheless the representation in question is there, and forces upon the mind a conviction that it records a fact, and a superhuman fact, just as the reflection of an object in a stream remains in its general form, however rapid the current, and however many the ripples, and is a sure warrant to us of the presence of the object on the bank, though that object be out of sight.

3.

Such, we conceive, though stated in our own words, **is** the argument drawn out in the pages before us, or rather such is the ground on which the argument is raised; and the interest which it has excited lies, not in its novelty, but in the particular mode in which it is brought before the reader, in the originality and precision of certain strokes by which is traced out for us the outline of the Divine Teacher. These strokes are not always correct; they are sometimes gratuitous, sometimes derogatory to their object; but they are always determinate; and, being such, they present an old argument before us with a certain freshness, which, because it is old, is necessary for its being effective.

We do not wonder at all, then, at the sensation which the Volume is said to have caused at Oxford, and among Anglicans of the Oxford school, after the wearisome doubt and disquiet of the last ten years; for it has opened the prospect of a successful issue of inquiries in an all-important province of thought, where there seemed to be no thoroughfare. Distinct as are the liberal and Catholicizing parties in the Anglican Church both in their principles and their policy, it must not be supposed that they are also as distinct in the members that compose them. No line of demarcation can be drawn between the one collection of men and the other, in fact; for no two minds are altogether alike; and individually, Anglicans have each his own shade of opinion, and belong partly to this school, partly to that. Or rather, there is a large body of men who are neither the one nor the other; they cannot be called an intermediate party, for they have no discriminating watchwords; they range from those who are almost Catholic to those who are almost Liberals. They are not Liberals, because they do not glory in a state of doubt; they cannot profess to be "Anglo-Catholics," because they are not prepared to give an internal assent to all that is put forth by the

Church as truth of revelation. These are the men who, if they could, would unite old ideas with new ; who cannot give up tradition, yet are loth to shut the door to progress ; who look for a more exact adjustment of faith with reason than has hitherto been attained ; who love the conclusions of Catholic theology better than the proofs, and the methods of modern thought better than its results ; and who, in the present wide unsettlement of religious opinion, believe indeed, or wish to believe, Scripture and orthodox doctrine, taken as a whole, and cannot get themselves to avow any deliberate dissent from any part of either, but still, not knowing how to defend their belief with logical exactness, or at least feeling that there are large unsatisfied objections lying against parts of it, or having misgivings lest there should be such, acquiesce in what is called a practical belief, that is, accept revealed truths, only because such acceptance of them is the safest course, because they are probable, and because to hold them in consequence is a duty, not as if they felt absolutely certain, though they will not allow themselves to be actually in doubt. Such is about the description to be given of them as a class ; though, as we have said, they so materially differ from each other, that no general account of them will apply strictly to any individual in their body.

Now, it is to this large class which we have been describing that such a work as that before us, in spite of the serious errors which they will not be slow to recognize in it, comes as a friend in need. They do not stumble at the author's inconsistencies or shortcomings ; they are arrested by his professed purpose, and are profoundly moved by his successful hits (as they may be called) towards fulfilling it. Remarks on the Gospel history, such as Paley's, they feel to be casual and superficial ;

such as Rousseau's to be vague and declamatory; they wish to justify with their intellect all that they believe with their heart; they cannot separate their ideas of religion from its revealed Object; but they have an aching dissatisfaction within them, that they should be apprehending Him so feebly, when they should fain (as *it* were) see and touch Him as well as hear. When, then, they have logical grounds presented to them for holding that the recorded picture of our Lord is its own evidence, that it carries with it its own reality and authority, that His "revelatio" is "revelata" in the very act of being a "revelatio," it is as if He Himself said to them, as He once said to His disciples, "It is I, be not afraid;" and the clouds at once clear off, and the waters subside, and the land is gained for which they are looking out.

The author before us, then, has the merit of promising what, if he could fulfil it, would entitle him to the gratitude of thousands. We do not say, we are very far from thinking that he has actually accomplished so high an enterprise, though he seems to be ambitious enough to hope that he has not come far short of it. He somewhere calls his book a treatise; he would have done better to call it an essay; nor need he have been ashamed of a word which Locke has used in his work on the Human Understanding. Before concluding, we shall take occasion to express our serious sense, how very much his execution falls below his purpose; but certainly it is a great purpose which he sets before him, and for that he is to be praised. And there is at least this singular merit in his performance, as he has given it to the public, that he is clear-sighted and fair enough to view our Lord's work in its true light, as including in it the establishment of a visible Kingdom or Church. In proportion, then, as we shall presently find it our duty to pass some severe remarks upon his Volume, as it comes before us, so do we feel bound, before doing so, to give some specimens of it in that point of view in which we consider it really to subserve the cause of Revealed Truth. And in the sketch which we are now about to give of the first steps of his investigation, we must not be understood to make him responsible for the language in which we shall exhibit them to our readers, and which will unavoidably involve our own corrections of his argument, and our own colouring.

4

Among a people, then, accustomed by the most sacred traditions of their Religion to a belief in the appearance, from time to time, of divine messengers for their instruction and reformation, and to the expectation of One such messenger still to come, the last and greatest of all, who should also be their king and deliverer as well as their teacher, suddenly is found, after a long break in the succession, and a period of national degradation, a prophet of the old stamp, in one of the deserts of the country —John, the son of Zachary. He announces the promised kingdom as close at hand, calls his countrymen to repentance, and institutes a rite symbolical of it. The people seem disposed to take him for the destined Saviour ; but, instead, he points out to them a private person in the crowd which is flocking about him ; and henceforth the interest which his own preaching has excited centres in that Other. Thus our Lord is introduced to the notice of His countrymen.

Thus brought before the world, He opens His mission. What is the first impression it makes upon us ? Admiration of its singular simplicity and directness, both as to object and work. Such of course ought to be its character, if it was to be the fulfilment of the ancient, long-expected promise; and such it was, as our Lord proclaimed it. Other men, who do a work, do not at once set about it as their object; they make several failures; they are led on to it by circumstances; they miscalculate their powers; or they are drifted from the first in a different direction from that which they had chosen; they do most where they are expected to do least. But our Lord said and did. "He formed one plan and executed it" (p. 18).

In the next place, what was that plan? Let us consider the force of the words in which, as the Baptist before Him, He introduced His ministry: "The kingdom of God is at hand." What was meant by the kingdom of God? "The conception was no new one, but familiar to every Jew" (p. 19). At the first formation of the nation and state of the Israelites, the Almighty had been their King; when a line of earthly kings was introduced, then God spoke by the prophets. The existence of the theocracy was the very constitution and boast of Israel, as limited monarchy, liberty, and equality are the boast respectively of certain modern nations. Moreover, the Gospel proclamation ran, " "Pœnitentiam agite; for the kingdom of heaven is at hand :" here again was another and recognized token of a theophany; for the mission of a prophet, as we have said above, was commonly a call to reformation and expiation of sin.

A divine mission, then, was a falling back upon the original covenant between God and His people; but again, while it was an event of old and familiar occurrence, it ever had carried with it in its past instances something new in connexion with the circumstances under which it took place. The prophets were accustomed to give interpretations, or to introduce modifications of the letter of the Law, to add to its conditions and to enlarge its application. It was to be expected, then, that now, when the new Prophet to whom the Baptist pointed, opened His commission, He too, in like manner, would be found to be engaged in a restoration, but in a restoration which should be a religious advance; and that the more, if He really was the special, final Prophet of the theocracy, to whom all former prophets had looked forward, and in whom their long and august line was to be summed up and perfected. In proportion as His work was to be more signal, so would His new revelations be wider and more wonderful.

Did our Lord fulfil these expectations? Yes; there was this peculiarity in His mission, that He came, not only as one of the prophets in the kingdom of God, but as the King Himself of that kingdom. Thus His mission involves the most exact return to the original polity of Israel, which the appointment of Saul had disarranged, while it recognizes also the line of Prophets, and infuses a new spirit into the Law. Throughout His ministry our Lord claimed and received the title of King, which no prophet ever had done before. On His birth, the wise men came to worship "the King of the Jews." "Thou art the Son of God, Thou art the King of Israel," cried Nathaniel after His baptism; and on His cross the charge recorded against Him was that He professed to be "King of the Jews." "During His whole public life," says the author, "He is distinguished from the other prominent characters of Jewish history by His unbounded personal pretensions. He claims expressly the character of that Divine Messiah for which the ancient prophets had directed the nation to look."—P. 25.

He is, then, a King, as well as a Prophet; but is He as one of the old heroic kings, David or Solomon? Had such been His pretension, He had not, in His own words, "discerned the signs of the times." It would have been a false step in Him, into which other would-be champions of Israel, before and after Him, actually fell, and in consequence failed. But here this young Prophet is from the first distinct, decided, and original. His contemporaries, indeed, the wisest, the most experienced, were wedded to the notion of a revival of the barbaric kingdom. "Their heads were full of the languid dreams of commentators, the unpracticable pedantries of men who live in the past" (p. 27). But He gave to the old prophetic promises an interpretation which they could undeniably bear, but which they did not immediately suggest; which we can maintain to be true, while we can deny it to be imperative. He had His own prompt, definite conception of the restored theocracy; it was His own, and not another's; it was suited to the new age; it was triumphantly carried out in the event.

5

In what, then, did He consider His royalty to consist? First, what was it not? It did not consist in the ordinary functions of royalty; it did not prevent His payment of tribute to Cæsar; it did not make Him a judge in questions of criminal or of civil law, in a question of adultery, or in the adjudication of an inheritance; nor did it give Him the command of armies. Then perhaps, after all, it was but a figurative royalty, as when the Eridanus is called "fluviorum rex," or Aristotle "the prince of philosophers." No; it was not a figurative royalty either. To call oneself a king, without being one, is playing with edged tools—as in the story of the innkeeper's son, who was put to death for calling himself "heir to the crown." Christ certainly knew what He was saying. "He had provoked the accusation of rebellion against the Roman government: He must have known that the language He used would be interpreted so. Was there then nothing substantial in the royalty He claimed? Did He die for a metaphor?" (p. 28.) He meant what He said, and therefore His kingdom was literal and real; it was visible; but what were its visible prerogatives, if they were not those in which earthly royalty commonly consists? In truth, He passed by the lesser powers of royalty to claim the higher. He claimed certain divine and transcendent functions of the original theocracy, which had been in abeyance since that theocracy had been infringed, which even to David had not been delegated, which had never been exercised except by the Almighty. God had created, first the people, next the state, which He deigned to govern. "The origin of other nations is lost in antiquity" (p. 33); but "this people," runs the sacred word, "have I formed for Myself." And "He who first called the nation did for it the second work of a king: He gave it a law" (p. 34). Now it is very striking to observe that these two incommunicable attributes of divine royalty, as exemplified in the history of the Israelites, are the very two which our Lord assumed. He was the Maker and the Lawgiver of His subjects. He said in the commencement of His ministry, "*Follow* Me;" and He added, and I will make you"—you in turn—"fishers of men." And the next we read of Him is, that His disciples came to Him on the Mount, and He opened His mouth and *taught* them. And so again, at the end of it, "Go ye, make *disciples* of all nations, *teaching* them." "Thus the very works for which the [Jewish] nation chiefly hymned their Jehovah, He undertook in His name to do. He undertook to be the Father of an ever-

lasting state, and the Legislator of a world-wide society"
(p. 36) ; that is, showing Himself, according to the
prophetic announcement, to be "*Admirabilis, consiliarius,
pater futuri sœculi, princeps pacis.*"

To these two claims He added a third: first, He chooses
the subjects of His kingdom ; next, He gives them a
law ; but thirdly, He judges them—judges them in a
far truer and fuller sense than in the old kingdom even
the Almighty judged His people. The God of Israel
ordained national rewards and punishments for national
obedience or transgression ; He did not judge His
subjects one by one ; but our Lord takes upon Himself
the supreme and final judgment of every one of His
subjects, not to speak of the whole human race (though,
from the nature of the case, this function cannot belong
to His present visible kingdom). "He considered, in
short, heaven and hell to be in His hand " (p. 40).

We shall mention one further function of the new King
and His new kingdom : its benefits are even bound up
with the maintenance of this law of political unity. "To
organize a society, and to bind the members of it together
by the closest ties, were the business of His life. For
this reason it was that He called men away from their
homes, imposed upon some a wandering life, upon others
the sacrifice of their property, and endeavoured by all
means to divorce them from their former connexions,
in order that they might find a new home in the Church.
For this reason He instituted a solemn initiation, and
for this reason He refused absolutely to any one a dispensation from it. For this reason, too . . . He established a common feast, which was through all ages to
remind Christians of their indissoluble union " (p. 92).
But *cui bono* is a visible kingdom, when the great end of
our Lord's ministry is moral advancement and prepara-

tion for a future state? It is easy to understand, for instance, how a sermon may benefit, or personal example, or religious friends, or household piety. We can learn to imitate a saint or a martyr, we can cherish a lesson, we can study a treatise, we can obey a rule; but what is the definite advantage to a preacher or a moralist of an external organization, of a visible kingdom? Yet Christ says, "Seek ye *first* the kingdom of God," as well as "His justice." Socrates wished to improve man, but he laid no stress on their acting in concert in order to secure that improvement; on the contrary, the Christian law is political, as certainly as it is moral.

Why is this? It arises out of the intimate relation between Him and His subjects, which, in bringing them all to Him as their common Father, necessarily brings them to each other. Our Lord says, "Where two or three are gathered together in My name, I am in the midst of them." Fellowship between His followers is made a distinct object and duty, because it is a means, according to the provisions of His system, by which in some special way they are brought near to Him. This is declared, still more strikingly than in the text we have just quoted, in the parable of the Vine and its Branches, and in that (if it is to be called a parable) of the Bread of Life. The almighty King of Israel was ever, indeed, invisibly present in the glory above the Ark, but He did not manifest Himself there or anywhere else as a present cause of spiritual strength to His people; but the new King is not only ever present, but to every one of His subjects individually is He a first element and perennial source of life. He is not only the head of His kingdom, but also its animating principle and its centre of power. The author whom we are reviewing does not quite reach the great doctrine here suggested, but he goes near it in the following passage: " Some men have appeared who have been 'as levers to uplift the earth and roll it in another course.' Homer by creating literature, Socrates by creating science, Cæsar by carrying civilization inland from the shores of the Mediterranean, Newton by starting science upon a career of steady progress, may be said to have attained this eminence. But these men gave a single impact like that which is conceived to have first set the planets in motion. Christ claims to be a perpetual attractive power, like the sun, which determines their orbit. They contributed to men some discovery, and passed away; Christ's discovery is Himself. To humanity struggling with its passions and its destiny He says, Cling to Me;—cling ever closer to Me. If we believe St. John, He represented Himself as the Light of the world, as the Shepherd of the souls of men, as the Way to immortality, as the Vine or Life-tree of humanity" (p. 177). He ends this beautiful passage, of which we have quoted as much as our limits allow, by saying that "He instructed His followers to hope for life from feeding on His Body and Blood."

6

O si sic omnia! Is it not hard, that, after following with pleasure a train of thought so calculated to warm all Christian hearts, and to create in them both admiration and sympathy for the writer, we must end our notice of him in a different tone, and express as much dissent from him and as serious blame of him as we have hitherto been showing satisfaction with his object, his intention, and the general outline of his argument? But so it is. In what remains to be said we are obliged to speak of his work in terms so sharp that they may seem to be out of keeping with what has gone before. With whatever abruptness, we must suddenly shift the scene, and manifest our disapprobation of portions of his book as plainly as we have shown an interest in it. We have praised it in various points of view. It has stirred the hearts of many; it has recognized a need, and gone in the right direction for supplying it. It serves as a token, and a hopeful token, of what is going on in the minds of numbers of men external to the Church. It is so far a good book, and, we trust, will work for good. Especially as we have seen, is it interesting to the Catholic, as acknowledging the visible Church to be our Lord's own creation, as the direct fruit of His teaching, and the destined instrument of His purposes. We do not know how to speak in an unfriendly tone of an author who has done so much as this; but at the same time, when we come to examine his argument in its details, and study his chapters one by one, we find, in spite of, and mixed up with, what is true and original, and even putting aside his patent theological errors, so much bad logic, so much of rash and gratuitous assumption, so much of half-digested thought, that we are obliged to conclude that it would have been much wiser in him, instead of publishing what he seems to confess, or rather to proclaim, to be the jottings of his first researches upon sacred territory, to have waited till he had carefully traversed and surveyed and mapped the whole of it. We now proceed to give a few instances of the faults of which we complain.

His opening remarks will serve as an illustration. In p. 41 he says, "We have not rested upon *single* passages, nor drawn from the *fourth Gospel.*" This, we suppose, must be his reason for ignoring the passage in Luke ii. 49 : "Did you not know that I must be about My Father's business ?" for he directly contradicts it, by gratuitously imagining that our Lord came for St. John's baptism with the same intention as the penitents around Him; and that, in spite of His own words, which we suppose are to be taken as another "single passage," "So it becometh us to fulfil all justice" (Matt. iii. 15). It must be on this principle of ignoring single passages such as these, even though they admit of combination, that he goes on to say of our Lord, that "in the agitation of mind caused by His baptism, and by the Baptist's designation of Him as the future Prophet, He retired into the wilderness," and there "He matured the plan of action which we see Him executing from the moment of His return into society" (p. 9); and that not till then was He "conscious of miraculous power" (p. 12). This neglect of the sacred text, we repeat, must be allowed him, we suppose, under cover of his acting out his rule of abstaining from single passages and from the fourth Gospel. Let us allow it; but at least he ought to adduce passages, single or many, for what he actually does assert. He must not be allowed arbitrarily to add to the history, as well as cautiously to take from it. Where, then, we ask, did he learn that our Lord's baptism caused Him "agitation of mind," that He "matured His plan of action in the wilderness," and that He then first was "conscious of miraculous power"?

But again: it seems he is not to refer to "single passages or the fourth Gospel;" yet, wonderful to say, he actually does open his formal discussion of the sacred history by referring to a passage from that very Gospel, —nay, to a particular text, which is not to be called "single," only because it is not so much as a single text, but an unfair half text, and half a text such, that, had he taken the whole of it, he would have been obliged to admit that the part which he puts aside just runs counter to his interpretation of the part which he recognizes. The words are these, as they stand in the Protestant version : " Behold the Lamb of God, which taketh away the sin of the world." Now, it is impossible to deny that " which taketh away," etc., fixes and limits the sense of "the Lamb of God ; " but our author notices the latter half of the sentence, only in order to put aside the light which it throws upon the former half; and instead of the Baptist's own interpretation of the title which he gives to our Lord, he substitutes another, radically different, which he selects for himself out of one of the Psalms. He explains " the Lamb " by the well-known image, which represents the Almighty as a shepherd and His earthly servants as sheep—innocent, safe, and happy under His protection. " The Baptist's opinion of Christ's character, then," he says, " is summed up for us in the title he gives Him—the Lamb of God, taking away the sins of the world. There *seems* to be, in the last part of this description, an allusion to the usages of the Jewish sacrificial system ; and, in order to explain it fully, it would be necessary to anticipate much which will come more conveniently later in this treatise. *But* when we remember that the Baptist's mind was *doubtless* full of imagery drawn from the Old Testament, and that the conception of a lamb of God makes the subject of one of the most striking of the Psalms, *we shall perceive what he meant to convey by this phrase*" (pp. 5, 6). This is like saying, to take a parallel instance, "Isaiah declares, 'Mine eyes have seen the King, the Lord of hosts ;' *but*, considering that doubtless the prophet was well acquainted with the first and second books of Samuel, and that Saul, David, and Solomon are the three great kings there represented, we shall easily perceive that, by ' seeing the King,' he meant to

say that he saw Uzziah, king of Judah, in the last year
of whose reign he had the vision. As to the phrase
'the Lord of hosts,' which seems to refer to the Almighty,
we will consider its meaning by-and-by:"—but, in truth,
it is difficult to invent a paralogism, in its gratuitous
inconsecutiveness parallel to his own.

7.

We must own that, with every wish to be fair to this
author, we never recovered from the perplexity of mind
which this passage, in the very threshold of his book,
inflicted on us. It needed not the various passages,
constructed on the same argumentative model, which
follow it in his work, to prove to us that he was not
only an *incognito*, but an enigma. "Ergo," is the symbol
of the logician:—what is the scientific method of a writer
whose symbols, profusely scattered through his pages
are "probably," "it must be," "doubtless," "on this
hypothesis," "we may suppose," and "it is natural to
think," and that at the very time that he pointedly
discards the comments of school theologians? Is it
possible that he can mean us to set aside, in his own
favour, the glosses of all that went before him, and to ex-
change our old lamps for his new ones? Men have been
at fault, when trying to determine whether he was an
orthodox believer on his road to liberalism, or a liberal
on his road to orthodoxy: this doubtless may be to
some a perplexity; but our own difficulty is, whether
he comes to us as an investigator or rather as a prophet,
as one unequal or superior to the art of reasoning.
Undoubtedly he is an able man; but what can he
possibly mean by startling us with such eccentricities
of argumentation as are quite familiar with him?
Addison somewhere bids his readers bear in mind,

that if he is ever especially dull, he always has a special reason for being so; and it is difficult to reconcile one's imagination to the supposition that this anonymous writer, with so much religious thought as he certainly evidences, is without some recondite reason for seeming so inconsequent, and does not move by some deep subterraneous process of investigation, which, if once brought to light, would clear him of the imputation of castle-building.

There is always a danger of misconceiving an author who has no antecedents by which we may measure him. Taking his work as it lies, we can but wish that he had kept his imagination under control; and that he had more of the hard head of a lawyer, and the patience of a philosopher. He writes like a man who cannot keep from telling the world his first thoughts, especially if they are clever or graceful; he has come for the first time upon a strange world, and his remarks upon it are too often obvious rather than striking, and crude rather than fresh. What can be more paradoxical than to interpret our Lord's words to Nicodemus, "Unless a man be born again," etc., of the necessity of external religion, and as a lesson to him to profess his faith openly and not to visit Him in secret? (p. 86). What can be more pretentious, not to say vulgar, than his paraphrase of St. John's passage about the woman taken in adultery? "In His burning embarrassment and confusion," he says, "He stooped down so as to hide His face. . . . They had a glimpse perhaps of the glowing blush upon His face," etc. (p. 104.)

We should be very sorry to use a severe word concerning an honest inquirer after truth, as we believe this anonymous writer to be; but we will confess that Catholics, kindly as they may wish to feel towards him, are scarcely even able, from their very position, to give his work the enthusiastic reception which it has received from some other critics. The reason is plain; those alone can speak of it from a full heart, who feel a need, and recognize in it a supply of that need. We are not in the number of such; for they who have found, have no need to seek. Far be it from us to use language savouring of the leaven of the Pharisees. We are not assuming a high place, because we thus speak, or boasting of our security. Catholics are both deeper and shallower than Protestants; but in neither case have they any call for a treatise such as this *Ecce Homo*. If they live to the world and the flesh, then the faith which they profess, though it is true and distinct, is dead; and their certainty about religious truth, however firm and unclouded, is but shallow in its character, and flippant in its manifestations. And in proportion as they are worldly and sensual, will they be flippant and shallow.* But their faith is as indelible as the pigment which colours the skin, even though it is skin-deep. This class of Catholics is not likely to take interest in a pictorial *Ecce Homo*. On the other hand, where the heart is alive with divine love, faith is as deep as it is vigorous and joyous; and, as far as Catholics are in this condition, they will feel no drawing towards a work which is after all but an arbitrary and unsatisfactory dissection of the Object of their devotion. Faith, be it deep or shallow, does not need Evidences. That individual Catholics may be harassed with doubts, particularly in a day like this, we are not denying; but, viewed as a body, Catholics, from their religious condition, are either too deep or too shallow to suffer from those elementary difficulties, or that distress of mind,

* [On this whole subject, *vide* "Difficulties felt by Anglicans," etc., Lecture IX.]

and need of argument, which serious Protestants so often experience.

We confess, then, as Catholics, to some unavoidable absence of cordial feeling in following the remarks of this author, though not to any want of real sympathy; and we seem to be justified in our indisposition by his manifest want of sympathy with us. If we feel distant towards him, his own language about Catholicity, and (what may be called) old Christianity, seems to show that that distance is one of fact, one of mental position, not any fault in ourselves. Is it not undeniable, that the very life of personal religion among Catholics lies in a knowledge of the Gospels? It is the character and conduct of our Lord, His words, His deeds, His sufferings, His work, which are the very food of our devotion and rule of our life. "Behold the Man," which this author feels to be an object novel enough to write a book about, has been the contemplation of Catholics from the first age when St. Paul said, "The life that I now live in the flesh, I live in the faith of the Son of God, who loved me, and delivered Himself for me." As the Psalms have ever been the manual of our prayer, so have the Gospels been the subject-matter of our meditation. In these latter times especially, since St. Ignatius, they have been divided into portions, and arranged in a scientific order, not unlike that which the Psalms have received in the Breviary. To contemplate our Lord in His person and His history is with us the exercise of every retreat, and the devotion of every morning. All this is certainly simple matter of fact; but the writer we are reviewing lives and thinks at so great a distance from us, as not to be cognizant of what is so patent and so notorious a truth. He seems to imagine that the faith of a Catholic is the mere profession of a formula. He

deems it important to disclaim, in the outset of his
work, all reference to the theology of the Church. He
eschews with much precision, as something almost
profane, the dogmatism of former ages. He wishes "to
trace" our Lord's "biography from point to point, and
accept those conclusions—not which Church doctors or
even Apostles have sealed with their authority—but
which the facts themselves, critically weighed, appear to
warrant."—(Preface.) Now, what Catholics, what Church
doctors, as well as Apostles, have ever lived on, is not any
number of theological canons or decrees, but, we repeat,
the Christ Himself, as He is represented in concrete
existence in the Gospels.* Theological determinations
about our Lord are far more of the nature of landmarks
or buoys to guide a discursive mind in its reasonings,
than to assist a devotional mind in its worship. Common sense, for instance, tells us what is meant by the
words, "My Lord and my God;" and a religious man,
upon his knees, requires no commentator; but against
irreligious speculators, Arius or Nestorius, a denunciation
has been passed, in Ecumenical Council, when "science
falsely so-called" encroached upon devotion. Has not
this been insisted on by all dogmatic Christians over and
over again? Is it not a representation as absolutely
true as it is trite? We had fancied that Protestants
generally allowed the touching beauty of Catholic hymns
and meditations; and after all is there not That in all
Catholic churches which goes beyond any written devotion, whatever its force or its pathos? Do we not believe in a Presence in the sacred Tabernacle, not as a
form of words, or as a notion, but as an Object as real
as we are real? And if before that Presence we need
neither profession of faith nor even manual of devotion,

* [*Vide* "Essay on Assent," ch. iv. and v.]

what appetite can we have for the teaching of a writer who not only exalts his first thoughts about our Lord into professional lectures, but implies that the Catholic Church has never known how to point Him out to her children ?

8.

It may be objected, that we are making too much of so accidental a slight as is contained in his allusion to " Church doctors," especially as he mentions Apostles in connexion with them ; but it would be affectation not to recognize in other places of his book an undercurrent of antagonism to us, of which the passage already quoted is but a first indication. Of course he has quite as much right as another to take up an anti-Catholic position, if he will ; but we understand him to be putting forth an investigation, not a polemical argument: and if, instead of keeping his eyes directed towards his own proper subject, he looks to the right or left, hitting at those who view things differently from himself, he is damaging the ethical force of a composition which claims to be, and mainly is, a serious and manly search after religious truth. Why cannot he let us alone ? Of course he cannot avoid see-ing that the lines of his own investigation diverge from those drawn by others ; but he will have enough to do in defending himself, without making others the object of his attack. He is virtually opposing Voltaire, Strauss, Renan, Calvin, Wesley, Chalmers, Erskine, and a host of other writers, but he does not denounce *them ;* why then does he single out, misrepresent, and anathematize a a main principle of Catholic orthodoxy. It is as if he could not keep his hand off us, when we crossed his path. We are alluding to the following magisterial passage :

" If He (our Lord) meant anything by His constant

denunciation of hypocrites, there is nothing which He could have visited with sterner censure than that *short cut to belief* which many persons take, when, overwhelmed with difficulties which beset their minds, and afraid of damnation, they *suddenly* resolve to strive no longer, but, giving their minds a holiday, to rest content with *saying* that they believe, and acting *as if* they did. A melancholy end of Christianity indeed ! Can there be such a disfranchised pauper class among the citizens of the New Jerusalem ? " (p. 79).

He adds shortly afterwards :

" Assuredly, those who represent Christ as presenting to man an abtruse theology, and saying to them peremptorily, ' Believe or be damned,' have the coarsest conception of the Saviour of the world " (p. 80).

Thus he delivers himself : Believe or be damned is so detestable a doctrine, that if any man denies that it *is* detestable, I pronounce him to be a hypocrite ; to be without any true knowledge of the Saviour of the world ; to be the object of His sternest censure ; and to have no part or place in the Holy City, the New Jerusalem, the eternal Heaven above.—Pretty well for a virtuous hater of dogmatism ! We hope we shall show less dictatorial arrogance than his in the answer which we proceed to make to him.

Whether or not there are persons such as he describes, Catholics, or, Protestant converts to Catholicism, —men who profess a faith which they do not believe, under the notion that they shall be eternally damned if they do not profess it without believing,—we really do not know—we never met with such ; but since facts do not concern us here so much as principles, let us, for argument's sake, grant that there are such men. Our author believes they are not only " many," but enough

to form a "class;" and he considers that they act in
this preposterous manner under the sanction, and in accordance with the teaching, of the religious bodies to
which they belong. Especially there is a marked allusion in his words to the Athanasian Creed and the
Catholic Church. Now we answer him thus :

It is his charge against the teachers of dogma that
they impose on men as a duty, instead of believing,
to "act as if they did" believe :—now in fact this is the
very kind of profession which, if it is all that a candidate
has to offer, absolutely shuts him out from admission
into Catholic communion. We suppose, that by belief
of a thing this writer understands an inward conviction of
its truth ;—this being supposed, we plainly say that no
priest is at liberty to receive a man into the Church who
has not a real internal belief, and cannot say from his
heart, that the things taught by the Church are true.
On the other hand, as we have said above, it is the very
characteristic of the profession of faith made by numbers
of educated Protestants, and it is the utmost extent to
which they are able to go in believing, to hold, not that
Christian doctrine is certainly true, but that it has such
a semblance of truth, it has such considerable marks of
probability upon it, that it is their duty to accept and
act upon it as if it were true beyond all question or
doubt : and they justify themselves, and with much
reason, by the authority of Bishop Butler. Undoubtedly,
a religious man will be led to go as far as this, if he
cannot go farther ; but unless he can go farther, he is no
catechumen of the Catholic Church. We wish all men to
believe that her creed is true ; but till they do so believe,
we do not wish, we have no permission, to make them
her members. Such a faith as this author speaks of to
condemn—(our books call it "*practical* certitude ")—does

not rise to the level of the *sine qua non*, which is the condition prescribed for becoming a Catholic. Unless a a convert so believes that he can sincerely say, "After all, in spite of all difficulties, objections, obscurities, mysteries, the creed of the Church undoubtedly comes from God, and is true, because He who gave it is the Truth," such a man, though he be outwardly received into her fold, will receive no grace from the sacraments, no sanctification in baptism, no pardon in penance, no life in communion. We are more consistently dogmatic than this author imagines; we do not enforce a principle by halves; if our doctrine is true, it must be received as such; if a man cannot so receive it, he must wait till he can. It would be better, indeed, if he now believed; but since he does not as yet, to wait is the best he can do under the circumstances. If we said anything else than this, certainly we should be, as the author thinks we are, encouraging hypocrisy. Nor let him turn round on us and say that by thus proceeding we are laying a burden on souls, and blocking up the entrance into that fold which was intended for all men, by imposing hard conditions on candidates for admission ; for, as we shall now show, we have already implied a great principle, which is an answer to this objection, and which the Gospels exhibit and sanction, but which he absolutely ignores.

9.

Let us avail ourselves of his own quotation. The Baptist said, "Behold the Lamb of God." Again he says, "This is the Son of God." "Two of his disciples heard him speak, and they followed Jesus." They believed John to be "a man sent from God" to teach them, and therefore they believed his word to be true.

We suppose it was not hypocrisy in them to believe in John's word; rather they would have been guilty of gross inconsistency or hypocrisy, had they professed to believe that he was a divine messenger, and yet had refused to take his word concerning the Stranger whom he pointed out to their veneration. It would have been "saying that they believed," and *not* "acting as if they did;" which at least is not better than saying and acting. Now was not the announcement which John made to them "a short cut to belief"? and what the harm of it? They believed that our Lord was the promised Prophet, without making direct inquiry about Him, without a new inquiry, on the ground of a previous inquiry into the claims of John himself to be accounted a messenger from God. They had already accepted it as truth that John was a prophet; but again, what a prophet said must be true; else he would not be a prophet; now, John said that our Lord was the Lamb of God; this, then, certainly was a sacred truth.

Now it might happen, that they knew exactly and for certain what the Baptist meant in calling our Lord "a Lamb;" in that case they would believe Him to be that which they knew the figurative word meant, as used by the Baptist. But, as our author reminds us, the word has different senses; and though the Baptist explained his own sense of it on the first occasion of using it, by adding "that taketh away the sin of the world," yet when he spoke to the two disciples he did not thus explain it. Now let us suppose that they went off, taking the word each in his own sense, the one understanding by it a sacrificial lamb, the other a lamb of the fold; and let us suppose that, as they were on their way to our Lord's home, they became aware of this difference between their several impressions, and disputed with each other which was the right interpretation. It is clear that they would agree so far as this, viz., that, in saying that the proposition was true, they meant that it was true in that sense in which the Baptist spoke it, whatever that was; moreover, if it be worth noticing, they did after all even agree, in some vague way, about the meaning of the word, understanding that it denoted some high characteristic, or office, or ministry. Anyhow, it was absolutely true, they would say, that our Lord was a Lamb, whatever it meant; the word conveyed a great and momentous fact, and if they did not know what that fact was, the Baptist did, and they would accept it in its one right sense, as soon as he or our Lord told them what that was.

Again, as to that other title which the Baptist gave our Lord, "the Son of God," it admitted of half a dozen meanings. Wisdom was "the only begotten;" the Angels were the sons of God; Adam was a son of God; the descendants of Seth were sons of God; Solomon was a son of God; and so is "the just man." In which of these senses, or in what sense, was our Lord the Son of God? St. Peter, as the after-history shows us, knew, but there were those who did not know; the centurion who attended the crucifixion did not know, and yet he confessed that our Lord was the Son of God. He knew that our Lord had been condemned by the Jews for calling Himself the Son of God, and therefore he cried out, on seeing the miracles which attended his death, "Indeed this *was* the Son of God." His words evidently imply, "I do not know precisely what He meant by so calling Himself; but this I do know,—what He said He was, that He is; whatever He meant, I believe Him; I believe that His word about Himself is true, though I cannot prove it to be so, though I do not even understand it; I believe His word, for I believe *Him*."

Now to return to the accusation which has led to these remarks. Our author says that certain persons are hypocrites, because they "take a short cut to belief, suddenly resolving to strive no longer, but to rest content with saying they believe." Does he mean by "a short cut," believing on the word of another? As far as we see, he can mean nothing else ; yet how *can* he really mean this and mean to blame this, with the Gospels before him? He cannot mean it, if he pays any deference to the Gospels, because the very staple of the sacred narrative, from beginning to end, is a call on all men to believe what is not proved, not plain, to them, on the warrant of divine messengers ; because the very form of our Lord's teaching is to substitute authority for argument ; because the very principle of His grave earnestness, the very key to His regenerative mission, is the intimate connexion of faith with salvation. Faith is not simply trust in His legislation, as the writer says ; it is definitely trust in His word, whether that word be about heavenly things or earthly ; whether it is spoken by His own mouth, or through His ministers. The Angel who announced the Baptist's birth, said, "Thou shalt be dumb, because thou believest not my words." The Baptist's mother said of Mary, "Blessed is she that believed." The Baptist himself said, "He that believeth on the Son hath everlasting life ; and he that believeth not the Son shall not see life, but the wrath of God abideth on him." Our Lord, in turn said to Nicodemus, "We speak that we do know, and ye receive not our witness ; he that believeth not is condemned already, because he hath not believed in the Name of the Only-begotten Son of God." To the Jews, "He that heareth My word, and believeth on Him that sent Me, shall not come into condemnation." To the Capharnaites, "He that believeth

on Me hath everlasting life." To St. Thomas, " Blessed
are they that have not seen, and yet have believed."
And to the Apostles, " Preach the Gospel to every creature ; he that believeth not shall be damned."

How is it possible to deny that our Lord, both in the
text and in the context of these and other passages, made
faith in a message, on the warrant of the messenger, to
be a condition of salvation, and enforced it by the great
grant of power which He emphatically conferred on His
representatives ? " Whosoever shall not receive you,"
He says, " nor hear your words, when ye depart, shake
off the dust of your feet." "It is not ye that speak, but the
Spirit of your Father." " He that heareth you, heareth
Me ; he that despiseth you, despiseth Me ; and he that
despiseth Me, despiseth Him that sent me." " I pray
for them that shall believe on Me through their word."
" Whose sins ye remit, they are remitted unto them ; and
whose sins ye retain, they are retained." "Whatsoever ye
shall bind on earth shall be bound in heaven." "I will give
unto thee the keys of the kingdom of heaven ; and what
soever thou shalt bind on earth shall be bound in heaven,
and whatsoever thou shalt loose on earth shall be loosed
in heaven." These characteristic and critical announcements have no place in this author's gospel ; and let it
be understood, that we are not asking why he does not
determine the exact doctrines contained in them—for
that is a question which he has reserved (if we understand him) for a future Volume—but why he does not
recognize the principle they involve—for that is a matter
which falls within his present subject.

10

It is not well to exhibit some sides of Christianity, and
not others ; this we think is the main fault of the author

we have been reviewing. It does not pay to be eclectic in so serious a matter of fact. He does not overlook, he boldly confesses, that a visible organized Church was a main part of our Lord's plan for the regeneration of mankind. "As with Socrates," he says, "argument is everything, and personal authority nothing ; so with Christ, personal authority is all in all, and argument altogether unemployed" (p. 94). Our Lord rested His teaching, not on the concurrence and testimony of His hearers, but on His own authority. He imposed upon them the declarations of a Divine Voice. Why does this author stop short in the delineation of principles which he has so admirably begun ? Why does he denounce "short cuts," as a mental disfranchisement, when no cut can be shorter that to "believe and be saved"? Why does he denounce religious fear as hypocritical, when it is written, "He that believeth not shall be damned"? Why does He call it dishonest in a man to sacrifice his own judgment to the word of God, when, unless he did so, he would be avowing that the Creator knew less than the creature ? Let him recollect that no two thinkers, philosophers, writers, ever did, ever will agree, in all things with each other. No system of opinions, ever given to the world, approved itself in all its parts to the reason of any one individual by whom it was mastered. No revelation then is conceivable, which does not involve, almost in its very idea as being something new, a collision with the human intellect, and demands accordingly, if it is to be accepted, a sacrifice of private judgment on the part of those to whom it is addressed. If a revelation be necessary, then also in consequence is that sacrifice necessary. One man will have to make a sacrifice in one respect, another in another, all men in some.

We say, then, to men of the day, Take Christianity, or leave it ; do not practise upon it ; to do so is as un-philosophical as it is dangerous. Do not attempt to halve a spiritual unit. You are apt to call it a dishonesty in us to refuse to follow out our reasonings, when faith stands in the way ; is there no intellectual dishonesty in your self-trust ? First, your very accusation of us is dishonest ; for you keep in the background the circumstance, of which you are well aware, that such a refusal on our part to back Reason against Faith, is the necessary con-sequence of our accepting an authoritative Revelation ; and next you profess to accept that Revelation your-selves, whilst you dishonestly pick and choose, and take as much or as little of it as you please. You either ac-cept Christianity, or you do not : if you do, do not garble and patch it ; if you do not, suffer others to submit to it ungarbled.

June, 1866,

EDITOR'S NOTES

Dedication:
Henry Arthur Woodgate (1801–1874), a friend of Newman from 1825, he became rector of Belbroughton in 1837. Newman visited him in 1874. (*L.D.* XXVII, p. 18)

PART I: HOW TO ACCOMPLISH IT

p. 1. *When I was at Rome*: Newman was there, together with Hurrell Froude and his father, from 2 March 1833 until 9 April (see *L.D.* III, pp. 228–82), during, what was for Newman, a seven-month tour of the Mediterranean. Newman pointed out in *Apo.*: 'We kept clear of Catholics throughout our tour ... I knew the Abbate Santini, at Rome, who did no more than copy for me the Gregorian tones. Froude and I made two calls upon Monsignore (now Cardinal) Wiseman at the Collegio Inglese, shortly before we left Rome ... I do not recollect being in a room with any other ecclesiastics ... As to Church Services, we attended the Tenebræ, at the Sestine for the sake of the Miserere; and that was all. My general feeling was, 'All, save the spirit of man, is divine.' (pp. 32–3).

p. 1. *an English acquaintance*: 'Whether Newman intended it or not, it is impossible not to recognize the views of Froude, and sometimes his very voice and personality, in the anonymous friend of the author who puts the case for Rome against Newman's ideal of the Anglican *Via Media* ... It is true that he speaks of him as though he was not a very intimate friend and as one whose ideas he disapproved of. But all his characteristics, his paradoxical opinions ... all suggest Froude, apart from the fact that he so often voices Froude's own opinions and arguments ... The paper was apparently written in 1835, and consequently may reflect the influence of his later discussions and arguments with Froude in that year rather than the earlier period at which the dialogue is supposed to have taken place.' Christopher Dawson, *The Spirit of the Oxford Movement*, London, 1933, p. 52.

p. 1. *his own county ... my own University*: Devon and Oxford (Froude was himself, of course, an Oxford man, and also a Fellow of Oriel).

p. 1. *"sacred right of private judgment"*: Keen to counter the abuse of the 'right' in his *Lectures on the Prophetical Office of the Church* (delivered in substance in 1836, and published in 1837), he offered the following definition: 'By the right of Private Judgment in matters of religious belief and practice, is ordinarily meant the prerogative, considered to belong to each individual Christian, of ascertaining and deciding for himself from Scripture what is Gospel truth, and what is not. This is the principle maintained in theory, as a sort of sacred possession or palladium, by the Protestantism of this day.' (*V.M.* I, p. 128).

p. 1. *"quot homines, tot sententiae"*: 'so many men, so many different opinions' (Terence, *Phormio*, p. 454).

p. 2. *sui simile*: 'like itself'. A phrase frequently used in classical and patristic writings, cf., e.g., Lucretius, *De Rerum Natura* VI, p. 1124.

p. 2. *meteoros*: 'lofty'.

p. 2. *the Prussian Minister*: Baron Christian Charles Josias von Bunsen (1791–1860), diplomat and scholar. He was Prussian Ambassador to Rome from 1823–38. He took a keen interest in ecclesiastical affairs, especially those of Prussia and Britain (on the former front he was a great friend of the future King Frederick William IV; and on the latter was intimate with Thomas Arnold), and was a prime mover in the Jerusalem Bishopric Scheme, which was to arouse the outraged opposition of Newman and some of the other Tractarians.

When in Rome in 1833 Newman called on Bunsen on seven occasions and met him incidentally on at least one other. He reported to Pusey on 19 March: 'We are much pleased with Mr Bunsen, tho' (to speak in confidence) I think he has not seen enough of the world – This seems a strange assertion, but he seems to me somewhat bigotted to views, *very* good in the main, but requiring in detail modifications, which he has never had the opportunity of entering into. It is curious to me to see a man somewhat of a *don* (tho' a most kind one) out of Oxford.' *L.D.* III, p. 262. Newman and Froude were to get some insight into Bunsen's plans which were to cause such uproar in 1841: 'He, together with the Prussian Court party, is anxious for the introduction of Episcopacy – and talks of getting it from England. Was not some such plan defeated in Archbishop Sharp's time, by the Prussians requiring us first to acknowledge their ministers as duly ordained? and would not the same objection occur now and wreck the plan?' *vol. cit.*, p. 280.

p. 2. *the staircase ... looked out over Rome*: The Caffarelli Palace on the Capitoline Hill. Under Bunsen's guidance, it developed also into an

Archaeological Institute. Murray's 1853 *Handbook for Travellers in Central Italy* reported that the Institute was 'founded a few years since under the auspices of the present king of Prussia, and maintained in the most efficient state by the Chevalier Bunsen, while Prussian Minister at Rome. It is also supported by the Hanoverian Minister, and by most of the distinguished resident foreigners. Travellers who are desirous of availing themselves of its advantages during their visit to Rome should not fail to become members. Many eminent Prussian scholars have become lecturers at the Institute, and the names of Platner, Bunsen, Röstell, Gerhard, Lepsius, and Braun, are to be found among the contributors to the transactions it has published (p. 230).

p. 3. *panoramic or dioramic descriptions*: A 'panorama' was a 'picture of a landscape, etc., either arranged on the inside of a cylindrical surface round the spectator as a centre …, or unrolled or unfolded so as to pass before him in successive portions.' A 'diorama' was a 'mode of scenic representation in which a picture, some portions of which are translucent, is viewed through an aperture, the sides are continued towards the picture; the light, which is thrown upon the picture from the roof, may be diminished or increased at pleasure' (*OED*). They both were developed, with great success, as forms of popular public entertainment in the eighteenth and early nineteenth centuries. See *L.D.* I, p. 7, regarding Newman's visits to the 'Panorama of Cadiz' and 'Panoramas of Malta and Flushing', on 24 and 28 January 1811.

p. 3. *the Capitol*: The south west summit of the Capitoline Hill in Rome on which, in imperial times, stood the great temple of Jupiter Optimus Maximus, the special guardian of the city. There sacrifice was offered by magistrates upon taking office, and generals returning from victory. It was on 4 March 1833 that Newman first 'mounted the Capitol' – the buildings he encountered being those designed in 1546 by Michelangelo, commissioned by the Farnese Pope Paul III.

p. 3. *News of public affairs had lately come from England*: A newly reformed Parliament had been presented on 12 February 1833 with the Irish Church Temporalities Bill, which proposed the abolition of ten of the twenty-two sees of the Established Church of Ireland, and a series of other trimmings and adjustments to the diocesan and parochial structure of that rather moribund institution. Newman was in Naples when he heard the news and, referring to Lord Grey, marked with vituperation, 'well done, my blind Premier, confiscate and rob, till, like Samson, you pull down the political structure on your own head, tho' without his deliberate purpose and his good cause!' (*L.D.* III, p. 224).

p. 3. *His eye glanced at St. Peter's*: The Basilica which had first been established to mark the grave of the Apostle at the time of his martyrdom during the reign of Nero, between AD 64 and 68. At first a small memorial, the Emperor Constantine initiated the construction of a grand edifice. With the election of Julius II to the papal throne in 1503, even more imperial visions for the Church were to be conjured up and, in 1506, the foundation stone for the new building was laid. Bramante was the first architect for the colossal project, Sangalle proved unable to cope, and in 1547 Michelangelo provided the design for the core of the Church we know today. Nearly another century was to await completion but the contributions of Maderno and Bernini (also remembered for his creation of the Piazza) were to bring one of the most titanic of building projects successfully into port. Newman made his first visit on Sunday 3 March 1833, and his impressions are recorded vividly in his letter of 20 March to his sister Jemima (*L.D.* III, pp. 262–6).

p. 3. *"Master, see what manner of stones and what buildings are here!"*: Mark 13:1.

p. 3. *I was in a retired parish in Berkshire*: Newman is presumably referring to the visit he made to Buckland on 1 July 1832 (see *L.D.* I, p. 62), preaching for Thomas Mozley. Mozley was acting as *locum tenens* for John Marriott, an Oriel pupil of Newman's who had just been appointed to the curacy.

p. 4. *the villa on the Palatine*: The house of Livia (built 75–50 BC).

p. 5. *"the seraph Abdiel"*: In Milton's *Paradise Lost*, Abdiel was the angel who

Among the faithless, faithful only he;
Among innumerable false, unmov'd,
Unshaken, unseduc'd, unterrified
His loyalty he kept, his love, his zeal. (Book V, 897–900)

Abdiel's loyalty was to his Maker when Satan was urging all the Angels to revolt.

p. 6. *"vaunteth not herself . . . unseemly"*: An adaptation by Newman of St Paul's words in I Corinthians 13:4–5.

p. 6. *some Romanist friend at the English College*: Nicholas Wiseman, see note to p. 1. Wiseman (1802–1865) was a talented theological and oriental scholar of Spanish/Irish extraction. He was Rector of the English

College in Rome from 1828–40, then came to England as Coadjutor to Bishop Walsh of the Midland District, and President of Oscott College. Moving to London in 1847, he succeeded as Ordinary in 1849, and in the following year became the first Archbishop of Westminster (and soon after Cardinal) in the newly re-established English Roman Catholic Hierarchy.

p. 7. *Donatist*: The Donatists were a body of schismatics which emerged in the North African Church in the early fourth century. The orthodox response to their position was first led by St Optatus and later by St Augustine. St Augustine's teaching against the Donatists was to have surprising effect on Newman's own theological development – see *Apo.*, pp. 109–11.

p. 7. *notes*: From the works of St Augustine (354–430), Bishop of Hippo and foremost Latin Doctor of the Church. Despite having a Christian mother and a Christian education, he abandoned the faith for Manichaeanism for a while, then turning to Neo-Platonism. The preaching of St Ambrose at Milan drew him back to the Church, and his conversion was complete by 386. Newman described him as The 'Bened'. This refers to the great edition of the works of the Fathers which was produced by the Benedictine Congregation of St Maur in the seventeenth and early eighteenth centuries. The project was based at the Abbey of St Germain-des-Pres, near Paris and the first two volumes of St Augustine's works, which contained the *Epistolae* from which the first quotation is taken, appeared in 1688–9. The second quotation is from St Augustine's apologetic work *De Vera Religione*, which was composed between 389 and 391, and was directed against Pagan and Manichaean philosophers.

p. 8. *Cyril's explanation*: St Cyril of Jerusalem (*c.* 315–87), who became Bishop of that city around 349. His *Catechetical Lectures* are one of the most valuable surviving works of fourth-century patristic writing. A translation of the *Lectures* was to form the second volume of the Oxford 'Library of the Fathers'. It appeared in 1838, translated by Richard William Church, recently elected Fellow of Oriel College (who was to remain a redoubtable friend to Newman, and later to become Dean of St Paul's Cathedral), and with a substantial Preface by Newman. The passage quoted (though slightly differently worded) appears on page 252.

p. 9. *"the Greek Communion to go for nothing"*: The supposed numerical and spiritual strength of the Greek and Russian Orthodox Churches was a favoured point of reference for Anglican apologists in their debates about Roman Catholicism. Newman's confidence in this strategy had weakened very considerably by the time he came to write his 1840 *British Critic* article on 'The Catholicity of the English Church', which itself had been

Editor's Notes

provoked by Wiseman's direct comparisn of the Donatists of the fourth century and the Church of England. Pusey complained: 'I only wish you had dwelt more upon the case of the Greek Church ... I think we might take refuge under the shadow of the Greek Church; people who might doubt whether we were not schismatical, on account of the smallness of our communion, ... would feel that the language of the Fathers would not apply, when it would cut off 90,000,000 in one Orthodox Church.' Newman was not so sanguine, and replied: 'Where you say 90,000,0000 do you include no schismatics or heretics? The whole of the lower part of European Russia (e.g.) ... is in schism with the orthodox Greeks. Then I want to hear signs of *life* among them.' (*L.D.* VII, p. 208).

p. 9. *the Armenian churches"*: At the beginning of the fourth century, Armenia became the first state to accept Christianity as its official religion. However, soon after, division of the Kingdom between the Byzantine and Persian Empires heralded discord over ecclesiology. In the ensuing centuries subjection to Arabs, Turks, and Russians did not help the recovery of an harmonious understanding of the locus of church authority. In 1307 the Christians of Little Armenia accepted union with Rome, but despite their attendance at the Council of Florence in 1438–9, the Christians of Greater Armenia shunned papal authority.

p. 9. *"the English Communion which has branched off"*: Much of this work was accomplished by the initiatives of the Society for the Propagation of the Gospel (S.P.G.) founded in 1701 to assist in the missionary work of the Society for the Promotion of Christian Knowledge (S.P.C.K.), which was addressed to the home territory. While having a particular remit to care for the spiritual needs of the British working or living abroad, the S.P.G. found its work most directly addressed to the evangelisation of the non-Christians who were subjects of the British Crown and the numbers of these had been increasing dramatically, particularly since the (from the British point of view) largely successful conclusion of the Seven Years War in 1763.

p. 9. *"India ... Nova Scotia"*: As the reputation and influence of Newman and the Tractarian Movement gained weight (and also as transport facilities advanced), Colonial ecclesiastical dignitaries were to find their way to Oxford and were regularly fêted at what Newman later termed 'gatherings', (for references to which see, e.g., *L.D.* VII, p. 533).

John Inglis (1777–1850), the third Bishop of Nova Scotia, was making a determined effort at the time of Newman's writing to reinforce Anglican discipline and traditions in his Diocese. Inglis passed through Oxford in 1839, and Newman visited him on 7 May.

p. 9. *"the Nestorians"*: Heretics who took the name from Nestorius (*c.* 382–*c.* 451), a monk and priest of Antioch who was to become Patriarch of Constantinople. 'The doctrine ... lay in the ascription of a human as well as a Divine Personality to Our Lord; and it showed itself in denying the title "Mother of God," ... to the Blessed Mary ... [T]he personality to which the ascribed unity must have laid in Our Lord's manhood, and not in His Divine Nature ... [A]s to the phrase "Mother of God," they rejected it as unscriptural; they maintained that St Mary was Mother of the humanity of Christ ...' (*Dev.*, pp. 294–5). With these principles, the Nestorians maintained that only the human nature of Christ suffered and died on the Cross. The heresy was condemned at the Council of Ephesus in 431. In January 1835, Newman had complained to Hurrell Froude: 'At present you hear Nestorianism preached in every other pulpit ... (and the more I think of those questions, the more I feel, that they are questions of *things* not *words*)' (*L.D.* V, p. 10).

p. 9. *"the Monophysites"*: The heretical Monophysites taught that Our Lord's personality was not in his manhood, but instead asserted that in the Person of the Incarnate Christ there was a single, and that a divine, Nature. Thus they rejected the teaching of the Council of Chalcedon (AD 451) which proclaimed that at the Incarnation Christ became one Person in two Natures, Divine and Human, which are united 'unconfusedly, unchangeably, indivisibly, inseparably'. Newman explained later in his life: 'When the Eternal Word decreed to come on earth, He did not purpose, He did not work, by halves; but He came to be a man like any of us, to take a human soul and body, and to make them His own ... He "was made flesh." He attached Himself to a manhood, and became as really and truly man as He was God, so that henceforth He was both God and man, or, in other words, he was One Person in two natures, divine and human' (*Mix.*, 345–6).

p. 9. *"the Protestants"*: Newman had explained the previous year in one of the *Tracts*, that: 'A number of distinct doctrines are included in the notion of Protestantism: and as to all these, our Church has taken the VIA MEDIA between it and Popery. At the present I will use it in the sense more apposite ... as the religion of so-called freedom and independence, as hating superstition, suspicious of forms, jealous of priestcraft, advocating heart-worship; characteristics, which admit of a good or a bad interpretation, but which, understood as they are instanced in the majority of persons who are zealous for what is called Protestant doctrine, are (I maintain) very inconsistent with the Liturgy of our Church' (*V.M.* II, pp. 41–2).

p. 10. *"the Nag's-head calumny"*: The 'Nag's Head story' was felt by Anglicans to be 'one of the most flimsy, as well as wicked inventions of the Romanists, to invalidate the orders of the Church of England. It refers to the consecration of Archbishop Parker, on which depends the validity of orders in the English Church ... The Papists assert that his consecration was irregular, both as to the place where it was performed, which they say was at the Nag's Head Tavern, Cheapside, and as to the manner of doing it, ... The story, ... was as follows: The queen [Elizabeth I] issued forth her warrant, directed to the Bishop of L[l]andaff: to Dr Scory, elect of Hereford; Dr Barlow, elect of Chichester; Dr Coverdale, elect of Exeter; and Dr Hodgkins, suffragan of Bedford. All these persons met at the Nag's Head Tavern, where it had been usual for the dean of the arches, and the civilians to refresh themselves, after any confirmation of a Bishop; and there one Neale, ... peeped through a hole in the door, and saw all the other Bishops very importunate with L[l]andaff, ...' (W. F. Hook, *A Church Dictionary*, fourth edition, London, 1840, p. 257). Newman explained the central point at issue in 1848: '... it is with extreme difficulty that a Catholic, ... can believe the validity of Anglican Orders; I mean, from the uncertainty that the Consecrators of Parker *intended* to make him a Bishop, ...' (*L.D.* XII, p. 235).

p. 10. *"in Scotland, dissent is the religion of that state"*: Though the Reformation had made uncertain progress in Scotland at first, the determination of John Knox and other Calvinists, led to the reformed Church of Scotland being established on Presbyterian principles in 1560. There followed a century of mixed fortunes, but, despite the efforts of the Stuarts to promote the Episcopal Kirk's interests, the 1560 settlement held through until the great 'Disruption' of 1843.

p. 11. *"the ten tribes"*: At the death of Solomon, ten of the twelve Hebrew tribes separated to form the Kingdom of Israel. The northerly position of the Kingdom meant that it bore the brunt of the Assyrian invasion of around 721 BC. The bulk of the population were deported and were assimilated into the gentile society of Assyria, though some may have been ancestors of the great northern and westward Diaspora of the Jewish people. The destiny of the tribes remained a subject of fascination for centuries, *see* e.g., *L.D.* VII, pp. 425–6.

p. 11. *"the Samaritans"*: The mixed people dwelling in the area of Palestine between Judæa and Galilee. Thought to be descended from the rump of the population of Israel after the Assyrian invasion. They were castigated by the Jews, before and after their own Babylonian captivity, for their syncretistic religious practices.

p. 11. *"the proselytes of the gate"*: Gentile converts to Judaism who did not subscribe to all the ordinances of the Law, especially circumcision, and thus did not share in all of the privileges of the born Jew.

p. 11. *"The early Christians had not the complete canon"*: 'This so called Canon did not exist at earliest till the fourth century . . .' *See* note to p. 203.

p. 12. *latitudinarianism*: A member of the Broad Church party.

p. 12. *"Forms are transitory – principles are eternal"*: Cf. p. 161.

p. 13. *"essentially conservative and aristocratic"*: Newman would remark that one of the marks of true development, in his *Essay* of 1845 would be 'conservative action on the past'.

p. 13. *"The orange ribbon ... badge of high tory confederations"*: In 1688, a cabal of Whig aristocrats set about the deposition of the Catholic King James II. They invited James's elder daughter Mary, together with her husband, Prince William of Orange (the royal house of Orange-Nassau was the ruling dynasty of Holland), to assume the throne upon their agreement to a 'Revolution Settlement'. The successful accession of William and Mary was a particular boon to the Protestants of Ireland, who took to celebrating the anniversary of the event by wearing orange badges or ribbons. The eighteenth century saw the establishment of an increasing number of Orange Lodges, influential clubs for businessmen, at first in Ireland and then over the whole Kingdom and across the globe. There was little doubt as to the Protestant and Tory allegiances of their members.

p. 14. *"the site of the Apollo library"*: Octavian, the future Augustus, was born on the Palatine Hill in Rome, and, on becoming emperor, built his personal palace there. Near to it he built a large temple dedicated to Apollo, to which he attached a fine Greek and Latin Library.

p. 14. *"Herod the Great"*: Herod the Great (73–4 BC) King of Judea from 37–4 BC, he was responsible for rebuilding the temple. His father, Antipater, was an Edomite. (qv. p. 15)

p. 14. *'Levites has been kept pure'*: *See* Leviticus 21:16 'Speak to Aaron and tell him: None of your descendants, who has any defect shall come forward to offer up the food of his God'.

p. 15. *'Asmoneans'*: Hasmoneans. A member of a Jewish priestly family in the 1st and 2nd century BC, which included the Maccabees. Cf. I Maccabees 2:1ff.

p. 15. *'A number of Jews once attempted'*: 1 Maccabees 2:32ff.

p. 15. *'there is a temple at Alexandria now'*: The Egyptian city, near to one of the mouths of the River Nile, was home to the largest and richest Jewish community of the later pre-Christian and early Christian world. There was a substantial temple, which, needless to say, became the focus for the anti-Jewish riots which broke out from time to time.

p. 15. *'another at Gerizim'*: Some time after the exile of the Jews, the Samaritans built a temple on Mt Gerizim. Though it was destroyed by the Hasmonaean King of Judah, John Hyrcanus, the mountain continued to be used as a place of worship, cf. John 4:20.

p. 15. *"St. Austin"*: St Augustine of Hippo. See note to p. 7.

p. 16. *a Tract that has fallen in my way*: John Keble, *Tracts for the Times*, 4, 'Adherence to the Apostolical Succession the safest Course'. The quotation occurs on p. 3.

p. 17. *"Andrewes"*: Lancelot Andrewes (1555–1626), one of the earliest and most influential of the famous seventeenth-century Anglican divines. A famed preacher, and learned patristic scholar, his works were the first to be published in the Library of Anglo-Catholic Theology, a project with which Newman had a loose connection. He was also a deeply spiritual man, and Newman translated and published his own version of Andrewes' *Preces Privatae* as No. 88 of the *Tracts for the Times*.

p. 17. *"Laud"*: William Laud (1573–1645), was appointed Archbishop of Canterbury by Charles I in 1633, and exercised enormous influence throughout that monarch's reign. He enforced strict adherence to the discipline and liturgy of the Church of England, thus attracting the enmity of the Puritan elements which had begun to develop in Elizabeth I's time. The ire of certain members of Parliament led to his impeachment on charge of treason in 1640, and eventual execution five years later. Newman and the other Tractarians held his memory in veneration. However, Newman later came to see that it was the theological methodology of the 'school of Laud gave birth to the latitudinarians; Hales and Chillingworth, their first masters, were personal friends of the Archbishop, whose indignation with them only proves his involuntary sense of the tottering state of his own theological position.' (*Diff.* I, p. 391).

p. 17. *"Ken"*: Thomas Ken (1637–1711), the devout and deeply spiritual Bishop of Bath and Wells, was also a celebrated preacher. He was one of the most famous of the Nonjuring bishops who refused to acknowledge the accession of William and Mary to the English throne in 1688. Of the Nonjurors, Newman wrote in 1850: 'There is something very venerable and winning in Bishop Ken; but this arises in part from the fact that he was so little disposed to defend any position, or oppose things as they were. He could not take the oaths, and was dispossessed; but he had nothing special to say for himself; he had no message to deliver; his difficulty was of a personal nature, and he was unwilling that the Non-juring Succession should be continued.' (*Diff.* I, p. 221).

p. 17. *"Butler"*: Joseph Butler (1692–1752) author of *The Analogy of Religion, Natural and Revealed* ... (1736) which had an influence on Newman's views of development. He became Bishop of Bristol in 1738 and of Durham in 1750.

p. 17. *"we are in the position of Abdiel"*: See note to p. 5.

p. 17. *"decrees of Trent, and that about images"*: The second decree of the twenty-fifth session dealt with 'the honour due to the relics of saints and the lawful use of images'.

p. 17. *"Stillingfleet"*: Edward Stillingfleet (1635–1699), an energetic controversialist and committed scholar of antiquities, was a popular London preacher, and was made Bishop of Worcester upon the accession of William and Mary. Despite his vigorous dispute with John Locke over the Doctrine of the Trinity, which he felt to be threatened by the latter's *Essay concerning Human Understanding*, he was very much a latitudinarian in theological matters. His *Irenicum* attempted to bridge differences between Episcopalians and Presbyterians, and his ecclesiology was minimalist.

p. 18. *"a fine-drawn theory, ... has slept in libraries"*: In the following year, Newman was to write in his *Lectures on the Prophetical Office of the Church* [*V.M.* I]: 'Protestantism and Popery are real religions; no one can doubt about them; they have furnished the mould in which nations have been cast: but the *Via Media* has never existed except on paper, it has never been reduced to practice; it is known, not positively but negatively, in its differences from the rival creeds, not in its own properties; and can only be described as a third system, neither the one nor the other, partly both, ... and boasting to be nearer Antiquity than either.' (p. 20 of 1837 edn). H. J. Rose's journal was indignant about this and, in a review, expressed a reservation about 'the allegation that the church-of-England system (the *Via Media*) is only a *theory*, existing in the writings of certain excellent divines, but never tried as a practical system.' The reviewer felt this 'not to be in harmony with history', and that 'the doctrines and teaching of Sanderson and Hammond, etc., were most widely influential – that perhaps half that party of the nation which attended to religious inquiries was ranged under their banners.' The reviewer's conviction was 'that the real and genuine product of "Anglicanism" is even now of large extent but went unnoticed as one of its chief characteristics was retirement.' See *British Magazine*, May 1837, pp. 546–7.

p.19. *"necessary development . . . except gradually"*: See note to p. 30.

p. 19. *note*: the Third volume of Newman's *Parochial Sermons* first appeared in 1836. He is here quoting from the 'Advertisement' which he prefaced to the second edition, published in the following year.

p. 20. *Hall of Norwich*: Joseph Hall (1574–1656), who achieved some fame as a satirist, was consecrated Bishop of Exeter in 1627, and translated to the see of Norwich in 1641. He had originally been eirenic towards Calvinists and Puritans, but pressure from Laud led to his adoption of a firmer position regarding church order, and in 1640 he published his *Episcopacy by Divine Right*. His criticisms of the Long Parliament led to his impeachment, and imprisonment in the Tower, in 1642. On his release he found that his revenues had been confiscated, his cathedral desecrated, and that he was barred from his episcopal palace.

p. 20. *addressed . . . to Laud*: In his *Christian Moderation* Bishop Hall wrote of that 'temper which is so offensive to the stomach'. *Works*, Oxford, 1837, 12 vols, vol. 6, p. 419.

p. 21. *the great Archbishop*: i.e. William Laud – see note to p. 17. In the early years of the Oxford Movement, Laud was venerated by some of the Tractarians as a martyr. Some of the younger and more eager Tractarians gave great emphasis to this theme. T. E. Morris, a tutor of Christ Church from 1838–45, was delated to the Vice-Chancellor of Oxford University for preaching a sermon in which he spoke of Laud as a martyr still interceding for the Church.

p. 21. *"a friend in need"*: In the original *British Magazine* letters this, and all other, even oblique, personal allusions were represented by a simple underscore.

p. 22. *"a King like the Martyr"*: Charles I (1600–1649), King of Britain and Ireland from 1625. Charles's overtly anti-Puritan ecclesiastical policies, promotion of High Churchmen, and the Roman Catholicism of his wife, Henrietta Maria, all conspired to arouse the hostility of a large section of Parliament. His inept Scottish policy only hastened the outbreak of Civil War in England. His defeat was to ultimately issue in his execution. From 1662 to 1856 a special service for 30 January, the day of his death, was annexed to the Book of Common Prayer, and the day decreed a national fast day. Just before his death a small work was secretly published, entitled

Eikon Basilike: The Poutraicture of His Sacred Majesty in his Solitudes and Sufferings. A great inspiration to royalists at the time, it remained popular among High Church Anglicans.

p. 22. *"Tis true . . . 'tis true'*: *Hamlet*, II, ii, 97.

p. 22. *"like Hagar, . . . in the wilderness"*: In Genesis, Hagar was an Egyptian servant of Abraham's wife, Sarah. Sarah's barrenness, and Abraham's need for a son and heir, led to Hagar's bearing a son to Abraham in Ishmael. Her success in this respect led to truculence, arousing the anger of Sarah, who drove Hagar out into the wilderness. However, the Lord appeared to her in a dream and told her to return to Abraham's household.

p. 23. *"when both Caesar . . . fulfil their office"*: Cf. Matthew 22:21; Mark 12:17; Luke 20:25.

p. 23. *"Oxford the sacred city"*: After the indecisive battle of Edge Hill in 1643, Charles I moved the Court to Oxford, which became the head-quarters of the Royal Army. The city remained the Cavalier capital until it fell to the Roundhead general Lord Fairfax in 1646.

p. 23. *"modern Paris of infidelity"*: Newman has in mind the legacy of 1789 (there was another revolution in 1830) and the proliferation of the ideas of Voltaire and the Encyclopedists. Cf. note p. 69.

p. 23. *"the eras of 1536, 1649, and 1688"*: Henry VIII had taken the title of 'Supreme Head of the Church of England' in 1535, and the following year saw the installation of an English translation of the Bible in churches, the acceleration of the attack on monasteries and religious houses, and the execution of Anne Boleyn. 1649 saw the execution of Charles I, and thus the full inauguration of the English Commonwealth. 1688 was the year of the deposition of James II and accession of William and Mary, these initi-ating the Whig-engineered 'Constitutional' Monarchy.

p. 24. *"Athanasius"*: St Athanasius (*c.* 296–373), Bishop of Alexandria. Newman wrote nearly ten years later: 'There has been a time in the history of Christianity, when it had been Athanasius against the world, and the world against Athanasius. The need and straitness of the Church had been great, and one man was raised up for her deliverance' (*Dev.*, p. 306). For Newman, Athanasius was, 'the foremost doctor of the Divine Sonship, being the most modest as well as the most authoritative of teachers', (*Ath.* II, pp. 56–7), and 'the first and the great teacher of "the revealed doctrine of the Incarnation"', (*Diff.* II, p. 87). On St Athanasius's astounding campaign against Arianism, see *Ari.*, pp. 282–92, 307–34, and 353–76.

p. 24. *"Basil"*: Basil the Great (330–379) wrote two rules which were a decisive influence on monasticism in the East. He succeeded Eusebius as Bishop of Caesarea in 370.

p. 24. *"Austin"*: See note to p. 7 on St Augustine of Hippo.

p. 25. *"Hildebrand"*: As Pope Gregory VII (1073–1085) he was responsible for many reforms in the Church. Newman is not correct in his dates.

p. 25. *"donations made by Pepin and Charlemagne"*: Promise made by Pepin III, King of the Franks to Pope Stephen II to win for him lands conquered by the Lombards in central Italy, embodied in a document in 756. This was further confirmed by his son, Charlemagne in 774. The donation was supposedly based on a grant originally made by Constantine I in the fourth century. See note p. 33.

p. 25. *"Gibbon tells us . . ."*: Edward Gibbon: *The Decline and Fall of the Roman Empire*, Bury's Edition, vol. III, p. 97. Marozia (892–937) was Theophylact and Theodora's daughter, and belonged to the powerful Crescenti family. She gave herself the title of Senator during the papacy of John X and her son was elected as John XI. She was overthrown by Albert II of Spoleto, a son of her first marriage who had her imprisoned, until her death.

p. 25. *"St Peter's chair"*: Besides its literal meaning, the term is a theological expression used for the teaching authority of the Pope as successor of St Peter which is symbolised by his chair (hence the expression 'ex cathedra'). The Feast of Cathedra Petri falls on 22 February.

p. 25. *"Guiberto"*: Guibert di Ravenna (1025–1100) was German Chancellor for Italy (1058–1063) and was then appointed Archbishop of Ravenna by Henry IV. He clashed with Gregory VII over his reforms and was excommunicated by him. He was elected antipope (as Clement III) in 1080 and crowned his patron, Henry IV, as emperor.

p. 25. *"Father Paul . . . with much anxiety towards the English hierarchy"*: Fr Paolo Sarpi (1552–1623) a Venetian, was Vicar General of the Servite Order and author of *Istoria del Concilio Tridentino* which appeared in English translation in 1620. He portrayed Trent as enhancing the power of the curia and the papacy. For this reason, he was often quoted by Anglican authors.

p. 26. *'Anglis nimium timeo . . .'*: Fr Sarpi does not fear the English but has reservations about the power of Anglican episcopacy and its possible tendency towards absolutism. An edition of his letters was published in 1677.

p. 26. *Sancroft ... was not alive to his position"*: William Sancroft (1616–1693), became Archbishop of Canterbury in 1677. He led those bishops who by their refusal to take the Oath of Allegiance to William and Mary were deprived of their offices, and became known as Nonjurors (see note to p. 17).

p. 26. *"genius loci"*: The guardian spirit or deity of a particular place.

p. 26. *"many Williams of Nassau"*: See note to p. 13.

p. 26. *"Leslie ... Case of the Regale and Pontificate"*: Charles Leslie (1650–1722), was a Nonjuror, a dexterous theologian, and redoubtable controversialist. Educated at Trinity College, Dublin, he was ordained, and presented to the Chancellorship of Connor. His refusal to take the 1688 Oaths of Allegiance meant the loss of his benefice. His *The Case of the Regale and the Pontificate* was an assertion of the divine rights and independence of the Church. Newman is quoting from pp. 266–7 of Volume III of the edition of Leslie's *Works* published in Oxford in seven volumes in 1832. H. E. Manning and S. F. Wood brought out a new edition of *The Case* on its own in 1838.

p. 26n. *Dr. Routh*: Martin Joseph Routh (1755–1854), President of Magdalen and author of *Reliquiae Sacrae* was, for years, Newman's friend and ally.

p. 27. *"Mr. Alexander Knox ..."*: Alexander Knox (1757–1831), was a devout Anglican layman, keenly interested in theological matters, who ended his days in Ireland leading a semi-eremitical life. In his insistence on the Catholicity, rather than Protestantism of the Church of England, he has been seen as a forerunner of Tractarianism. Newman acknowledged this but with qualification, insisting that writers such as Knox, 'are to be noticed far more as indications of what was secretly going on in the minds of men than as causes of it', (*Ess.* I, p. 269). J. J. Hornby collected together his scattered miscellaneous writings and published them in four volumes of *Remains* between 1834 and 1837. Newman is here quoting from pp. 51 ff. of the first volume.

p. 28. *"does not acknowledge our Orders"*: See note to p. 10.

p. 28. *"refuses us the Cup"*: In the twenty-first session of the Council of Trent on 16 July, 1562, Canon 3 says: 'If anyone denies that the whole and entire Christ, the source and author of all graces, is received under the species of bread alone, alleging, as some falsely do, that such a reception is not in accord with Christ's institution of the sacrament under both species: let him be anathema'.

p. 29. *"we are concerned not with illusions"*: The French expression 'nous ne nourissons pas d'illusions'.

p. 29. *"the two brothers in the seventeenth century"*: John Rainolds (1549–1607) President of Corpus Christi College, Oxford and Dean of Lincoln, mastermind of the King James version of the Bible, and his brother William (?1544–1594), co-editor of the Douai Bible. The fact of their disputation seems apocryphal.

p. 30. *"doctrinaire"*: Doctrinaires, or Doctrinists, were a political grouping in post-Napoleonic France, who emphasised the compatibility of liberty and monarchical government. The statesman and historian François Guizot, in whose works Newman was interested, was one of their number.

p. 30. *"observance of the Lord's Day"*: Sabbatarianism began with the Scottish Presbyterians (under John Knox) and continued under the Puritans who took it to the American colonies where they imposed the Blue Laws. The Society for Promoting the Observance of the Lord's Day, founded in the 1830s, continued the tradition in England.

p. 30. *"the State's interference with the distribution of Church property"*: This would seem a reference to the Irish Temporalities Bill which passed in 1833. Cf. note p. 3.

p. 30. *"Hildebrand found the Church provided"*: In 1075, he excommunicated King Henry IV who then did penance before the Pope at Canossa.

p. 30. *"St Paul . . . preaching at Athens"*: See Acts 17:15–34.

p. 30. *"persuading his countrymen"*: See, e.g., Acts 13:46–51.

p. 32. *of a Florentine, . . . school*: A reference to Niccolò Macchiavelli (1469–1527), and his doctrine of 'reason of state', most famously expounded in his treatise *Il Principe*, which was written in 1513–14, but only published after his death.

p. 32. *"St. Paul says that everyone should remain"*: I Cor. 7:17.

p. 32. *"we find the Church and State united"*: The Church of England is the

Church by law established with the monarch as supreme governor. 'Such is St Paul's view. Hence we give our Kings the power over the Church which they possess – we allow them to choose our Bishops and to legislate for us, but only on this ground – that they are God's ministers.' Newman, MS Sermon 376, 30 January 1835.

p. 32. *"in the house of bondage"*: Cf., e.g., Exodus 13:3; 20:2; Deuteronomy 5:6; 6:12; 8:14.

p. 32. *'Stand still, and see salvation of God.'*: Exodus 14:13.

p. 33. *'the Lord delivered Sisera ... of a woman'*: Cf. Judges 4:9.

p. 33. *'to know the times ... His own power'*: Acts 1:7.

p. 33. *"Daniel ... prayed towards the Temple"*: Cf. Daniel 6:10.

p. 33. *the terrace walk overlooking the Trastevere*: The Trastevere, or 'Regio Transtiberina', is the district on the right of the River Tiber, south of the Vatican, and was only annexed to the city during the reign of the Emperor Augustus. It is a suburb which has always retained a distinctive individuality, and its inhabitants have often claimed to be the most direct descendants of the ancient Romans. The terrace Newman is here talking about is no doubt that on the Janiculum Hill, the striking, and once fortified, hill behind the area.

p. 33. *the Montorio*: The church of San Pietro in Montorio was founded by Constantine, near to the spot where St Peter was crucified. It fell into complete disrepair during the papacy's Avignon exile of the later fourteenth and early fifteenth century. The Franciscans began its rebuilding in 1475, with Ferdinand and Isabella of Spain providing the money. Newman had visited the Trastevere on 15 March 1833, and had returned to visit San Pietro in Montorio on 9 April.

p. 33. *"Hildebrand"*: See note to p. 25.

p. 33. *"The Exarchate of Ravenna"*: The outlying districts of the Byzantine Empire were governed by Exarchs. Ravenna managed to hold out in its allegiance to Constantinople during the first stages of the Lombard conquest of Italy, but fell to them around 753. The Lombard kingdom itself was to fall to Charlemagne and the Franks only a little over twenty years later.

p. 33. *"The supposed donation of Constantine and the Decretals"*: The 'False Decretals' were a collection of Canon Law documents, purporting to be from the very earliest centuries, but actually drawn up in the midst of the ninth century. However, their authority regarding questions of ecclesiastical jurisdiction was respected throughout the Middle Ages. The 'Donation of Constantine' was a document drawn up in the later ninth century, alleged to have been drawn up by the Emperor Constantine after his conversion, and listing all the privileges he granted to the popes, particularly their primacy over the Churches of Antioch, Jerusalem, Alexandria and Constantinople. The pope was also asserted to be the supreme judge of all the clergy.

p. 34. *"Magna-Chartas"*: See note to p. 314.

p. 34. *"Coronation oaths"*: The oath administered to every monarch on accession to the English throne. The monarch agrees to administer the Kingdom of England (and its dominions), according to the statutes agreed in Parliament, and the laws and customs of the same. The monarch is to cause law and justice in mercy to be upheld, to maintain the laws of God, the true profession of the gospel, and to support the reformed Protestant religion as established by law. They are also to preserve to the bishops and clergy of the realm, and the churches, all their rights and privileges as established by law.

p. 34. *"that commanding moral influence which attended the early Church"*: A subject which Newman wrote about and was fascinated by for nearly all his life. Perhaps his greatest treatments are to be found in the second and fifth of his *University Sermons* ('The Influence of Natural and Revealed Religion Respectively', 13 April 1830; 'Personal Influence the Means of Propagating the Truth', 22 January 1832), and in the tenth chapter of the *Grammar of Assent*.

p. 34. *"we have the Ordination Service"*: The preface of the Book of Common Prayer says 'The Holy Scriptures and ancient Christian writers make it clear that from the apostles' time, there have been different ministries within the Church.'

p. 34. *"the strong language of the services"*: In *The Communion* the priest says: 'My duty is to exhort you in the mean season to consider the dignity of that holy mystery, and the great peril of the unworthy receiving thereof.'

p. 34. *Confirmation and Matrimony . . . spiritual ordinances"*: Only two are considered truly sacramental: Baptism and the Lord's Supper.

p. 35. *"forms of absolution and blessing"*: In *The Visitation of the Sick*, and after the General Confession at *Evensong*.

p. 35. *"the injunction of daily service"*: The Introduction to Volume I of the Tracts, published in 1834, spoke of the 'neglect of the daily service'.

p. 35. *"the solemnization of fast and festival days"*: from the Book of Homilies, Homily 23: That the duty of fasting is a truth more manifest than it should need to be proved. Cf. Tracts 18 and 66 'On the Benefits of the System of Fasting'.

p. 35. *"a yearly confession"*: John Keble complained to J. T. Coleridge on 29 December 1843 about the neglect of Confession, as did Pusey. The reference is to the Book of Common Prayer 'Commination or Denouncing of God's anger and judgments against sinners ... to be used on the first day of Lent'.

p. 35. *"The Church of England ... How to do it"*: Hurrell Froude, putting his own gloss on Keble's *Assize Sermon* of 1833 writing to Christie, said 'He calls the Ministers Libertines and the Parliament Erastian and implies that the Bishops are such a set that he hardly knows whether we ought to remain in Communion with them'. *BOA*

p. 35. *"Hildebrand"*: see n. p. 25.

p. 36. *"In planting his lever"*: Archimedes (287–212 BC), the Greek mathematician and inventor is supposed to have said: 'Give me a fulcrum on which to rest and I could move the world'.

p. 36. *"The power of the keys"*: The power to absolve or excommunicate, derived from Matthew 16:19.

p. 37. *"the meeting house"*: The reference is to the Society of Friends' place of prayer, but also to any religious meeting place where the emphasis was on 'enthusiasm' rather than an ordered form of words.

p. 37. *"Religious Institutions"*: Newman makes clear (p. 42) that he is thinking of Religious Congregations and Orders in the Roman Catholic sense.

p. 38. *"Te Deum."*: A Christian hymn of praise composed around AD 400 which begins 'We praise you, God, we acknowledge you as Lord'.

p. 38. *Watts*: Isaac Watts (1674–1748) became pastor of Mark Lane Independent Chapel in 1702. He published many of his hymns in 1706 and 1707, including 'When I survey the wondrous Cross' and 'O God, our help in ages past'.

p. 38. *Newton*: John Newton (1725–1807), the former slave trader who became the Curate of Olney in 1764, and in collaboration with the poet William Cowper (1731–1800), published The Olney hymns. One of his most famous is 'Amazing Grace'.

p. 38. *Wesley*: John Wesley (1707–1791) brother of Charles and regarded as leader of the Methodists, originally a reformist movement within the Anglican Church (they fasted twice a week and encouraged frequent Communion), but which eventually broke away. He published 'Rules for Methodist Societies' in 1743.

p. 39. *"The Easter anthem"*: The *Exultet*, which begins 'Rejoice choirs of angels ...' now sung on Holy Saturday night in the Roman liturgy.

p. 39. *"The Venite"*: The opening word of Psalm 95 'O Come, let us sing unto the Lord ...' used as a Canticle at Morning Prayer.

p. 39. *"Jeremy Taylor"*: Bishop of Down and Connor (1613–1667) famous for his two books *Rule and Exercises of Holy Living* and *Rule and Exercises of Holy Dying* published in 1650 and 1651.

p. 39. *the Wesleyans*: Alternative name for Methodists whose founder was John Wesley. (qv above)

p. 40. *"religious Sisterhoods"*: The first Anglican Sisterhood was the Community of the Holy Cross at Park Village, London in 1845; the Community of St Mary the Virgin followed in 1848 and the Community of St John the Baptist at Clewer in 1851. Newman would write to Tom Mozley on 12 December 1839, 'Women would be going to Rome unless nunneries are soon held out to them *in* our Church'. *L.D.* VII, p. 263.

p. 41. *"A high episcopal system"*: Newman is appealing to the principle of levelling up in accord with the teaching of the Caroline divines.

p. 41. *"Arianism"*: The fourth-century heresy which affirmed that the Son of God 'came from another substance than that of the Father'. See n. p. 58.

p. 41. *"Associated Brethren of Egypt and Syria prophesying"*: In the second persecution of The Emperor Constantius as related by St Athanasius in his *History of the Arians*, Part IV.

p. 43. *"monachism"*: The establishment of monasteries. Newman was himself accused when he retired to Littlemore, of setting up a monastery, and did refer to it as such in private correspondence.

PART 2: THE PATRISTIC IDEA OF ANTICHRIST

p. 44. *"Let no man deceive ... son of perdition"*: 2 Thessalonians 2:3.

p. 45. *"One more than a prophet"*: Mathew 11:9.

p. 45. *being universally held*: The passage is very much a summary of the 'Rule of Faith' of Vincent of Lerins: 'quod ubique, quod semper, quod ab omnibus creditum est'. It was a formula most dear to many Anglican apologists from the mid-seventeenth century onwards, and especially so to the Newman of 1833–9, and to all of the early Tractarians.

p. 46. *St. Paul says, "Remember ... these things?"*: 2 Thessalonians 2:5.

p. 47. *the Fathers do not convey to us the interpretation*: Three and a half years later, Newman was to expand the argument of these paragraphs in his essay on the 'Prospects of the Anglican Church', in which he pointed out that, 'this age is a practical age: the age of the Fathers was more contemplative; their theology, consequently, had a deeper, more mystical, more subtle character about it, than we with our present habits of thought can readily enter into. We lay greater stress than they on proofs from definite verses of Scripture, or what are familiarly called texts, and we build up a system upon them; they rather recognized a certain truth lying hid under the tenor of the sacred text as a whole, and showing itself more or less in this verse or that as it might be. We look on the letter of Scripture more as a foundation, they as an organ of truth ... The Fathers might have traditionary information of the general drift of the inspired text which we have not. Moderns argue from what alone remains to them; they are able to move more freely. Moreover, a certain high moral state of mind, which times of persecution alone create, may be necessary for a due exercise of mystical interpretation.' (*Ess.* I, pp. 286–7).

p. 47. *"That Day shall not come ... falling away first"*: 2 Thessalonians 2:3.

p. 47. *"false prophets ... even at the doors"*: Matthew 24:24, Mark 13:22; Matthew 24:12; Matthew 24:33, Mark 13:29.

p. 48. *by the brightness of Christ's coming*: 2 Thessalonians 2:8.

p. 48. *"a time, ... dividing of time"*: Daniel 7:25.

p. 48. *"forty-two months"*: Cf. Revelations 13:5.

p. 48. *"the mystery of iniquity doth already work"*: 2 Thessalonians 2:7.

p. 49. *the types of Christ went before Christ*: The examination of Old Testament characters as 'types of Christ' was to become a recurrent theme in Newman's preaching. Cf. especially, *S.D.* 12, 'Joshua a Type of Christ and His Followers' (13 June 1841), and *S.D.* 13, 'Elisha a Type of Christ and His Followers (14 August 1836).

p. 49. *the judicial destruction of the Jewish Church*: In his later Anglican preaching, Newman was to lay greater stress on the positive connection between Judaism and Christianity. See especially *S.D.* 14, 'The Christian Church a Continuation of the Jewish' (13 November 1842), and *S.D.* 15, 'The Principle of Continuity between the Jewish and Christian Churches (20 November 1842). He came increasingly to emphasise that Christ's mission was a completion of that of the Jewish Dispensation.

p. 49. *"Now ye know . . . revealed in his time"*: 2 Thessalonians 2:6.

p. 49. *"He that now withholdeth, . . . out of the way"*: 2 Thessalonians 2:7.

p. 49. *this restraining power*: Cf. *Idea*, p. 443: 'It was once an opinion, . . . drawn from the sacred text, that the Christian Dispensation was to last a thousand years, and no more; the event disproved it. A still more exact and plausible tradition, derived from Scripture, was that which asserted that, when the Roman Empire should fall to pieces, Antichrist should appear, who should be followed at once by the Second Coming. Various Fathers thus interpret St. Paul, and Bellarmine receives the interpretation as late as the sixteenth century. The event alone can decide if, under any aspect of Christian history, it is true; but at present we are at least able to say that it is not true in that broad plain sense in which it was once received.'

p. 49. *"hindereth"*: Isaiah 14:6.

p. 50. John Chrysostom, Homily 76 on Matthew 24:16–18.

p. 50. *"ten kings that shall rise"*: Daniel 7:24.

p. 50. *"I considered the horns, . . . speaking great things"*: Daniel 7:8.

p. 51. *"the mystery of iniquity doth* already *work"*: 2 Thessalonians 2:7.

p. 51. note 'ο ἄνομος: 'wicked or lawless'.

p. 52. *"That day shall not come, . . . signs and lying wonders"*: 2 Thessalonians 2:3–4; 8–9.

p. 52. *"Another shall rise after them"*: Daniel 7:24–5.

p. 53. *Xerxes, Darius and Alexander*: Darius (521–486) followed Xerxes (519–465) as King of Persia, and Alexander (356–323) was the conqueror of the country.

p. 54. *"In those days ... to do mischief"*: 1 Maccabees 1:11–15.

p. 54. *"After that Antiochus ... spoken very proudly"*: 1 Maccabees 1:20–4.

p. 54. *"and pulled down the houses ... therein"*: 1 Maccabees 1:31, 33, 35.

p. 54. *"King Antiochus wrote ... profaned the sabbath"*: 1 Maccabees 1:41–3.

p. 55. *"profane the sabbath ... uncircumcised"*: 1 Maccabees 1:45–8.

p. 55. *"the Abomination of Desolation ... with fire"*: 1 Maccabees 1:54, 56.

p. 55. *"Howbeit ... upon Israel"*: 1 Maccabees 1:62–4.

p. 55. *the apostate emperor Julian*: Flavius Claudius Julianus (331–363) see note p. 389. He attempted to reintroduce paganism – see pp. 57–8, 67.

p. 56. *"Theodoret"*: Theodoret (*c.* 393–*c.* 460) became Bishop of Cyrrhus in Syria in 423, and proved a wise and competent ordinary, as well as a keen rebutter of paganism and heretics. However, he found himself embroiled in the controversy between Nestorius and St Cyril of Alexandria, and, while not endorsing the doctrines of the former, had reservations about the counter-arguments of the latter, and this was to lead ultimately to his deposition. He was a talented apologist, but also the finest exegete of the Eastern Church of Antiquity, and his commentary on Daniel was just one of the many commentaries on the books of the Bible which he composed. Though not in any substantial agreement with his views, Newman always felt an instinctive sympathy for him, as is evident in his later essay on the 'Trials of Theodoret', included in *H.S.* II.

p. 57. *called by St. Paul*: 2 Thessalonians 2:3.

p. 58. *Nestorianism*: See note to p. 9.

p. 58. *Eutychianism*: 'In A.D. 448 Eutyches, the abbot of a monastery in the suburbs of Constantinople, was condemned by a synod held in that city, and presided over by St. Flavian, Patriarch of Constantinople, for teaching the doctrine of One, not Two, Natures in Christ. Eutyches was a *persona grata* at court, and St. Flavian was not. In consequence the affair soon became one of the first magnitude, and the Emperor, Theodosius II, determined upon a General Council to settle it. Meanwhile both the Emperor and Eutyches wrote to the Pope, St. Leo the Great, but no report came from St. Flavian. The Pope wrote somewhat sharply to the last named. It was from him that he ought first to have heard of the scandal, and it was not clear that Eutyches had been justly condemned. "Send therefore," the letter continued, "to give us a full account of what has occurred." On hearing from St. Flavian, the Pope, now fully informed, wrote his *Epistola Dogmatica ad Flavianum*, generally known as the Tome of St. Leo, in which Eutyches was condemned, and the Catholic doctrine of the Two Natures was set forth.' *K.C.*, pp. 2–3. For Newman's first encounter with the figure of Eutyches during his pivotal studies in the Long Vacation of 1839, see *Apo.*, pp. 114–15.

p. 58. *the heresy of Arius*: Arius (*c.* 260–336) was a priest of Alexandria, who became embroiled in controversy with his orthodox bishop, Alexander, over the distinctions between God the Father and God the Son. The most famous of all heresies in the history of Christianity, Arianism is often confused with Socinianism and Unitarianism, though the three are completely distinct. Strictly speaking, Arians are those who believe Jesus Christ to be a secondary deity; one who has existed since before creation, but not co-eternally with God the Father.

p. 58. note: See note to p. 8 for the background to the Oxford translation of the *Catechetical Lectures* of St Cyril of Jerusalem. St Cyril's fifteenth lecture was 'On the Second Advent, the Last Judgment, and the Perpetuity of Christ's Kingdom', and the reference alluded to here is to be found on p. 189. Newman himself seems to have compiled many of the footnotes, and used them to pull together all the patristic references he had sourced when writing these four sermons.

p. 59. *Societies ... principles of utility*: No doubt Newman had at the fore-front of his mind the Society for the Diffusion of Useful Knowledge, of which, in 1827, Henry Peter Brougham was one of the founding fathers. See notes to pp. 255 and 257.

p. 61. *have lot or part in this matter?*: Cf. Acts 8:21.

p. 61. *"O my soul ... be not thou united"*: Genesis 49:6.

p. 61. *"What fellowship hath ... be ye separate"*: Cf. 2 Corinthians 6:14–17.

p. 62. *"every spirit that confesseth ... is in the world"*: 1 John 4:3.

p. 64. *"The mystery of iniquity doth* already *work"*: 2 Thessalonians 2:7.

p. 64. *"he is the Antichrist that* denieth the Father and the Son": 1 John 2:22.

p. 64. "the adversary and rival ... *himself that he is God"*: Cf. 2 Thessalonians 2:4.

p. 64. *"The king* ... *himself* above all": Daniel 11:36–7.

p. 66. *"I am Christ"*: Matthew 24:5.

p. 66. *"whose coming* ... *in unrighteousness"*: 2 Thessalonians 2:9–12.

p. 66. *"sit in the Temple of God"*: 2 Thessalonians 2:4.

p. 66. *"the Abomination of Desolation* ... *standing in the* holy place": Matthew 24:15.

p. 66. *"Their dead bodies* ... *our Lord was crucified"*: Revelation 11:8.

p. 67. note: The anti-Gnostic *Adversus Haereses* of St Irenaeus of Lyons (*c.* 130–*c.* 200) were probably composed between 174 and 189 AD. The fifth book, which Newman is quoting from here and a little later is devoted to solely eschatological themes. St Hippolytus (*c.* 170–*c.* 236) was the foremost third century theologian of the Latin Church. He was a prolific writer but few of his works have survived, one exception being the *De Antichristo* referred to here. The St Cyril of Jerusalem reference occurs on pp. 191–2 of the Oxford translation (see note to p. 8).

p. 68. *"exalt himself over all that is called God or worshipped"*: 2 Thessalonians 2:4.

p. 69. *that great and famous nation over against us*: i.e. France, particularly since the Revolution of 1789. At the beginning of the nineteenth century, many in England identified Napoleon with the Antichrist, and his rise to power spurred on some extreme forms of millenarianism. Almost ironically, France took over the role of Antichrist from the Pope in the English imagination. The July Revolution of 1830 was to inspire equally intense feelings in Newman, who reflected that: 'At the first revolution they were wild beasts let loose; and now they are more like evil spirits' (*BOA*). Only a few years later Newman was to see clearer marks of the Antichrist in the growing scepticism and commercial greed of contemporary society, and in 1838 reflected that, 'London has, at this moment, many of the tokens of the Apocalyptic Babylon' (*Letter to Faussett*, second edition, Oxford 1838, p. 40 n.).

p. 69. *"a strange worship"*: Cf. Psalms 81:9; Isaiah 43:10. Theophilanthropism. Deistic sect formed in France during the latter part of the Revolution by disciples of Rousseau and Robespierre. They originally met in the church of St Catherine in Paris.

p. 69. *wretched man . . . a fable*: Jean Baptiste Gobel of Paris, who declared in 1797 'There is no other cult than liberty and holy equality', before resigning.

p. 69. *like Belshazzar*: Cf. Daniel 5:1–4.

p. 70. *The remains of the two principal of these*: Both were disinterred and were brought into the Pantheon: Voltaire in July 1791 and Rousseau in October 1794. Cf. note p. 288.

p. 73. *Irenaeus and Hippolytus*: See note to p. 67.

p. 73. *"Here is wisdom, . . . threescore and six"*: Revelation 13:18.

p. 75. *"think it strange"*: Cf. 1 Peter 4:12.

p. 77. *"The woman which thou sawest . . . of the earth"*: Revelation 17:18.

p. 77. *His mother the Blessed Virgin . . . taxed by the Roman governor*: Cf. Luke 2:1–5.

p. 77. *under Pontius Pilate, the Roman governor*: Cf. Matthew 27:2.

p. 77. *St. Paul . . . being a Roman citizen*: Cf. Acts 22:25–9.

p. 77. *by the Roman governors . . . sent to Rome himself*: Cf. Acts 25:12, 21.

p. 78. *represented by St. John as an abandoned woman*: Cf. Revelation 17:4–7.

p. 79. *the figure of four beasts*: Daniel 7:3–6.

p. 79. *"diverse . . . it had ten horns"*: Daniel 7:7.

p. 79. *the very same beast which St. John saw*: Cf. Revelation 13:1.

p. 79. *"ten kings that shall arise"*: Daniel 7:24.

p. 79. *"The ten horns . . . one hour with the beast"*: Revelation 17:12.

p. 79. *"The ten horns . . . burn her with fire"*: Cf. Revelation 17:16.

p. 80. *"Another shall arise after them . . . the dividing of time"*: Daniel 7:24–5.

p. 80. *"the ten horns shall hate and devour" the woman*: Cf. Revelation 17:16.

p. 80. *"I considered the horns . . . plucked up by the roots"*: Daniel 7:8.

p. 80. *"desolated, devoured, and burned with fire"*: Cf. Revelation 17:16.

p. 81. *"a golden cup in her hand full of abominations"*: Revelation 17:4.

p. 81. *"the inhabitants of the earth drunk with the wine of her fornication"*: Revelation 17:2.

p. 81. *seven hills of which St. John spake*: Cf. Revelation 17:9.

p. 81. *The Prophet Daniel . . . the ten kings*: Cf. Daniel 7:24.

p. 82. *"The wild Beast . . . and yet is"*: Revelation 17:8.

p. 82. *"The ten kings . . . one hour with the beast"*: Cf. Revelation 17:12.

p. 83, n.3. *Gibbon, Hist . . .*: Newman is referring to the twelve volume, London 1813, edition of Edward Gibbon's *The History of the Decline and Fall of the Roman Empire*, Vol. V, pp. 224–8 [Bury's edn, III, pp. 269–71].

p. 84. *a modern writer, who is neither favourable to Christianity, nor credulous*: Edward Gibbon (1737–94), the celebrated historian and author, whose scepticism is evidenced in his critical attitude towards Christianity. In the Long Vacation of 1818 Newman had been 'taken up with Gibbon' (*A.W.*, p. 40). In the following year, Newman proclaimed: 'A second perusal . . . has raised him in my scale of merit. With all his faults, his want of simplicity, his affectation, and his monotony, few can be put in comparison with him; and sometimes, when I reflect on his happy choice of expressions, his vigorous compression of ideas, and the life and significance of his every word, I am prompted indignantly to exclaim that no style is left for historians of an after day. O who is worthy to succeed our Gibbon! Exoriare aliquis! and may he be a better man!' (*L.D.* I, p. 67). Despite appreciation of Gibbon's skills, he became increasingly critical of, 'his cold heart, impure mind, and scoffing spirit', (*U.S.*, p. 126). Nevertheless, in 1841 he pointed out: 'It is notorious that the English Church is destitute of an Ecclesiastical History; Gibbon is almost our sole authority for subjects as near the heart of a Christian as any can well be.' (*Ess.* II, p. 186).

p. 84, n.1. *Ibid.*: Vol. VI, pp. 12–32 on the invasions of Genseric and the Vandals [Bury's edn, III, pp. 400–415].

p. 84, n.3. *Ibid.*: Vol. IV, pp. 338–40 [Bury's edn, III, pp. 69–70].

p. 84, n.3. *Ibid.*: Vol. VII, pp. 418–24 [Bury's edn, IV, pp. 436–40].

p. 85. *"that which withholdeth . . . taken away"*: Cf. 2 Thessalonians 2:7.

p. 85. *"make her desolate and burn her with fire"*: Revelation 17:16.

p. 86. *"she shall be . . . who judgeth her"*: Revelation 18:8.

p. 86. *a mighty Angel . . . found no more at all"*: Revelation 18:21.

p. 86. *the prophecy ascribed to St. Malachi*: 'It is perhaps not generally known, that the Roman Catholics possess in anticipation a list of all the popes who are to reign till the end of the world. A countryman of our own has the merit of having drawn up this prophetic catalogue. St Malachy was born in Armagh in 1094, and became archbishop of that see in 1127: he resigned his honours in 1135, and, after working many miracles, he died in 1148 at Clairvaux in France. It may be remarked, that he was the first saint regularly canonised by the Romish Church. Among other proofs of his supernatural powers, he left a list of all the popes from Celestin II. 1143, to the end of time. The fact is pretty well ascertained, that this was an invention of the cardinals assembled in conclave to elect a pope upon the death of Urban VII, in 1590. The partisans of Cardinal Simoncelli, afterwards Gregory XIV, brought forward this list as a prophecy of St Malachy; and the words which were considered indicative of his election were, "de Antiquitate Urbis," as the Cardinal was a native of Orvieto, the Latin name of which was *Urbs Vetus*. No mention is made of the existence of such a prophecy till 1600, . . . The concluding words of the prophecy are these: "In the last persecution of the holy Roman Church, Peter of Rome shall be on the throne, who shall feed his flock in many tribulations. When these are past, the city upon seven hills shall be destroyed, and the awful Judge shall judge the people."' Edward Burton, *A Description of the Antiquities and other Curiosities of Rome*, Oxford, 1821, pp. 472–5.

p. 87. *Abraham's intercession for Sodom*: Cf. Genesis 18:22–33.

p. 88. *"If He be . . . come down from the Cross"*: Cf. Luke 23:39; Matthew 27:40.

p. 88. *"to respect the Churches . . . sanctuaries"*: The History of the Decline and Fall of the Roman Empire, London, 1813, Vol. V, p. 312 [Bury's edn, III, p. 322].

p. 89. *when Attila . . . the captives from torture*: Ibid., Vol. VI, pp. 130–2, 151 [Bury's edn, III, pp. 472–3, IV, p. 5].

p. 90. *The destruction of Jerusalem in our Lord's prophecy*: Cf. Matthew 24:1–22; Mark 13:1–23; Luke 21:5–24.

p. 91. *"the righteous men"*: Cf., e.g., 2 Peter 2:8–10.

p. 93. *"Blessed are they . . . the kingdom of heaven"*: Matthew 5:10.

p. 94. *"There shall be a time of trouble, . . . in the Book"*: Daniel 12:1.

p. 96. *"There shall be great tribulation . . . shortened"*: Matthew 24:21–2.

p. 97. *"There shall arise false Christs . . . the very elect"*: Matthew 24:24.

p. 97. *"There shall be a time of trouble . . . in the book"*: Daniel 12:1.

p. 97. *"They shall take away the Daily Sacrifice"*: Daniel 11:31.

p. 97. *that Antichrist will suppress for three years and a half*: Cf. Augustine, *City of God*, Book XX, Ch 13.

p. 97. *St. Augustine questions*: 'And thus they shall be snatched from him (Satan) even though unbound'. Augustine, *City of God*, Book XX, Ch 8.

p. 98. *our Saviour declares the same*: Cf. Matthew 24:15.

p. 98. *the magicians of Egypt effected against Moses*: Exodus 7:11.

p. 98. *"Signs and wonders"*: Matthew 24:24.

p. 99. *"They were tortured . . . tormented"*: Cf. Hebrews 11:35–7.

p. 100. *It is written by eye-witnesses*: Pseudo-Irenaeus, Letter of the Churches of Vienna and Lugdunum to the Churches of Asia and Phrygia.

p. 101. n. *Op. cit.*, Vol. VI, p. 284 [Bury's edn, IV, p. 8].

p. 103. *the night is far spent*: Cf. Romans 13:12.

p. 103. *the approaching destruction of the Mahometan power*: The Ottoman Empire was already bruised by the outcome of the Greek War on Independence and was even more so by the defeats suffered, in 1832–3, by Turkish forces in Syria and Adana at the hands of the vassal Mohammed Ali Pasha, ruler of Egypt. Western Governments were acting increasingly on the assumption that the Ottoman regime would soon collapse.

p. 104. *Satan, being loosed . . . Gog and Magog*: Cf. Revelation 20:7–8.

p. 104. *used by the prophet Ezekiel*: Cf. Ezekiel 38:2–3; 39:1–7.

p. 104. *the sons of Japheth*: Genesis 10:2.

p. 104. *Goths and Vandals*: Both were Germanic tribes; the Goths settled near the Black Sea in the 3rd century AD and the Vandals moved from Eastern Europe in the 5th century AD through Gaul and Spain to Africa, sacking Rome in 455.

p. 105. *to use our Lord's instance*: Cf. Luke 12:54–6.

p. 105. *our rock of strength*: Cf. Psalms 62:6–7.

p. 107. *Bishop Horsley*: Samuel Horsley (1733–1806) was rector of Newington from 1759–93. He became Bishop of St David's, then Rochester and St Asaph. He devoted much of his life to a controversy with Joseph Priestley on the divinity of Christ.

p. 107. *British Magazine*: It was founded to promote High Church views in 1832 by Hugh James Rose (1795–1838). He had become acquainted while spending a year in Germany with rationalist theology and biblical higher criticism. A meeting at his rectory in Hadleigh in July 1833 marked the beginning of the Oxford Movement.

PART 3: HOLY SCRIPTURE IN ITS RELATION TO THE CATHOLIC CREED

LECTURE 1: DIFFICULTIES IN THE SCRIPTURE PROOF OF THE CATHOLIC CREED

p. 111. *Jebusites*: The tribes which occupied the city of Jerusalem at the time of David's conquest (2 Samuel 4:6ff.).

p. 111. *like haughty Haman*: King Ahasuerus' high official who was described as 'outstanding in devotion and steadfast loyalty, and who has gained the second rank in the kingdom' (Esther 8:3) which enabled him to plot the destruction of the Jews.

p. 111. *an argumentum ad hominem*: 'to the man', appealing to one's prejudice.

p. 113. *the Apostolical Succession of the Ministry*: That bishops have succeeded to the place of the apostles, possessing authority over the people entrusted to them.

p. 113. *to deny that the Holy Ghost is God*: Christianity expresses its belief in the divinity of the Holy Spirit by saying that 'with the Father and the Son he is worshipped and glorified' (Nicene Creed).

p. 115. *"on the duty of fasting"*: 'When you fast, do not look gloomy like the hypocrites . . .' (Matthew 6:16). 'The day will come when the bridegroom is taken away from them, and then they will fast' (Matthew 9:15).

p. 118. *planting groves*: Cf. Isaiah 1:29; 65:3; 66:17; Ezekiel 6:13; 20:28; Hosea 4:13; Judith 3:8. The groves may have been connected with the worship of Asherah/Ashtaroth, a semitic fertility goddess identified with the Phoenician goddess, Astarte.

p. 118. *consecrating ministers*: Abijah, King of Judah tells Jeroboam, King of Israel, 'Have you not expelled the priests of the Lord, the sons of Aaron, and the Levites, and made for yourselves priests like the people of foreign lands?' (2 Chronicles 13:9).

p. 119. *"the communication of the Body of Christ"*: 1 Corinthians 10:16.

p. 119. *"We have an Altar"*: Hebrews 13:10.

p. 120. *There is not a single text*: Not explicity, but the practice of baptizing whole households (Acts 16:15.33; 18:8; I Cor. 1:16) points towards infants being baptized. It is certainly part of apostolic tradition. Origen (writing in the third century) stated that the practice came from the apostles in his *Commentary on Romans* 5, 9. However *The Record* (an evangelical paper) demanded that patristic authority as used by Tractarians 'be cast away as the dust in the balance' (22 August 1836).

p. 121. *St. Paul happens in one place*: Hebrews 13:15.

p. 121. *Our Saviour says that where two or three*: Matthew 18:20.

p. 121. *"good* for the present distress": I Corinthians 7:26.

p. 122. *The words of our Lord and St. James*: Matthew 5:34; James 5:12.

p. 122. *"Whoso sheddeth man's blood"*: Genesis 9:6.

p. 122. *"he (the magistrate) beareth not"*: Romans 13:4.

p. 123. *St. James actually denies that it is*: James 2:24.

p. 124. *"articulus stantis aut cadentis ecclesiae"*: An article of belief by which the Church stands or falls. Justification by faith identified as such in Luther's Smaller Catechism of 1529.

p. 125. *"My Lord and my God"*: John 20:28.

p. 125. *"I ascend to my Father and your Father"*: John 20:17.

p. 125. *"Lord, Thou knowest all things."*: John 21:17.

LECTURE 2: THE DIFFICULTIES OF LATITUDINARIANISM

p. 126. *Latitudinarianism*: The broad Church view. Cf. 'Liberalism in religion is the doctrine ... that ... one creed is as good as another' Newman's *Biglietto* Speech May 12 1879.

p. 126. *Lutherans*: The followers of Martin Luther (1483–1546) the German theologian and reformer.

p. 126. *Presbyterianism*: A Church which is governed by presbyters or elders.

p. 126. *Independency*: A self-governing Church, such as Congregationalist or Baptist.

p. 126. *the religion of Lutherans*: The followers of Martin Luther (1483–1546) the German theologian, and founder of the Protestant Reformation.

p. 126. *of ... Baptists*: The followers believe in baptism by immersion, but not of infants. The first Church was founded by Thomas Helwys in London in 1611, and a breakaway community, called the Particular Baptists, founded across the river in Southwark by John Spilsbury in 1638.

In Newman's time the Baptists were re-founded with Methodist theology in 1770.

p. 126. *of ... Wesleyans*: Followers of John Wesley (1703–1791) or Methodists. Cf. note p. 38 and Tract 36 for an account of religious sects 'at present existing'.

p. 126. *of ... Friends*: The Religious Society of Friends (or Quakers) founded by George Fox *c*. 1650. Its members believe in the 'Inner Light' and come together for 'meetings'. They have no ecclesiastical structure, are pacifists and are opposed to oath-taking. William Penn (1644–1718) set up the colony of Pennsylvania as a refuge for those seeking religious toleration.

p. 127. *the ground of the Roman Church*: That revelation is contained in Scripture and Tradition.

p. 128. *the doctrine of the Atonement*: That humanity is reconciled to God through Christ, and in particular his saving death and Resurrection.

p. 128. *the doctrine of spiritual influence*: After reading the first volume of Newman's *Parochial Sermons* upon its publication in 1834, Samuel Wilberforce complained to Newman: 'The *single* point which has most continually met and surprized me is an apparently studied effort to suppress the doctrine of spiritual influences.' Newman responded: 'If I must express broadly my view of spiritual influences on the heart and will etc. I should say, that they were vouchsafed *according to the constitution of man's nature* – i.e. so as not to change it *from* its ordinary workings, but to make use of these. The Holy Spirit addresses us thro' our reason.'

p. 128. *the Catholic doctrine of the Trinity is not ... upon the surface of Scripture*: The doctrine of the Trinity although hinted at especially in John 16:12–16 was clarified in the Councils of the Church and especially in the Nicene and Athanasian Creeds.

p. 129. *the Gospel ... scarcely more than the republication of the law of nature*: This is the philosophy of John Jacques Rousseau (1712–1778) as expressed in *Le Contrat Social* and *Emile*.

p. 130. *Romanists or Protestants*: Romanists are Roman Catholics. Protestants adhere strictly to the Thirty-Nine Articles, and abhor any popish tendencies, cf. note p. 9.

p. 130. *Catholics or Heretics*: Catholics, in Newman's view, are those who accept the substance of the Apostles' Creed and Apostolic Succession. Heretics are those who deny any or all of these.

p. 130. *Calvinists or Arminians*: Calvinists, the followers of John Calvin (1509–1564) believe in the predestination of the righteous, whereas Arminians, who follow Jacob Harmonsen (1560–1609) believe that Christ died for all.

p. 130. *Anglicans or Dissenters*: Anglicans are members of the Church of England and Dissenters are those who refuse to take the Thirty-Nine Articles.

p. 130. *High Churchmen or Puritans*: High Churchmen give a high place to the authority of the episcopate and priesthood and to the inherent grace of the sacraments and the Church structure. Puritans believe in a strict moral and disciplinary code without hierarchy and with emphasis on the faith of the believer.

p. 130. *Episcopalians or Independents*: Episcopalians belong to a Church structured on an episcopacy. Independents are self-governing (and dissenters).

p. 130. *Wesleyans or Socinians*: Wesleyans (=Methodists) accept the Christian Creed, but not the Episcopacy as opposed to the followers of Fausto Sozzini (1539–1604), who reject the divinity of Christ and many Christian teachings.

p. 130. *"hold"* ... *"hold fast"*: Cf. 2 Timothy 1:13; Hebrews 10:23.

p. 131. *the doctrine is not written on the sun*: Cf. Thomas Paine, *The Age of Reason. Part the Third . . .*, London, 1811, p. 88: 'Now had the news of salvation by Jesus Christ been inscribed on the face of the Sun and the Moon, ... the whole earth had known it in twenty-four hours, and all nations would have believed it ...' See *Apo.*, p. 17, for Newman's recollection of reading the work of the infidel Paine (1737–1809) in his youth. Tom Mozley recorded that, at Oriel, Newman 'had Tom Paine's works under lock and key, and lent them with much caution to such as could bear the shock ...' *Reminiscences, chiefly of Oriel College and the Oxford Movement*, London, 1882, I, p. 40. See also *L.D.* I, p. 103, and *G.A.*, p. 378.

p. 132. *it limits ... our liberty of thought*: 'A man who fancies he can find out truth by himself, disdains revelation. He who thinks he *has* found it out, is *impatient* of revelation.' *P.S.* I, p. 318.

p. 132. *You tell me ... "no creed is to be found in Scripture"*: 'When our Saviour promises that the Holy Spirit, whom the Father should send in Christ's name, should teach them all things ... these words of His are not to be explained as relating merely to a system of doctrines and motives – to an abstract religious principle, – but to a real, individual personal agent.' Richard Whately, *Detached Thoughts and Apothegms*, London, 1854, p. 172.

p. 133. *antecedent improbability*: Contrast with Newman's antecedent probability. Cf. note p. 295.

p. 134. *Religion cannot but be dogmatic; it ever has been*: The first 'Council' of Jerusalem occasioned by new Gentile converts made decisions which were conveyed to them by letter. Acts 15:19–21.

p. 134. *it will have anathemas*: The accompaniment of dogmatism is the authority to proscribe the contrary error. The majority of the Church Councils have followed their doctrinal decrees with a series of anathemas directed against those who held the opposing errors. 'Excommunication is as much a spiritual act as administering the Eucharist and Ordination.' Newman to A. P. Perceval, 20 March 1835, *L.D.* V, p. 49.

p. 134. *a rule of faith as well as of conduct*: 'The Gospel is not a mere scheme or doctrine, but a reality and a life; not a subject for books only, for private use, for individuals, but for public profession, for combined action ...' *S.D.*, p. 115.

p. 134. *Presbyterians ... Wesleyans*: Cf. note pp. 126, 130.

p. 135. *"He who believeth ... shall be damned"*: Cf. Mark 16:16.

p. 135. *"the doctrine of Christ"*: 2 John 9.

p. 135. *"keeping the faith"*: Cf. 2 Timothy 3:7.

p. 135. *"the faith once delivered to the saints"*: Cf. Jude 3.

p. 135. *"delivering that which has been received"*: Cf. 1 Corinthians 11:23.

p. 136. *other branches of the Church*: The Via Media theory has the Anglican Church between the Roman and the Protestant. Cf. note pp. 9.18.

p. 136. *St. Paul speaks of one faith, one baptism, one body*: Cf. Ephesians 4:4–5.

p. 136. *"The rest will I set in order when I come"*: 1 Corinthians 11:34.

p. 136. *"I had* many things *to write . . . we shall* speak *face to face"*: Cf. 2 John 12; 3 John 13.

p. 137. *antecedent disposition*: See note to p. 295.

p. 137. *"the whole counsel of God"*: Acts 2:23.

p. 137. *Whether we adopt our Sixth Article or not*: 'Of the Sufficiency of the holy Scriptures for salvation.'

p. 139. *The Epistles of St. Ignatius . . . the longer Epistles of St. Paul*: St Ignatius in his Epistle to the Ephesians says, 'There is only one physician . . . who is at once fleshly and spiritual, uncreated, yet born, God in man, true life in death, born of Mary and of God, first passable, then impassible, Jesus Christ our Lord.' (n. 7).

p. 140. *Christianity is . . . social*: Newman preached on 7 June 1835: 'Surely the whole Church living and dead is bound together in one communion and whenever we baptize our children, or receive the Blessed Eucharist, we admit souls and unite ourselves more deeper into the fellowship of the dead as well as the living.' MS Sermon 389. Cf. also note p. 232.

p. 140. *There has been an uninterrupted maintenance . . . from the beginning*: 'The idea of disbelieving, or criticizing the great doctrines of the faith from the nature of the case, would scarcely occur to the primitive Christians. These doctrines were the subject of Apostolical Tradition; they were the very truths which had been lately revealed to mankind.' *Ari.*, p. 134.

p. 141. *We must submit to the indirectness of Scripture*: Cf. Newman's Letter to Mrs Froude, note p. 238.

LECTURE 3: ON THE STRUCTURE OF THE BIBLE, ANTECEDENTLY CONSIDERED

p. 142. *professing Christians . . . whatever their particular denomination*: The word 'denomination' was first used of a sect in the seventeenth century.

p. 143. *Lutherans . . . Independents*: Cf. note pp. 126, 130.

p. 143. *consubstantiation with Luther*: The belief that the reality of bread co-exists with the Body of Christ in the Eucharist.

p. 143. *absolute predestination of individuals, with Calvin*: The doctrine that the elect are pre-ordained to eternal happiness and the lost, to eternal damnation by a divine decree.

p. 143. *"as He liveth . . . rather that he should live"*: Ezekiel 18:23.

p. 143. *the Church's being "the pillar and ground of the Truth"*: I Timothy 3:15.

p. 143. *Baptism is . . . always connected with it in Scripture*: Cf. John 3:5, 'No one can enter the kingdom of God without being born of water and Spirit', and Rom. 6:4. 'We were buried therefore with him by baptism into death, so that as Christ was raised from the dead by the glory of the Father, we too might walk in newness of life.'

p. 143. *Friends . . . contrary to St. Paul's plain prohibition*: I Corinthians 14:34–5. Cf. note p. 123. See *L.D.* VIII, p. 448, for Newman's reaction to Elizabeth Fry's leading of a prayer service at Newgate in the presence of the King of Prussia in 1842.

p. 143. *our Saviour's plan declaration . . . His Kingdom is not of this world*: John 18:36.

p. 143. *the woe denounced against riches*: Luke 6:24.

p. 143. *praise bestowed on celibacy*: Cf. I Corinthians 7:25–38.

p. 144. *Churchmen, Presbyterians*: Cf. note pp. 126, 130.

p. 144. *Unitarians*: A religion which owes much to Socianism (qv. note p. 130). John Biddle (1615–1662) a Socinian, is credited as the founder of Unitarianism in England. The first place of worship was the Essex Street chapel in London founded by Theophilus Lindsey in 1774. Most influential was James Martineau (1805–1900) from his base in Birmingham. Unitarianism encouraged freedom of religious thought rather than acceptance of Creeds or Confessions, with a reliance on science rather than Tradition or authority. A humanitarian Christology with a liberal emphasis resulted. Newman's colleague at Oriel, Joseph Blanco White and Newman's own brother, Francis, became Unitarians (Francis describes this in *Phases of Faith*, published in 1850).

p. 144. *in a former lecture*: Cf. p. 128ff.

p. 148. *the* onus probandi: 'The burden of proof'.

p. 148. *"the whole counsel of God"*: Cf. Acts 20:27.

p. 149. *"the certainty of the things in which they had been instructed"*: Luke 1:4.

p. 149. *as the Homilies show*: Homily 12: They declare that, not only the holy Apostles and disciples of Christ, but the godly Fathers also, before and since Christ, were endued without doubt with the Holy Ghost.

p. 150. *this beautiful and fully-furnished surface ... a series of accidents*: Sir Charles Lyell (1797–1875) in his *Principles of Geology* (1830–33) developed the earlier theories of James Hutton that the earth was shaped over a long period of time by natural processes. Newman attended his lectures as an undergraduate.

LECTURE 4: STRUCTURE OF THE BIBLE IN MATTER OF FACT
p. 155. *the fifth chapter of Genesis*: The chapter contains a full genealogy from Adam to Noah.

p. 156. *the devil is called "that old serpent"*: Revelation 12:9; 20:2.

p. 156. *two accounts of Abraham denying his wife*: Genesis 12:10–20; 20:1–14. The former is ascribed to the Yahwist Tradition, and the latter to the Elohistic.

p. 156. *one instance of Isaac*: Genesis 26:7–11. This passage is considered a conflation of the Yahwist and Priestly Traditions.

p. 156. *"Confess your faults one to another"*: James 5:16.

p. 157. *we read that Moses fasted*: Deuteronomy 9:25; 10:10. Exodus 32:1–14. The former passages belong to the Deuteronomic Tradition, and the latter is a conflation of the Yahwist and Elohistic.

p. 157. *Deacons are spoken of by St. Paul ... Bishops*: 1 Timothy 3:8; 10:12–13; Philippians 1:1; I Timothy 3:1–2; Titus 1:7.

p. 157. *two kinds of Bishops ... overseers*: Bishop from the Greek episkopos.

p. 158. *the fourth commandment*: Exodus 20:8–11; Deuteronomy 5:12–15.

p. 159. *'My Father worketh hitherto, and I work'*: John 5:17.

p. 159. *"communication of the body and blood of Christ"*: Cf. I Corinthians 10:16.

p. 161. "the rest *will I set in order when I come"*: I Corinthians 11:30.

p. 162. *freethinkers have before now attributed*: The traditional opinion was that Chronicles were written by Ezra the scribe.

p. 163. *substantive additions or simply developments*: Newman would pursue the matter in his Lectures on the Prophetical Office of the Church (=*V.M.* I) where he sees a role for apostolic and prophetical tradition. The Roman Catholic doctrine as set out in the Council of Trent was that revelation is partly (*partim*) in written books and partly in unwritten tradition.

p. 163. *David's great sin, and Solomon's fall*: See II Samuel 24:10 regarding David's census of Israel; and I Kings 11:6–11, on Solomon's offering sacrifice to the gods of his various foreign wives.

p. 165. *"If thou bring thy gifts to the* altar ... *If thou wouldst be* perfect": Matthew 5:23; 19:21.

p. 166. *the raising of Lazarus*: John 11:1–44.

p. 166. *parallel miracles ... of Elijah and Elisha*: I Kings 17:17–24; 15–16; II Kings: 4:32–7; 2–7.

p. 166. *the feeding of the 4,000 with seven loaves*: Cf. Matthew 15:34–9; 16:20; Mark 8:5–9.

p. 167. *Simon of Cyrene ... Christ Himself bore it*: Matthew 27:32; Mark 15:21; Luke 23:26; John 19:17.

p. 167. *St Paul says, "Ye do* shew forth *the Lord's death till He come"*: I Corinthians 11:26.

p. 168. *Judas is represented ... bowels gushing out*: Matthew 27:5; Acts 1:16–19.

p. 168. *Confirmation*: See Newman's long and important letter to his sister Jemima of 4 June 1837 (*L.D.* VI, pp. 78–81), for Newman's understanding of the rite, and the gifts conveyed, at this time. He gives references to authorities, both Scriptural and Anglican, for his view.

p. 168. *the intermediate state*: the Anglican term which is designed to eliminate the need for the Catholic doctrine of Purgatory, deemed in Article 22 'a fond thing vainly invented'. Newman's views on Purgatory and his objections are in Tract 79 published in March 1837.

LECTURE 5: THE IMPRESSION MADE ON THE READER BY THE STATEMENTS OF SCRIPTURE

p. 171. *"We are told, . . . in the Prayer Book"*: Cf. Articles XIX and XXV. The reference is to Wheatley's *Rational Illustration of the Book of Common Prayer*, London, 1839.

p. 172. *'Upon the first day of the week, . . . break bread'*: Acts 20:7.

p. 172. *'Christ our Passover . . . sincerity and truth'*: I Corinthians 5:7–8.

p. 173. *"Do not many most excellent men now alive"*: Godfrey Fausset, Lady Margaret Professor of Divinity preached 'The real and unqualified and therefore ambiguous expression "real presence" in relation to the Eucharist' in *The Revival of Popery* (A Sermon preached at St Mary's 20 May, 1838) directed against the Tractarians. Cf. also Tract 73, *On the Introduction of Rationalistic Principles into Religion*, *Ess.* I, p. 30ff.

p. 174. *his half sentences . . . have a meaning in them independent of the context*: Cf. *G.A.*, pp. 78–9, and Newman's remarks about Virgil, '. . . as if a prophet or magician; his single words and phrases, his pathetic half lines, giving utterance, as the voice of Nature herself, to that pain and weariness, yet hope of better things, which is the experience of her children in every time.'

p. 174. *when a writer is deep*: Cf. *G.A.*, p. 47, '. . . when some one said, perhaps to Dr. Johnson, that a certain writer (say Hume) was a clear thinker, made answer, "All shallows are clear." But supposing Hume to be in fact both a clear and a deep thinker, yet supposing clearness and depth are incompatible in their literal sense, . . . and still in their full literal sense were to be ascribed to Hume, then our reasoning about his intellect has ended in the mystery, "Deep Hume is shallow"; whereas the contradiction lies not in the reasoning, but in the fancying that inadequate notions can be taken as the exact representations of things.'

p. 175. *when the prophet Isaiah told Ahaz*: Isaiah 7:12.

p. 175. *his zeal led him to smite the Egyptian*: Exodus 2:12.

p. 176. *the account of Jeroboam's conduct*: Jeroboam advised King Rehoboam to pursue a harsh policy (beating with scorpions) and 'all Israel went off to their tents. Rehoboam therefore, reigned only over those Israelites who lived in the cities of Judah'. 2 Chronicles 10:16–17.

p. 176. *the old prophet who dwelt in Samaria*: 2 Kings 5:3.

p. 177. *the ancient Martyrologies*: i.e. the registers of martyrs that began to be drawn up locally in the fourth century. The eighth and ninth centuries saw the appearance of the more detailed historical martyrologies of writers such as Bede, Ado, and Usuard. That of the latter was revised and expanded in the sixteenth century to form the Roman Martyrology.

p. 177. *the persecution at Lyons and Vienne*: In the summer of 177 Lyons and then nearby Vienne saw the outbreak of one of the earliest and most horrendous persecutions of Christians. The communities seem to have been founded by missionaries from the eastern Mediterranean, and the Christian faith took root succesfully among the mainstream of the community. Jealousy led to trumped up charges which formed the excuse for savage punishments.

p. 178. *Agabus at Caesarea*: See Acts 21:8–11, regarding St Paul's encounter with the prophet.

p. 178. *his cleverly dividing the Jewish council*: See Acts 23:6–9 on St Paul's appearance before the high priest Ananias.

p. 178. *Lot ... "a just man"*: Cf. 2 Peter 2:7.

p. 178. *Ehud's assassination of Eglon*: See Judges 3:12–23 on the judge of Israel's killing of the King of Moab.

p. 178. *the praise given to Jael for killing Sisera*: Jael was the wife of Heber the Kenite, who found herself giving refuge to the Canaanite King Sisera, and, realising who he was, killing him with a hammer and tent peg. The incident is recounted in Judges 4:17–21. The 'praise' occurs in the 'Song of Deborah and Barak' which forms the fifth chapter of Judges.

p. 179. *the account of Jacob's wresting with the Angel*: See Genesis 32:24–30.

p. 179. *Or how simply and abruptly the narrative runs*: Genesis 3:1.2ff.

p. 180. *"And when He had thus spoken"*: St Paul after the storm. Acts 27:35.

p. 180. *a very high meaning put on them in our Prayer Book*: In 'The Order for the Administration of the Lord's Supper, or Holy Communion' in *The*

Book of Common Prayer. 'And this is certainly a very essential part of the service. For during the repetition of these words, the priest performs to God the representative sacrifice of the death and passion of his Son. By taking the *bread into his hands*, and *breaking* it, he makes a memorial to him of our Saviour's body broken upon the cross; ... For this reason we find, that it was always the practice of the ancients, in consecrating the Eucharist, to break the bread, (after our Saviour's example,) to represent his passion and crucifixion.' Charles Wheatley, *A Rational Illustration of the Book of Common Prayer of the Church of England*, Oxford, 1839, p. 292.

p. 181. *"Neither in this mountain ... worship the Father"*: Cf. John 4:21.

p. 181. *to speak about all religious things at once*: Many years later, Newman described his dislike of 'what, when I was young, R. Wilberforce and H. Froude used to call "180 degree sermons," that is, sermons which were resolved to bring in the whole circuit of theology in the space of twenty minutes. We used to think it was the great fault of Evangelicals – that they would not let religious topics come in naturally, but accused a man of not being sound in religion if he dared to speak of sanctification without justification, regeneration, etc., etc.'

p. 182. *St. Peter struck off the ear of Malchus*: John 18:10; Matthew 26:51; Mark 14:47.

p. 182. *our Lord's miracle in healing the ear*: Luke 22:51.

p. 182. *to be tribulation, want, contempt, persecution*: Cf., e.g., John 16:33; Acts 14:22; Philippians 4:11; Matthew 5:10–11; Luke 6:22.

p. 183. *that the world was soon to come to an end*: Cf., e.g., Matthew 13:40, 49; John 7:6; Revelation 1:7; 12:12.

p. 183. *the danger of sin after baptism*: Newman, like most Anglicans and Protestants, held no doctrine of the remission of post-baptismal sin. This lacuna suggested terrifying consequences. In a series of sermons which he included in *P.S.* IV, Newman attempted to ameliorate some of the extreme severity of his earlier preaching, while refusing to accept the Roman Catholic doctrine, e.g.: 'It is said if a man be changed in heart and life, this is a plain proof that he has been visited by God's grace; ... his past sins are already forgiven him. I answer by denying what is here assumed; I would say, then, that a man may be in God's favour, yet his sins not absolutely forgiven ...'; 'When Christians have gone wrong in any way ... it seems that pardon is not explicitly and definitely promised them in Scripture as a matter of course ...', (*vol. cit.* pp. 191, 114). A few years later, Newman began to see the impossibility of such a position and turned to the mind of the early Church: 'It is not necessary here to enlarge on the benefits which the primitive Church held to be conveyed to the soul by means of the Sacrament of Baptism. Its distinguishing gift ... was the plenary forgiveness of sins past. It was also held that the Sacrament could not be repeated. The question immediately followed, how, since there was but "one Baptism for the remission of sins," the guilt of such sin was to be removed as was incurred after its administration ... When ... an answer had to be made to the question, how is post-baptismal sin to be remitted, there was an abundance of passages in Scripture to make easy to the faith of the inquirer the definitive decision of the Church', (*Dev.*, pp. 384, 393).

p. 184. *falling away is spoken of, and excommunication*: Cf., e.g., 2 Thessalonians 2:3; Matthew 18:15–18; 1 Corinthians 5:13.

p. 184. habitat: (Latin) 'it inhabits'. Used to refer to the location where any genus or species dwell and flourish.

p. 184. *"called to be saints"*: Cf. Romans 1:7; 1 Corinthians 1:2.

p. 184. *our Saviour was a superhuman being*: The belief of Unitarians.

p. 185. *the same Apostle's Epistle to the Hebrews*: See note to p. 206.

p. 185. *"He who has begun ... the Lord Jesus"*: Cf. Philippians 1:6.

p. 185. *"Who are kept ... unto salvation"*: 1 Peter 1:5.

p. 185. *the Book of Canticles*: Or Song of Songs, or, Song of Solomon, the latter pseudonymous ascription arising from the King's reputation as a prolific lover and the suggestively erotic nature of much of the contents. The latter had often been used to throw doubt on the book's legitimate canonicity, but for centuries allegorical interpretations had been found to detach the work from its apparent literal meaning.

p. 185. *two Messiahs*: No doubt Newman is referring to the 'Suffering Servant' who appears in various poems in Books 40–55 of Isaiah, and the 'Son of Man' of Book 7 of the prophet Daniel.

p. 185. *the impression which David's history*: The picture of David to be found running from 1 Samuel 16 right through to 1 Kings 2 is distinctly critical, whereas that found in 1 Chronicles 2–29 is very favourable.

p. 187. *the Socinians*: followers of Fausto Sozzini (1539–1604), the Italian

Protestant theologian. Newman uses the term often with reference to liberal theologians. See note to p. 130.

p. 187. *the historian Gibbon*: On Edward Gibbon, and Newman's view of him, see note to p. 84. Gibbon began to explore, albeit tendentiously, the influence of Platonism on Christian doctrine, particularly on the Divinity and Sonship of Christ, in Chapter XXI of *The Decline and Fall of the Roman Empire*. See Vol. III, London, 1813, 314–22 (Bury's edn, II, 335–40).

p. 187. *the mustard-seed, or the labourers of the vineyard*: See Matthew 13:31–2; Mark 4:30–32; Luke 13:18–19; Matthew 20:1–16.

p. 187. *His discourse at Nazareth ... wrought upon Gentiles*: Luke 4:16–18, 24–27.

p. 188. *the prayer of the Canaanitish woman*: Matthew 15:22–28.

p. 188. *His condescension towards the centurion*: Matthew 8:5–13.

p. 188. *"and to go teach all nations, baptizing them"*: Cf. Matthew 28:19.

p. 188. *we have now the gift of the Holy Spirit*: See note to p. 128.

p. 188. *"Ye shall be witnesses ..."*: Acts 1:8.

p. 189. *"And St. Peter's address ... Bithynia"*: I Peter 1:1.

p. 190. *"preach the Gospel to every creature"*: Mark 16:15.

p. 190. *"who being in the form of God"*: Philippians 2:6.

p. 190. *"If thou bring thy gift to the Altar"*: Cf. Matthew 5:23.

p. 191. *"I am with you alway," or, "Receive ye the Holy Ghost"*: Matthew 28:10; John 20:22.

p. 191. *St. Peter at Joppa*: See Acts 9:36–42; 10:7–22.

p. 191. *St. Paul on his journeys*: See Acts 13–14; 15:36–18:21; 18:23–21:14. For St. Paul's reflections on his journeys and their trials, see 2 Corinthians *passim*.

p. 191. *"I am the God of Abraham"*: Exodus 3:6. Cf. also, e.g.: Matthew 22:32; Mark 12:26; Luke 20:37.

p. 191. *called the pillar and ground of the Truth*: 1 Timothy 3:15.

p. 191. *"But ye are clean, but not all"*: Cf. John 13:10.

p. 191. *His riding on an ass*: See John 12:14.

p. 191. *"Destroy this Temple ... the Temple of His Body"*: John 2:19, 21.

p. 192. *Isaiah said to Ahaz*: Isaiah 7:14. Cf. also Matthew 1:23.

p. 192. *How different persons are ... their writings!*: Cf. *U.S.*, pp. 309–10: 'Another striking proof of narrowness of mind among us may be drawn from the alteration of feeling with which we often regard members of this or that communion, before we know them and after.' ('Wisdom, as contrasted with Faith and with Bigotry', preached on 1 June 1841). The sermon was preached just after he had received the first of several letters from Charles W. Russell, the Catholic priest and Maynooth professor, which were 'gentle, mild, unobtrusive, uncontroversial'. Newman later admitted that Russell, 'had, perhaps, more to do with my conversion than any one else', (*Apo.*, p. 194).

p. 193. *Bp. Butler ... a Cross in his chapel at Bristol*: The chapel at Littlemore had a stone cross on the wall behind the altar also. 'This was considered exceedingly popish'. Meriol Trevor, *Newman the Pillar of the Cloud* (London, 1962), p. 196. Cf. also note p. 17. Bishop Butler's work *Analogy of Religion, Natural and Revealed, to the Constitution and Course of Nature* was published in 1736 and defended revealed religion against the theories of the Deists.

p. 193. *Greek historians ... the gravest and severest of them*: Thucydides (460–404 BC) is the author of the *History of the Peloponnesian War*.

p. 194. *Sophocles*: (496–406 BC) The greatest of Greek tragic poets. His verse plays include *Antigone*, *Oedipus the King* and *Electra*.

p. 194. *Pericles* (494–429) Athenian statesman – one of the ten *strategi* who managed home and foreign affairs, who was elected continuously for thirty years. He was responsible for the beautification of the Acropolis.

p. 194. *Cicero*: Marcus Tullius (106–43 BC) A lawyer (he prosecuted Catiline) and Roman statesman (he became consul in 63 BC) as well as noted orator. His "Offices" are his Moral Lectures.

p. 195. *for the early Church did ... conceal high truths*: 'This self-restraint and abstinence, practised, at least partially, by the Primitive Church in the publication of the most sacred doctrines of our religion, is termed, in theological language, the *Disciplina Arcani …*' (*Ari.*, p. 51). At that point Newman saw such a withholding of doctrine as a primarily catechetical strategy. He later came to suggest that it accounted for the 'instinctive feeling' that gave rise to the 'deep silence which Scripture observes concerning the Blessed Virgin after the Resurrection' (*Ath.* II, p. 209). Discussing the Real Presence in *G.A.*, Newman suggests that the omission is owing to the ancient 'Disciplina Arcani', which withheld the Sacred Mystery from catechumens and heathen, 'to whom the creed was known', (p. 145).

LECTURE 6: EXTERNAL DIFFICULTIES OF THE CANON AND THE CATHOLIC CREED COMPARED

p. 197. *our Article says it "contains"*: The sixth of the 'Thirty-Nine Articles of Religion' declared that: 'Holy Scripture containeth all things necessary to salvation: so that whatsoever is not read therein, nor may be proved thereby, is not to be required of any man, that it should be believed as an Article of the Faith, or be thought requisite or necessary to salvation.'

p. 200. *"clothed upon," "that mortality may be swallowed up of life"*: 2 Corinthians 5:4.

p. 200. *St Paul's … controversy at Athens*: Acts 17:17–33.

p. 203. *The language of St. Austin is favourable to the admission of the Apocrypha*: On St Augustine, see note to p. 7. His exegetical treatise *De Doctrina Christiana* was begun about 397 and finished around 426. In the eighth chapter, 'The Canonical Books', he noted: 'There are … books which seem to follow no regular order, and are connected neither with the order of the preceding books nor with one another, such as Job, and Tobias, and Esther, and Judith, and the two books of Maccabees, and the two of Ezra, … Next are the Prophets, … two books, one called Wisdom and the other Ecclesiasticus, are ascribed to Solomon from a certain resemblance of style, but the most likely opinion is that they were written by Jesus the son of Sirach. Still they are to be reckoned among the prophetical books, since they have attained recognition as being authoritative … The authority of the Old Testament is contained within the limits of these forty-four books.' (*Nicene and Post-Nicene Fathers* Vol. II, p. 539). The 'Thirty-Nine Articles' recognised only thirty eight of the books as canonical.

p. 204. *at the end of the prayer for the Church Militant*: The Prayer forms part of the 'Communion Service' of *The Book of Common Prayer*. The conclusion reads: 'And we also bless the holy Name for all thy servants departed this life in thy faith and fear; beseeching thee to give us grace, so to follow their good examples, that with them we may be partakers of thy heavenly kingdom'. Charles Wheatley remarked, 'though the direct petition for the *faithful departed* is still discontinued, yet, were it not for the restriction of the words, *militant here on earth*, they might be supposed to be implied in our present form, when we beg of God that *we* WITH THEM *may be partakers of his heavenly kingdom.*' (*A Rational Illustration of the Book of Common Prayer of the Church of England*, Oxford, 1839, p. 279).

p. 204. *Tertullian, about a hundred years after St John's death: Against Marcion*, Book V, ch. 10.

p. 204. *St. Paul's Epistle to Philemon*: Tertullian, *Against Marcion*, Book V, Ch 21. In 1892, J. B. Lightfoot commented: 'The estimate formed of this epistle at various epochs has differed widely. In the fourth century there was a strong bias against it. The "spirit of the age" had no sympathy with either the subject or the handling. Like the spirit of more than one later age, it was enamoured of its own narrowness, which it mistook for large-ness of view, and it could not condescend to such trivialities as were here offered to it ... Of what account was the fate of a single insignificant slave, long since dead and gone, to those before whose eyes the battle of the creeds was still raging? This letter taught them nothing about questions of theological interest, nothing about matters of ecclesiastical discipline; and therefore they would have none of it. They denied that it had been written by St Paul. It mattered nothing to them that the Church from the earliest ages had accepted it as genuine, that even the remorseless "higher criti-cism" of a Marcion had not ventured to lay hands on it. It was wholly unworthy of the Apostle. If written by him, they contended, it must have been written when he was not under the influence of the Spirit: its contents were altogether so unedifying. We may infer from the replies of Jerome, of Chrysostom, and of Theodore of Mopsuestia, that they felt themselves to be stemming a fierce current of prejudice which had set in this direction. But they were strong in the excellence of their cause, and they nobly vindicated this epistle against its assailants.

In modern times there has been no disposition to under-rate its value. Even Luther and Calvin, whose bias tended to the depreciation of the ethical as compared with the doctrinal portions of the scriptures, show a true appreciation of its beauty and significance.' *St. Paul's Epistles to the Colossians and to Philemon*, pp. 314–15.

p. 204. *Caius*: A Roman priest of the early third century, well known for his learning, and his controversy with the Montanist Proclus. The refer-ence is to be found in Book II, Chapter 5, of Eusebius's *Ecclesiastical History*.

p. 204. *follows Eusebius*: Ecclesiastical History, Book III, Chapter 2.

p. 204. *Further, St. Jerome observes*: He mentions Paul's *thirteen* Epistles in *Lives of Illustrious Men*, ch. 59.

p. 204. *Aerius*: A fourth-century priest of Pontus, whose life and writings are only known of through the works of St Epiphanius. As well as prayers for the dead, he also opposed prescribed fasts, any distinction between priests and bishops, and dismissed the observance of Easter as a Jewish superstition.

p. 206. *"Eusebius . . . speaks of fourteen Epistles"*: Ecclesiastical History, Book III, ch. 2.

p. 206. *Ignatius . . . speaks in the clearest*: 'See that you all follow the bishop even as Christ Jesus does the Father.' *Letter to the Smynaeans*, ch. 8.

p. 206. *St. Jerome, in writing controversially*: It can hardly be said that Jerome does not uphold the principle of apostolic succession, but in individual cases he is scathing: 'It is a monk who menaces monks . . . and who boasts that he holds an apostolic chair'. *Letter 82 to Theophilus, Bishop of Alexandria.*

p. 207. *Tertullian ascribes it to St. Barnabas*: On Modesty, ch. 20. Cf. Newman's letter to Mrs Froude in note p. 238.

p. 207. *the Epistles to the Thessalonians . . . Irenaeus*: Adversus Haereses, Book V, ch. 25; Tertullian *Scorpiace*, ch. 49; Origen Against Celsus *II*, ch. 49.

p. 207. *the Lord's table is always called an Altar . . . Apostolic*: Newman seems to have taken most of his references from chapter II, Section 3, of the early eighteenth-century theologian John Johnson's *The Unbloody Sacrifice, and Altar Unvail'd and Supported*, London, 1724, I, pp. 305–19. Ignatius *to Philadelphians*, ch. 4; Clement, *Stromata*, Book 7; Irenaeus, *Adversus Haereses*, Book IV, ch. 18; Tertullian, *Against Marcion*, Book IV, ch. 39; Cyprian, *Letter to Stephen*, p. 71; Origen, *De Principiis*, IV, ch. 1; Eusebius, *Oration in praise of Emperor Constantine*, ch. 16; Athanasius, *Against the Arians*, ch. 6; Ambrose, *Letter 18*; Gregory Nazianzen, *Orations* II, p. 61; Jerome, *Letter 66 to Pammachus*; Augustine, *Tract 26 on John*, ch. 6. However, Cyril of Jerusalem in his Catechetical Lectures talks of a 'mystical and spiritual Table' (Lecture 22) and Chrysostom says 'call them to his Table with the king' (*Commentary on I Thessalonians*).

p. 208. *that the Eucharist is a Sacrifice*: For references, again Newman seems to have made good use of Johnson, *vol. cit.*, pp. 1–304.

p. 209. *real Presence in the Holy Eucharist*: Johnson again seems to be the source for references here, *vol. cit.*, pp. 180–235, especially pp. 191–4 for Johnson's careful examination of the understanding of St Irenaeus.

p. 210. *a deeper and hidden sense*: The mystical or spiritual sense can be either allegorical (a sign of some later Christian practice or teaching), moral (drawing a moral lesson) or anagogical (as a sign or Christ's Second Coming).

p. 210. *our Saviour, in St. Luke's Gospel*: To the disciples on the road to Emmaus Luke 24:27.

p. 211. *an infidel historian accuses St. John*: See note to p. 187 regarding Gibbon's suggestions.

p. 211. *a theory has been advocated, – by whom I will not say*: The advocate was Michael Russell, on whom see note to p. 213 below. He drew the argument out in pp. 254–82 of Volume I of his *Connection of Sacred and Profane History, from the Death of Joshua to the Decline of the Kingdoms of Israel and Judah*, London, 1827.

p. 213. *a writer, not of the English Church*: Tom Mozley was intrigued by this allusion, and quizzed Newman as to whether he was referring to Whately. Newman explained: 'The person I allude to ... is not the Archbishop of Dublin, (whom I would not allude to, if I could help) but Bishop Russell of Scotland.' (*L.D.* VII, p. 33). Michael Russell (1781–1848) was Bishop of Glasgow and Galloway, and a theological liberal. The quotation is from *A Connection of Sacred and Profane History*, London, 1827, I, p. 259.

p. 213. *the Book of Job ... an Eastern story*: In 1839 Newman received, as editor of the *British Critic*, a copy of Thomas Wemyss's *Job and his Times, or a Picture of the Patriarchal Age*, London, 1839, which adopted just such an argument. For Wemyss, Job was an 'Arabian Prince, or Emir', and the Old Testament book was littered with 'Arabisms'.

p. 215. *St. Peter ... "be not afraid"*: Cf. Matthew 14:26–31; Mark 6:49–51; John 6:20.

LECTURE 7: INTERNAL DIFFICULTIES OF THE CANON AND THE
CATHOLIC CREED, COMPARED

p. 216. *priestcraft*: The most notorious being John Toland (1670–1721) in
his *Christianity not Mysterious* (London, 1696) which was an outspoken
attack on all aspects of the priesthood. The book was condemned to be
burnt by the hangman.

p. 218. *the account of the serpent speaking to Eve*: Genesis 3:1–5.

p. 219. *the devils being sent into the swine*: Matthew 8:30–32; Mark 5:11–13;
Luke 8:32–3.

p. 219. *the history of Balaam's ass speaking*: See Numbers 22:28–30.

p. 219. *the Holy Ghost ... a dove*: Cf. Matthew 3:16; Mark 1:10; Luke
3:22; John 1:32.

p. 219. *"glory and honour" ... the Throne and to the Lamb*: Cf. Revelation
5:13.

p. 220. *acrostic*: A poem or arrangement of words in which certain letters
in each line, taken in order, spell out a name or motto. That which
Newman is referring to here stands for 'Ἰησούς Χριστος Θεού Υἱος
Σωτήρ', or 'Jesus Christ, Son of God and Saviour'.

p. 220. *pseudo-sibyls*: Sibyls were the divinely inspired seeresses of classical
antiquity, the most famous being that of Cumae who, in Book VI of
Virgil's *Aeneid*, introduced Aeneas to the vision of the future Rome that it
was his destiny to found (as well as to the dead figures of his past). The
Sibylline Oracles proved very persuasive over the religious views of the
people, and the Hellenistic Jews of Alexandria copied their form to
produce verses aimed at proselytizing Pagans. The practice lasted into the
second and third centuries, and then started to be emulated by Christian
writers.

p. 220. *"four beasts"*: Cf. Revelation 4:6–9.

p. 220. *the figure of the Cherubim*: Celestial beings who first appear in the
Old Testament as guardians of the Tree of Life in Genesis 3:24. Like the
Cherubim, they had six wings, six hands, and six feet. Christian commentators assigned them to the orders of Angels. Whereas the Seraphim
were known for the intensity of their love, the Cherubim excelled in
knowledge.

p. 221. *oil . . . in the case of a coronation*: The oil in the ampula is blessed by the Archbishop of Canterbury.

p. 221. *at Bethesda*: John 5:4.

p. 221. *Naaman bathing seven times in the Jordan*: On the cure of the Syrian general from leprosy, see 2 Kings 5.

p. 221. *the tree which Moses cast into the waters*: On the miracle at Marah, see Exodus 15:25. See also *L.D.* VII, p. 108, where Newman points out these references to Pusey, when the latter was preparing a new edition of his three part *Tract* on Baptism.

p. 221. *Elisha's throwing meal into the pot*: See 2 Kings 4:41.

p. 221. *our Saviour's breathing, making clay*: John 20:22; 9:6.

p. 222. *the woman with the issue of blood*: Matthew 9:22; Mark 5:25–9; Luke 8:43–4.

p. 222. *handkerchiefs and aprons*: Acts 19:12.

p. 222. *St. Peter's shadow being earnestly sought out*: Acts 5:15.

p. 223. opus operatum: A term used by theologians since the thirteenth century to describe the efficacy of sacraments independently of minister and recipient. The teaching of the Eastern Church, while rejecting the idea of the sacraments working automatically believes that they are the principle means of communicating grace 'in the Spirit'. (Symeon, 'The New Theologian', *Ethical Orations*, I.10.3.).

p. 223. *they deny that the Blessed Virgin*: See note to p. 9 on Nestorianism.

p. 223. *to her in whose bosom He lay*: Cf. *U.S.*, pp. 312–14.

p. 224. *the "number of the beast"*: Revelation 13:18.

p. 224. *St. Peter's cure of the impotent man*: Acts 3:6; 3:16.

p. 224. *"By what power . . . must be saved"*: Cf. Acts 4:7–12.

p. 224. *not "speak . . . in the Name of Jesus"*: Cf. Acts 5:28.

p. 224. *"that signs and wonders . . . Holy Child Jesus"*: Acts 4:30.

p. 224. *the visitation of the Blessed Virgin to Elizabeth*: See Luke 1:40–56.

p. 225. *the account of Christ's ascending into heaven*: See Luke 24:50–1; Acts 1:9–11.

p. 225. *He be on God's right hand in heaven*: Cf. Acts 7:55; Romans 8:34; Ephesians 1:20; Colossians 3:1.

p. 225. *St. Peter catch a fish . . . to pay tribute with*: See Matthew 17:24–7.

p. 225. *the blood and water which issued from our Saviour's side*: See John 19: 34; 1 John 5:6–8.

p. 226. *Martyrologies*: See note to p. 177.

p. 226. *the history of the Deluge, the ark, and its inhabitants*: See Genesis 6:5–9, 14–22.

p. 226. *the narrative of Jonah and the whale*: See Jonah 1:17–2:10.

p. 227. *Men of this age are full of their dread of priestcraft and priestly ambition*: The reference is to Thomas Arnold's 'The Oxford Malignants and Dr Hampden' *Edinburgh Review* 63 (April 1836) pp. 225–39. Cf. *L.D.* V, p. 125.

p. 227. *"given such power unto men"*: Matthew 9:8.

p. 228. *the Shunammite was a great woman*: See 2 Kings 4:8–36.

p. 228. *Naaman was angered*: See 2 Kings 5:11–12.

p. 229. *filled with the loaves and the fishes*: Cf. Matthew 15:36; John 6:9.

p. 229. *quickening of the dead soul*: Cf. 1 Corinthians 15:45.

p. 230. *a man living on locusts and wild honey*: Cf. Matthew 3:4; Mark 1:6.

p. 230. *"then shall they fast"*: Matthew 9:15.

p. 230. *St. John's character*: It is interesting to note that the frontispiece adopted for the Oxford 'Library of the Fathers' was a print of the figure of St John the Baptist on a rock in the wilderness, holding a cross and pointing to the motto 'Vox clamantis in Deserto'. See *L.D.* VII, p. 470.

p. 230. *St. Paul's spiritualizing the history of Sarah and Hagar*: Cf. Galatians 4:22–31.

p. 231. *fire trying every man's work*: Cf. 1 Corinthians 3:13.

p. 231. *"because of the Angels"*: 1 Corinthians 11:10.

p. 231. *"before the elect Angels"*: Cf. 1 Timothy 5:21.

p. 231. *"the pillar and ground of the Truth"*: 1 Timothy 3:15.

p. 231. *his observations on celibacy*: See, e.g., 1 Corinthians 7 *passim*.

p. 231. *"the mystery of iniquity"* ... *"already working"*: Cf. 2 Thessalonians 2:7.

p. 231. *St. John's remarkable agreement of tone with him*: See, e.g., Revelation 16:14; 18:5.

p. 231. *Our Lord's account of the sin ... falling away*: See Matthew 12:31; 2 Thessalonians 2:3.

p. 231. *St. John's notice of a sin which is unto death*: 1 John 5:16.

p. 231. *the arduousness of a rich man's getting to heaven*: Matthew 19:16–24.

p. 231. *what He says about binding and loosing*: See Matthew 16:19.

p. 231. *evil spirit going out only by fasting and prayer*: See Matthew 17:21; Mark 9:29.

p. 231. *command to turn the left cheek*: See Matthew 5:39; Luke 6:29.

p. 231. *St. Peter's saying ... "going and preaching to the spirits in prison"*: See 2 Peter 1:4; 1 Peter 3:19.

p. 231. *St. Matthew's account of the star*: Matthew 2:2, 9–10.

p. 231. *a woman is saved through childbearing*: See 1 Timothy 2:15.

p. 231. *how to treat those who hold not "the doctrine of Christ"*: 2 John 9–11.

p. 232. *Christianity has been cast into any particular social mould*: In his long letter of 10 November 1840 to his brother Francis, who had challenged the historical authenticity of the 'Apostolical' Christianity that Newman and the Tractarians were promulgating, Newman asserted: 'Evidence of any other system of religion, (i.e. in temper, principle, doctrine, conduct) calling itself Christianity, is altogether unproducible. Either this is Christianity, or we do not know (historically) *what* Christianity is. Everything else is the history of mere sects with known authors. The Christian religion, when traced back from the fourth century, vanishes in this form from the pages of history. In proportion as it is known, it is this ... There is no reason why this should not be Apostolic Christianity; as it does not differ from Scripture more than the parts of Scripture differ from each other, and does not resemble foreign systems, which came in contact with it between the first and fourth centuries, more than systems resemble each other which are acknowledged by all to be independent and distinct ... This temper, cast of principle, doctrine, conduct, are singularly consistent with each other, or *one*; so that the existence of e.g. the temper, makes the co-existence of the doctrine at least not improbable ... The *temper and principles* of the Church have been precisely the same from first to last, from the Apostolic age to this; viz what her enemies call dogmatic, mystical, credulous, superstitious, bigoted, legal. I consider no persons doubt this great fact.' (*L.D.* VII, p. 440).

p. 233. *Pantheism ... awaits the Age to come*: The Dutch philosopher Spinoza (1632–1671) adopted Descartes' view of substance as needing nothing else for its existence. He argued that it exists necessarily, is therefore infinite and unique and is God or Nature.

LECTURE 8: DIFFICULTIES OF JEWISH AND OF CHRISTIAN FAITH COMPARED

p. 237. Exceptio probat regulam: 'The exception proves the rule'. A legal tag indicating that the identification of an exception proves that a rule was in existence.

p. 237. *The fifth century acts as a comment on the obscure text*: In his letter of 10 November 1840 to his brother (on which see note to p. 232 above), Newman pointed out that: 'From the first, running up into the obscurity of the Apostolic century, there has been a large body called the Church, claiming the exclusive dispensation of the gospel; and there has been but one such, – large, continuous and commanding ... This body, in centuries iv and v, is known to have been of a certain temper, cast of principle, system of doctrine, and character of conduct; in a word of a certain *religion* ... On tracing backwards, the evidences of the existence of this religion are fainter, but they exist in their degree.' (*L.D.* VII, p. 440).

p. 238. *there were about the Epistle to the Hebrews or the Apocalypse*: Newman explained in a letter of 8 November to Mrs William Froude: 'I do not think the Canon was settled till the fifth century really. Up to the end of the 4th the Latin Church did not receive the Hebrews, nor the Greek the Apocalypse.' Exploring the question of the status of the Apocrypha further, Newman pointed out: '... the evidence for the Apocalypse is not equal to that for St Matthew's gospel etc etc. But on the whole for a variety of reasons we think that Apocryphal books fall below the line of Canonicity. They have far *more* objections to their authority than the corresponding books of the Apocalypse etc etc. ... What the Apocrypha is to the Pentateuch, Prophets and Psalms, such are the Hebrews, Apocalypse, St. James, 2 and 3 St. John, 2 St. Peter to the Gospels, Acts and Epistles.' (*L.D.* VII, p. 435).

p. 238. *Origen's about eternal punishment*: Origen had sought to emphasise the remedial nature of punishment after death, rather than eternal damnation, thus suggesting the possibility of universal restoration and salvation. His views were widely condemned from the sixth century, but were to enjoy a considerable revival in the centuries after Erasmus.

p. 241. *the custom of the Sign of the Cross*: High Church, but nevertheless staunchly Protestant, W. F. Hook, explained that: 'The cross was the instrument of death to our most blessed LORD and SAVIOUR, and it has been considered by all ages by the Church as the most appropriate emblem, or symbol, of the Christian religion. The sign of the cross was made in the primitive Church at some part of almost every Christian office. In the Church of England it is commanded to be used only in the Sacrament of Baptism, when the newly signed person is baptized with the sign of the cross, in token that hereafter he shall not be ashamed of CHRIST crucified; and perhaps in the Sacrament of the Eucharist, where it may be implied in the direction, that the priest shall lay his hand on the bread and wine when he consecrates them.' (*A Church Dictionary*, fourth edition, London, 1840, p. 286).

p. 241. *the Baptism of infants*: See note to p. 120.

p. 241. *the Sacrifice or the Consecration of the Eucharist*: Cf. p. 123.

p. 241. *Episcopal Ordination*: See note to p. 34.

p. 241. *the Acts of the Apostles is written by St. Luke*: Though the Lucan authorship of Acts was almost universally accepted from the middle of the second century, occasional doubts have been cast over the centuries, chiefly on the grounds that he features nowhere himself in the book, and is an almost invisible presence in the history of the Apostolic Church (excepting for mentions by St Paul in Colossians, Philemon, and Timothy). However, the similarity of style of Acts and the third Gospel, and the dedication of both to Theophilus for his instruction, make the traditional case the strongest one.

p. 242. *children of wrath*: Cf. Ephesians 2:3.

p. 244. *"Search the Scriptures"*: John 5:39.

p. 244. *the Berœans, who* "searched *the Scriptures daily"*: Acts 17:11.

p. 244. *The Sun of Righteousness:* Cf. Malachi 4:2.

p. 246. *"the hidden man of the heart"*: 1 Peter 3:4.

p. 246. *"I am the God of Abraham"*: Genesis 26:24. Cf. also Matthew 22:32.

p. 246. *"I am with you alway"*: Matthew 28:20.

p. 246. 'their *God*': Cf. Hebrews 11 *passim*.

p. 247. *the Sadducees* did *profess*: The Sadducees were a Jewish sect of the New Testament era, who comprised a large section of the priestly elite. They insisted on the authority of the Mosaic Torah alone, denying, unlike the Pharisees, any authority to the traditions of the elders and rabbis. Similarly, they did not acknowledge the possibility of any resurrection of the dead, or of the future coming of a Messiah.

p. 247. *"the glory of His people Israel"*: Cf. Luke 2:32.

p. 248. *"How long dost Thou . . . tell us plainly"*: John 10:24.

p. 249. *parable of the Talents*: Matthew 25:14–30. See Newman's 1824 sermon on the parable, which he continued to use for some years later. (*BOA*)

p. 249. *talent in a napkin*: Cf. Luke 19:20.

p. 249. *"Will ye also go away?" . . . "Lord* to whom *shall we go?"*: John 6:67–8.

p. 250. *Simon the sorcerer*: See Acts 8:9–24.

p. 250. *vagabond Jews*: Acts 19:13.

p. 251. *"Thou hast the words of eternal life"*: John 6:68.

p. 251. and note *"love is the parent of faith"*: Throughout the 1830s, and principally in his *Lectures on Justification*, Newman had been assimilating the theology of the Caroline divines, particularly Jeremy Taylor and George Bull, with their emphasis on 'fides formata charitate' (and his so doing has made him the target of criticism, particularly by Alister E. McGrath in *Iustitia Dei*, Cambridge, 1998, pp. 308–21). Even before he left the Church of England, Newman had begun to see the unsatisfactory incompleteness of such ideas. In his 1850 *Lectures on the Difficulties of Anglicans*, he explained that, 'Protestants, . . . consider that faith and love are inseparable; where there is faith, there, they think, are love and obedience; and in proportion to the strength and degree of the former, are the strength and degree of the latter. They do not think the inconsistency possible of really believing without obeying; and, where they see disobedience, they cannot imagine there the existence of real faith. Catholics, on the other hand, hold that faith and love, faith and obedience, faith and works, are simply separable, and ordinarily separated, in fact; that faith does not imply love, obedience, or works; that the firmest faith, so as to move mountains, may exist without love, that is, real faith, as really faith in the strict sense of the word as the faith of a martyr or doctor. In other words when Catholics speak of faith they are contemplating the existence of a gift which Protestantism does not even imagine. Faith is a spiritual sight of the unseen; and since in matter of fact Protestantism does not impart this sight, does not see the unseen, has no experience of this habit, this act of the mind – therefore, since it retains the word "faith," it is obliged to find some other meaning for it; and its common, perhaps its commonest, idea is, that faith is substantially the same as obedience; at least, that it is the impulse, the motive of obedience, or the fervour and heartiness which attend good works. In a word, faith is hope or it is love, or it is a mixture of the two. Protestants define or determine faith, not by its nature or essence, but by its effects.' (*Diff.* I, pp. 269–70).

PART 4: THE TAMWORTH READING ROOM

p. 254. *Sir Robert Peel*: The founder of the Conservative party (1788–1850) became MP for Oxford University in 1817. He was Prime Minister from 1834–5 and, with a majority of 70, from 1841–6. He repealed the Corn Laws in 1846.

p. 254. *in the Address*: It was made at the Town Hall in Tamworth, a town in the West Midlands at the heart of the Black Country, where the Industrial Revolution began.

p. 255. *Gower Street*: The site of London University.

p. 255. *Mr. Brougham*: A lawyer and Whig politician, Henry Peter Brougham (1778–1868). A co-founder of the *Edinburgh Review* (with Sidney Smith) in 1802. He also created London University and was Lord Chancellor (1830–34).

p. 255. *Dr. Lushington*: Stephen Lushington (1782–1873). Barrister and MP, judge of The High Court of Admiralty (1838–67) and Dean of Arches (1858–67).

p. 255. *Education . . . Useful Knowledge*: Mr Brougham founded the Society for the Diffusion of Useful Knowledge which made books available to the working classes.

p. 256. *Discources upon Science*: *A Discourse of the Objects, Advantages, and Pleasures of Science*, London, 1827.

p. 256. *Pursuit of Knowledge . . .*: *The Pursuit of Knowledge under Difficulties*, George L. Craik, London, 1830.

p. 256. *"a great experimentalist . . . closed to him"*: The reference is to Sir Humphrey Davy (1778–1829) the English chemist and inventor of the miner's lamp.

p. 257. *Paris and Helen*: Paris was the son of Priam, King of Troy who seduced Helen, the wife of the King of Sparta.

p. 257. *Hero and Leander*: Leander fell in love with Hero, a priestess of Aphrodite and drowned swimming the Hellespont. Hero drowned herself in consequence.

p. 257. *". . . and railroads"*: 2,400 miles of rail had been constructed, by 1840. In 1840 Samuel Cunard founded the transatlantic steamship line.

p. 258. *Newton*: Sir Isaac (1642–1727) English physician and mathematician, inventor of the binomial theorem and discoverer of universal gravitation. He published *Philosophiae Naturalis Principia Mathematica* in 1687 and *Optics* in 1704. He built the first reflecting telescope and separated light into its component colours. He was made Lucasian Professor of Mathematics at Cambridge in 1699 and became President of the Royal Society.

p. 258. *La Place*: Pierre-Simon, Marquis de Laplace (1749–1827) French astronomer and mathematician.

p. 258. *Mr. Brougham talked at Glasgow*: Inaugural Discourse, ... Wednesday 16 April 1825, Glasgow, 1825.

p. 258. *Pascal*: Blaise (1623–62) French philosopher and mathematician. He was the inventor of the digital calculator (1644) and author of *Les Provinciales* and *Les Pensees*. He abandoned controversy at the end of his life and devoted himself to spiritual reflection.

p. 260. *Such is the reward in 1841*: Peel resigned from George Canning's Cabinet in 1827 over the issue of Catholic Emancipation. He was returned as Prime Minister in 1841 with a majority of 70.

p. 261. *A distinguished Conservative statesman*: Sir Robert Peel.

p. 262. *Mr Bentham*: Jeremy Bentham (1748–1832) English philosopher and economist. He coined the philosophy of utilitarianism saying 'every man is the best judge of his own advantage'.

p. 263. obiter: 'by the way'.

p. 263. *"signifying nothing"*: Macbeth says, '... a tale, told by an idiot, full of sound and fury, signifying nothing': Shakespeare's *Macbeth*, Act 5, Scene 5.

p. 264. *Tully*: a disciple of the Porch. Marcus Tullius Cicero (106–43 BC), a follower of the Stoics (Stoa = porch). Newman uses similar expressions in *Idea* and *H.S.* I, pp. 264–275.

p. 264. "O philosophia, vitae dux": 'O philosophy, life's guiding light.' Cicero, *Tusculanae Disputationes*, ch. 5, p. 2.

p. 265. extra artem: 'beyond artifice'.

p. 265. *White Ladies or Undines*: White Ladies are ghosts which inhabit castles or manor houses in Britain. Undines are elemental beings that live in water (according to Paracelsus).

p. 265. *Cicero outwitted by Caesar*: He was persuaded against his better judgement to join with Pompey and Crassus and then found he had to undertake distasteful legal defences. Cf. e.g. *Letters to Atticus* X, p. 8.

p. 265. *treatise on Consolation*: The lost *De Consolatione*.

p. 265. *Lydian city*: Herodotus mentions it in his *Histories* I, p. 94.

p. 265. *Cowper*: William (1730–1800) English poet, and a favourite of Newman.

p. 266. pro re nata: 'as occasion may require'.

p. 266. *gin-palaces*: Ornately designed shops, selling gin.

p. 266. *Rasselas*: Samuel Johnson's novel (1759) *The Prince of Abissinia: A Tale* which uses an oriental context to express the futility of questing for happiness.

p. 267. *King Canute*: Henry of Huntingdon in the twelfth century, relates that Canute or Cnut the Great (995–1035) sat at the edge of the waves at Gainsborough near Lincoln (where there was a tidal bore).

p. 267. *Aspasia*: Athenian courtesan (470–410 BC), the mistress of Pericles.

p. 272. *French Tyrant*: Probably Louis XI (1461–1483) who figures in Scott's *Quentin Durward*.

p. 273. Naturam expellas furca ... recurret: Even though you drive out nature with a pitchfork, she will always return. Horace, *Epistles* I, p. 24.

p. 274. *Dugald Stewart*: Scottish philosopher (1753–1828). He was Professor of Moral Philosophy at Edinburgh University, 1785–1820.

p. 275. *Arcesilas into Berkeley*: Arcesilaus (315–240 BC) was the sixth head of Plato's Academy, credited with turning it into a sceptical direction. George Berkeley (1685–1753) was an Irish bishop and philosopher who inclined towards extreme subjectivism.

p. 277. *says Lord Bacon*: *Novum Organum* II, p. 7, and III, p. 1. (*The Works of Francis Bacon*, London, 1815, IV, pp. 16, 30–1).

p. 280. "non omnia possumus omnes": Virgil, *Eclogues* VIII, p. 63.

p. 283. *"party feeling"*: No doubt Newman had at the back of his mind here the teaching of his early mentor, Richard Whately, for whom 'party spirit' was something of a *bête noire*, and who devoted his 1822 Bampton Lectures to a supposed examination of the subject. Though he had come to agree with his master in the mid-1820s, he speedily took up an opposite position, starkly asserting that 'Christ undeniably made a party the vehicle of His doctrine', (*U.S.*, p. 174).

p. 283. *a hole-and-corner meeting, or a parish job*: 'Done and happening in a "hole and corner", or place which is not public; private and the Society's book policy, secret, clandestine, underhand' (*OED*). A 'parish job' was akin to a meeting of a parish or vestry meeting or council.

p. 284. *the Reform Bill*: The Reform Bill of 1832 sought to redress the voting anomalies which existed between the small 'rotten' and 'pocket' boroughs controlled by the aristocracy or the gentry and the large industrial towns. London only merited four members of parliament whereas the under-populated county of Cornwall returned 44.

p. 284. *Lord Melbourne*: William Lamb (1779–1848), Second Viscount Melbourne, a Whig politician, who entered Parliament as a supporter of Charles James Fox in 1805, and held high offices in the Canning and Grey governments. He was Prime Minister from 1834–5, and again from 1835–41.

p. 285. *as chalk is to cheese*: To 'know the difference between chalk and cheese' is, proverbially, to be able to distinguish between what is valuable and what is worthless.

p. 287. *Vitae Sanctorum*: 'Lives of the Saints'. Newman was by this time familiar with the 1615 work of the Jesuit Heribert Rosweyde of the same title, which served to break the ground for the huge and comprehensive work of the Bollandist community.

p. 287. *"the Pursuit of Knowledge under difficulties"*: See note under p. 257. As Newman notes earlier, the author was not Lord Brougham but George Lillie Craik (1798–1866), one of the many followers of Samuel Smiles' philosophy of self-help.

p. 288. *Pantheon*: Literally, a temple for all the Gods, the most famous being that built in Rome by Augustus's son-in-law, Agrippa, and completed in 27 BC. It was rebuilt in the following century by the Emperor Hadrian, and at the beginning of the seventh century was consecrated as a Christian church. The term also came to be applied to any building used for the burial of the famous dead heroes of a nation, such as St Geneviève in Paris, or even Westminster Abbey in London.

p. 288. *Alfred*: Alfred the Great, King of the West Saxons, was born in 849, and succeeded his brother Ethelred to a throne threatened by internal unrest, and the threat of Danish invasion. The latter he countered in a remarkable series of military engagements. He then turned his attention to domestic reform, including the establishment of a stable social order, the creation of a national fleet, and the encouragement of learning. He died in 901, with the reputation of a deeply religious man.

p. 289. *Lorenzo de Medicis*: Lorenzo (1448–1492), 'il Magnifico', achieved power in Florence by putting down, in 1478, the Pazzi who had murdered his brother. Alliance with Venice and Milan provoked the wrath of the Papacy and brought excommunication upon the city. Reconciliation followed under Pope Innocent VIII. He was a great patron of learning and collector of manuscripts.

p. 289. *Edward VI*: Son of Henry VIII and Jane Seymour, was born in 1537 and succeeded to the English throne upon the death of his father in 1547. Though intelligent, he lacked strength of either body or character, and government fell largely into the hands of his uncle, the Duke of Somerset, provoking aristocratic resentment, and so then supplanted by the Duke of Northumberland. A more distinctly Protestant Church establishment took root in his reign. However, he was a great patron of education, as the great number of distinguished schools carrying his name bears testimony.

p. 289. *Haroun al Raschid*: Born in 763, he succeeded to the Caliphate of Baghdad and successfully reorganised his territories so as to be able to resist the raid of the Eastern Empire. He forced the Byzantine Emperor Nicephorus I to resume the payment of tribute, and invaded the Empire when the said Emperor failed to observe the terms of the peace. He sent an embassy to Charlemagne.

p. 289. *Dr. Johnson*: Samuel Johnson (1709–1784), son of a Lichfield bookseller, was educated at Pembroke College, Oxford. A brief period of schoolmastering was followed by work in a Birmingham bookshop, marriage to an older widow, a failed attempt to found a school, and then a move to London. He combined journalistic work with the authorship of several small literary items. He then founded journals of his own, the *Rambler* and the *Idler*, and in 1755 published his famous *Dictionary*. He founded the Literary Club in 1764, and its members included Goldsmith, Burke, and Reynolds. In 1773 he published his *Journey to the Hebrides*, describing a tour of Scotland he made with his friend and disciple, James Boswell. The latter immortalised his memory in his classic *Life*. His deep Christian moralism had always attracted Newman, who thought that in spirit he was almost a Catholic.

p. 289. *Dr. Franklin*: Benjamin Franklin (1706–1790), statesman, philosopher, and scientist, was one of seventeen children of a Boston soap boiler. A serious quarrel with a brother led to his moving to Philadelphia, where he became a successful printer, publisher of the *Pennsylvania Gazette* and began to acquire political influence. In 1753 he became deputy Postmaster General for British North America, and visited Europe several times as the Seven Years War began to loom. On a visit to England in 1764 he obtained the repeal of the Stamp Act. Upon the quarrel with England he was elected to the American Congress, and was a signatory of the Declaration of Independence. In 1776 he was appointed American Ambassador to France, returning to the States in 1785 to assume the office of president of Pennsylvania. The most famous of his scientific discoveries was the identity of lightning (for which he was awarded the Copley Gold medal of the Royal Society), which he arrived at by means of the famous kite experiment.

p. 289. *Newton*: Sir Isaac Newton (1642–1727). Cf. note p. 258.

p. 289. *Protagoras*: A Greek Sophist philosopher, who flourished in the mid-fifth century BC. An extoller of practical excellence, as opposed to dogmatism, and of practical and rhetorical skill. Though none survive, he was evidently the author of several works on logic, and also on practical philosophy. He was banished from Athens on a charge of atheism. One of his dicta was: 'Man is the measure of all things, of the existence of things that are and the non-existence of the things that are not'.

p. 289. *Pascal*: Blaise Pascal (1623–1662). His spirituality influenced John and Charles Wesley. Cf. note p. 258.

p. 289. *Julian the Apostate*: Flavius Claudius Julian (331–363), was a nephew of Constantine the Great. Though he was brought up a Christian, the study of Greek philosophy at Athens and elsewhere turned his allegiances in a different direction. In 355 he was made Caesar, was sent to Gaul, and was hailed as Emperor there in 361. He lost his life two years later during an expedition against the Persians. Newman wrote perceptively about Julian on many occasions, e.g.: 'The event of his experiment refuted the opinion which led to it. The impartial toleration of all religious persuasions, malicious as was its intent, did but contribute to the ascendancy of the right faith, … which can be held as a principle as well as an opinion, and which influences the heart to suffer and to labour for its sake' (*Ari.*, pp. 354–5).

p. 289. *Joseph Milner*: A highly effective Evangelical preacher (1704–1782), who did much to help to secure that school within the Anglican establishment. His five-volume *History of the Church of Christ* was influential, not least on Newman, who 'was nothing short of enamoured of the long extracts from St. Augustine, St. Ambrose, and the other Fathers which I found there.' (*Apo.*, p. 7).

p. 289. *Lord Byron*: George Noel Gordon, Lord Byron (1788–1824), the Romantic poet, who first started to achieve fame with the publication of the first cantos of his *Childe Harold* in 1812. This was followed by an unsuccessful marriage, which was in turn followed by the resumption of earlier continental travels. He took a fitful interest in politics, with markedly liberal views, and Newman declared: 'I have no sympathy with the philosophy of Byron', (*Apo.*, p. 261). Newman contrasted the case of St Augustine with, 'the case of a popular poet, an impressive instance of a great genius throwing off the fear of God, seeking for happiness in the creature, roaming unsatisfied from one object to another, breaking his soul upon itself, and bitterly confessing and imparting his wretchedness to all around him.' (*H.S.* II, p. 144).

p. 289. *Cromwell*: Oliver Cromwell (1599–1658), 'the Protector'. He was always of Puritan views, and veered more towards Independency as opposed to Presbyterianism. First elected to the House of Commons for Huntingdon in 1628, he represented Cambridge in the Short and Long Parliaments, and was noted for his zealotry on behalf of parliamentary liberty. On the outbreak of the English Civil War, it was he who galvanised the parliamentary troops, with ultimate success. By ejecting certain members in 'Pride's Purge', he cleared the way for the trial and execution of King Charles I. He reduced Ireland to submission by savage means, and then defeated the Scottish Royalists. Attempts at constitutional government failing to run smoothly, he assumed the title of Protector and ruled as a military despot.

p. 289. *Ovid*: Publius Ovidius Naso (43 BC–AD 17), Roman poet, who was for a while patronised by the Emperor Augustus. He fell sharply from favour and was exiled to a town near the north west coast of the Black Sea. His chief works are the *Amores*, *Fasti*, and above all, the *Metamorphoses*.

p. 289. *Bayle*: Pierre Bayle (1647–1706) held the Professorship of Philosophy at the Protestant Academy of Sedan, and commenced a career of controversial writing. The Academy being suppressed he accepted the Chair of History and Philosophy at the University of Rotterdam, and while there more than raised eyebrows with his attack on the French Jesuit Louis Maimbourg's *History of Calvinism*. He started a new periodical, *Les Nouvelles de la République des Lettres*, in 1684. In 1697 he produced his great work, the *Dictionnaire Historique et Critique*, which almost acted as a standard bearer for what was to become a distinctively French version of Enlightenment.

p. 289. *Boyle*: Robert Boyle (1626–1691), the eminent scientist, who was one of the very early members of the Royal Society. He was also deeply interested in religious and scriptural matters, and studied Hebrew and Oriental languages so as to aid his apologetics. As a defence of Christian Evidences, he founded the Boyle Lectures. He is best remembered for his chemical and physical research, most notably the establishment of 'Boyle's Law' regarding gases.

p. 289. *Adrian pope*: Pope Hadrian IV, Nicholas Breakspear (*c.* 1100–1159), was Pope from 1154, and the only Englishman to have occupied the Apostolic throne. His outstanding talents led Pope Eugenius III, to retain him in Italy when on a visit to Rome, and make him Cardinal. He showed diplomatic prowess when sent to Scandinavia as Papal Legate. He was elected pope unanimously in 1154. An active five years were marred by an escalating feud with the Emperor Frederick Barbarossa.

p. 289. *Adrian emperor*: Hadrian (76–138), was proclaimed Emperor of Rome in 117, and ruled with outstanding versatility. He visited all parts of the Empire, as is attested by the wall that bears his name, which divides England and Scotland. A great patron of learning, he established various libraries and founded the famous Athenaeum in Rome.

p. 289. *Lady Jane Grey*: Lady Jane Grey (1537–1554), a great-niece of Henry VIII, was made heir to the English throne by Edward VI, despite an earlier settlement of the succession. She was Queen for ten days, after which she was beheaded along with the Duke of Northumberland, her father-in-law, who had been assiduous in supporting her cause.

p. 289. *Madame Roland*: Marie Jeanne Philipon Roland (1754–1793), wife of a leading French revolutionary, she herself was committed to the ideals of the Revolution, and exerted much influence over the policies of the moderate republican Girondist party. She was imprisoned upon the proscription of the Girondists, and later executed. She is a leading character in Thomas Carlyle's *French Revolution*, and Newman deplored Carlyle's idealisation of her.

p. 289. *The persecuting Marcus*: Antoninus Marcus (121–80), was the adopted son of the Emperor Antoninus Pius, succeeding to his throne in 161. His reign was beset by a series of wars with the German tribes. He was a deeply committed disciple of the Stoic creed (hence his determination in visiting Athens on return from an Eastern campaign), as is attested by his surviving and long much-admired *Meditations*. Despite the enlightened and tolerant principles espoused in the work, he was a ruthless persecutor of Christians.

p. 289. *whence St. Paul was driven in derision*: Following his speech on the Areopagus. See Acts 17:16–34.

p. 289. *The royal Alphery ... to the throne of the Czars*: Russia had begun to import British medicines during the reign of Ivan the Terrible, and such contact with the West was to continue under the regime of Boris Godunov. Eighteen young Russian men from royal and aristocratic circles were sent to France and Britain to pursue studies. After the horrors of Ivan's reign, Russia was plunging into her 'Time of Troubles', and this induced several of the students to remain in the West. He graduated from Cambridge, and, to Moscow's horror, abandoned Orthodoxy in favour of Anglicanism. In 1618 he became vicar of Woolley in Huntingdonshire.

p. 289. *West*: Benjamin West (1738–1820), historical painter, born in Pennsylvania, and self-taught. He came to England, and was made President of the Royal Academy in 1792. Some of his best known paintings include 'The Death of Wolfe', and 'Orestes and Pylades'. He was notable for his abandonment of classical in favour of contemporary costume in his portraits.

p. 289. *Kirke White*: Henry Kirke White (1785–1806), born in Nottingham, commenced a minor legal career, but began to compose and publish verses, which were to attract the favourable attention of Robert Southey. He attained a Sizarship of St John's College, Cambridge, but overwork led to a premature death. Southey personally edited and saw to the publication of his *Remains*.

p. 289. *Roger Bacon*: Scientific investigator (1214–1292), who studied theology at Oxford and Paris. He entered the Franciscan Order in 1240, and gave all his attention to physical science, going on to make several original discoveries. His zeal for reform of the clergy made him enemies, and his works were outlawed. Papal intervention led to his exoneration, but a change in popes led to the revival of the condemnations, and he even had to endure a period of imprisonment.

p. 289. *Belzoni*: Giovanni Battista Belzoni (1778–1823), an explorer with a particular interest in archaeology. Originally destined for the religious life, the French occupation of Rome in 1798 turned his attentions elsewhere. Travels to France and Holland, were followed by a lengthier visit to England, where he married. Both he and his wife were of massive build, and this helped them to improve their circumstances by appearances at Astley's. He focussed his attentions increasingly on Egypt and explored Thebes, and the Valley of the Tombs of the Kings. An attempt to penetrate West Africa from the Guinea Coast led to his contracting a fatal disease.

p. 289. *Astley's*: Philip Astley (1742–1814), was a champion horseman, who had given outstanding service in the Seven Years War. In 1806, he opened a remarkable theatre, which he had had constructed from the timbers of an old captured French warship. Named 'Astley's Middlesex Amphitheatre', boxing matches and the like were hosted, but without spectacular success, and he put the premises (near Drury Lane) up for sale.

p. 289. *Duval*: Alexandre Vincent Pineux Duval (1767–1842), was a French dramatist who rose to eminence during the First Empire. He had earlier worked as an actor, theatre manager, sailor, and architect.

p. 289. *Mr. Davy*: William Davy (1743–1826), was educated at Ballliol College, Oxford, entered holy orders, and became a prolific homilist. He was encouraged to publish the fruits of his preaching as a multi-volume *System of Divinity*, and to finance the project by subscription. Many subscribers failed to honour their commitment, and Davy lost a good deal of money. His vision extended to a much larger project, but, unwilling to risk a second serious financial loss, he set about printing the work himself, with his maid's help.

p. 290. *Raleigh*: Sir Walter Raleigh (1552–1618), was educated at Oriel College, Oxford. He saw military action, in support of the Protestants of France, in 1569 and against Irish insurgency in 1580–1, and thus rose in Queen Elizabeth I's favour. His 1585 expedition to America led to the discovery of Virginia, and it was as a result of this voyage that potatoes and tobacco were introduced into England. He took part in the repulsion of the Spanish Armada in 1588, and eight years later led the attack on Cadiz. He fell from favour with the death of the Queen, James I suspecting him of favouring a rival to the throne, and was imprisoned in the Tower of London from 1603–16, during which time he completed his *History of the World*. Released to lead an expedition against the Spaniards in Guiana, its failure led to his execution.

p. 290. *"Apart sat on a hill . . . false philosophy."*: *Paradise Lost*, II, pp. 557–9, 564–5.

p. 290. *Society for Promoting Christian Knowledge*: The S.P.C.K. was founded by the Reverend Thomas Bray in 1698. Its aim was the Christian education of poor children and the publication of religious literature.

p. 290. *singularly irreligious work*: George Lillie Craik, *The Pursuit of*

Knowledge under Difficulties, two volumes, London 1830–1. On the controversy over this work and the Society's book policy in general, see *L.D.* IV,
pp. 264–5.

p. 291. in usum laicorum: 'for the use of lay people'.

p. 293. in posse: 'in a state of possible existence'.

p. 295. *"in the lowest depth a lower deep"*: *Paradise Lost*, IV, p. 76. Milton's
text reads, 'in the lowest deep a lower deep'.

p. 295. *to act you must assume*: Newman had been exploring the nature of
antecedent probability, and the relationship of such probabilities to faith,
in a series of University Sermons in the two years before the appearance of
these letters. See, e.g., *U.S.*, pp. 187–200, 203–4, 213–32, and also *L.D.*
XV, p. 381.

p. 298. *to say that he is unreal*: Cf. *Idea* p. xvii, *P.S.* V, p. 36.

p. 298. *"The natural philosophies ... perpetually inculcating."*: *Of the
Advancement of Learning*, Book II, in *The Works of Francis Bacon*, London,
1824, I, p. 106.

p. 299. *La Place ... had a formula*: In his *Traité de Mécanique Céleste*
(1799–1825). Cf. note to p. 258

p. 299. *Divine Fiat*: 'Direct command of God'.

p. 301. *"O Lord, how glorious are Thy works!"*: 'How *great* are Thy works'
(Ps. 92:5).

p. 302. *the god of a watch*: The language of the Deists. Dr Richard Dawkins
goes one stage further in his book *The Blind Watchmaker* (1987).

p. 302, note. *Idea*, pp. 19–42.

p. 305. *Sir Robert Peel* had just issued his Tamworth Manifesto containing
the guiding principles for the new Conservative Party.

PART 5: WHO'S TO BLAME?
p. 306. *THE CATHOLIC STANDARD*: Newman's letters appeared in
the issues for 3, 10, 17, 24, 31 March, and 7, 14, 21, April, 1855.

p. 306. *the running comments of the Press*: Newman himself cut out a series of extracts from *The Times*, which he pasted into a large album. Newman possessed a small work by A. Fonblanque (revised by W. A. Holdsworth) entitled *The Government of the Country. How we are Governed*, London, 1865. At the end of his chapter on the Constitution the author quotes, 'Mr Canning, who said that, "He who, speculating on the British Constitution, should emit from his enumeration the mighty powers of public opinion embodied in a free press, which pervades and checks, and perhaps in the last resort nearly governs the whole, would give but an imperfect view of the government of England."'

p. 306. *the British Constitution*: Newman's nephew Herbert explained that, while countries such as the United States and Switzerland had inviolable written constitutions, 'as applied to the legislation of the British Parliament, the words in question are words of vague and indefinite import; they are often used as signifying merely approval or aversion, as the case may be. Sometimes they are used with greater precision, to indicate conformity with, or variation from, some traditional maxim of legislation, especially in reference to the *constitution* of the supreme legislative body.' H. N. Mozley and G. C. Whiteley, *A Concise Law Dictionary*, London, 1876, p. 86.

p. 306. *Mr. Editor*: Henry William Wilberforce (1807–1873): 'From 1854 to 1863 he was the proprietor and editor of the *Catholic Standard*; afterwards called the *Weekly Register*. In this, as in all his undertakings, he was actuated by an earnest desire to promote the interests of religion, though at the sacrifice of his own.' 'Memoir' prefaced to *The Church and the Empires. Historical Periods*, H. W. Wilberforce, London, 1874.

p. 307. *no wish for "reforms . . . to democracy or to absolutism"*: Reform of the franchise had been a topic of debate ever since Lord John Russell's 1848 announcement that he no longer thought of the 1832 Reform Act as a 'final' measure. Proposals that kept cropping up were the secret ballot and an extension of the borough franchise. A Bill was proposed by Russell's Liberal Administration in 1852, towards the end of its term of office, and another had been introduced early in 1854 by the Aberdeen Coalition. Lord John Russell had mischievously raised the matter again in Cabinet in the December of that year.

p. 307. *tyranny . . . of autocrat or mob*: The memory of Napoleon is still fresh in the mind and also the Chartist riots which terrorised London in June 1848 when Wellington mobilised troops in the capital. Dickens portrays mob rule (in the Gordon riots) in *Barnaby Rudge*.

p. 307. *whirled off to Siberia*: After the tumultous events of the revolutionary year 1848, the Russian Police, who had grown more oppressive and arbitrary, resorted ever more frequently to sentences of exile to the vast wastes for all suspected dissidents. The number of those sentenced to confinement in a Siberian penal colony, or 'katorga', increased dramatically.

p. 307. *tarred and feathered*: A punishment prescribed in the reign of Richard I for any robbery committed on board the ships of the Crusaders.

p. 307. *the blind fanaticism of a certain portion of my countrymen*: The bitterly anti-Catholic zealotry among Protestants, which had exploded so noisily in 1850, and which Newman satirised so mercilessly in his *Lectures on the Present Position of Catholics*. The ground is summarised excellently in pp. vii–xxi of the Editor's Introduction of the work, which comprises the first volume of the present series.

p. 307. *in the German Sea!*: The contemporary name for the North Sea.

p. 307. *by a lucky accident, the Duke of Wellington . . . military prestige*: Arthur Wellesley, Duke of Wellington (1759–1852), said that the result of Waterloo was 'a damn close thing'.

p. 308. *the bigotry of our middle class*: Congregationalists, Baptists and Unitarians were among the noisiest opponents of popery, and were also proud to regard themselves as predominantly middle class. It was the middle classes that were to be the most vocal in their criticism of the stalemate in which the Crimean Expedition had so quickly become locked, seeing the problem as lying in the ineptitude of Lord Raglan and the other figures who had achieved commanding posts through their traditional aristocratic connections.

p. 308. *the heights of Inkerman*: The British forces in Crimea had established a position on Inkerman Heights, and the Russian army, boosted by successes in the early stages of the Battle of Balaklava, attacked them on 5 November 1854. For four hours the British were in a very precarious position, until the arrival of French troops enabled the allies to defeat the Russians. The Battle was the bloodiest of the whole war.

p. 308. *the depths of Exeter Hall*: Exeter Hall in the Strand was opened in 1831 and was used especially in May and June for religious conventions – the 'May meetings'. Newman was always suspicious of 'enthusiasm' as a substitute for solid faith in God's Church and in the sound words of Christian services.

p. 308. *fowling-pieces*: Light guns used for shooting wild fowl.

p. 308. *like Philoctetes . . . with bow and arrows*: The famous Greek archer, to whom Hercules, at his death, gave his bow and arrows. He joined the allied Greek forces in the expedition to Troy, but, on the way, was bitten in the foot by a snake. The subsequent ulceration became so fetid that the Greeks left him on the island of Lemnos. After ten years of siege, a seer told Odysseus that Troy would only be taken with the help of the bow of Hercules. Philoctetes was sent for, slew Paris, and so helped to achieve the downfall of the city.

p. 309. *as we treated the Pope four years before*: Pope Pius IX (1846–1878) constituted the hierarchy of England and Wales on 29 September 1850. Lord John Russell, the Prime Minister wrote to the Bishop of Durham 'I agree with you in considering "the late aggression of the Pope upon our Protestantism" as "insolent and insidious"' (*O.S.* p. 20). The Pope and Cardinal Wiseman were burnt in effigy on Guy Fawkes Day (5 November).

p. 309. *The* Times *put out feelers, this time last year*: The Times drew attenton to 'the perseverance with which we have thought it our duty to advocate every exertion that could be made for the preservation of peace' (7 February 1855) and called for a Grand European Tribunal (16 February).

p. 309. *the British Lion*: A term used to describe the pugnacity and indomitability of the British Nation. Phrases such as 'twisting the Lion's tail', and 'rousing the British Lion', refer to attempts to fly a red flag in John Bull's face, provoking him even to war.

p. 309. *neither the Duke nor Sir Robert Peel would have let him do*: The Duke of Wellington had died in 1852; Sir Robert Peel had died in 1850.

p. 309. *the knout and the tar barrel*: The knout was a knotted bunch of thongs of hide. A Tartar invention, it was used by the Russians as a scourge for punishment. Cf. note to p. 307

p. 310. *rescuing Turkey from the Russo-Greeks*: British, Russian and French forces defeated the Ottomans and Egypt at Navareno and as a result Greek autonomy was recognised in 1832. At the Treaty of Edime in 1829 the Ottoman had to cede the mouth of the Danube and parts of Asia Minor to Russia.

p. 310. *form of government less favourable to the Church . . . planting Protestant Liberalism there instead*: Newman prefers the status quo of an Established Church to a completely liberal, and presumably disestablished, Church with a government freed to embrace the doctrines of Voltaire and Rousseau and not hindered by the need to act in a totalitarian fashion if they thought it was necessary.

p. 313. *A lively illustration ... by a classical historian*: Herodotus, *Histories*, I, pp. 96–7.

p. 314. *the Horse in the fable*: The thirty-fourth of Aesop's *Fables* recounted how: 'The stag, with his sharp horns, got the better of the horse, and drove him clear out of the pasture where they used to feed together. So the latter craved the assistance of man; and in order to receive the benefit of it, he suffered him to put a bridle into his mouth, and a saddle upon his back. By this way of proceeding, he entirely defeated his enemy; but was mightily disappointed, when, upon returning thanks, and desiring to be dismissed, he received this answer: – "No, I never knew before how useful a drudge you were: now I have found what you are good for, you may depend upon it I will keep you to it."' The fable was intended to warn people against agreeing to anything which might prejudice public liberty.

p. 314. *"Quis custodiat ipsos custodes?"*: Juvenal, *Satires*, VI, p. 347: 'Who is to guard the guards themselves?'

p. 314. in statu: 'in being'.

p. 314. *as Cromwell did*: Oliver Cromwell dissolved the Rump Parliament (so called because it was the 'rump' of the Long Parliament of 141 members) in 1648 with the words 'Ye have sat here long enough'.

p. 314. *Magna Charta*: The 'Great Charter' of English 'liberties', which the barons of the nation forced King John to agree to at Runnymede on 15 June 1215, despite the disapproval of Pope Innocent III. It guarantees the independence of the Church and the right of habeas corpus. Subsequent monarchs re-issued it.

p. 314. *the Bill of Rights*: The declaration delivered to William, Prince of Orange, on his election to the British throne, confirming the rights and privileges of the English people. William and Mary accepted it on 13 February 1689, and were duly declared monarchs.

p. 314. *the Reform Bill*: See note to p. 284.

p. 315. modus vivendi: 'way of living', often used to refer to a compromise agreed in the interest of harmony.

p. 315. diathesis: Permanent condition of the body rendering it vulnerable to certain diseases.

p. 315. *first principles*: Newman had offered a searching analysis of such in his 1851 *Lectures on the Present Position of Catholics in England*: 'As the Prejudice is the rejection of reason altogether, so Bigotry is the imposition of private reason, – that is, of our own views and theories of our own First Principles, as if they were the absolute truth, and the standard of all argument, investigation, and judgment ... There are principles ... such as the First Principles of Morals, not peculiar or proper to the individual, but the rule of the world, because they come from the Author of our being, and from no private factory of man.' (*Prepos.*, pp. 291–2). Newman wrote angrily in 1877 of the 'philosophists of the day', who 'coolly and contemptuously ignore religious first principles', while 'they assume first principles of their own, without any compunction' (*L.D.* XXVIII, p. 278).

p. 318. *You will say ... must have a Constitution*: See note to p. 306.

p. 318. *These expedients ... the Turks*: Conspiracies to depose the Tsar, even to assassinate him, had not been uncommon in eighteenth-century Russia. The most recent occasion had been in 1801. The rumour had been put about that Tsar Paul I was mad; the Tsarevitch had been sounded out, and, led by the ex-foreign minister, Count Panin, a group of plotters planned a forced deposition. Nothing came of this but at the end of 1800 the project was revived, and, on 23 March 1801, the Tsar was not only deposed but also strangled. Similar incidents litters the history of the Ottoman dynasty. In 1622, Sultan Osman II was deposed and later executed. In 1648 a mutiny led to the deposition, and then execution, of Sultan Ibrahim I.

p. 318. *some of our self made politicians ... to the triumph of the allied*: A further assassination attempt on the Tsar was made by the Decembrists in 1825.

p. 318. *specimen of a Constitutional principle ... in the Medo-Persian Empire*: i.e. unalterable laws. Cf. Daniel 6:8: 'Now, O king, establish the decree, and sign the writing, that it be not changed, according to the law of the Medes and Persians, which altereth not.'

p. 318. *Alexander ... killed his friend in the banquet*: Cleitus 'the Black' (*c*. 380–328 or 327 BC) was a distinguished Macedonian cavalry leader, who saved Alexander the Great's life at the Battle of Granicus. Seven years later, disliking the increasing Orientalism of Alexander, he fell into a drunken argument and was killed by the latter.

p. 319. *the unpolite proverb*: i.e. allow a person to continue committing a wrong, until the consequences catch up with them.

p. 319. *when Darius would have saved the prophet Daniel*: See Daniel 6:1–29. Darius, King of the Medes and Persians, had issued an edict forbidding prayer to any but himself for thirty days. Daniel was alleged to have broken the law and was thrown into a den of lions. Darius recognised the miracle when Daniel remained unharmed, and had Daniel's accusers cast into the den.

p. 319. *It is said a king of Spain was roasted to death*: This was mentioned in a leading article in *The Times* 7 February 1855. Maréchal Bassompierre tells the story of Philip III, who caught a fever from a brazier left too close to him, which the Duke of Alba would not move without orders from the Duke of Uceda, Head of the Royal Household, who was out of the palace. Cf. Elliott J., *Spain and its World 1500–1700*, (1989), p. 151.

p. 319. *so necessary for Sancho Panza, governor of Barataria, to eat his dinner*: Sancho Panza was squire to Don Quixote in Cervantes' novel. In the second part of the work, a duke whom they encounter appoints Sancho governor of Barataria for a few days.

p. 320. *"the king can do no wrong"*: A quotation from that classic authority on English Law, Sir William Blackstone's *Commentaries on the Laws of England* (1765–9). Newman had used this and other quotations from Blackstone with dramatic satirical effect in the first of his *Lectures on the Present Position of Catholics in England* four years earlier (*see Prepos.*, pp. 29–41).

p. 321. *in the history both of Israel and of Judah the tyranny of kings brought within due limits by the priests and the prophets*: Samuel tells Saul that he is rejected by God (I Samuel 13:14; 15:26); Nathan tells King David from the Lord: 'I will be a Father to him, and he shall be a son to me. And if he does wrong I will correct him with the rod of men and with human chastisements' (2 Samuel 7:14). Nathan later tells him 'The sword shall never depart from your house because you have despised me' (2 Samuel 12:10). Hanani tells King Asa 'Because you relied on the King of Aram and did not rely on the Lord your God, the army of the King of Aram has escaped your hand' (2 Chronicles 16:7).
    Jehoiada the priest and the Levites put an end to the domination of The Queen Mother Athaliah and install Joash as king (2 Chronicles 23); Elijah anoints Jehu, son of Nimshi, King of Israel (2 Kings 9); Hilkiah the priest and the scribe Shaphan help King Josiah to bring reform according to the Book of the Law (2 Kings 22).

p. 321. *"If the Christian Church had not existed,"* says M. *Guizot* in his *History of Civilisation* (3 vols, London, 1846) Volume I, p. 38. Cf. note p. 30 'doctrinaire'.

p. 321. the suzerain: Technically, a feudal overlord, though in modern history the term came to be applied to any monarch or state which had supremacy over another state which, though having its own ruler, was not able to act independently.

p. 322. *barons*: The level of nobility next in rank to that of viscount. Soon after the Conquest it became customary for the barons to attend meetings of the Upper House of what was an embryonic Parliament. When too many barons began to attend, the King would issue a writ inviting attendance 'for this occasion only'. The rank of baron became less significant and therefore some of their number had their baronetcy confirmed by letters patent, so that their title could be passed on to heirs; these barons came to be known as Lords of Parliament.

p. 322. *soldiers*: Strictly, one who gives military service in return for pay, as opposed to the performance of a feudal duty.

p. 322. *serfs*: Slaves or bondmen.

p. 322. *Thus the Roman Dictator . . . during the term of his rule*: In Republican Rome, a dictator was a magistrate elected to serve for six months during grave emergencies of State. He was granted supreme power, and an absolute 'carte blanche'. Some of the most famous of the early dictators were Cincinnatus and Q. Fabius Maximus Cunctator. The office lapsed around the end of the 3rd century BC, but was revived by Sulla in 82, and, in 49 BC, Julius Caesar was appointed Dictator.

p. 323. *the remedy against seditious, libellous . . . publications*: Once again, strongly resonant of the Achilli Trial, and Newman's conviction for libel, and sentencing in Westminster Hall on 31 January 1853.

p. 323. *Instead of making a venture . . . safe mediocrity*: Newman's sermons are filled with calls for his hearers to make 'Ventures of Faith' (the title of one of his best known sermons, *P.S.* IV, p. xx). Soon after becoming a Catholic, Newman urged another prospective convert, 'the merit of faith consists in making ventures' (*L.D.* XI, pp. 60–1).

p. 323. *the Aulic Council in Germany, which virtually co-operated with Napoleon*: The Aulic Council, or 'Reichshofrat', was the Court Council of the Holy Roman Emperor from 1498 until 1806, when the Empire was dissolved upon Francis II's renunciation of the Imperial Crown in 1806. Instituted by the Emperor Maximilian I, it was responsible for all matters except finance and diplomacy. Napoleon had demanded that several princes of the southern and western parts of the Empire form a Confederation of the Rhine, and support him. The Confederation essentially abrogated the constitution of the Empire.

p. 323. *committees of taste*: With the fast growing number of Victorian public buildings, the decline of aristocratic patronage, and the professionalisation of the architectural profession, cities, towns, and boroughs, were increasingly relying on committees of middle class men to oversee the despatch of such commissions.

p. 325. *Power, when freely developed*: Newman remarks that the Constitution is 'jealous' of the centralization of power 'as hostile to the liberty of the subject'. Letter on Centralization to the *British Magazine* 19 October 1834 *L.D.* IV, p. 340.

p. 325. *The Man promised to kill the Stag*: See note to p. 314.

p. 326. *"Britannia, rule the waves ... slaves"*: The words were written for the Masque, 'Alfred' (first performed in 1740), by James Thomson (1700–1748) and David Mallet, and were most probably penned by the former. The air was composed by Thomas Augustine Arne (1710–1778).

p. 327. *The age of Philip and Demosthenes ... such a foe as Macedon*: Philip II, acceded to the Macedonian throne in 360 BC. Having subjugated Thrace and Thessaly, he defeated Athens at the Battle of Chæronea in 338, but was assassinated two years later, being succeeded by his son Alexander (the Great). Demosthenes (*c.* 395–322 BC, the famous Athenian orator, whose Philippics and Olynthiacs were directed against the former.

p. 328. *that similarly small strip of land in Syria*: i.e. Palestine.

p. 328. *friendly and hostile orators in the pages of her great historian*: Thucydides (*c.* 460–400 BC), the historian, whose *History of the Peloponnesian War* quickly achieved almost immortal status. Most of the work was completed during a twenty-year exile, and, recalling the views of the participants, he recounted the arguments pro and contra in the form of speeches.

p. 328. *the grace and poetry ... if Pericles is to be believed*: The end of chapter VI of the *History* contains the funeral oration which Pericles pronounced for the first dead in the war, and embodies a eulogy of the people, constitution, and civilisation, of Athens.

p. 328. *as Russia now*: The introduction of railways in the late 1830s had helped Russia to speed up and consolidate the policy of expansion and colonisation which Catherine the Great had struck out on so determinedly in the previous century. Notable gains had been made in these decades at the expense of the Caucasian peoples and Persia.

p. 328. *Socrates . . . died under a judicial sentence*: In 399 BC, the philosopher was charged with importing new deities and corrupting youth. At the conclusion of a trial (memorably recounted in Plato's *Apology*), he was condemned to death by drinking hemlock.

p. 329. *Xenophon conducted his memorable retreat across Asia Minor*: Xenophon (*c*. 430–*c*. 355 BC), Athenian historian, general, and philosopher. He joined the Greek forces in Asia Minor, who were acting as mercenaries of Cyrus who was trying to seize control of the Persian throne. He successfully led the 10,000 Greek troops back to the Argive mainland, and he memorably recounted the expedition in his *Anabasis*. On his own return, his friendship with various leading Spartans led to his exile, and it was not until near the end of his life that he was allowed back to Athens.

p. 329. *Miltiades*: (5th century BC), of an Athenian family. His uncle, Cypselus, had led an expedition to found an Athenian colony by the Hellespont, which he had then ruled like a tyrant. He himself repeated such an exercise in the Crimean peninsula. Though he participated with note in the Battle of Marathon, later incompetence led to his impeachment.

p. 329. *Themistocles had a double drift . . . the victory of Salamis*: Themistocles (*c*. 514–449 BC), was an Athenian statesman and general who led his country's forces to victories against Xerxes at Artemisium and Salamis during the Second Persian War. However, he made enemies in Athens, was exiled, and ultimately took refuge at the court of the Persian King Artaxerxes, and was reputed to have eventually poisoned himself.

p. 329. *what took place . . . when Hannibal threatened the city*: Hannibal (247–183 BC), the great Carthaginian general, who committed his life from an early age to the downfall of Rome. His expedition against Rome, through Spain and across the Alps is legendary. His forces arrived in Italy in 218, achieved several victories, culminating in his great triumph at Cannae in 216. He then camped at Capua to prepare for an assault on Rome. He found no success in his quest and arrived back in Carthage in ignominy in 203.

p. 329. *their conduct at Pylos . . . the orders of the elder Demosthenes*: Pylos ws the scene of an important Athenian victory over Sparta in 425 BC. Demosthenes, father of the famous orator, was the leading Athenian general of the day.

p. 329. *"They are fond of change," say their Corinthian opponents in the Lacedemonian Council*: Lacedaemon was a name for Sparta, and the Council was a league, consisting of Thebes, Corinth, Argos and Athens, formed to resist the hegemony which Sparta had achieved with eventual victory over Athens in the Peloponnesian War. There were initial military successes in 396 and 397, but by 387, with the help of the King of Persia, Sparta had resumed her supremacy.

p. 331. *Letter-carriage . . . involves an extent of system*: The British national postal system was introduced in 1840 by Rowland Hill, with a flat-rate postage.

p. 331. *the care of Religion . . . is left to private competition in the United States*: Under the *Establishment Clause* state funding for religious education is barred.

p. 332. *according to the proverb*: i.e. 'live within your means'; adapted from the Latin phrase, 'si non possis quod velis, velis id quod possis'.

p. 333. *"Optat ephippia bos"*: Horace, *Epistles*, I, pp. xiv, 43: 'The lazy ox longs for the horse's trappings'.

p. 333. *forte*: 'strength', and that ability in which a person or nation excels most, and displays their powers to the greatest.

p. 333. *and literary men . . . the Herald's College*: The College of Arms or the Herald's College dates from 1483; it grants armorial bearings and has three Kings of Arms, and four pursuivants.

p. 333. *like Attica*: A region in South East Greece, surrounding Athens in ancient times.

p. 333. *their wooden walls, to use the Athenian term*: The 'wooden walls of Old England', were the ships of war.
   As Xerxes approached, the Athenians sent to Delphi to ask how they should defend themselves. The reply was to the effect that 'Pallas hath, urged, and Zeus, the sire of all, Hath safety promised in a wooden wall.'

p. 333. *be he Dane, or Norman, or Dutch*: The first Danish King was Canute

(1016), the first Norman King was William I (1066–1087) and the Dutch King was William III (1689–1702).

p. 334. *the death of the sons of Oedipus*: Eteocles and Polyneices, who after their father's death agreed to reign in Thebes in alternate years. When his brother refused to give up the throne at the appointed time, Polyneices advanced on the city with the help of the Argive army, which was led by seven heroes. After indecisive fighting, it was decided that the contest should be settled by the brothers in single combat, and they slew each other. The war formed the subject of Aeschylus's play *The Seven against Thebes*.

p. 334. *Walter Scott's "Two Drovers"*: A short story which appeared in 1827 as one of the *Chronicles of Canongate*. The story's central character, Robin Oig M'Combich, is a Highland drover, who ventures off to England with his cattle in the company of his friend, a Yorkshire drover. On reaching England, the latter contrives to land Robin in an argument with an Englishman who ridiculed the Highland character, thus hoping to start a fight. Robin is not drawn, but returns homewards, fetches his dagger, murders the Yorkshireman, but honourably gives himself up to justice.

p. 335. *the Saxon Heptarchy*: The division of England into seven parts, each of which had a separate ruler; the seven being Kent, Sussex, Essex, Wessex, East Anglia, Mercia, and Northumbria. The division began to take shape in the later part of the sixth century AD, and, at different times before the Scandinavian invasions, different kingdoms were to gain ascendant positions.

p. 335. *as they do now under Queen Victoria*: Theodore Hoppen has pointed out that: 'The legislative steps which led to the creation of the United Kingdom of Great Britain and Ireland on 1 January 1801 – namely, the acts of union with Wales (1536), Scotland (1707), and Ireland (1800) – were less comprehensive than is commonly supposed. Late Victorian disputes over Home Rule disguise the fact that the "new" kingdom's actual, as distinct from its supposed, condition was always one of quasi-devoluton. That, in the event, it often proved difficult to give formal recognition to this state of things had less to do with the smaller nations ... than with England's overweening and relatively increasing power, wealth, and size. In 1841 80.2 per cent of Britain's and 55.7 per cent of the United Kingdom's inhabitants lived in England. Sixty years later these figures had grown to 82.5 and 73.6 per cent respectively. Given the absence of demands for regional autonomy within England, this presented devolutionists of all kinds with almost insuperable difficulties. Home Rule, therefore was at heart always more an English problem than an Irish,

Scottish, or Welsh one.' *The Mid-Victorian Generation: 1846–1886*, Oxford, 1998, p. 513.

p. 336. *use their Ruler as their mere manager and man of business*: *The Government of the Country*, London, 1865 (see note to p. 306), explained that: 'England is under a "limited monarchy." The sovereigns of other countries often assert a "divine right" to govern; a sovereign of the house of Hanover can put forth no such pretensions, because he holds his crown under, and by virtue of, the act of settlement, and strictly subject to the conditions which it imposes' (p. 24).

p. 336. *What a place is London in its extent*: The population of London in 1841 was 2,207,653. The subterranean works, or underground, between Farringdon Street and Bishop's Road, Paddington (3.75 miles) was the first in the world.

p. 336. *Waterloo Bridge . . . built by shares*: Designed by John Rennie and opened in 1817, Waterloo Bridge, with its nine huge stone arches was for many years regarded as one of the finest in the world.

p. 337. *A famine threatens*: Ireland was afflicted with famine in 1822 and more seriously in 1845. Commercial interests exacerbated the catastrophe, and ignorance of the scale of the disaster prevented organized Poor Law relief becoming available. It is chronicled by Cecil Woodham Smith in *The Great Hunger*.

p. 337. *Emigration is in vogue*: Archbishop Whately addressed a meeting of the Society for the Promotion of the Gospel in Foreign Parts at Enniskerry in County Wicklow in which he said 'that the present emigration imposed upon the Mother Country and Church the strongest obligation to provide the blessing of Religious Instruction for those who go forth to people our colonies'. *The Times*, 26 August 1854.

p. 337. *the Prytaneum*: The Prytanaeum was the Town Hall of major ancient Greek cities, and under the protection of Hestia, Goddess of the Hearth. And it was at the hearth that guests of state were entertained.

p. 337. *Suddenly a youth, the castaway of his family*: Robert Clive (1725–1774) was sent to India at the age of eighteen. He joined the army and won the victory of Plassey. He became Governor of Bengal in 1755 and later Baron Plassey and was known as 'Clive of India'.

p. 337. *a mighty empire over the graves of Mahmood and Aurungzebe*: Mahmood (998–1030) ruled over Kabul, Peshawar and Lahore. At his court in Ghazni was the philosopher Avicenna. His dynasty lasted until 1184. Aurangzeb (1658–1707) was the great-grandson of Akbar. As a sunni Moslem, he ruled an empire which stretched from Assam in the North to Thanjavur in the South.

p. 339. *the Horse ... the Stag*: Cf. note p. 314.

p. 340. *For a year past ... on our Constitutional* routine: The Bill to reform the British Civil Service, the permanent establishment which advises government ministers, introduced in 1853. The unreformed state of the Civil Service is described in Anthony Trollope's *Three Clerks* (1857).

p. 340. Deus è machina: 'A God out of a machine', i.e. someone who saves a situation in a crisis.

p. 340. *The present Parliamentary Committee of Inquiry*: The Committee of Inquiry into the Crimean War was called for by Roebuck, the MP for Sheffield. It caused the downfall of Lord Aberdeen's government.

p. 341. *Wellington's question in opposition to the Reform Bill*: The Reform Bill passed in the House of Commons in March 1832. The opposition carried an amendment on 7 May. Lord Grey, the Prime Minister, proposed to the King that fifty peers should be created to ensure passage of the original Bill. Wellington said that this was completely unconstitutional; the proper course of action would have been to modify the Bill. The government resigned on 9 May.

p. 342. *title of John Bull*: The English national nickname, encapsulating the figure of a bluff but bull-headed farmer. The sobriquet was first used by John Arbuthnot in his satirical *The History of John Bull* of 1712, which advocated England's withdrawal from the War of Spanish Succession. In the same satire, France was portrayed as Lewis Baboon, and the Dutch as Nicholas Frog. Newman felt that John Bull was, 'a spirit neither of heaven nor hell.' (*Apo.*, p. 29). Though himself a John Bull in many mundane matters, Newman abhorred the English tendency to give priority to domestic and commercial matters over religious truth.

p. 343. *your store-keepers and harbour-masters at Balaklava*: A sea port on the Black Sea and the site of a battle in the Crimean War fought on 25 October 1854.

p. 343. *with the* Times *to see the world by*: *The Times* had installed eight-feed rotary presses in 1849 which could produce 9,600 copies an hour.

p. 343. *Aberdeen, Gladstone, Sidney Herbert, Newcastle*: George Hamilton Gordon, Lord Aberdeen (1784–1860) was Foreign Secretary under Wellington and Peel, and Prime Minister in 1852–55. Sidney Herbert, later Baron Herbert (1810–1861) was Secretary for War at the time of the Crimean War; Henry Pelham Fiennes Pelham Clinton Duke of Newcastle (1811–1864) was Secretary for War in 1852 and 1855 and Colonial Secretary from 1859–64.

p. 343. *their regular quarter-day*: Lady Day (25 March); Midsummer Day (24 June); Michaelmas Day (29 September); and Christmas Day (25 December). The four days, fixed by custom as marking off quarters of the year, on which the tenancy of houses usually begins and ends, and rent and other charges fall due (and sometimes, as here, payment of salary).

p. 343. *Raglan, Burgoyne, Dundas*: Fitzroy James Henry Somerset, Lord Raglan (1788–1855) was Commander of British forces in the Crimean War; John Burgoyne (1722–1792) a soldier and dramatist surrendered British forces to General Gates at Saratoga in 1777. Henry Dundas, Lord Melville (1742–1810) was Home Secretary in 1791 and Secretary for War 1794–1801. He was impeached over a financial scandal when he was Treasurer of the Admiralty, but was acquitted.

p. 343. *fetters of Constitutional red tape*: Tape used by lawyers and government officials to secure their papers together. Colloquially, excessive attention to routine and formality, or mechanical observance of rules and details. It figures prominently in Dickens' *Little Dorrit*.

p. 344. *my workhouse apprentices*: Children from the poorhouse who have been placed in apprenticeships – the lowest of the low in society.

p. 345. *From the Irish famines of 1822 to that of 1845 and following years*: Cf. note p. 337.

p. 345. *in spite of the many millions voted to them by Parliament*: Lord John Russell wrote to Lord Clarendon on 13 August 1848: 'Eight million pounds had been advanced after the failure of 1846 to enable the Irish to supply the loss of the potato crop' (Clarendon Papers IA).

p. 346. *John, Duke of Marlborough . . . a monopoly of blanket-making*: A woollen industry had been established in the Oxfordshire town in Anglo-Saxon times. Blanket-makers had become predominant in the seventeenth century, and in 1711 they obtained a charter making them into a company, consisting of master, assistants, two wardens, and a commonalty.

p. 348. *the Sovereign . . . as Tudor monarchs asserted, and Constitutional lawyers have handed down to us*: Newman is drawing on Sir William Blackstone's *Commentaries on the Laws of England*. Cf. note p. 319.

p. 348. *as the Merovingian king, not the Mayor of the Palace*: The Merovingians were the Frankish dynasty that ruled from 500–750.

p. 348. *as the Great Mogul, not the Company . . . Hindostan*: The great Mongol rulers in what is now North India and Pakistan. The Company is the East India Company based on the spice trade in South India. It became a government department in 1835 and ceased to exist in 1873.

p. 348. *which slipped out of the hands of the Stuarts*: The power to rule without parliament, which was curtailed by their need of finance, for which the consent of parliament was necessary.

p. 348. motu proprio: 'On one's own initiative'.

p. 349. *I recollect being shocked . . . the ends of the Law*: The source cannot be traced but Newman at one time considered that the law was to be his intended profession and was entered as a student at Lincoln's Inn in June 1819.

p. 349. *the Star Chamber*: English law court which incuded members of the monarch's Privy Council, sitting without a jury. It was abolished in 1641.

p. 350. *the Committee of Privy Council on the baptismal controversy*: The Privy Council was called on to decide whether Revd. G. C. Gorham, who denied baptismal regeneration, could be instituted to the parish of Bramford Speke which Phillpots, the Bishop of Exeter refused to do, upheld by the Court of Arches. The Privy Council overturned the judgement on 8 March 1850.

p. 350. *I have been told by an eminent lawyer . . . the precedents of several centuries*: The eminent lawyer was probably James Robert Hope Scott (1823–1873) whom Newman knew when he was at Merton College. He married Charlotte Lockhart, grand-daughter of Sir Walter Scott, in 1847 and would be Newman's counsel at the Achilli trial for libel in 1852.

p. 350. *Queen's Bench*: The highest British court of Common Law dealing with civil and criminal cases.

p. 351. *the public meeting held to thank . . . Mr. Maurice*: F. D. Maurice,

Professor at King's College London, had argued in *Theological Essays* (1853) that future endless punishment was superstitious.

p. 351. *buying a seat in Parliament . . . purchase of an eligible incumbency*: The first Reform Bill of 1832 sought to redress the issue of 'pocket boroughs' which were in the hands of the landed gentry who instructed their voters accordingly. Anthony Trollope describes the scene in '*Can you forgive her?*' which was serialised in 1862 and published in 1865.

p. 351. *from the time of Sir Robert Walpole*: Sir Robert Walpole (1676–1745) was Britain's first Prime Minister (1715–17; 1721–42).

p. 352. *having died away with Bolingbroke's "Patriot King"*: Henry Bolingbroke, Henry IV (1366–1413).

p. 352. *knout and the tar-barrel*: Cf. note p. 307.

p. 352. *que voulez vous?*: A French expression often accompanied by a shrug of the shoulders: 'What do you expect?'

p. 354. *"l'Etat c'est moi"*: 'I am the State'; a remark attributed to Louis XIV in his address to the Parlement de Paris on 13 April 1655. An ironic inversion of the fabled statement of one of Britain's perennially most legendary enemies.

p. 354. *the fable of Menenius Agrippa*: Consul of Rome in 593 BC, Menenius Agrippa was reputed to have persuaded the plebeians to return to the city by relating the fable of 'The Belly and its Members': once upon a time, the members refused to work for the lazy belly, but, finding the supply of food stopped, they realised there was a mutual dependence. The story is related by Shakespeare in Coriolanus, I, i.

p. 354. *"cuius participatio eius in id ipsum"*: Each has a share in the other.

p. 355. *"Old England"*: The term first came into use in 1641, twenty-one years after the American colony of New Virginia received the sobriquet 'New England'. The expression features in numerous quotations. One of the most familiar to Newman would have been Samuel Johnson's remark of May 1776: 'Sir, it is not to be lamented so much that Old England is lost, as that the Scotch have found it.'

p. 355. chef-d'oeuvres: 'masterpieces'.

p. 355. ultima ratio: 'last reason' or 'last expedient'.

p. 355. *haphazard and pell-mell fighting*: the walls of Troy "As foe with foe grappled in murderous fight ... Men stabbed with swords, and men impaled on spears/Lay all confusedly ... *Iliad*, Book XI.

p. 356. *the Pretorians, the Gothic mercenaries, the medieval Turks, and later Janizzaries*: The personal body guards of the ruler. Mahud II the Ottoman ruler had massacred his Janisseries for mutiny in 1826 in what was known as 'The Auspicious Incident'.

p. 356. *the Horse, the Stag, and the Man*: Cf. note to p. 314.

p. 356. an imperium in imperio: 'a government within a government', i.e. a body existing within, but operating wholly independently of, a larger authorised body. Such an accusation had been made against the East India Company in its heyday.

p. 357. *an intense* esprit de corps: Literally, 'spirit of the body', but commonly meaning 'brotherhood' or brotherly feeling, referring to the zeal for mutual honour found in collective bodies.

p. 357. *Instead of one corporation in religion ... as chapters and rectories*: Cathedral chapter of canons and groups of rectories under a rural dean.

p. 357. *recognize the Dissenting bodies*: Dissenters were only reluctantly admitted to Oxford and Cambridge in 1871, when they were no longer required to take the Thirty-nine Articles as a requirement of obtaining their degree.

p. 358. ex abundanti cautela: 'On account of extreme caution'.

p. 358. *that clothing and fuel shall oscillate to and fro between Balaklava and Malta*: Malta, a British possession, possessed the Grand Harbour for vict-ualling the fleet; Balaklava was the sea port for the Crimea.

p. 358. *the use of the bag in making a pudding*: A muslin bag is used for steaming the contents in suet and Christmas puddings.

p. 358. *field-pieces*: Small cannon brought by an army into the field of battle.

p. 358. *sisters of charity*: Florence Nightingale sent for Sisters of Charity to staff her hospital at Scutari in the Crimea. She was high in their praises.

p. 359. *two sacraments, neither being really dangerous*: Baptism and the

Eucharist. Homily 19 of *The Book of Homilies* states 'That there are other Sacraments besides "Baptism and the Lord's Supper", though not "such as" they'.

p. 359. *the stubbornness of the Guards at Inkerman*: 8000 British troops were involved in hand-to-hand combat against 50,000 Russians, among them the Grenadier Guards and Coldstream Guards at 'The Sandbag battery'. See note p. 308.

p. 359. *A general good education, a public school*: Clergymen of the Church of England were ordained normally after the completion of their university degree, as was Newman himself. Bishop Law of Chester founded St Bees as a Theological College for University men in 1815. The CMS founded a College for non-University men in Islington in 1825.

p. 360. *like the dog in the fable*: Aesop's fable 'The Dog and the Shadow' in which the dog who has stolen some meat sees his shadow in the stream and being greedy tries to eat the reflection and loses the meat in his mouth.

p. 360. *There was Dr. Whately in 1826 ... keeping the endowments*: in his *Letters on the Church, by an Episcopalian*.

p. 361. *there is the* Times *newspaper in 1855, which would reorganize the army*: The dispatches of their correspondent, William Howard Russell, were judged by a French officer to be so prejudicial to the allies that they positively assisted the enemy.

p. 361. *That of Arragon*: Aragon, once a kingdom ruled by Ferdinand V (1474–1504) jointly with Isabella I of Castille (now a province), is in North East Spain.

p. 361. *Mr. Macaulay gives us a warning from history*: Thomas Macaulay (1800–1859) was a lawyer and historian. He became secretary to the Board of Control and advisor to the Supreme Council of India. From his essay on Mr Hallam's History in *Critical & Historical Essays* Vol 1, London Everyman, 1966, pp. 30–31, 33, 34.

p. 362. *Gustavus Adolphus*: Gustavus II, King of Sweden (1611–1632), great military commander, called 'The Lion of the North'.

PART 6: AN INTERNAL ARGUMENT FOR CHRISTIANITY
p. 363. *a recent work, called "Ecce Homo"*: Sir John Seeley, Professor of Latin at Cambridge University published a work with this title in 1865. Newman is reviewing it here.

p. 364. *doubt and devotion are incompatible with each other*: Newman writes in *V.M.* I 'If by "unclouded certainty" is meant the absence of all involuntary misgivings, or a sense of imperfection or incompleteness in the argumentative grounds of religion, a certitude so circumstanced is *not* (according to Catholic teaching) "necessary for a Christian's faith and hope". Nor can real "doubt" be anything short of a deliberate withholding of assent to the Church's teaching.' *V.M.* I, p. 85 n. 4.

p. 365. *at this time, its divine authority is the very point to be determined*: 'It is frightful to think where England would be, as regards Revelation, if it once got to disbelieve or to doubt the authority of Scripture.' To Charles Crawley, 17 March 1861 (in reference to the publication of *Essays and Reviews* in 1860) *L.D.* XIX, p. 482.

p. 366. *St. Augustine's well-known words*: From 'Against the Epistle of Manichaeus', ch 5.

p. 366. *the young man in the Gospel*: 'Good Master . . .' Luke 18:28.

p. 366. *"went about doing good"*: Acts 10:38.

p. 366. *"Si la vie . . ." says Rousseau*: 'If the life and death of Socrates are those of a sage, the life and death of Jesus are those of a God.' In his novel, *Emile* I.4.

p. 367. *"l'inventeur en serait . . . le héros"*: 'The one who invented it would be more amazing than the hero himself.'

p. 367. *In theological language, it is the* motivum credibilitatis, *the* objectum materiale, *and the* formale: The motive of credibility, the material and the formal object.

p. 367. in Deo vivo et vero: 'the living and true God', I Thessalonians 1:9.

p. 367. *"We now believe, . . . have heard Him"*: Cf. John 4:42.

p. 367. *Paley . . . the auxiliary Evidences of Christianity*: The classic apologetic work of William Paley, the theological utilitarian, was first published in 1794, and was to retain a dominant role in Anglican religious writing for many decades. Paley's opus was divided into three parts, the second given over to an examination 'Of the Auxiliary Evidences of Christianity'. The fourth and fifth chapters of the second part focussed on the 'Identity of Christ's character' and the 'Originality of Christ's character', respectively.

p. 368. *Socrates . . . Zeno*: Greek philosophers. Socrates 469–399, Zeno of Elea 490–430 and Epicurus 342–270.

p. 368. per impossibile: 'if by impossibility'.

p. 369. sui generis: 'Of its own kind', or 'of a kind distinctive to itself'.

p. 370. *"Anglo-Catholics"*: Newman was one of the first to use the term. He defines Anglo-Catholicism in his introduction to *Lectures on the Prophetical Office of the Church* (= *V.M.* I) as 'the religion of Andrewes, Laud, Hammond, Butler, and Wilson [and] is capable of being professed, acted on, and maintained on a large sphere of action, or whether it be a mere modification or transition-state of either Romanism or popular Protestantism'.

p. 372. *work on the Human Understanding*: John Locke (1644–1718) English philosopher published his *Essay Concerning Human Understanding* in 1690 as an attempt to detect the limits of human knowledge.

p. 373. *John . . . announces the promised kingdom as close at hand*: Matthew 3:2.

p. 373. *a rite symbolical of it*: i.e. baptism. Cf. Matthew 3:11; Mark 1:8; Luke 3:16; John 1:36. On the wider implication of the rite, see e.g., Acts 11:16–17.

p. 373. *points out to them a private person*: Cf. Matthew 3:13–17; Mark 1:9–15; Luke 3:21.

p. 374. *"Poenitentiam agite; for the kingdom of heaven is at hand"*: Matthew 3:2: 'Repent ye'. Cf. also Matthew 4:17.

p. 375. *which the appointment of Saul had disarranged*: By becoming King of Israel. I Samuel 10:17ff.

p. 375. *received the title of King*: See John 1:49, 12:13; Matthew 2:2; Matthew 25:11, 29; Mark 15:18, 26; Luke 23:3, 38; John 19:19, 21.

p. 376. *"discerned the signs of the times"*: Cf. Matthew 16:3.

p. 376. *it did not prevent His payment of tribute*: Matthew 22:21.

p. 376. *the Eridanus is called "fluviorum rex"*: The King of greatly flowing waters otherwise known as the celestial river. The Eridanus is a large constellation between Cetus and Orion, second in size to Hydra, so termed because of its star formation in the skies.

p. 376. *the inkeeper's son, ... "heir to the crown"*: Perkin Warbeck (1474–1499) impersonated Richard Duke of York in 1497, one of the princes in the Tower. He was hanged two years later.

p. 377. *"Follow Me;" ... "fishers of men"*: Matthew 4:19; Mark 2:14; Luke 5:27.

p. 377. *"Go ye, ... teaching them"*: Matthew 28:19–20.

p. 377. *... for which the [Jewish] nation ... Jehovah*: Cf. Pss 32:8, 132:12; Isaiah 2:3.

p. 378. *"Admirabilis, consiliarius ..."*: Wonderful counsellor, father of the world to come, Prince of Peace. Isaiah 9:6.

p. 378. *cui bono*: 'for whose good or benefit'.

p. 379. *"Seek ye first the kingdom of God"*: Matthew 6:33.

p. 379. *"Where two or three are gathered together"*: Matthew 18:20.

p. 379. *"parable of the Vine ... of the Bread of Life"*: John 15:1ff; John 6:22ff.

p. 380. *'as levers to uplift the earth'*: A reference to Archimedes. Cf. note p. 36.

p. 380. *O si sic omnia!*: 'If all things were like that!'

p. 383. *"Behold the Lamb of God"*: John 1:29.

p. 383. *"Mine eyes have seen the King"*: Isaiah 6:5.

p. 384. *that he saw Uzziah*: Isaiah 1:1.

p. 384. *Addison*: Joseph Addison (1672–1719) English essayist. Publisher with Sir Richard Steele of *The Spectator*.

p. 385. *"Unless a man be born again"*: John 3:5.

p. 385. *"He stooped down to hide His face"*: Cf. John 8:6.

p. 387. *"Behold the Man"*: Pilate's words to the crowd (John 19:5) as well as the title of Sir John Seeley's book.

p. 387. *"The life that I now live in the flesh"*: Gal. 2:20.

p. 387. *In these latter times especially since St. Ignatius*: The Jesuit method of meditation, following *The Exercises of St Ignatius* involves 'points' for reflection, which often consist of short passages from the Gospels.

p. 387. *which the Psalms have received in the Breviary*: The Psalms are divided into sections spread over the days of the week in the daily prayers said by the Catholic clergy, known also as the Liturgy of the Hours.

p. 388. *"My Lord and my God"*: The words of Thomas after the Resurrection (John 20:28).

p. 388. *Arius*: Cf. note p. 58.

p. 388. *Nestorius*: Patriarch of Constantinople (428–431). Cf. note p. 9.

p. 389. *Voltaire*: aka Francois Marie Arouet (1694–1778) writer and philosopher who was a career anti-cleric who adopted the ideas of Reimarus. The German exegete had declared that Jesus was an impostor, whose disciples had continued his work by similar methods.

p. 389. *Strauss*: David Friedrich (1808–1874) a pupil of Schliermacher, he wrote a rationalist account of Jesus' life, *Leben Jesu kritisch bearbeitet* in 1835; it was translated by George Eliot in 1846–50. Strauss portrays Christ not as an individual but as an idea – the miracles attributed to him are myths.

p. 389. *Renan*: Ernest (1823–1863) wrote *La Vie de Jesus* in 1863. He extols the character of Jesus but considers a Christ who is part of the march of history – a stage on the road to a 'God who is not yet, but who may be one day'.

p. 389. *Calvin*: Jean (1509–1564) French theologian who preached his reformed religion from Geneva in Switzerland. Cf. note p. 130.

p. 389. *Wesley*: Cf. note p. 38.

p. 389. *Chalmers*: Thomas (1780–1847) was the founder of the Free Chuch of Scotland, the breakaway group from the Presbyterians. They were more extreme Calvinists.

p. 389. Erskine: Ebenezer (1680–1754) published his *Marrow of Modern Divinity* in which he expounds his unorthodox theology and for which he was expelled from the Church.

p. 391. *Bishop Butler*. See note p. 17.

p. 391. "practical *certitude*": As opposed to a theoretical assent to truth.

p. 392. sine qua non: Something indispensable.

p. 392. *"Two of his disciples heard him speak"*: John 1:37.

p. 392. *"a man sent from God"*: John 1:6.

p. 393. *"that taketh away the sin of the world"*: John 1:29.

p. 394. *Wisdom was the "only begotten . . . sons of God"*: Proverbs 8:22; Job 1:6; Genesis 6:2; I Chronicles 28:6; Wisdom 2:18.

p. 394. *"Indeed this was the Son of God"*: The centurion on Calvary (Matt. 27:54).

p. 395. *"Thou shalt be dumb"*: Luke 1:20.

p. 395. *"Blessed is she that believed"*: Luke 1:45.

p. 395. *"He that believeth on the Son"*: John 3:36.

p. 395. *"We speak that we do know"*: John 3:11.18.

p. 395. *"He that heareth My word"*: John 5:24.

p. 395. *"He that believeth on Me hath everlasting life"*: John 6:47.

p. 396. *"Blessed are they that have not seen"*: John 20:29.

p. 396. *"Preach the Gospel . . . shall be damned"*: Mark 16:15–16.

p. 396. *"Whosoever shall not receive you . . . dust of your feet"*: Mark 6:11.

p. 396. *"It is not ye that speak . . . your Father"*: Matthew 10:20.

p. 396. *"He that heareth you . . . Him that sent me"*: Luke 10:16.

p. 396. *"I pray for them . . . through their word"*: John 17:20.

p. 396. *"Whose sins ye remit . . . they are retained"*: Matthew 18:18.

p. 396. *"Whatsoever ye shall bind on earth"*: Matthew 18:19.

p. 396. *"I will give unto thee the keys . . . in heaven"*: Matthew 16:19.

p. 397. *He imposed upon them the declarations of a Divine Voice*: He told them that He was Lord of the Sabbath, that before Abraham was I AM, that he had authority on earth to forgive sins and that they would see the Son of Man at the right hand of the Power of God.

DATE DUE

			Printed in USA

HIGHSMITH #45230